The Manager's Bookshelf

Ninth Edition

The Manager's Bookshelf

A MOSAIC OF CONTEMPORARY VIEWS

Jon L. Pierce
University of Minnesota Duluth

John W. Newstrom
University of Minnesota Duluth

Prentice Hall

Boston   Columbus   Indianapolis   New York   San Francisco   Upper Saddle River
Amsterdam   Cape Town   Dubai   London   Madrid   Milan   Munich   Paris
Montreal   Toronto   Delhi   Mexico City   Sao Paulo   Sydney
Hong Kong   Seoul   Singapore   Taipei   Tokyo

Editorial Director: Sally Yagan
Editor in Chief: Eric Svendsen
Acquisitions Editor: Kim Norbuta
Product Development Manager: Ashley Santora
Editorial Project Manager: Claudia Fernandes
Editorial Assistant: Meg O'Rourke
Director of Marketing: Patrice Lumumba Jones
Marketing Manager: Nikki Ayana Jones
Marketing Assistant: Ian Gold
Production Project Manager: Renata Butera
Operations Specialist: Renata Butera
Creative Art Director: Jayne Conte
Cover Designer: Bruce Kenselaar

Manager, Visual Research: Beth Brenzel
Photo Researcher: Karen Sanatar
Manager, Rights and Permissions: Zina Arabia
Image Permission Coordinator: Suzanne Deworken
Manager, Cover Visual Research & Permissions:
  Karen Sanatar
Cover Photo: July Flower/Shutterstock
Full-Service Project Management: Hemalatha, Integra
  Software Services, Ltd.
Composition: Integra Software Services, Ltd.
Printer/Binder: Courier, Stoughton
Cover Printer: Courier, Stoughton
Text Font: 10/12 Times

Library of Congress Cataloging-in-Publication Data

The manager's bookshelf : a mosaic of contemporary views / Jon L. Pierce, John W. Newstrom. — 9th ed.
  p. cm.
 Includes bibliographical references and index.
 ISBN-13: 978-0-13-612250-0 (alk. paper)
 ISBN-10: 0-13-612250-7 (alk. paper)
 1. Management literature—United States. I. Pierce, Jon L. (Jon Lepley)
 II. Newstrom, John W.
HD70.U5M32 2011
658—dc22

2010009419

10 9 8 7 6 5 4 3 2

Prentice Hall
is an imprint of

www.pearsonhighered.com

ISBN 10:   0-13-612250-7
ISBN 13: 978-0-13-612250-0

We dedicate this book to our beloved grandchildren—Madison, Peter, Eric, Sawyer, William, Graham, Ruth Emma, and Ruth Lillian—who give us great pleasure and strong hope for the future.

BRIEF CONTENTS

CONTENTS

PREFACE

The last several decades were marked by a proliferation of books published on topics in management, leadership, and various organizational issues. This explosion of products apparently reflects an intense and continuing fascination by managers, future managers, and the general public with the inner workings of organizations and their managers, work teams and their leaders, and employees. Bookstores around the country and distribution sources on the Internet continue to offer a large number of management books, and many of these books have appeared on various "best-seller" lists—some remaining there for months and years at a time. Clearly, managers and others (including business school students at both graduate and undergraduate levels, as well as liberal arts students who are headed for a career in business or public organizations) remain intrigued by, and are searching for insights, perspectives, and answers in, the popular business literature.

We prepared *The Manager's Bookshelf: A Mosaic of Contemporary Views* to serve the needs of both managers and management students. A significant number of individuals in both of these groups do not have sufficient time to read widely, yet many people find themselves involved in conversations where someone else refers to ideas like evidence-based management, vision, self-directed work teams, ethics, fun at work, organizational politics, or spirituality. We believe that a laudable and critical goal for managers, as well as all students of management, is to remain current in their understanding of the wide range of views being expressed about organizational and management practices. To help you become a better-informed organizational citizen, we prepared *The Manager's Bookshelf,* which introduces you to more than 50 popular management books—both recent and "classic."

NEW TO THIS EDITION

The ninth edition of *The Manager's Bookshelf* introduces a fresh new set of readings into the book. A broad array of 18 new best sellers is included, replacing numerous other books that had become somewhat dated. The goal of this (and previous) revisions was to make *The Manager's Bookshelf* an undeniably comprehensive and up-to-date compendium of highly readable book summaries. Here are the major changes we designed and built into the new edition:

- In response to user feedback, we abbreviated and streamlined Part I so that it now contains only two readings: (1) our Introduction (exploring the popularity of best sellers, the rationale for the book, the typical contents of the best sellers, a structured format for critiquing them, our selection strategy, and commentary on the authors of the best sellers) and (2) a summary of Chris Argyris' intriguing book, *Flawed Advice and the Management Trap.*
- We changed the thrust of Part III from an emphasis on highly effective firms to a more balanced set of perspectives on both those that succeed and those that decline sharply and fall from grace. We now include the most recent book by noted author/consultant Jim Collins, *How the Mighty Fall.*
- We included new material (see Part XI) on "Spirituality at Work." This appears in a book summary of *Lead Like Jesus,* which is written by one of the all-time best-selling authors of business books, Ken Blanchard (along with Phil Hodges).

- An exciting development for this edition is the creation of Part IX, "'Undiscussable' Issues at Work." This section includes new summaries of both *Workplace Survival* (by Van Fleet and Van Fleet) and *The No-Asshole Rule* (by Sutton).
- Another new chapter (Part X) is titled "The Managerial Brain," and focuses on ways that managers can (and should) think. *Gut Feelings* (by Gigerenzer) accents the intuitive side of managerial decision making, while *Five Minds for the Future* (by Gardner) introduces a typology of thinking processes that managers can draw upon.
- To round out the collection of book summaries and point the way to the future, we included two other unconventional books in Part XV, "Contemporary Thinking about Management." Jeff Pfeffer's *What Were They Thinking?* challenges many of the common organizational practices that have been blindly adopted by practitioners, while *Hard Facts, Dangerous Half-truths, & Total Nonsense* (by Pfeffer and Sutton) introduces the reader to the valuable field of "evidence-based management."
- Part XVI closes out the book with some cautionary perspectives urging readers to be aware of the shortcomings of books that don't always have a sound empirical basis for their conclusions.
- Other new inclusions in this edition accent themes of Fun at Work, Social Technologies, Positive Leadership, Psychological Capital, and Followership.

A COLLAGE AND A MOSAIC

The Manager's Bookshelf, as a book of concise *summaries*, does not express the views of just one individual on the management of organizations, nor does it attempt to integrate the views of several dozen authors. Instead, *this book is a collage*—a composite portrait constructed from a variety of classic and contemporary sources (approximately 90 percent of the books summarized here were published in the twenty-first century). *The Manager's Bookshelf* provides you with insights into many aspects of organizational management from the perspectives of a diverse and sometimes provocative group of management writers, including some highly regarded authors such as Peter Drucker, Jim Collins, Barbara Kellerman, Thomas Friedman, Edward Lawler III, Malcolm Gladwell, Jeffrey Pfeffer, Stephen Covey, John Kotter, Clayton Christensen, Spencer Johnson, Michael Porter, and Marcus Buckingham. Through this collection we will introduce you to the thoughts, philosophies, views, and experiences of a number of authors whose works have caught the attention of today's management community—and often captivated them in the process.

This book contains a rich array of pieces—a veritable *mosaic* that provides a fascinating overall portrait of management. From a topical perspective, its inclusions focus on motivation, ethics, global perspectives, environmental trends, inclusiveness, corporate strategy, leadership styles, and other key concerns of managers. This collection includes the views from a variety of individuals—some practitioners (e.g., Bill George), some philosophers (e.g., Peter Drucker), some management consultants (e.g., Jim Collins or Marcus Buckingham), and some organizational scholars (e.g., Ed Lawler or John Kotter). The selections reflect a wide variety in terms of their tone and tenor, as well as the diverse bases for their conclusions. Indeed, critics have praised some of the authors' works as passionate, invaluable, stimulating, and insightful, whereas other business books have been attacked as being overly academic, superficial, redundant, glib, or unrealistic.

NATURE OF THE INCLUSIONS

The nature and source of the ideas expressed in this collection are diverse. Some inclusions are prescriptive in nature, whereas others are more dispassionately descriptive; some are thoughtful and philosophical, whereas others limit themselves to reporting directly on their personal or organizational experiences; some of these works represent armchair speculation, whereas others are based on empirical study. Finally, the selections take a variety of forms. Some of the readings are articles written by the book's author in which part of their overall perspective on management is revealed, while the majority of the inclusions are concise and objective summaries of popular books that have been specially prepared for inclusion in *The Manager's Bookshelf.*

This mosaic of readings can provide you with useful insights, provoke your own reflective thinking, and spark stimulating dialogue with your colleagues about the management of today's organizations. We expect that these readings will prompt you to raise questions of yourself and your peers about the viability of many of the ideas expressed by these authors regarding the practice of organizational management. We hope and predict that these readings will prompt you to read the full text of many of the authors' works; these books often contain rich anecdotes, compelling stories, provocative assertions, and detailed data that are not possible to include in our summaries. Finally, we hope that these summaries will encourage you to continue your managerial self-development through a variety of avenues, including ongoing reading of both the popular and scientific (research-based) literature. If these goals are met, our purpose for assembling this collection will be realized.

INSTRUCTOR'S MANUAL

This book offers an Instructor's Manual that includes suggestions for using best sellers in the classroom, a sample classroom assignment, and provocative questions for each reading to guide instructors in classroom discussion.

The instructor's manual is available to adopting instructors for download at www. pearsonhighered.com/irc. Registration is simple and gives the instructor immediate access to other titles and new editions. Instructors should visit http://247.pearsoned.com/ for answers to frequently asked questions and for toll-free user support phone numbers.

COURSESMART

CourseSmart textbooks online is an exciting new choice for students trying to economize. As an alternative to purchasing the print textbook, students can subscribe to the same content online and save up to 50 percent off the suggested list price of the print text. With a CourseSmart e-textbook, students can search the text, make notes online, and bookmark important passages for later review. For additional information on this option, visit www.coursesmart.com.

Jon L. Pierce
John W. Newstrom

ACKNOWLEDGMENTS

We express our sincere and very warm appreciation to several colleagues who played key roles in the preparation of this edition of *The Manager's Bookshelf: A Mosaic of Contemporary Views*. Their commitment and dedication to students of organizations and management, coupled with their efforts, made this improved and updated edition possible.

We would also like to single out our late friend and colleague, Larry L. Cummings (Carlson School of Management at the University of Minnesota and "The Institute"), for his "Reflections on the Best Sellers" contained Part XVI of in our book. We also value the additional comments provided on managerial best sellers offered by Brad Jackson and Anne Cummings, which greatly enrich the discussion in that section.

CONTRIBUTORS TO THIS EDITION

We extend our thanks to a number of individuals who provided us with a great deal of assistance and support for the preparation of this book. Many of our management colleagues, former students, and professional managerial associates took the time and effort—always under tight time pressures—to contribute to this book by carefully reading and preparing a summary of one of the selected books. Many of these individuals wanted to offer their personal opinion, add their endorsements or criticisms, and surface elements of their own management philosophies, but at our urging they stuck to their task. To them we express our thanks for their time, energy, and commitment to furthering management education.

The following individuals prepared book summaries for this edition of *The Manager's Bookshelf:*

Introduction

Kelly Nelson, AK Steel—Argyris's *Flawed Advice and the Management Trap*

Best Seller "Classics"

John D. Stavig and Shaker A. Zahra, University of Minnesota—Drucker's *The Practice of Management*

William B. Gartner, Georgetown University, and M. James Naughton, Expert-Knowledge Systems, Inc.—Deming's *Out of the Crisis*

Gayle Porter, Rutgers University—McGregor's *The Human Side of Enterprise*

Dorothy Marcic, Vanderbilt University—Senge's *The Fifth Discipline*

Sara A. Morris, Old Dominion University—Porter's *Competitive Advantage*

High- (and Low-) Performing Organizations

Kristie J. Loescher, University of Texas at Austin—Buckingham's *The One Thing You Need to Know About Great Managing, Great Leading, and Sustained Individual Success*

Allen Harmon, University of Minnesota Duluth and WDSE-TV—Marcus' *Big Winners and Big Losers*

Tanya Pietz, Riverwood Healthcare Center—Collins' *How the Might Fall*

David L. Beal, formerly with Consolidated Papers, Inc.—Beyerlein, Freedman, McGee, and Moran's *Beyond Teams*

Organizational Strategy and Execution

Allen Harmon, University of Minnesota Duluth and WDSE-TV—Raynor's *The Strategy Paradox*

Allen Harmon, University of Minnesota Duluth and WDSE-TV—Joyce, Nohria, and Roberson's *What (Really) Works*

Stephen Rubenfeld, University of Minnesota Duluth—Cascio's *Responsible Restructuring*

Focusing on the Human Dimension

Jodi Nelson, SISU Medical Solutions, LLC—Cameron's *Positive Leadership*

Danielle DuBois Kerr, Uponor, Inc.—Lawler's *Treat People Right!*

Kelly Nelson, AK Steel—Csikszentmihalyi's *Good Business*

Motivation

Shelley Ovrom, City of Azusa—Sirota, Mischkind, and Meltzer's *The Enthusiastic Employee*

Cathy A. Hanson, City of Manhattan Beach—Luthans, Youssef, and Avolio's *Psychological Capital*

AnneMarie Kaul, Arthritis Foundation (North Central Chapter)—Katzenbach's *Why Pride Matters More than Money*

Leadership

Rebecca M. C. Boll, Central Minnesota Federal Credit Union—Dean's *Leadership for Everyone*

Warren Candy, Allete/Minnesota Power—Kellerman's *Bad Leadership*

Claudia PlauntMartin, University of Minnesota Duluth—Kellerman's *Followership*

Organizational Change

Peter Stark, University of Minnesota Duluth—Quinn's *Building the Bridge as You Walk On It*

Warren L. Candy, Allete/Minnesota Power—Christensen, Raynor, and Anthony's *The Innovator's Solution*

Martha Golden, University of Minnesota Duluth/Wintergreen Northern Wear—Lawler & Worley's *Built to Change*

David L. Beal, formerly of Consolidated Papers, Inc.—Kotter's *A Sense of Urgency*

"Undiscussable" Issues at Work

Kelly L. Nelson, AK Steel—Van Fleet and Van Fleet's *Workplace Survival*

Stephen Rubenfeld, University of Minnesota Duluth—Sutton's *The No-Asshole Rule*

AnneMarie Kaul, Arthritis Foundation (North Central Chapter)—Reardon's *It's All Politics*

The Managerial Brain

Rebecca M. C. Boll, Central Minnesota Federal Credit Union—Gigerenzer's *Gut Feelings*

Meghan Keil, Target Corporation—Gardner's *Five Minds for the Future*

Cheri Stine, Stampin' Up!—Gladwell's *Blink!*

Ethics, Values, and Spirituality in the Workplace

Adam Surma, Target Corporation—Lennick and Kiel's *Moral Intelligence*

Linda Hefferin, Elgin Community College—Kidder's *The Ethics Recession*

Randy Skalberg, University of Minnesota Duluth—George's *Authentic Leadership*

Kevin Wold, WSB Engineering—Blanchard and Hodge's *Lead Like Jesus*

Emotions at Work

Beverly Frahm, Frahm Consulting—Boyatzis and McKee's *Resonant Leadership*

Gary J. Colpaert, Milwaukee's Eye Institute—Frost's *Toxic Emotions at Work*

Gary P. Olson, Center for Alcohol and Drug Treatment—Pattakos' *Prisoners of Our Thoughts*

Emerging Dimensions of Organizational Environments

Bob Stine, University of Minnesota College of Natural Resources—Friedman's *Hot, Flat, and Crowded*

Amber Christian, Phoenix Endeavors, LLC—Li and Bernoff's *Groundswell*

Management Fables and Lessons for Personal Success

Charles C. Manz, University of Massachusetts, Amherst—Blanchard and Johnson's *The One Minute Manager*

Gary Stark, Northern Michigan University—Johnson's *Who Moved My Cheese?*

David L. Beal, formerly with Consolidated Papers, Inc.—Covey's *The 8th Habit*

John W. Newstrom, University of Minnesota Duluth—Pike, Ford, and Newstrom's *The Fun Minute Manager*

Contemporary Thinking About Management

Adam Surma, Target Corporation—Pfeffer's *What Were They Thinking?*

Jannifer David, University of Minnesota Duluth—Pfeffer and Sutton's *Hard Facts, Dangerous Half-Truths, and Total Nonsense*

Several persons provided gracious and constructive feedback on the previous edition and offered useful suggestions for improvement; the reviewers include Barry Brock, Maria Cuddy-Casey, Jeffrey Farhenwald, Philip Hess, Sharon Lind, George Lough, Brian Russell, and Fred Ziolkowski. We also appreciate the recommendations for inclusions in this ninth edition made by several reviewers, adopters, and friends. To Connie Johnson, who provided always-patient administrative support, we want to say "Thank you" for helping us complete this project—and many others over the past two decades—in a timely fashion. We appreciate the supportive environment provided by Dean Kjell Knudsen of the Labovitz School of Business and Economics, and our colleagues in the Department of Management Studies here at the University of Minnesota Duluth. We gratefully acknowledge the continued project commitment from Eric Svendsen and the editorial support and assistance that we have received from Kim Norbuta, Ashley Santora, and Claudia Fernandes, all at Prentice Hall.

Jon L. Pierce
John W. Newstrom

ABOUT THE EDITORS

Jon L. Pierce is a Morse-Alumni Distinguished Teaching Professor of Management and Organization in the Labovitz School of Business and Economics at the University of Minnesota Duluth (UMD). He received his Ph.D. in management and organizational studies at the University of Wisconsin-Madison. He is the author of more than 60 papers that have been published or presented at various professional conferences. His publications have appeared in the *Academy of Management Journal, Academy of Management Review, Journal of Management, Journal of Organizational Behavior, Journal of Applied Behavioral Science, Journal of Social Psychology, Journal of Occupational and Organizational Psychology, Organizational Dynamics, Organizational Behavior and Human Decision Processes, Personnel Psychology,* and *Review of General Psychology.*

His research interests include sources of psychological ownership, employee ownership systems, and organization-based self-esteem. He has served on the editorial review board for *the Academy of Management Journal, Personnel Psychology, Journal of Management,* and the *Scandinavian Management Journal.* He is the coauthor of six other books: *Management, Managing, Management and Organizational Behavior: An Integrated Perspective,* and along with John W. Newstrom, *Alternative Work Schedules, Windows into Management,* and *Leaders and the Leadership Process* (now in its sixth edition). In 2000, he was inducted into the *Academy of Management Journal*'s Hall of Fame; in 2005, he received UMD's prestigious Chancellor's Award for Distinguished Research. Dr. Pierce may be contacted at jpierce@d.umn.edu.

John W. Newstrom is a Morse-Alumni Distinguished Teaching Professor Emeritus of Management in the Labovitz School of Business and Economics at the University of Minnesota Duluth. Prior to that, he completed his doctoral degree in Management and Industrial Relations at the University of Minnesota and then taught at Arizona State University for several years. His work has appeared in publications such as *Academy of Management Executive, Personnel Psychology, California Management Review, Journal of Management, Academy of Management Journal, Human Resource Planning, Supervision, Business Horizons,* and the *Journal of Management Development.* He has served as an editorial reviewer for *the Academy of Management Review, Academy of Management Journal, Academy of Management Executive, Human Resource Development Quarterly, Advanced Management Journal,* and the *Journal of Management Development.*

He is the author or coauthor of over 40 books in various editions, including *The Fun Minute Manager* (with Bob Pike and Robert C. Ford), *Organizational Behavior: Human Behavior at Work* (13th edition), *Supervision* (9th edition), *Transfer of Training* (with Mary Broad), *Leading With a Laugh* (with Robert C. Ford), and *The Big Book of Teambuilding Games* (with Ed Scannell). He is a member of the University of Minnesota's Academy of Distinguished Teachers and has served on the Boards of Directors for several nonprofit organizations. He has also actively served as a seminar leader for leadership development programs around the country and as a consultant to many other organizations. One of his current interests lies in helping managers create and sustain a fun work environment for their employees. Dr. Newstrom may be contacted at jnewstro@d.umn.edu.

I

Introduction

Part I contains two readings. The first, *Understanding and Using the Best Sellers*, prepared by us (Pierce and Newstrom), the editors of *The Manager's Bookshelf*, provides insight into why such a large number of management-oriented books have found themselves in bookstores, on coffee tables in homes, on Internet bookselling sites, and on the bookshelves of those who manage today's organizations. Four elements stand out in Reading 1:

1. We discuss the rationale for this mosaic of contemporary views on organizations and management and provide you with insight into the nature and character of (and authors in) *The Manager's Bookshelf*.
2. We challenge you to read and critically reflect upon this collection of thoughts and experiences.
3. We invite you to debate the ideas and philosophies that are presented here.
4. We encourage you to let these contemporary management books stimulate your thinking, to motivate you to look more systematically into the science of organizations and management, and to provide you with the fun of learning something new.

As a result of our substantial concern that these contemporary books will be seen as "quick and dirty" cures for organizational woes, we encourage you to read books such as Ralph H. Kilmann's *Beyond the Quick Fix: Managing Five Tracks to Organizational Success*. In it, the author provides a valuable message that should serve as the backdrop to your consumption and assessment of all of the purported "one minute" cures for organizational problems and for the management of today's complex organizations. Kilmann encourages managers to *stop perpetuating the myth of organizational and management simplicity* and to develop a more complete and integrated approach to the management of today's complex organizations.

Many other writers have echoed these thoughts and cautions. For example:

- Marcus Alexander and Harry Korine (*Harvard Business Review*, December 2008, p. 74) contended that the unquestioned assumptions underlying management trends/fads "often lead to sloppy thinking" and "preclude careful examination of the pros and cons of the specific choices made by a single company in a particular context."

- John Hollon (*Worforce Management*, June 9, 2008, p. 42) concluded that "Everyone is looking for the magic formula that will help make them a great manager who can drive workers (and the organization) to the next level."
- Jeffrey Pfeffer and Robert I. Sutton (*Harvard Business Review*, January 2006, p. 63) asserted that "Executives routinely dose their organizations with strategic snake oil: discredited nostrums, partial remedies, or untested management miracle cures."
- Robert J. David and David Strand (*Academy of Management Journal*, 2006, 49:2, p. 215) asserted that "Management fashions are a striking feature of contemporary organizational life (but) . . . enthusiasm soon wanes, skepticism mounts, and yesterday's panacea becomes today's run-of-the-mill application."
- Eric W. Ford and colleagues (*Academy of Management Executive*, 2005, 19:4, p. 24) contended that "rather than being interested in systematic and long-term solutions, managers are generally infatuated with the latest fads and fashions in their search for quick fixes."
- Geoffrey Colvin (*Fortune*, June 28, 2004, p. 166), in "A Concise History of Management Hooey," suggested that "Idea-starved managers . . . were so hungry they created an entirely new phenomenon in publishing, the business bestseller."
- Danny Miller and associates (*Business Horizons*, July–August 2004, p. 7) begin their condemnation of management fads by getting right to the point: "Many popular administrative ideas are epitomized by a search for the quick fix—a simple solution that all organizations can embrace to make employees more productive, customers happier, or profits greater."
- Michael Harvey (*SAM Advanced Management Journal*, Autumn 2001, p. 37) concluded that "there is an immense wrong-headedness or slipperiness in most normative approaches" to management as portrayed in various management best sellers.
- Shari Caudron (*TD*, June 2002, p. 40) noted that the fads presented in management best sellers are taken up with great enthusiasm for a short while and then quickly discarded. This, she suggests, is done because "the tools were sold into companies by charlatans who didn't understand the concepts but knew the right buzzwords."
- Kristine Ellis (*Training*, April 2001, p. 41) concluded that the worst of the best sellers are promoted as "magic bullets" to solve organizational problems but often become little more than the prevailing "flavor of the month."
- Business columnist Dale Dauten (*The Arizona Republic*, February 19, 2004, p. D3) suggested that there are three types of business books on the market to avoid: the Obvious (compilations of clichéd truths), the Envious (stories of successful businesspeople), and the Obnoxious (books that insult your intelligence).
- Danny Miller and Jon Hartwick (*Harvard Business Review*, October 2002, p. 26) noted that management fads usually have short life cycles and are quickly replaced by new ones. Typical fads, according to Miller and Hartwick, are simple, prescriptive, falsely encouraging, broadly generic, overly simplistic, closely matched to contemporary business problems, and novel and fresh appearing, and achieve their legitimacy through the status and prestige of gurus (as opposed to the merits of empirical evidence).
- Jeffrey Pfeffer (*Harvard Business Review*, February 2005, p. 54) surveyed the 30,000-plus business books in print and concluded that "Much of this advice is, at best, a waste of time. At worst, it can—if followed—create more problems than it solves."
- Another cautionary perspective is provided in *The Witch Doctors*. After systematically and objectively reviewing a wide array of popular management books, authors John Micklethwait and Adrian Wooldridge concluded that managers must become critical consumers of these products. Being critical means being suspicious of the faddish contentions,

remaining unconvinced by simplistic argumentation by the authors, being selective about which theory might work for you, and becoming broadly informed about the merits and deficiencies of each proposal.

Readers interested in more comprehensive and critical portraits of the management best-seller literature are encouraged to read "Management Fads: Emergence, Evolution, and Implications for Managers" by Jane Whitney Gibson and Dana V. Tesone (*Academy of Management Executive*, 2001, 15:4, pp. 122–133) and the reviews of four books on management fads in "Resource Reviews" (*Academy of Management Learning and Education*, 2003, 2:3, pp. 313–321).

In an explicit attempt to provoke your critical thinking about management fads, we have included (as Reading 2) a summary of *Flawed Advice and the Management Trap*. Noted Harvard University professor Chris Argyris presents two models of behavior. He voices a cautionary note when it comes to the managerial advice that is presented through the "popular management" press. Much of these prescriptions, such as those presented in Stephen R. Covey's *The Seven Habits of Highly Effective People* (see Reading 4 in Part XIV), are presented as though they are sound and valid principles of management, when in fact they cannot be tested and therefore proven correct (workable). In order to avoid the management trap that stems from the adoption of "flawed advice," Argyris offers an alternative through Model II behavior.

Argyris has received numerous awards and is the recipient of 11 honorary degrees from universities around the world. He is the James Bryant Conant Professor Emeritus of Education and Organizational Behavior at Harvard's Graduate School of Business. He has written more than 400 articles and 30 books across a 45-year career, including *The Next Challenge for Leadership: Learning, Change, and Commitment* and (with Donald Schon) *Organizational Learning: A Theory of Action Perspective*. Interested readers may wish to read the "retrospective" comments on his career by Argyris and others in the *Academy of Management Executive* (2003, 17:2, pp. 37–55).

1

Understanding and Using the Best Sellers

Jon L. Pierce and John W. Newstrom

For several decades now, a large number of newly published books have focused on various aspects of management. These books have been in high demand at local bookstores and on the Internet. Several individuals have authored books that have sold millions of copies, among them Peter Drucker (*The Practice of Management*), Tom Peters and Bob Waterman (*In Search of Excellence*), Spencer Johnson (*Who Moved My Cheese?*), Jim Collins (*Good to Great*), Stephen Covey (*The Seven Habits of Highly Effective People*), Kenneth Blanchard and Spencer Johnson (*The One Minute Manager*), Malcolm Gladwell (*Blink!*), and Thomas Friedman (*The World Is Flat*).

Some of these books have stayed on "best-seller" lists for many weeks, months, and even years. What are the reasons for their popularity? Why have business books continued to catch the public's attention through both good economic times and bad?

We have all read newspaper stories about (and many have felt the shock waves and personal impact of) downsizing, pension fund losses, restructuring, corporate ethical scandals, outsourcing of jobs, globalization, and excessive executive compensation and benefits. We have all read stories about the success of foreign organizations—especially in the automotive and electronics industries. We have continued to watch bigger and bigger portions of our markets being dominated by foreign-owned and foreign-controlled organizations. We have witnessed foreign interests purchase certain segments of America, while more and more jobs have been moved offshore. Perhaps in response to these trends, a tremendous thirst for *American* success stories and a desire to learn what would prevent some of these negative phenomena have arisen. In essence, the public is receptive and the timing is right for the writing, publication, and sale of popular management books.

A second reason for the upsurge in management books stems from another form of competition. Many management consultants, fighting for visibility and a way to differentiate their services, have written books they hope will become best sellers. Through the printed word they hope to provide a unique take-home product for their clients, communicate their management philosophies, gain wide exposure for themselves or their firms, and profit handsomely.

Third, the best sellers also provide an optimistic message to a receptive market. In difficult economic times or under conditions of extreme pressure to produce short-term results, managers may be as eager to swallow easy formulas for business success as sick patients are to consume their prescribed medicines. Sensing this propensity, the authors of the best sellers (and of many other books with lesser records) often claim, at least implicitly, to present managers with an easy cure for their organizational woes, or with an easy path to personal success. In a world characterized by chaos, environmental turbulence, and intense global competition, managers are driven to search for the ideas provided by others that might be turned into a competitive advantage.

Fourth, we are witnessing an increased belief in and commitment to proactive organizational change and a search for differentiating one's approach. An increasing number of managers are rejecting the notion that "if it ain't broke, don't fix it," and instead are adopting what Peters and Waterman portrayed as a bias toward action. These managers are seriously looking for and experimenting with different approaches toward organizational management. Many of the popular books provide managers with insights into new and different ways of managing. At a minimum, readers are engaging in the process of benchmarking their competition and adopting "best practices" that have worked for others; hopefully, they are using the established practices of others as a springboard to developing even better ideas themselves.

In their search for the "quick fix," generations of risk-taking American managers have adopted a series of organizational management concepts, such as management by objectives, job enlargement, job enrichment, sensitivity training, flextime, and a variety of labor-management participative schemes, such as quality circles, total quality management, and quality of work-life programs. Each has experienced its own life cycle, often going through the stages of market discovery, wild acceptance by passionate believers, careful questioning of it by serious critics, broad disillusionment with its shortcomings, and sometimes later being abandoned and replaced by another emerging management technique (while a few advocates remain staunchly supportive of the fad).[1]

As a consequence of this managerial tendency to embrace ideas and then soon discard them, many viable managerial techniques have received a tarnished image. For example, many of the Japanese participative management systems that were copied by American managers found their way into the garbage cans of an earlier generation of American managers. The continuing demand for quick fixes stimulates a ready market for new, reborn, and revitalized management ideas. We encourage you to read and seriously reflect on the questionable probability of finding a legitimate quick fix. The search for solutions to major organizational problems in terms of "one-minute" answers reflects a Band-Aid® approach to management—one that is destined to ultimately fail and one that we condemn as a poor way to enrich the body of management knowledge and practice.

We alert you to this managerial tendency to look for "new" solutions to current organizational problems. The rush to resolve problems and take advantage of opportunities frequently leads to the search for simple remedies for complex organizational problems. Yet few of today's organizational problems can be solved with any single approach. The high-involvement management, the learning organization, and the compassionate corporate culture advocated in today's generation of popular management books may also join the list of tried-and-abandoned solutions to organizational woes if implemented without a broader context and deeper understanding. We especially hope that the quick-fix approach to organizational problem solving that characterizes the management style of many will not be promoted as a result of this mosaic (i.e., *The Manager's Bookshelf*) of today's popular business books.

RATIONALE FOR THIS BOOK

The business world has been buzzing with terms like *vision, alignment, flow, pride, authenticity, innovation, credibility, narcissism, paradigms, stewardship, the learning organization, the spirit of work, the soul of business, transformational and charismatic leaders, knowledge management, high-involvement management and organizations,* and *corporate cultures.* On the negative side, these terms feed the management world's preoccupation with quick fixes and the perpetuation of management fads. On the positive side, many of these concepts serve as catalysts to the further development of sound management philosophies and practices.

In earlier decades, a few books occasionally entered the limelight (e.g., *Parkinson's Law, The Peter Principle, The Effective Executive,* and *My Years with General Motors*), but for the most part they did not generate the widespread and prolonged popularity of the current generation of business books. Then, too, many were not written in the readable style that makes most contemporary books so easy to consume.

Managers find the current wave of books not only interesting but also enjoyable and entertaining to read. A small survey conducted by the Center for Creative Leadership found that a significant number of managers who participated in a study of their all-around reading selections chose one or more management books as their favorite.[2] In essence, many of the popular management books are being read by managers—probably because the books are often supportive of their present management philosophies! Many managers report that these books are insightful, easily readable, interestingly presented, and seemingly practical. Whether the prescriptions in these books have had (or ever will have) a real and lasting impact on the effective management of organizations remains to be determined.

Despite the overall popularity of many business best sellers, some managers do not read *any* current management books, and many others have read only a limited number or small parts of a few.* Similarly, many university students studying management have heard about some of these books, but not read them. *The Manager's Bookshelf* presents perspectives from (but not a criticism of) a number of those popular management books. *The Manager's Bookshelf* is designed for managers who are interested in the best sellers but do not have time to read all of them in their entirety and for students of management who want to be well informed as they prepare to enter the work world. Reading about the views expressed in many of the best sellers will expand the knowledge and business vocabulary of both groups and enable them to engage in more meaningful conversations with their managerial colleagues.

Although reading the 52 summaries provided here can serve as a useful introduction to this literature, they should not be viewed as a substitute for immersion in the original material, nor do they remove the need for further reading of the more substantive management books and professional journals. The good news is that the popularity of these books suggests that millions of managers are reading them and are exhibiting an interest in learning about what has worked for other managers and firms. This is an important step toward the development of an open-system paradigm for themselves and for their organizations.

We strongly advocate that both managers and students be informed organizational citizens. Therefore, we believe it is important for you to know and understand what is being written about

---

* For a discussion on incorporating these types of management books into management training programs, see John W. Newstrom and Jon L. Pierce, "The Potential Role of Popular Business Books in Management Development Programs," *Journal of Management Development,* 8 (2, 1989), 13–24.

organizations and management. We also believe that it is important for you to know what is being read by the managers who surround you, some of which is contained in best sellers, and much of which is contained in more traditional management books, as well as in professional and scientific journals.[3]

CONTENTS OF THE BEST SELLERS

What topics do these best-selling books cover, what is their form, and what is their merit? Although many authors cover a wide range of topics and others do not have a clear focus, most of these books fall into one of several categories. Some attempt to describe the more effective and ineffective companies and identify what made them successes or failures. Others focus on "micro" issues in leadership, motivation, or ethics. One group of authors focuses their attention on broad questions of corporate strategy and competitive tactics for implementing strategy. Some focus on pressing issues facing the contemporary organization such as social responsibility, globalism, the natural environment, workforce diversity, and the virtual workplace.

In terms of form, many contain apparently simple answers and trite prescriptions. Others are built around literally hundreds of spellbinding anecdotes and stories. Some have used interviews of executives as their source of information; others have adopted the parable format for getting their point across. As a group, their presentation style is rich in diversity. As editors of this mosaic, we have necessarily had to exclude thousands of books while attempting to provide you with a rich exposure to an array of perspectives. For the most part, we have not included books that focus on a single executive's career success (e.g., Jack Welch or Steve Jobs), a single successful firm (e.g., Wal-Mart or Southwest Airlines) or failed organization (e.g., Enron), or a historical reinterpretation of a key person's practices (e.g., *Leadership Secrets of Sitting Bull* [or Sir Ernest Shackleton, Sun Tzu, General George Patton, William Shakespeare, or the Sopranos!]).

Judging the merits of best sellers is a difficult task (and one that we will leave for readers and management critics to engage in). Some critics have taken the extreme position of calling these books "intellectual wallpaper" and "business pornography." Certainly labels like these, justified or not, should caution readers. A better perspective is provided by an assessment of the sources, often anecdotal, of many of the books. In other words, much of the information in business best sellers stems from the experiences and observations of a single individual and is often infused with the subjective opinions of that writer. Unlike the more traditional academic literature, these books do not all share a sound scientific foundation. Requirements pertaining to objectivity, reproducibility of observations, and tests for reliability and validity have not guided the creation of much of the material. As a consequence, the authors are at liberty to say whatever they want (and often with as much passion as they desire).

Unlike authors who publish research-based knowledge, authors of management best sellers do not need to submit their work to a panel of reviewers who then critically evaluate the ideas, logic, and data. The authors of these popular management books are able to proclaim as sound management principles virtually anything that is intuitively acceptable to their publisher and readers. Therefore, readers need to be cautious consumers who are vigilant about being misled. The ideas presented in these books need to be critically compared with the well-established thoughts from more traditional sources of managerial wisdom.

CRITIQUING THESE POPULAR BOOKS

Although the notion of one-minute management is seductive, we may safely conclude that there are no fast-acting cures to deep and complex business problems. Recognizing that simple solutions are not likely to be found in 200 pages of anecdotal stories and that the best sellers frequently present (or appear to present) quick fixes and simple solutions, we strongly encourage you to read these popular books, looking less for simple solutions and more toward using them to stimulate your thinking and challenge the way you go about doing your business. We encourage you not only to achieve comprehension and understanding but ultimately to arrive at the level of critique and synthesis—far more useful long-term skills.

To help you approach these works more critically, we encourage you to use the following questions to guide your evaluation:[4]

- **Author credentials:** How do the authors' backgrounds and personal characteristics uniquely qualify them to write this book? What relevant experience do they have? What unique access or perspective do they have? What prior writing experience do they have, and how was it accepted in the marketplace? What is their research background (capacity to design, conduct, and interpret the results of their observations)?
- **Rationale:** Why did the authors write the book? Is their self-proclaimed reason legitimate?
- **Face validity:** On initial examination of the book's major characteristics and themes (but before reading the entire book and actually examining the evidence provided), do you react positively or negatively? Are you inclined to accept or reject the authors' conclusions? Are the major contentions believable? Does it fit with your prior experience and expectations, or does it rock them to the core?
- **Target audience:** For whom is this book uniquely written? What level of manager in the organizational hierarchy would most benefit from reading the book and why? Is it for *you*?
- **Integration of existing knowledge:** A field of inquiry can best move forward only if it draws upon and then extends existing knowledge. Was this book written in isolation of existing knowledge? Do the authors demonstrate an awareness of and build upon existing knowledge, while giving appropriate credit to other sources of ideas?
- **Readability/interest:** Do the authors engage your mind? Are relevant, practical illustrations provided that indicate how the ideas have been or could be applied? Are the language and format used appealing to you?
- **Internal validity:** To what degree do the authors provide substantive evidence that the phenomenon, practice, or ideas presented actually and directly produce a valued result? Does an internally consistent presentation of ideas demonstrate the processes through which the causes for their observations are understood?
- **Reliability/consistency:** To what degree do the authors' conclusions converge with other sources of information available to you, or with the product of other methods of data collection? Do the authors stay internally consistent in their "pitch" from beginning to end of the book?
- **Distinctiveness:** Is the material presented new, creative, and distinctive (providing you with "value added"), or is it merely a presentation of "old wine in new bottles"?
- **Objectivity:** To what extent do the authors have a self-serving or political agenda, or have the authors presented information that was systematically gathered and objectively evaluated? Have the authors offered both the pros and cons of their views?
- **External validity:** Are the ideas likely to work in your unique situation, or are they bound to the narrow context within which the authors operated? What are the similarities that give

you confidence that the recommendations made can be safely and effectively applied to your context?

- **Practicality:** Are the ideas adaptable? Do the authors provide concrete suggestions for application? Are the ideas readily transferable to the workplace in such a way that the typical reader could be expected to know what to do with them a few days later at work? Is it possible to produce an action plan directly from the material that you have read?

These are only some of the questions that should be asked as you read and evaluate any popular management book.

NATURE OF THIS BOOK

This is the ninth edition of *The Manager's Bookshelf.* Recent language editions have also appeared in Italian, Spanish, and Chinese, pointing to the international popularity of these books. The current edition includes many books that were not previously summarized, representing a substantial revision. *The Manager's Bookshelf* provides a comprehensive introduction to many of the major best sellers in the management field during recent years.

The selections contained in this book are of two types: excerpts of original material and summaries prepared by a panel of reviewers. In some cases, we provide the reader with not only the main ideas presented by the author of a best seller but also the flavor (style or nature) of the author's literary approach. For some selections, we obtained permission to excerpt directly a chapter from the original book—particularly chapters that are the keystone presentation of the author's major theme. In one case, the author's original thoughts and words were captured by selecting an article (representing part of the book) that the author had written for publication in a professional journal. Here again, the reader will see the author's ideas directly, though only sampled or much condensed from the original source.

The major format chosen for inclusion is a comprehensive, but brief and readable, summary of the best seller prepared by persons selected for their relevant expertise, interest, and familiarity. These summaries are primarily descriptive, designed to provide readers with an overall understanding of the book. These summaries are not judgmental in nature, nor are they necessarily a complete or precise reflection of the book author's management philosophy.

Determining what constituted a management best seller worthy of inclusion was easy in some cases and more difficult in others. From the thousands of books available for selection, the ones included here rated highly on one or more of these criteria:

1. *Market acceptance:* Several books have achieved national notoriety by selling hundreds of thousands, and, occasionally, millions, of copies.
2. *Provocativeness:* Some books present thought-provoking viewpoints that run counter to "traditional" management thought.
3. *Distinctiveness:* A wide variety of topical themes of interest to organizational managers and students of management is presented.
4. *Representativeness:* In an attempt to avoid duplication from books with similar content within a topical area, many popular books were necessarily excluded.
5. *Author reputation:* Some authors (e.g., John Kotter and Edward E. Lawler III) have a strong reputation for the quality of their thinking and the insights they have generated; therefore, some of their newer products were included.

AUTHORS OF THE BEST SELLERS

It is appropriate for a reader to examine a management best seller and inquire, "Who is the author of this book?" Certainly the authors come from varied backgrounds, which can be both a strength and weakness for the best sellers as a whole. Their diversity of experience and perspective is rich, yet it is possible that some authors are ill-qualified to speak and portray themselves as experts.

Some of the authors have been critically described as self-serving egotists who have little to say constructively about management, but who say it with a flair and passion such that reading their books may appear to be very exciting. Some books are seemingly the product of armchair humorists who set out to entertain their readers with tongue in cheek. Other books on the best-seller lists have been written with the aid of a ghostwriter (i.e., by someone who takes information that has been provided by another and then converts it into the lead author's story) or a professional writer who helps a busy executive organize and present his or her thoughts. Other books are the product of a CEO's reflection on his or her career or heartfelt positions on contemporary issues in organizations (e.g., author Bill George). A rather new and refreshing change has been the emergence in the best-seller literature of books prepared by respected academic professionals who have capably applied the best of their substantive research to pressing management problems and subsequently integrated their thoughts into book form. (Examples in this edition of such academics include Edward E. Lawler III, Wayne Cascio, Alfred Marcus, Kim Cameron, Jeffrey Pfeffer, and John Kotter.) In summary, it may be fascinating to read the "inside story" or delve into a series of exciting anecdotes and "war stories," but the reader still has the opportunity and obligation to challenge the author's credentials for making broad generalizations from that experience base.

Conclusions

We encourage you to read and reflect on this collection of thoughts from the authors of today's generation of management books. We invite you to expand and enrich your insights into management as a result of learning from this set of popular books. We challenge you to question and debate the pros and cons of the ideas and philosophies that are presented by these authors. We hope you will ask when, where, how, and why these ideas are applicable. Examine the set of readings provided here, let them stimulate your thinking, and, in the process, learn something new. You'll find that learning—and especially critical thinking—can be both fun and addictive!

Notes

1. See, for example, Barbara Ettore, "What's the Next Business Buzzword?" *Management Review*, 1997, 86:8, 33–35; "Business Fads: What's In—and Out," *Business Week*, January 20, 1986; W. W. Armstrong, "The Boss Has Read Another New Book!" *Management Review*, June 1994, 83:6, 61–64.
2. Frank Freeman, "Books That Mean Business: The Management Best Sellers," *Academy of Management Review*, 1985, 10, 345–350.
3. See, for example, a report on executive reading preferences by Marilyn Wellemeyer in "Books Bosses Read," *Fortune*, April 27, 1987.
4. See John W. Newstrom and Jon L. Pierce, "An Analytic Framework for Assessing Popular Business Books," *Journal of Management Development*, 1993, 12:4, 20–28.

Flawed Advice and the Management Trap

Chris Argyris

Summary Prepared by Kelly Nelson

Kelly Nelson is a 1991 graduate of the University of Minnesota Duluth. Since graduation, she has served in various operating management and human resource positions in the steel industry. She is currently working as general manager, Human Resources, at AK Steel in Ohio. She is committed to dispensing "unflawed" advice as often as possible, particularly when dispensing parenting knowledge to her son John.

Many individuals receive and accept advice that is fundamentally flawed, which leads to counterproductive consequences. The acceptance of flawed advice stems from Model I behaviors that strive to protect oneself, while unilaterally treating all others the same (i.e., not dealing specifically and directly with behaviors in order to effect change). Model II behaviors, on the other hand, provide organizations the opportunity to share information, act cooperatively, and deal directly and firmly with behaviors in order to effect change. Organizations that adopt Model II behaviors also provide themselves the opportunity to analyze advice to ensure it is not flawed, thereby avoiding the "management trap."

INCONSISTENT AND UNACTIONABLE ADVICE

Stephen Covey's *The Seven Habits of Highly Effective People* (1989) is based upon a set of principles that direct individuals to effectiveness through **inside-out management**, one that begins with a focus on one's self. The goal is to develop a positive attitude through developing trust, generating positive energy, and sidestepping negative energy. Covey's strategy suggests suppressing negative feelings and putting on a "false face" of positive feedback. However, the premise of this suppression flies

---

Chris Argyris. *Flawed Advice and the Management Trap: How Managers Can Know When They're Getting Good Advice and When They're Not.* New York: Oxford University Press, 2000.

in the face of Covey's basic principles (i.e., to develop trust). Furthermore, the "theory" espoused by Covey cannot be tested; therefore, it cannot be proven.

This inconsistent and unactionable advice is also demonstrated by Doyle and Strauss (*How to Make Meetings Work*, 1982), management consultants who advise groups on actions to produce effective meetings. According to Doyle and Strauss, if a group is having difficulty deciding where to begin and how, it is best to wait until the group is convinced it needs the consultant (or leader). The group will then ask for assistance and the consultant can take control and give direction to the group. In any group, this tactic may become a self-fulfilling prophecy. Further, Doyle and Strauss do not give specific guidelines on the point at which the consultant should intervene. Also, the actual behaviors of the consultant are not detailed. Similar to Covey's theory, Doyle and Strauss's theory cannot be tested; therefore, it cannot be proven.

As demonstrated by the examples of Covey and Doyle and Strauss, popular management advice is published as valid and actionable and is widely adopted. However, the advice reveals a pattern of gaps and inconsistencies, leading to unintended consequences and an inability to systematically correct the deficiencies.

ORGANIZATIONAL CONSEQUENCES OF USING INCONSISTENT ADVICE

The most common advice for designing and implementing programs for organizational change and improvement involves the following four elements:

1. Define a vision.
2. Define a competitive strategy that is consistent with the vision.
3. Define organizational work processes that, when carried out, will implement the strategy.
4. Define individual job requirements so that employees can produce the processes effectively.

The elements are sound and understandable. However, they lead to inconsistencies when the vision, strategy, work processes, and job requirements are developed to support contradictory goals. For example, a 1996 study concluded that a vast majority of companies held only a superficial commitment to internal participative decision making. Eighty-three percent of the middle managers responding favored more involvement; yet, their supervisors did not know it. Top managers were not committed to the strategy, nor were they aware of the lack of credibility they were demonstrating.

For the four elements to succeed and to lead to consistent improvement, *internal commitment* of every employee (gained through intrinsic motivation) is needed. However, most organizations attempt to develop the elements' **external commitment** (top–down policies). This inherent inconsistency lays the groundwork for failure. The failure is demonstrated through the organization's failure to improve performance, increase profits, and develop cooperative behaviors.

WHY FLAWED ADVICE EXISTS

If so much professional advice, even if implemented correctly, leads to counterproductive consequences, why have so many users found that advice to be helpful? Because people hold two different "theories of action" about effective behavior—one they *espouse* and one they actually *use* (i.e., *Model I*). While using Model I, people strive to satisfy their actions when they

- Define goals and try to achieve them. (They don't try to develop, with others, a mutual definition of shared purpose.)

- Maximize winning and minimize losing. (They treat any change in goals, once they are decided on, as a sign of weakness.)
- Minimize the generation or expression of negative feelings. (They fear this would be interpreted as showing ineptness, incompetence, or lack of diplomacy.)
- Be rational. (They want to remain objective and intellectual, and suppress their feelings.)

To accomplish these ends, under Model I, people will seek to

- Design and manage the environment unilaterally, that is, plan actions secretly and persuade or cajole others to agree with one's definition of the situation.
- Own and control the task.
- Unilaterally protect themselves, that is, keep from being vulnerable by speaking in abstractions, avoiding reference to directly observed events, and withholding underlying thoughts and feelings.
- Unilaterally protect others from being hurt, in particular, by withholding important information, telling white lies, suppressing feelings, and offering false sympathy. Moreover, they do not test the assumption that the other person needs to be protected or that the strategy of protection should be kept secret.

Following Model I behavior leads to a self-sealing loop in which the individual treats others unilaterally while protecting himself or herself. As individuals follow Model I behavior, they become skilled and their actions will appear to have "worked" in that they achieve their intended objectives while appearing spontaneous and effortless. Model I behaviors are performed not only by individuals but also by groups. This provides an organization-wide network of Model I behavior in which all members are protecting themselves (whether individually or as a group). Furthermore, the Model I behaviors are enforced and perpetuated by Human Resource Department individuals who also practice Model I behaviors.

On the other hand, **Model II** behaviors involve sharing power with anyone who has competence and is relevant to deciding about implementing the action in question. Defining and assigning tasks are shared by all decision makers. In the Model II method, decision-making networks are developed with the goal of maximizing the contribution of each member.

Model I behaviors allow individuals to remain within their comfort zones and encourage all to place responsibility on problems "out there" instead of on the systematic faults of the advice being used. Hence, it is attractive and still widely used. Model II behavior forces individual behavioral change and accepts all participants as equals in the process. While pulling individuals out of their comfort zones, it requires individuals to face up to their own commitments and reflect upon their own assumptions, biases, and reasoning.

VALIDITY AND ACTIONABILITY LIMITS TO MODEL I

The four main reasons Model I behavior produces unskilled awareness and incompetence are as follows:

1. The advice represents **espoused theories** of effectiveness.
2. The advice, as crafted, contains evaluations and attributions that are neither tested nor testable.
3. The advice is based on self-referential logic that produces limited knowledge about what is going on.
4. The advice does not specify causal processes.

Critiquing Advice

How can managers determine if the advice they are receiving is Model I-based advice? It is important that individuals focus on reducing inconsistencies, closing knowledge gaps, and addressing personal fear. Instead of judging others as defensive, wrong, and/or unjust, the individual must request illustrations of evaluations and attributions and craft tests of their validity. Instead of judging others as naïve, complainers, or crybabies, one should request illustrations and tests, then inquire about how others responded to test attempts. One must also illustrate how the gaps and inconsistencies in the reasoning process are likely to back-fire. Finally, evaluations and attributions about counterproductive actions must be illustrated and testing encouraged.

If most of the advice is abstract and does not specify the theory required to implement it, Model I behaviors will result. Some may espouse Model II behavior, but they will be unaware of and unable to explain the gaps. Finally, Model II behavior is more direct and much tougher on holding people responsible for true changed behaviors.

Model I is often integrated in performance review systems. Often performance appraisals are "eased into" by the appraiser in order to save the recipient's feelings. Also, negative feedback is given in general terms, and quickly followed by positive reinforcement (often given only to get away from the negative portion of the review). Performance evaluations such as these are classic Model I examples, with inconsistencies, information gaps, and behavior not changed as a result.

On the other hand, performance evaluations based in Model II are specific, direct, and produce discussion about tough, productive reasoning that results in compelling decisions. It also facilitates change of the organization to generating internal commitment to organization values.

Generating Internal Commitment to Values to Produce Desired Outcomes

In order for an organization's values to become internal commitments on an individual level, Model II behavior needs to be practiced at all levels of the organization. Nondefensive information sharing and decision making, along with individual awareness of their own gaps and inconsistencies, provide the culture in which value commitment becomes internal to the individual.

The organization's values lead to strategic choices. High-quality choices possess four key attributes:

1. They are genuine.
2. They are sound.
3. They are actionable.
4. They are compelling.

Obstacles to high-quality strategic choices include politics, bad analyses, turbulent markets and, most commonly, flawed processes. In flawed processes, choices either do not get framed, do not get made, appear to get made but fall apart, are made but are not sound, or get made but the subsequent action is not timely.

To ensure strategic choices are of high quality and meet the internal commitment to values adopted by individuals, a **choice-structuring process** is necessary. The goal of a choice-structuring process is to produce sound strategic choices that lead to successful action.

The strategic choice-structuring process has five steps:

1. Frame the choice.
2. Brainstorm possible options.
3. Specify conditions necessary to validate each option.
4. Prioritize the conditions that create the greatest barrier to choice.
5. Design valid tests for the key barrier conditions.

Summary

Model I behaviors prohibit strategic choice structuring because protectionism and defensiveness are the bases for the behavior. In Model II environments, successful strategic choice structuring is possible because the advice adopted is not flawed. The advice adopted stipulates that (1) the **theories in use** should specify the sequence of behavior required to produce the intended consequences or goals; (2) the theories in use should be crafted in ways that make the causality transparent; (3) the causalities embedded in the theories in use are testable robustly in the context of everyday life; and (4) actionable knowledge must specify the values that underlie and govern the designs in use.

Model II behaviors provide organizations with the opportunity to analyze advice directly to ensure advice adopted by the organization is not flawed.

II

Best-Seller "Classics"

Many of the books contained in earlier editions of *The Manager's Bookshelf* as a part of our mosaic of contemporary views continue to have a message that many managers reference frequently and still want to study. As a result, for the ninth edition of *The Manager's Bookshelf* we have included summaries of six key books published in earlier years that continue to be popular references for managers today. (Note: additional "classics" such as *The One Minute Manager*, *Who Moved My Cheese?* and *The Seven Habits of Highly Effective People* are included in Part XIV of this book.)

Peter F. Drucker—a writer, consultant, and teacher—was the Marie Rankin Clarke Professor of Social Sciences and Management at Claremont Graduate University and previously taught at New York University. He received his doctorate from University of Frankfurt, Germany, in 1931. Having awed the world with his writings across a half-century until his death at age 95 in 2005, Drucker was variously described as "the man who invented management," "the patron saint of socially aware executives," a "prolific and profound management thinker," "The Dr. Spock of American business," and "the world's foremost pioneer of management theory." He was the author of 40 books and an astounding 35 articles that appeared in the prestigious *Harvard Business Review* journal. In 2002, he was awarded the Presidential Medal of Freedom, the nation's highest civilian award.

In *The Practice of Management*, Drucker suggests that executives ask several penetrating questions, such as, What is our business? Who is our customer? What does our customer value most? He argues that management is a distinct (but previously underappreciated) function that is practice oriented and can be improved through education. He emphasizes the importance of the external environment, pursuing multiple goals, accenting innovation and knowledge workers, acting with integrity, following a systematic decision-making process, and viewing the firm as a social institution. He also pioneered the concept of management by objectives (MBO).

Quality, customer service, total quality management, and continuous improvement have been organizational buzzwords for the past several years. One of the leaders in developing strategies for building quality into manufacturing processes was the late W. Edwards Deming. During the 1950s, Deming went to Japan to teach statistical control, where his ideas received a very warm reception. The Japanese built on Deming's ideas and moved the responsibility for quality from the ranks of middle management down to the shop floor level. Deming's ideas on quality control soon became an integral feature in Japanese management. Deming has been hailed by his admirers both as the "prophet of quality" and the "man of the century." He certainly demonstrated a powerful force of personality and singular focus.

Total quality control (TQC) means that responsibility for quality is a part of every employee's job. Deming's *Out of the Crisis* calls for long-term organizational transformation through the implementation of a 14-step plan of action focusing on leadership, constant innovation, and removal of barriers to performance. Interested readers may also wish to examine other works about Deming and his influence in *The World of W. Edwards Deming, The Deming Dimension, Thinking About Quality,* and *Deming's Road to Continual Improvement.*

A true classic in the management literature is Douglas McGregor's *The Human Side of Enterprise*, first published in 1960. Because of the book's popularity, its timeless theme, and genuine relevance for organizations in the twenty-first century, McGregor's seminal work continues to be valuable reading.

McGregor explores alternative assumptions that managers might hold and that drive different approaches to the management of organizations and their employees. Through the presentation of two sets of assumptions—labeled Theory X and Theory Y—McGregor urges managers to see employees as capable of innovation, creativity, commitment, high levels of sustained effort, and the exercise of self-direction and self-control.

Douglas McGregor received his doctorate at Harvard University. Before his death in 1964, he served on the faculties of Harvard University and the Massachusetts Institute of Technology and was president of Antioch College. McGregor is also the author of *The Professional Manager.*

A contemporary of McGregor, Abraham Maslow has sometimes been called the "greatest psychologist since Freud," and a "significant contributor to the humanistic psychology movement." He is well known to psychology students for his books *Toward a Psychology of Being* and *The Psychology of Science.* However, he is equally well known to most business students for his highly popularized and defining work on postulating a hierarchy of human needs, beginning at the physiological level and proceeding up through safety, social, esteem, and self-actualizing levels and suggesting that any need level, when fully satisfied, can no longer be a powerful motivator. Maslow also published *Eupsychian Management* (which received little acclaim in the 1960s), but has been republished (with additional material from a variety of his admirers) as *Maslow on Management.* In this book, Maslow lays out the underlying assumptions for a eupsychian (humanistic) organization. Maslow taught at Brooklyn College and Brandeis University and, while writing his final book, was an in-depth observer of worker behaviors at the Non-Linear Systems plant in Del Mar, California. For an illustration of Maslow's enduring impact on management, see Chip Conley's recent book, *Peak: How Great Companies Get Their Mojo from Maslow.*

Peter M. Senge is the Director of the Systems Thinking and Organizational Learning Program at MIT's Sloan School of Management. His book *The Fifth Discipline* emphasizes the importance of organizations developing the capacity to engage in effective learning. Senge identifies and discusses a set of disabilities that are fatal to organizations, especially those operating in rapidly changing environments. The fifth discipline—systems thinking—is presented as the cornerstone for the learning organization. Personal mastery, mental models, shared vision, and team learning are presented as the core disciplines and the focus for building the learning organization. Senge has also published *The Fifth Discipline Fieldbook* and *The Dance of Change.*

Michael E. Porter, a Harvard Business School faculty member and holder of the Bishop Lawrence University Professorship, continues to make contributions to our understanding of organizations and their competitive strategies. He received the 1986 George R. Terry book award for his book *Competitive Advantage*, which was published in 1985. *Competitive Advantage* was a follow-up to his earlier book *Competitive Strategy*. Porter is also the author of *Competitive Advantage of Nations*. He has argued that firms can achieve above-average profits by synthesizing and applying their unique strengths effectively within their industry. They can do this either through creating a cost advantage or by differentiating a product or service from that of their competitors. The key, which some firms seemingly ignore, is to link strategy formulation successfully with strategy implementation. Porter encouraged managers to study their industry in depth, select a course of competitive advantage, develop a set of strategies that adapt the firm to its external environment, and draw on their executive leadership talents.

In *Competitive Advantage*, Porter provides insight into the complexity of industry competition by identifying five underlying forces. Low cost, differentiation, and focus are presented as generic strategies for the strategic positioning of a firm within its industry. The popularity of this book is revealed by its widespread adoption by managers and academics, as it has undergone its 16th printing in English and translation into 17 languages. Interested readers might wish to explore "An Interview with Michael Porter" by Nicholas Argyres and Anita M. McGahan in the *Academy of Management Executive*, 2002, 16:2, pp. 43–52.

The Practice of Management

Peter F. Drucker

Summary Prepared by John D. Stavig and Shaker A. Zahra

John D. Stavig is the professional director of the Center for Entrepreneurial Studies at the Carlson School of Management, University of Minnesota. He holds a BSB from the Carlson School and an MBA from the Wharton School. John has over 15 years of experience in management consulting, private equity, and industry. As a founding principal of a $100 million private equity fund, he sourced and managed investments in numerous early-stage communications firms. John also served as CEO, CFO, and board member for several start-up and early-stage technology firms, and led numerous investments, acquisitions, and divestitures. As a principal at Gemini Consulting and Arthur Andersen, he provided strategic and financial consulting services to senior executives in Fortune 1000 firms throughout the world. John has also taught in the MBA program at the University of St. Thomas.

Shaker A. Zahra is the Robert E. Buuck Chair of Entrepreneurship and professor of Strategy at the Carlson School of Management at the University of Minnesota. He is also the codirector of the Center for Entrepreneurial Studies and codirector of the Integrative Leadership Center. His research has appeared in leading journals. He has also published or edited 10 books. His research has received several major awards. He is the chair for the Entrepreneurship Division of the Academy of Management. His teaching, research, and service activities have received several awards.

Management is the brain of an enterprise and the primary source of long-term differentiation between firms. It is the disciplined and integrated practice of managing business, managers, workers, and work. It is also the creative process that drives **innovation** (the process of transforming discoveries into products, goods, and services) and entrepreneurship in a company. Management is entrusted with the responsibility for directing resources for the attainment of profits and the betterment of society.

Peter F. Drucker. *The Practice of Management.* New York: Harper & Row Publishers, Inc., 1954.

Management is a practice, rather than an exact science or profession. As such, it requires judgment. *Management represents a systematic and fluid process of establishing and pursuing shared objectives for the enterprise, managers, and workers.* The role of management is to create a customer and organize the firm's resources toward the attainment of shared objectives. Managers must live in both the present and the future by balancing often-conflicting objectives. They need also to develop and maintain the logical linkages among strategy, objectives, and incentives throughout the enterprise.

The quality and performance of management are the only sustainable advantages for a business. A business is a social institution, created and managed by people. Rather than adapting to external conditions, management is creative and forward looking. It is the proactive creator of economic growth by deliberate action. Managing a business must always be entrepreneurial, focusing on creating customers through innovation and marketing. Management drives continued improvements and avoids inertia.

A CONCEPT OF THE FIRM

Organizations—and their managers—should be

- Outward looking—both influenced by and shaping their external environment.
- A social institution—created by people; contributing to society.
- Pursuing multiple goals——both financial and nonfinancial.
- Innovative—emphasizing creativity, innovation, and entrepreneurship.
- Focused—answering and aligning resources to the question, What is our primary business?
- Spirited—creating self-controlled and motivated managers.

Management has important economic and social responsibilities. Though economic performance is the first priority and management must make a profit to cover its risk premium, it must also consider the impact of its policies and decisions on society.

Advances in technology and automation will challenge managerial capabilities. These advances will lead to a more highly skilled workforce and the growth of **knowledge workers** (employees with high levels of education, skills, and competencies) and create demand for managers with better capabilities to lead these employees. Rank-and-file jobs will become increasingly managerial, resulting in a displacement of jobs, rather than replacement. Properly executed, the application and management of automation will drive productivity and wealth creation.

THE JOBS OF MANAGEMENT

Determining the Business and Purpose

Management's first responsibility is to answer the question, *What is our business?* This is a challenging question that requires deliberate analysis based upon a thorough understanding of who the customers are, what they're actually buying, and what they value. Customers must be the foundation of the business, based upon the value they receive. Forward-looking companies seek to assess market potential and structure and introduce innovations that deliver value to customers, a process that determines what the business should be long term. Therefore, a company's entrepreneurial functions of innovation and marketing must cut across the entire business in order to satisfy customer needs. Customer satisfaction should be a company's primary goal.

Profit is not the purpose of business, but rather a test of the validity of the business. *A firm's objective cannot simply be profit maximization.*

Setting and Measuring Progress Against the Objectives of a Business

Fundamental to the management of the business is the development of shared objectives. This must be derived from a creative and fluid process of deliberate goal setting. Objectives are required in every area of the business where performance impacts the survival and success of the business. Objectives determine what action to take today to obtain results tomorrow. Objectives must be forward looking, and management should anticipate the future and be prepared to respond. Deliberate emphasis on innovation in setting objectives can be most valuable in areas where it appears less obvious. Management must implement regular, systematic, and unbiased measurements against set objectives, ideally based on feedback from the customer. Objectives should include areas of manager performance and development, worker performance and attitudes, and social responsibility. **Social responsibility** is simply the contribution a firm makes to its society. To some, this means making a profit, while others expect the firm to do more than this by ameliorating social problems. Setting objectives to improve worker performance and attitudes is one of the greatest challenges for management.

Balancing objectives across the different parts of a business is a critical role of management and requires judgment. Objectives can be changing, conflicting, intangible, and of differing duration. Objectives must be balanced based on organizational priorities and timing. A balanced set of objectives can serve as the "instrument panel" for piloting business.

Managing Managers by Objectives

Managers are the basic resource of business. They depreciate the fastest and require the greatest nourishment. **Management by objectives (MBO)** is the process in which employees set goals, justify them, determine resources needed to accomplish them, and establish timetables for their completion. These goals reflect the overall objectives of the organization. MBO develops individual responsibility toward a common direction. For an enterprise to grow beyond a single leader, an organized and integrated team that focuses on shared objectives is needed. Also required is the regular, systematic, and unbiased measurement of performance and the results against established objectives.

Being a manager means sharing in the responsibility for the enterprise. Every manager should responsibly participate in the development of the objectives in the unit he or she works for. Objectives must be clear and specific. They should be balanced and incorporate short- and long-term, tangible and intangible objectives. Objectives must be measurable—clear, simple, rational, relevant, reliable, and understandable.

Using MBO, emphasis on teamwork and shared goals should occur at every level of management. To ensure cooperation, individual managers should be measured on the following: performance from the individual unit, contribution to help other units achieve their objectives, and contribution expected from other units. MBO fosters self-control and motivation. This requires managers to convert objectives into personal goals, enabling them to direct, measure, and motivate themselves. To be in control and motivated, a manager's job should have the following characteristics: clear and measurable contribution to the success of the enterprise; directed and controlled by objectives, rather than the boss; broad scope and authority—decisions pushed down as far as possible; and duty to assist subordinates and peer managers to attain their objectives.

Productively Utilizing All Resources

Management is responsible for the productive utilization of all resources to meet their overall objectives. It should create a desired balance between all factors of production that will give the greatest output for the smallest effort. Productivity must incorporate both direct labor and managerial talent, because management is the scarcest and most expensive resource in the organization. Management should be the creative driver of increased productivity, rather than parasitical overhead. Companies should focus on increasing contributed value and the proportion of this value retained as profit.

Management should also understand company capabilities and consider outsourcing certain activities, even if potentially profitable. By evaluating this process mix, management will focus its resources on the activities that the company is best at performing, enabling it to create the most value for its customers.

Fostering a Positive Spirit

The spirit of the organization determines the motivation of its managers. It must be built on integrity and demonstrated by the actions of its leaders. Excellence and continuous improvement of the performance of the whole group must be encouraged, recognized, and rewarded. Managerial focus should underscore strengths, not weaknesses. Recognition, promotion, and financial incentives need to be tied to objectives and team performance. A positive spirit prepares a person for leadership, enabling the execution of objectives and the attainment of superior results.

Developing Managers

Managers are the firm's scarcest and most expensive resource. Management must challenge employees at all levels to pursue self-development to meet future managerial requirements. While management should encourage and direct the development of employees, the responsibility for development must remain with the subordinate manager. This development should place a large number of individuals in positions with general management responsibility across the business, rather than in a rotational program that promotes functional specialization for a select few. It is imperative that management create the opportunities and test the ability of its future managers to run and lead a whole business long before they reach the top.

Management of the Worker and Work

A key role for management is to define the nature of work, create a stimulating work environment, set standards, and train employees to assume progressively higher and more challenging responsibilities. Work should be rewarding—both financially and psychologically—in order to improve productivity.

Structure of Management

The **management structure** of an organization—the way managers divide, share, coordinate, and evaluate the work they do in planning and organizing the firm's overall operations—must facilitate the achievement of its objectives. *Structure does not always create good performance, but it can certainly inhibit results.* The structure should be flat, simple, and focused on performance. In determining the appropriate structure, management should consider the following: What activities are needed to achieve objectives? What decisions, and at what level, are necessary to achieve objectives? To what degree are activities and decisions interdependent?

Management structure should focus on business performance and results, contain the least possible number of levels, and enable the training and testing of future managers. When possible, autonomous product businesses are superior in meeting these requirements. A functional organization, even when decentralized, encourages specialization at the expense of company-wide perspective, adds unnecessary levels of management, and limits the development of future general managers.

2

Out of the Crisis

W. Edwards Deming

Summary Prepared by William B. Gartner and M. James Naughton

William B. Gartner is a professor at Georgetown University.

M. James Naughton is the owner of Expert-Knowledge Systems, Inc.

Deming provides an ambitious objective for his book when he begins by saying:

> The aim of this book is transformation of the style of American management. Transformation of American style of management is not a job of reconstruction, nor is it revision. It requires a whole new structure, from foundation upward. *Mutation* might be the word, except that *mutation* implies unordered spontaneity. Transformation must take place with directed effort.

Few individuals have had as much positive impact on the world economy as Dr. W. Edwards Deming. With the broadcast of the NBC white paper "If Japan Can, Why Can't We?" on June 24, 1980, Dr. Deming gained national exposure as the man responsible for the managerial theory that has governed Japan's transformation into a nation of world leaders in the production of high-quality goods. This transformation did not happen overnight. Since 1950, when Dr. Deming first spoke to Japan's top managers on the improvement of quality, Japanese organizations have pioneered in the adaptation of Dr. Deming's ideas.

As a result of his seminars, Japan has had an annual national competition for quality improvement (the Deming Prize) since 1951. Japan has numerous journals and books devoted to exploring and furthering the implications of Deming's theory. However, it has only been within the last few years that a number of books have been published in the United States on "the Deming Theory of Management." An overview of the ideas that underlie Deming's theory, which cut across all major topical areas in management, will be provided here.

W. Edwards Deming. *Out of the Crisis.* Cambridge, MA: MIT Press, 1986.

DISEASES AND OBSTACLES

Deming's book is not merely about productivity and quality control; it is a broad vision of the nature of organizations and how organizations should be changed. Deming identifies a set of chronic ailments that can plague any organization and limit its success. These, which he calls "deadly diseases," include an overemphasis on short-term profits, human resource practices that encourage both managers and employees to be mobile and not organizationally loyal, merit ratings and review systems that are based on fear of one's supervisor, an absence of a single driving purpose, and management that is based on visible figures alone.

The reason that managers are not as effective as they could be is that they are the prisoners of some structural characteristics and personal assumptions that prevent their success. Among the obstacles that Deming discusses are the insulation of top management from the other employees in the organization, lack of adequate technical knowledge, a long history of total reliance on final inspection as a way of ensuring a quality product, the managerial belief that all problems originate within the workforce, a reliance on meeting specifications, and the failure to synthesize human operators with computer systems for control.

THE CONCEPT OF VARIABILITY

The basis for Deming's theory is the observation that variability exists everywhere in everything. *Only through the study and analysis of variability, using statistics, can a phenomenon be understood well enough to manipulate and change it.* In many respects, using statistics is not very radical. Statistics are fundamental to nearly all academic research. But Deming asks that the right kind of statistics (analytical) be applied to our everyday lives as well. And that is the rub. To recognize the pervasiveness of variability and to function so that the sources of this variability can be defined and measured are radical. In Deming's world, the use of statistical thinking is not an academic game; it is a way of life.

The concept of variability is to management theory and practice what the concept of the germ theory of disease was to the development of modern medicine. Medicine had been "successfully" practiced without the knowledge of germs. In a pregerm theory paradigm, some patients got better, some got worse, and some stayed the same; in each case, some rationale could be used to explain the outcome. With the emergence of germ theory, all medical phenomena took on new meanings. Medical procedures thought to be good practice, such as physicians attending women in birth, turned out to be causes of disease because of the septic condition of the physicians' hands. Instead of rendering improved health care, the physicians' germ-laden hands achieved the opposite result. One can imagine the first proponents of the germ theory telling their colleagues who were still ignorant of the theory to wash their hands between patients. The pioneers must have sounded crazy. In the same vein, managers and academics who do not have a thorough understanding of variability will fail to grasp the radical change in thought that Deming envisions. Deming's propositions may seem as simplistic as "wash your hands!" rather than an entirely new paradigm of profound challenges to present-day managerial thinking and behaviors.

An illustration of variability that is widely cited in the books on Deming's theory is the "red bead experiment." Dr. Deming, at his four-day seminar, asks for 10 volunteers from the attendees. Six of the students become workers, two become inspectors of the workers' production, one becomes the inspector of the inspectors' work, and one becomes the recorder. Dr. Deming mixes together 3,000 white beads and 750 red beads in a large box. He instructs the workers to scoop out beads from the box with a beveled paddle that scoops out 50 beads at a time. Each scoop of the paddle is treated as a day's production. Only white beads are acceptable. Red beads are defects. After each worker scoops a paddle of beads from the box, the two inspectors count the defects, the inspector of the inspectors inspects the inspectors' count, and the recorder writes down the inspectors' agreed-upon number of defects. Invariably, each worker's scoop contains some red beads. Deming plays the role of the manager by exhorting the workers to produce no defects. When a worker scoops few red beads, he may be praised. Scooping many red beads brings criticism and an exhortation to do better, otherwise "we will go out of business." The manager reacts to each scoop of beads as if it had meaning in itself rather than as part of a pattern.

Dr. Deming's statistical analysis of the workers' production indicates that the process of producing white beads is in statistical control; that is, the variability of this production system is stable. The near-term prediction about the *pattern,* but not the individual draws, of the system's performance can be made. Near-future draws will yield an average, over many experiments, of 9.4 red beads. Any one draw may range between 1 and 18 red beads. In other words, the actual number of red beads scooped by each worker is out of that worker's control. The worker, as Dr. Deming says, "is only delivering the defects." Management, which controls the system, has caused the defects through design of the system. There are a number of insights people draw from this experiment. Walton lists the following:

- Variation is part of any process.
- Planning requires prediction of how things and people will perform. Tests and experiments of past performance can be useful, but not definitive.
- Workers work within a system that—try as they might—is beyond their control. It is the system, not their individual skills, that determines how they perform.
- Only management can change the system.
- Some workers will always be above average, some below.[1]

The red bead experiment illustrates the behavior of systems of stable variability. In Deming's theory, a system is all of the aspects of the organization and environment—employees, managers, equipment, facilities, government, customers, suppliers, shareholders, and so forth—fitted together, with the aim of producing some type of output. Stability implies that the output has regularity to it, so that predictions regarding the output of the system can be made. But many of these systems are inherently unstable. Bringing a system into stability is one of the fundamental managerial activities in the Deming theory.

In Deming's theory, a stable system, that is, a system that shows signs of being in statistical control, behaves in a manner similar to the red bead experiment. In systems, a single datum point is of little use in understanding the causes that influenced the production of that point. It is necessary to withhold judgment about changes in the output of the system until sufficient evidence (additional data points) becomes available to suggest whether or not the system being examined is stable. Statistical theory provides tools to help evaluate the stability of systems. Once a system is stable, its productive capability can be determined; that is, the average output of the system and the spread of variability around that average can be described. This can be used to predict the near-term future behavior of the system.

The inefficiencies inherent in "not knowing what we are doing," that is, in working with systems not in statistical control, might not seem to be that great a competitive penalty if all organizations are similarly out of control. Yet we are beginning to realize that the quality of outputs from organizations that are managed using Deming's theory are many magnitudes beyond what non-Deming organizations have been producing. The differences in quality and productivity can be mind boggling.

For example, both Scherkenbach[2] and Walton[3] reported that when the Ford Motor _pany began using transmissions produced by the Japanese automobile manufacturer, Mazda, Ford found that customers overwhelmingly preferred cars with Mazda transmissions to cars with Ford-manufactured transmissions—because the warranty repairs were 10 times lower, and the cars were quieter and shifted more smoothly. When Ford engineers compared their transmissions to the Mazda transmissions, they found that the piece-to-piece variation in the Mazda transmissions was nearly three times less than in the Ford pieces. Both Ford and Mazda conformed to the engineering standards specified by Ford, but Mazda transmissions were far more uniform. More uniform products also cost less to manufacture. With less variability there is less rework and less need for inspection. Only systems in statistical control can begin to reduce variability and thereby improve the quality and quantity of their output. Both authors reported that after Ford began to implement Deming's theory over the last five years, warranty repair frequencies dropped by 45 percent and "things gone wrong" reports from customers dropped by 50 percent.

FOURTEEN STEPS MANAGEMENT MUST TAKE

The task of transformation of an entire organization to use the Deming theory becomes an enormous burden for management, and Deming frequently suggests that this process is likely to take a minimum of 10 years. The framework for transforming an organization is outlined in the 14 points (pp. 23–24):

1. Create constancy of purpose toward improvement of product and service, aiming to become competitive, to stay in business, and to provide jobs.
2. Adopt the new philosophy. We are in a new economic age. Western management must awaken to the challenge, must learn their responsibilities, and must take on leadership in order to bring about change.
3. Cease dependence on inspection to achieve quality. Eliminate the need for inspection on a mass basis by building quality into the product in the first place.
4. End the practice of awarding business on the basis of the price tag. Instead, minimize total cost. Move toward a single supplier for any one time and develop long-term relationships of loyalty and trust with that supplier.
5. Improve constantly and forever the systems of production and service in order to improve quality and productivity. Thus, one constantly decreases costs.
6. Institute training on the job.
7. Institute leadership. Supervisors should be able to help people to do a better job, and they should use machines and gadgets wisely. Supervision of management and supervision of production workers need to be overhauled.
8. Drive out fear, so that everyone may work effectively for the company.
9. Break down barriers between departments. People in research, design, sales, and production must work as a team. They should foresee production problems and problems that could be encountered when using the product or service.
10. Eliminate slogans, exhortations, and targets that demand zero defects and new levels of productivity. These only create adversarial relationships because frequently the cause of low quality and low productivity is the system, and not the workforce.
11. **a.** Eliminate work standards (quotas) on the factory floor. Substitute leadership.
    b. Eliminate **management by objectives**. Eliminate management by numbers or numerical goals. Substitute leadership.

12. **a.** Remove barriers that rob hourly workers of their right to pride of workmanship. The responsibility of supervisors must be changed from sheer numbers to quality.

   b. Remove barriers that rob people in management and in engineering of their right to pride of workmanship. This means, *inter alia,* abolishing the annual merit rating and management by objectives.

13. Institute a vigorous program of education and self-improvement.

14. Put everybody in the company to work to accomplish the transformation. The transformation is everybody's job.

As mentioned earlier, these 14 points should not be treated as a list of aphorisms, nor can each of them be treated separately without recognizing the interrelationships among them.

Conclusions

Out of the Crisis is full of examples and ideas, and Deming calls for a radical revision of American management practice. To his credit, Deming constantly recognizes ideas and examples from individuals practicing various aspects of his theory. This constant recognition of other individuals provides a subtle indication that a body of practitioners exists who have had successful experiences applying his 14 steps and other ideas.

A transformation in American management needs to occur; it can take place, and it has begun already in those firms applying Deming's theory. Deming offers a new paradigm for the practice of management that requires a dramatic rethinking and replacement of old methods by those trained in traditional management techniques. In conclusion, Deming recognizes that "it takes courage to admit that you have been doing something wrong, to admit that you have something to learn, that there is a better way" (Walton, 1986, p. 223).

Notes

1. William B. Gartner and M. James Naughton, "The Deming Theory of Management," *Academy of Management Review,* January 1988, 138–142.

2. William W. Scherkenbach. *The Deming Route to Quality and Productivity: Roadmaps and Roadblocks.* Milwaukee, WI: ASQC, 1986.

3. Mary Walton. *The Deming Management Method.* New York: Dodd, Mead & Company, 1986.

3

The Human Side
of Enterprise

Douglas McGregor

Summary Prepared by Gayle Porter

Gayle Porter obtained her doctorate from the Ohio State University in Organizational Behavior and Human Resource Management and is now at Rutgers University—Camden. Articles and ongoing research interests include the effects of dispositional differences in the workplace; group perceptions of efficacy and esteem; and the comparison of influence on employees through reward systems, leadership, and employee development efforts. Her prior experience includes positions as Director of Curriculum Development for a human resource management degree program; consultant on training programs, financial operations, and computer applications; financial manager for an oil and gas production company; and financial specialist for NCR Corporation.

The Human Side of Enterprise was written during an ongoing comparative study of management development programs in several large companies. In McGregor's view, the making of managers has less to do with formal efforts in development than with how the task of management is understood within that organization. This fundamental understanding determines the policies and procedures within which the managers operate and guides the selection of people identified as having the potential for management positions. During the late 1950s, McGregor believed that major industrial advances of the next half century would occur on the human side of enterprise, and he was intrigued by the inconsistent assumptions about what makes managers behave as they do. His criticism of the conventional assumptions, which he labels Theory X, is that they limit options. Theory Y provides an alternative set of assumptions that are much needed due to the extent of unrealized human potential in most organizations.

Douglas McGregor. *The Human Side of Enterprise.* New York: McGraw-Hill, 1960.

THE THEORETICAL ASSUMPTIONS OF MANAGEMENT

Regardless of the economic success of a firm, few managers are satisfied with their ability to predict and control the behavior of members of the organization. Effective prediction and control are central to the task of management, and there can be no prediction without some underlying theory. Therefore, *all managerial decisions and actions rest on a personally held theory, a set of assumptions about behavior.* The assumptions management holds about controlling its human resources determine the whole character of the enterprise.

In application, problems occur related to these assumptions. First, managers may not realize that they hold and apply conflicting ideas and that one may cancel out the other. For example, a manager may delegate based on the assumption that employees should have responsibility, but then nullify that action by close monitoring, which indicates the belief that employees can't handle the responsibility. Another problem is failure to view control as **selective adaptation**, when dealing with human behavior. People adjust to certain natural laws in other fields; for example, engineers don't dig channels and expect water to run uphill! With humans, however, there is a tendency to try to control in direct violation of human nature. Then, when they fail to achieve the desired results, they look for every other possible cause rather than examine the inappropriate choice of a method to control behavior.

Any influence is based on dependence, so the nature and degree of dependence are critical factors in determining what methods of control will be effective. Conventional organization theory is based on authority as a key premise. It is the central and indispensable means of managerial control and recognizes only upward dependence. In recent decades, workers have become less dependent on a single employer, and society has provided certain safeguards related to unemployment. This limits the upward dependence and, correspondingly, the ability to control by authority alone. In addition, employees have the ability to engage in countermeasures such as slowdowns, lowered standards of performance, or even sabotage to defeat authority they resent.

Organizations are more accurately represented as systems of **interdependence**. Subordinates depend on managers to help them meet their needs, but managers also depend on subordinates to achieve their own and the organization's goals. While there is nothing inherently bad or wrong in the use of authority to control, in certain circumstances it fails to bring the desired results. Circumstances change even from hour to hour, and the role of the manager is to select the appropriate means of influence based on the situation at a given point in time. If employees exhibit lazy, indifferent behavior, the causes lie in management methods of organization and control.

Theory X is a term used to represent a set of assumptions. Principles found in traditional management literature could only have derived from assumptions such as the following, which have had a major impact on managerial strategy in organizations:

1. The average human being has an inherent dislike of work and will avoid it if possible.
2. Because of this human characteristic of dislike of work, most people must be coerced, controlled, directed, and threatened with punishment to get them to put forth adequate effort toward the achievement of organizational objectives.
3. The average human being prefers to be directed, wishes to avoid responsibility, has relatively little ambition, and wants security above all.

These assumptions are not without basis, or they would never have persisted as they have. They do explain some observed human behavior, but other observations are not consistent with this view. Theory X assumptions also encourage us to categorize certain behaviors as human nature, when they may actually be symptoms of a condition in which workers have been deprived of an opportunity to satisfy higher-order needs (social and egoistic needs).

A strong tradition exists of viewing employment as an employee's agreement to accept control by others in exchange for rewards that are only of value outside the workplace. For example, wages (except for status differences), vacation, medical benefits, stock purchase plans, and profit sharing are of little value during the actual time on the job. Work is the necessary evil to endure for rewards away from the job. In this conception of human resources we can never discover, let alone utilize, the potentialities of the average human being.

Many efforts to provide more equitable and generous treatment to employees and to provide a safe and pleasant work environment have been designed without any real change in strategy. Very often what is proposed as a new management strategy is nothing more than a different tactic within the old Theory X assumptions. Organizations have progressively made available the means to satisfy lower-order needs for subsistence and safety. As the nature of the dependency relationship changes, management has gradually deprived itself of the opportunity to use control based solely on assumptions of Theory X. A new strategy is needed.

Theory Y assumptions are dynamic, indicate the possibility of human growth and development, and stress the necessity for selective adaptation:

1. The expenditure of physical and mental effort in work is as natural as play or rest.
2. External control and the threat of punishment are not the only means for bringing about effort toward organizational objectives. People will exercise self-direction and self-control in the service of objectives to which they are committed.
3. Commitment to objectives is a function of the rewards associated with their achievement (*satisfaction of ego and self-actualization needs can be products of effort directed toward organizational objectives*).
4. The average human being learns, under proper conditions, not only to accept but also to seek responsibility.
5. The capacity to exercise a relatively high degree of imagination, ingenuity, and creativity in the solution of organizational problems is widely, not narrowly, distributed in the population.
6. Under the conditions of modern industrial life, the intellectual potentialities of the average human being are only partially utilized.

The Theory Y assumptions challenge a number of deeply ingrained managerial habits of thought and action; they lead to a management philosophy of integration and self-control. Theory X assumes that the organization's requirements take precedence over the needs of the individual members, and that the worker must always adjust to needs of the organization as management perceives them. In contrast, the principle of *integration* proposes that conditions can be created such that individuals can best achieve their own goals by directing their efforts toward the success of the enterprise. Based on the premise that the assumptions of Theory Y are valid, the next logical question is whether, and to what extent, such conditions can be created. How will employees be convinced that applying their skills, knowledge, and ingenuity in support of the organization is a more attractive alternative than other ways to utilize their capacities?

THEORY IN PRACTICE

The essence of applying Theory Y assumptions is guiding the subordinates to develop themselves rather than developing the subordinates by telling them what they need to do. An important consideration is that the subordinates' acceptance of responsibility for self-developing (i.e., self-direction and self-control) has been shown to relate to their commitment to objectives. But the overall aim is to further the growth of the individual, and it must be approached as a managerial strategy rather than simply as a personnel technique. Forms and procedures are of little value. Once the concept is provided, managers who welcome the assumptions of Theory Y will create their own processes for implementation; managers with underlying Theory X assumptions cannot create the conditions for integration and self-control no matter what tools are provided.

The development process becomes one of role clarification and mutual agreement regarding the subordinate's job responsibilities. This requires the manager's willingness to accept some risk and allow mistakes as part of the growth process. It also is time consuming in terms of discussions and allowing opportunity for self-discovery. However, it is not a new set of duties on top of the manager's existing load. It is a different way of fulfilling the existing responsibilities.

One procedure that violates Theory Y assumptions is the typical utilization of performance appraisals. Theory X leads quite naturally into this means of directing individual efforts toward organizational objectives. Through the performance appraisal process, management tells people what to do, monitors their activities, judges how well they have done, and rewards or punishes them accordingly. Since the appraisals are used for administrative purposes (e.g., pay, promotion, retention decisions), this is a demonstration of management's overall control strategy. Any consideration of personal goals is covered by the expectation that rewards of salary and position are enough. If the advancement available through this system is not a desired reward, the individuals are placed in a position of acting against their own objectives and advancing for the benefit of the organization only. The alternative (e.g., turning down a promotion) may bring negative outcomes such as lack of future options or being identified as employees with no potential.

The principle of integration requires active and responsible participation of employees in decisions affecting them. One plan that demonstrates Theory Y assumptions is *The Scanlon Plan*. A central feature in this plan is the cost-reduction sharing that provides a meaningful cause-and-effect connection between employee behavior and the reward received. The reward is directly related to the success of the organization, and it is distributed frequently. This provides a more effective learning reinforcement than the traditional performance appraisal methods. The second central feature of the Scanlon Plan is effective participation, a formal method through which members contribute brains and ingenuity as well as their physical efforts on the job. This provides a means for social and ego satisfaction, so employees have a stake in the success of the firm beyond the economic rewards. Implementation of the Scanlon Plan is not a program or set of procedures; it must be accepted as a way of life and can vary depending on the circumstances of the particular company. It is entirely consistent with Theory Y assumptions.

Theory X leads to emphasis on tactics of control, whereas Theory Y is more concerned with the nature of the relationship. Eliciting the desired response in a Theory Y context is a matter of creating an environment or set of conditions to enable self-direction. The day-to-day behavior of an immediate supervisor or manager is perhaps the most critical factor in such an environment. Through sometimes subtle behaviors superiors demonstrate their attitudes and create what is referred to as the psychological "climate" of the relationship.

Management style does not seem to be important. Within many different styles, subordinates may or may not develop confidence in the manager's deeper integrity, based on other behavioral cues. Lack of confidence in the relationship causes anxiety and undesirable reactions from the employees. No ready formula is available to relay integrity. Insincere attempts to apply a technique or style—such as using participation only to manipulate subordinates into believing they have some input to decisions—are usually recognized as a gimmick and soon destroy confidence.

In addition to manager–subordinate relationships, problems connected to Theory X assumptions can be observed in other organizational associations such as staff-line relationships. Upper management may create working roles for staff groups to "police" line managers' activities, giving them an influence that equates psychologically to direct line authority. Top management with Theory X assumptions can delegate and still retain control. The staff function provides an opportunity to monitor indirectly, to set policy for limiting decisions and actions, and to obtain information on everything happening before a problem can occur.

Staff personnel often come from a very specialized education with little preparation for what their role should be in an organization. With full confidence in their objective methods and training to find "the best answer," they often are unprepared for the resistance of line managers who don't share this confidence and don't trust the derived solutions. The staff may conclude that line managers are stupid, are unconcerned with the general welfare of the organization, and care only about their own authority and independence. They essentially adopt the Theory X assumptions and readily accept the opportunity to create a system of measurements for control of the line operations.

To utilize staff groups within the context of Theory Y, managers must emphasize the principle of self-control. As a resource to all parts and levels of the organization, staff reports and data should be supplied to all members who can use such information to control their own job— not subordinates' jobs. If summary data indicate something wrong within the manager's unit of responsibility, the manager would turn to subordinates, not to the staff, for more information. If the subordinates are practicing similar self-control using staff-provided information, they have most likely discovered the same problem and taken action before this inquiry occurs. There is no solution to the problem of staff-line relationships in authoritative terms that can address organizational objectives adequately. However, a manager operating by Theory Y assumptions will apply them similarly to all relationships—upward, downward, and peer level—including the staff-line associations.

THE DEVELOPMENT OF MANAGERIAL TALENT

Leadership is a relationship with four major variables: the characteristics of the leader; the attitudes, needs, and other personal characteristics of the followers; the characteristics of the organization, such as its purpose, structure, and the nature of its task; and the social, economic, and political environment in which the organization operates. Specifying which leader characteristics will result in effective performance depends on the other factors, so it is a complex relationship. Even if researchers were able to determine the universal characteristics of a good relationship between the leader and the other situational factors, there are still many ways to achieve the same thing. For example, mutual confidence seems important in the relationship, but there are a number of ways that confidence can be developed and maintained. Different personal characteristics could achieve the same desired relationship.

Also, because it is so difficult to predict the situational conditions an organization will face, future management needs are unpredictable. The major task, then, is to provide a heterogeneous supply of human resources from which individuals can be selected as appropriate at a future time. This requires attracting recruits from a variety of sources and with a variety of backgrounds, which complicates setting criteria for selection. Also, the management development programs in an organization should involve many people rather than a few with similar qualities and abilities. Finally, management's goal must be to develop the unique capacities of each individual, rather than common objectives for all participants. We must place high value on people in general—seek to enable them to develop to their fullest potential in whatever role they best can fill. Not everyone must pursue the top jobs; outstanding leadership is needed at every level.

Individuals must develop themselves and will do so optimally only in terms of what each of them sees as meaningful and valuable. What might be called a "manufacturing approach" to management development involves designing programs to build managers; this end product becomes a supply of managerial talent to be used as needed. A preferred alternative approach is to "grow talent" under the assumption that people will grow into what they are capable of becoming, if they are provided the right conditions for that growth. There is little relationship (possibly even a negative one) between the formal structure for management development and actual achievement of the organization, because programs and procedures do not *cause* management development.

Learning is fairly straightforward when the individual desires new knowledge or skill. Unfortunately, many development offerings soon become a scheduled assignment for entire categories of people. Learning is limited in these conditions, because the motivation is low. Further, negative attitudes develop toward training in general, which interferes with creating an overall climate conducive to growth. In many cases, managers may have a purpose in sending subordinates to training that is not shared with or understood by that individual. This creates anxiety or confusion, which also interferes with learning. It is best if attendance in training and development programs is the result of joint target setting, wherein the individual expresses a need and it can be determined that a particular program will benefit both the individual and the organization.

Classroom learning can be valuable to satisfying needs of both parties. However, it can only be effective when there is an organizational climate conducive to growth. Learning is always an active process, whether related to motor skills or acquisition of knowledge; it cannot be injected into the learner, so motivation is critical. Practice and feedback are essential when behavior changes are involved. Classroom methods such as case analysis and role playing provide an opportunity to experiment with decisions and behaviors in a safe environment, to receive immediate feedback, and to go back and try other alternatives. Some applications of classroom learning may be observed directly on the job. In other cases, the application may be more subtle, in the form of increased understanding or challenging one's own preconceptions. Care must be taken so that pressures to evaluate the benefits of classroom learning don't result in application of inappropriate criteria for success while the true value of the experience is overlooked.

Separate attention is given to management groups or teams at various levels. Within Theory X assumptions, direction and control are jeopardized by effective group functioning. On the other hand, a manager who recognizes interdependencies in the organization—one who is less interested in personal power than in creating conditions so human resources will voluntarily achieve organization objectives—will seek to build strong management groups. Creating a managerial team requires unity of purpose among those individuals. If the group is nothing more than several individuals competing for power and recognition, it is not a team. Again, the climate of the relationships and the fundamental understanding of the role of managers in the organization will be critical. One day the hierarchical structure of reporting relationships will disappear from organizational charts and give way to a series of linked groups. This shift in patterns of relationships will be a slow transition, but will signify recognition of employee capacity to collaborate in joint efforts. Then we may begin to discover how seriously management has underestimated the true potential of the organization's human resources.

Conclusion

Theory X is not an evil set of assumptions, but rather a limiting one. Use of authority to influence has its place, even within the Theory Y assumptions, but it does not work in all circumstances. A number of societal changes suggest why Theory X increasingly may cause problems for organizations needing more innovation and flexibility in their operating philosophy. It is critically important for managers to honestly examine the assumptions that underlie their own behavior toward subordinates. To do so requires first accepting the two possibilities, Theory X and Theory Y, and then examining one's own actions in the context of that comparison. Fully understanding the implications on each side will help identify whether the observed choices of how to influence people are likely to bring about the desired results.

4

Maslow on Management

Abraham H. Maslow

It should be possible to implement an enlightened management policy into an organization, where employees can *self-actualize* (institute their own ideas, make decisions, learn from their mistakes, and grow in their capabilities) while creating *synergy* (attaining beneficial results simultaneously for the individual and the organization). Such a policy (and associated practices) would not necessarily apply to all people, because everyone is at a different level on the motivational hierarchy (from physiological to safety to love to esteem to self-actualization). Nevertheless, the assumptions that would need to be true in order to create an ideal (eupsychian) society can be identified and then explored. They include the following dimensions. People are

- psychologically healthy;
- not fixated at the safety-need level;
- capable of growth, which occurs through delight and through boredom;
- able to grow to a high level of personal maturity;
- courageous, with the ability to conquer their fears and endure anxiety.

They have

- the impulse to achieve;
- the capacity to be objective about themselves and about others;
- the capacity to be trusted to some degree;
- a strong will to grow, experiment, select their own friends, carry out their own ideas, and self-actualize;
- the ability to enjoy good teamwork, friendships, group spirit, group harmony, belongingness, and group love;
- the capacity to be improved to some degree;
- the ability to identify with a common objective and contribute to it;
- a conscience and feelings.

Abraham H. Maslow. *Maslow on Management.* New York: Wiley & Sons, Inc., 1998.

Everyone prefers

- to love and to respect his or her boss;
- to be a prime mover rather than a passive helper;
- to use all their capacities;
- to work rather than being idle;
- to have meaningful work;
- to be justly and fairly appreciated, preferably in public;
- to feel important, needed, useful, successful, proud, and respected;
- to have responsibility;
- to have personhood, identity, and uniqueness as a person;
- to create rather than destroy;
- to be interested rather than bored;
- to improve things, make things right, and do things better.

Given this portrait of a certain type of individual described by these assumptions, we can conclude the following:

- Authoritarian managers are dysfunctional for them;
- People can benefit by being stretched, strained, and challenged once in a while;
- Everyone should be informed as completely as possible;
- These types of persons will do best at what they have chosen, based on what they like most;
- Everybody needs to be absolutely clear about the organization's goals, directions, and purposes.

In conclusion, *enlightened management is the wave of the future.* It will be seen more and more for a very simple reason that can be stated as a fundamental principle of human behavior: "Treating people well spoils them for being treated badly." In other words, once employees have experienced any aspect of enlightened management, they will never wish to return to an authoritarian environment. Further, as other workers hear about enlightened work organizations, they will either seek to work there or demand that their own workplaces become more enlightened.

The Fifth Discipline

Peter M. Senge

Summary Prepared by Dorothy Marcic

Dorothy Marcic is adjunct professor at Vanderbilt University's Owen Graduate School of Management. Previously, she served as Director of Graduate Programs in Human Resource Development at Peabody College and Fulbright Scholar at the University of Economics—Prague, and held academic appointments at Arizona State University and the University of Wisconsin—La Crosse. Dorothy's research and consulting interests include how to develop the kinds of structures, values, and systems that help create learning organizations that are uplifting to employees. Addressing that issue is one of the 10 books she has authored—Managing With the Wisdom of Love: Uncovering Virtue in Organizations.

Learning disabilities can be fatal to organizations, causing them to have an average life span of only 40 years—half a human being's life. *Organizations need to be learners, and often they are not.* Somehow some survive, but never live up to their potential. What happens if what we term *excellence* is really no more than mediocrity? Only those firms that become learners will succeed in the increasingly turbulent, competitive global market.

LEARNING DISABILITIES

There are seven learning disabilities common to organizations.

IDENTIFICATION WITH ONE'S POSITION[1]   American workers are trained to see themselves as what they do, not who they are. Therefore, if laid off, they find it difficult, if not impossible, to find work doing something else. Worse for the organization, though, is the limited thinking this attitude creates. By claiming an identity

---

Peter M. Senge. *The Fifth Discipline: The Art and Practice of the Learning Organization.* New York: Doubleday, 1990.

related to the job, workers are cut off from seeing how their responsibility connects to other jobs. For example, one American car had three assembly bolts on one component. The similar Japanese make had only one bolt. Why? Because the Detroit manufacturer had three engineers for that component, while a similar Japanese manufacturer had only one.

EXTERNAL ENEMIES   This belief is a result of the previously stated disability. *External enemies* refers to people focusing blame on anything but themselves or their unit. Fault is regularly blamed on factors like the economy, the weather, or the government. Marketing blames manufacturing, and manufacturing blames engineering. Such external faultfinding keeps the organization from seeing what the real problems are and prevents them from tackling the real issues head-on.

THE ILLUSION OF TAKING CHARGE   Being proactive is seen as good management—doing something about "those problems." All too often, though, being proactive is a disguise for reactiveness against that awful enemy out there.

THE FIXATION ON EVENTS   Much attention in organizations is paid to events—last month's sales, the new product, who just got hired, and so on. Our society, too, is geared toward short-term thinking, which in turn stifles the type of generative learning that permits a look at the real threats—the slowly declining processes of quality, service, or design.

THE PARABLE OF THE BOILED FROG   An experiment was once conducted by placing a frog in boiling water. The frog, sensing danger in the extreme heat, immediately jumped out to safety. However, placing the frog in cool water and slowly turning up the heat resulted in the frog getting groggier and groggier and finally boiling to death. Why? Because the frog's survival mechanisms are programmed to look for sudden changes in the environment, not gradual changes. Similarly, during the 1960s, the U.S. auto industry saw no threat by Japan, which had only 4 percent of the market. Not until the 1980s when Japan had over 21 percent of the market did the Big Three begin to look at their core assumptions. Now with Japan holding about 30 percent share of the market, it is not certain if this frog (U.S. automakers) is capable of jumping out of the boiling water. Looking at gradual processes requires slowing down our frenetic pace and watching for the subtle cues.

THE DELUSION OF LEARNING FROM EXPERIENCE   Learning from experience is powerful. This is how we learn to walk and talk. However, we now live in a time when direct consequences of actions may take months or years to appear. Decisions in R&D may take up to a decade to bear fruit, and their actual consequences may be influenced by manufacturing and marketing along the way. Organizations often choose to deal with these complexities by breaking themselves up into smaller and smaller components, further reducing their ability to see problems in their entirety.

THE MYTH OF THE MANAGEMENT TEAM   Most large organizations have a group of bright, experienced leaders who are supposed to know all the answers. They were trained to believe there are answers to all problems and they should find them. People are rarely rewarded for bringing up difficult issues or for looking at parts of a problem that make them harder to grasp. Most teams end up operating below the lowest IQ of any member. What results are "skilled incompetents"—people who know all too well how to keep *from* learning.

SYSTEMS THINKING

Five disciplines are required for a learning organization: personal mastery, mental models, shared vision, team learning, and systems thinking. The fifth one, systems thinking, is the most important. Without systems thinking, the other disciplines do not have the same effect.

The Laws of the Fifth Discipline

TODAY'S PROBLEMS RESULT FROM YESTERDAY'S SOLUTIONS   A carpet merchant kept pushing down a bump in the rug, only to have it reappear elsewhere, until he lifted a corner and out slithered a snake. Sometimes fixing one part of the system only brings difficulties to other parts of the system. For example, solving an internal inventory problem may lead to angry customers who now get late shipments.

PUSH HARD AND THE SYSTEM PUSHES BACK EVEN HARDER   Systems theory calls this compensating feedback, which is a common way of reducing the effects of an intervention. Some cities, for example, build low-cost housing and set up job programs, only to have more poor people than ever. Why? Because many moved to the cities from neighboring areas so that they, too, could take advantage of the low-cost housing and job opportunities.

BEHAVIOR GETS BETTER BEFORE IT GETS WORSE   Some decisions actually look good in the short term, but produce *compensating feedback* and crisis in the end. The really effective decisions often produce difficulties in the short run but create more health in the long term. This is why behaviors such as building a power base or working hard just to please the boss come back to haunt you.

THE BEST WAY OUT IS TO GO BACK IN   We often choose familiar solutions, ones that feel comfortable and not scary. But the effective ways often mean going straight into what we are afraid of facing. What does *not* work is pushing harder on the same old solutions (also called the "what we need here is a bigger hammer" syndrome).

THE CURE CAN BE WORSE THAN THE DISEASE   The result of applying nonsystematic solutions to problems is the need for more and more of the same. It can become addictive. Someone begins mild drinking to alleviate work tension. The individual feels better and then takes on more work, creating more tension and a need for more alcohol, and the person finally becomes an alcoholic. Sometimes these types of solutions only result in shifting the burden. The government enters the scene by providing more welfare and leaves the host system weaker and less able to solve its own problems. This ultimately necessitates still more aid from the government. Companies can try to shift their burdens to consultants, but then become more and more dependent on them to solve their problems.

FASTER IS SLOWER   Every system, whether ecological or organizational, has an optimal rate of growth. Faster and faster is not always better. (After all, the tortoise finally did win the race.) Complex human systems require new ways of thinking. Quickly jumping in and fixing what *looks* bad usually provides solutions for a problem's symptoms and not for the problem itself.

CAUSE AND EFFECT ARE NOT ALWAYS RELATED CLOSELY IN TIME AND SPACE   *Effects* here mean the symptoms we see, such as drug abuse and unemployment, whereas *causes* mean the interactions of the underlying system that bring about these conditions. We often assume cause is near to effect. If there is a sales problem, then incentives for the sales force should fix it, or if there is inadequate housing, then build more houses. Unfortunately, this does not often work, for the real causes lie elsewhere.

TINY CHANGES MAY PRODUCE BIG RESULTS; AREAS OF GREATEST LEVERAGE ARE FREQUENTLY THE LEAST OBVIOUS   System science teaches that the most obvious solutions usually do not work. While simple solutions frequently make short-run improvements, they commonly contribute to long-term deteriorations. The *nonobvious* and *well-focused* solutions are more likely to provide leverage and bring positive change. For example, ships have a tiny trim tab on one edge of the rudder that has great influence on the movement of that ship, so small changes in the trim tab bring big shifts in the ship's course. However, there are no simple rules for applying leverage to organizations. It requires looking for the structure of what is going on rather than merely seeing the events.

YOU CAN HAVE YOUR CAKE AND EAT IT TOO—BUT NOT AT THE SAME TIME   Sometimes the most difficult problems come from "snapshot" rather than "process" thinking. For example, it was previously believed by American manufacturers that quality and low cost could not be achieved simultaneously. One had to be chosen over the other. What was missed, however, was the notion that improving quality may also mean eliminating waste and unnecessary time (both adding costs), which in the end would mean lower costs. Real leverage comes when it can be seen that seemingly opposing needs can be met over time.

CUTTING THE ELEPHANT IN HALF DOES NOT CREATE TWO ELEPHANTS   Some problems can be solved by looking at parts of the organization, whereas others require holistic thinking. What is needed is an understanding of the boundaries for each problem. Unfortunately, most organizations are designed to prevent people from seeing systemic problems, either by creating rigid structures or by leaving problems behind for others to clean up.

THERE IS NO BLAME   Systems thinking teaches that there are no outside causes to problems; instead, you and your "enemy" are part of the same system. Any cure requires understanding how that is seen.

THE OTHER DISCIPLINES

Personal Mastery

Organizations can learn only when the individuals involved learn. This requires personal mastery, which is the discipline of personal learning and growth, where people are continually expanding their ability to create the kind of life they want. From their quest comes the spirit of the learning organization.

Personal mastery involves seeing one's life as a creative work, being able to clarify what is really important, and learning to see current reality more clearly. The difference between what's important, what we want, and where we are now produces a "creative tension." Personal mastery means being able to generate and maintain creative tension.

Those who have high personal mastery have a vision, which is more like a calling, and they are in a continual learning mode. They never really "arrive." Filled with more commitment, they take initiative and greater responsibility in their work.

Previously, organizations supported an employee's development only if it would help the organization, which fits in with the traditional "contract" between employee and organization ("an honest day's pay in exchange for an honest day's work"). The new, and coming, way is to see it rather as a "covenant," which comes from a shared vision of goals, ideas, and management processes.

Working toward personal mastery requires living with emotional tension, not letting our goals get eroded. As Somerset Maugham said, "Only mediocre people are always at their best." One of the worst blocks to achieving personal mastery is the common belief that we cannot have what we want. Being committed to the truth is a powerful weapon against this, for it does not allow us to deceive ourselves. Another means of seeking personal mastery is to integrate our reason and intuition. We live in a society that values reason and devalues intuition. However, using both together is very powerful and may be one of the fundamental contributions to systems thinking.

Mental Models

Mental models are internal images of how the world works and can range from simple generalizations (people are lazy) to complex theories (assumptions about why my coworkers interact the way they do). For example, for decades the Detroit automakers believed people bought cars mainly for styling, not for quality or reliability. These beliefs, which were really unconscious assumptions, worked well for many years, but ran into trouble when competition from Japan began. It took a long time for Detroit even to begin to see the mistakes in their beliefs. One company that managed to change its mental model through incubating a business worldview was Shell.

Traditional hierarchical organizations have the dogma of organizing, managing, and controlling. In the new learning organization, though, the revised "dogma" will be values, vision, and mental models.

Hanover Insurance began changes in 1969 designed to overcome the "basic disease of the hierarchy." Three values espoused were

1. *Openness*—seen as an antidote to the dysfunctional interactions in face-to-face meetings.
2. *Merit,* or making decisions based on the good of the organization—seen as the antidote to decision making by organizational politics.
3. *Localness*—the antidote to doing the dirty stuff the boss does not want to do.

Chris Argyris and colleagues developed "action science" as a means for reflecting on the reasoning underlying our actions. This helps people change the defensive routines that lead them to skilled incompetence. Similarly, John Beckett created a course on the historical survey of main philosophies of thought, East and West, as a sort of "sandpaper on the brain." These ideas exposed managers to their own assumptions and mental models and provided other ways to view the world.

Shared Vision

A shared vision is not an idea. Rather it is a force in people's hearts, a sense of purpose that provides energy and focus for learning. Visions are often exhilarating. Shared vision is important because it may be the beginning step to get people who mistrusted each other to start working together. Abraham Maslow studied high-performing teams and found that they had a shared vision. Shared visions can mobilize courage so naturally that people don't even know the extent of their strength. When John Kennedy created the shared vision in 1961 of putting a man on the moon by the end of the decade, only 15 percent of the technology had been created. Yet it led to numerous acts of daring and courage.

Learning organizations are not achievable without shared vision. Without that incredible pull toward the deeply felt goal, the forces of *status quo* will overwhelm the pursuit. As Robert Fritz once said, "In the presence of greatness, pettiness disappears." Conversely, in the absence of a great vision, pettiness is supreme.

Strategic planning often does not involve building a shared vision, but rather announcing the vision of top management, asking people, at best, to enroll, and, at worst, to comply. The critical step is gaining commitment from people. This is done by taking a personal vision and building it into a shared vision. In the traditional hierarchical organization, compliance is one of the desired outcomes. For learning organizations, commitment must be the key goal. Shared vision, though, is not possible without personal mastery, which is needed to foster continued commitment to a lofty goal.

Team Learning

Bill Russell of the Boston Celtics wrote about being on a team of specialists whose performance depended on one another's individual excellence and how well they worked together. Sometimes that created a feeling of magic. He is talking about *alignment,* where a group functions as a whole unit, rather than as individuals working at cross purposes. When a team is aligned, its energies are focused and harmonized. They do not need to sacrifice their own interests. Instead, alignment occurs when the shared vision becomes an extension of the personal vision. Alignment is a necessary condition to empower others and ultimately empower the team.

Never before today has there been greater need for mastering team learning, which requires mastering both dialogue and discussion. *Dialogue* involves a creative and free search of complex and even subtle issues, whereas *discussion* implies different views being presented and defended. Both skills are useful, but most teams cannot tell the difference between the two. The purpose of dialogue is to increase individual understanding. Here, assumptions are suspended and participants regard one another as on the same level. Discussion, on the other hand, comes from the same root word as *percussion* and *concussion* and involves a sort of verbal ping-pong game whose object is winning. Although this is a useful technique, it must be balanced with dialogue. A continued emphasis on winning is not compatible with the search for truth and coherence.

One of the major blocks to healthy dialogue and discussion is what Chris Argyris calls *defensive routines.* These are habitual styles of interacting that protect us from threat or embarrassment. These include the avoidance of conflict (smoothing over) and the feeling that one has to appear competent and to know the answers at all times.

Team learning, like any other skill, requires practice. Musicians and athletes understand this principle. Work teams need to learn that lesson as well.

OTHER ISSUES

Organizational politics is a perversion of truth, yet most people are so accustomed to it, they do not even notice it anymore. A learning organization is not possible in such an environment. In order to move past the politics, one thing needed is openness—both speaking openly and honestly about the real and important issues and being willing to challenge one's own way of thinking.

Localness, too, is essential to the learning organization, for decisions need to be pushed down the organizational hierarchy in order to unleash people's commitment. This gives them the freedom to act.

One thing lacking in many organizations is time to reflect and think. If someone is sitting quietly, we assume he or she is not busy and feel free to interrupt. Many managers, however, are too busy to "just think." This should not be blamed on the tumultuous environment of many crises. Research suggests that, even when given ample time, managers still do not devote any of it to adequate reflection. Therefore, habits need to be changed, as well as how we structure our days.

Competitive Advantage

Michael E. Porter

Summary Prepared by Sara A. Morris

Sara A. Morris received her Ph.D. in Business Policy and Strategy from the University of Texas at Austin. Now on the faculty at Old Dominion University, she teaches capstone courses in strategic management and graduate seminars in competitive strategy. Her current research is in business ethics and social responsibility and concerns CEO misconduct and the use of unethical techniques for obtaining competitor information.

How can a firm obtain and maintain an advantage over its competitors? The answer lies in an understanding of industries, the five forces that drive competition in an industry, and three generic strategies that a firm can use to protect itself against these forces. An industry is a group of firms producing essentially the same products and/or services for the same customers. The profit potential of an industry is determined by the cumulative strength of five forces that affect competition in an industry.

1. Jockeying for position on the part of current competitors in the industry
2. Potential for new competitors to enter the industry
3. The threat of substitutes for the industry's products or services
4. The economic power of suppliers of raw materials to the industry
5. The bargaining power of the industry's customers

Three strategies that a firm can use to neutralize the power of these five forces are low costs, differentiation, and focus. Several specific action steps are required to execute each of these three generic strategies.

Michael E. Porter. *Competitive Advantage: Creating and Sustaining Superior Performance.* New York: Free Press, 1985.

PRINCIPLES OF COMPETITIVE ADVANTAGE

A firm creates a competitive advantage for itself by providing more value for customers than competitors provide. Customers value either (1) equivalent benefits at a lower price than competitors charge or (2) greater benefits that more than compensate for a higher price than competitors charge. Thus, there are two possible competitive advantages, one based on costs and the other on differentiation (benefits). Each of these tactics will be discussed in detail, following an examination of the value chain.

THE VALUE CHAIN

The *value chain,* consisting of value-producing activities and margin, is a basic tool for analyzing the large number of discrete activities within a firm that are potential sources of competitive advantage. The inclusion of margin in the value chain is a reminder that, in order for a firm to profit from its competitive advantage, the value to customers must exceed the costs of generating it. Value-producing activities fall into nine categories—five categories of primary activities and four categories of support activities. Primary activities include inbound logistics, operations, outbound logistics, marketing/sales, and service. Support activities include procurement (of all of the inputs used everywhere in the value chain), technology development (for all of the myriad of technologies that are used in every primary and support activity), human resource management (of all types of personnel throughout the organization), and the firm infrastructure (general management, planning, finance, accounting, legal and government affairs, quality management, etc.).

Firms perform hundreds or thousands of discrete steps in transforming raw materials into finished products. The value chain decomposes the nine value-producing activities into numerous subactivities because each separate subactivity can contribute to the firm's relative cost position and create a basis for differentiation. In most subactivities, the firm is not significantly different from its rivals. The strategically relevant subactivities are those that currently or potentially distinguish the firm from competitors.

Value chain activities are not independent from one another, but interrelated. The cost or performance of one activity is linked to many other activities. For example, the amount of after-sale service needed depends on the quality of the raw materials procured, the degree of quality control in operations, the amount of training given to the sales force regarding matching customer sophistication and model attributes, and other factors. Competitive advantage can be created by linkages among activities as well as by individual activities. Two ways that firms can derive competitive advantage from linkages are through optimization of linkages and coordination of linkages.

The configuration and economics of the value chain are determined by the firm's *competitive scope.* By affecting the value chain, scope also affects competitive advantage. Four dimensions of scope are as follows:

1. *Segment scope*—varieties of products made and buyers served
2. *Vertical scope*—the extent of activities performed internally rather than purchased from outside
3. *Geographic scope*—the range of locations served
4. *Industry scope*—the number of industries in which the firm competes

Broad-scope firms operate multiple value chains and attempt to exploit interrelationships among activities across the chains to gain competitive advantages. Narrow-scope firms use focus strategies to pursue competitive advantages; by concentrating on single value chains, they attempt to perfect the linkages within the value chain.

COMPETITIVE ADVANTAGE THROUGH LOW COST

The starting point for achieving a cost advantage is a thorough analysis of costs in the value chain. The analyst must be able to assign operating costs and assets (fixed and working capital) to each separate value chain activity. There are 10 major factors that are generally under the firm's control and which drive costs:

1. Economies (or diseconomies) of scale
2. Learning, which the firm can control by managing with the learning curve and keeping learning proprietary
3. Capacity utilization, which the firm can control by leveling throughput and/or reducing the penalty for throughput fluctuations
4. Linkages within the value chain, which the firm can control by recognizing and exploiting
5. Interrelationships between business units (in multi-industry firms), which the firm can control by sharing appropriate activities and/or transferring management know-how
6. The extent of vertical integration
7. Timing, which the firm can control by exploiting first-mover or late-mover advantages, and/or timing purchases over the business cycle
8. Discretionary policies (regarding products made, buyers served, human resources used, etc.)
9. Location
10. Institutional factors imposed by government and unions, which the firm can influence if not control outright

Moreover, costs are dynamic; they will change over time due to changes in industry growth rate, differential scale sensitivity, differential learning rates, changes in technology, aging, and the like. Each individual value chain activity must be analyzed separately for its cost drivers and cost dynamics.

By definition, the firm has a cost-based competitive advantage if the total costs of all its value chain activities are lower than any competitor's. A firm's cost position relative to competitors depends on the composition of its value chain compared to competitors' chains, and the firm's position relative to its competitors vis-à-vis the cost drivers of each value chain activity. Two ways that a firm can achieve a cost advantage, therefore, are (1) by controlling cost drivers and (2) by reconfiguring the value chain through means such as changing the production process, the distribution channel, or the raw materials. A cost-based competitive advantage will be sustainable only if competitors cannot imitate it. The cost drivers that tend to be harder to imitate are economies of scale, interrelationships, linkages, proprietary learning, and new technologies that are brought about through discretionary policies.

COMPETITIVE ADVANTAGE THROUGH DIFFERENTIATION

Successful *differentiation* occurs when a firm creates something unique that is valuable to buyers and for which buyers are willing to pay a price premium in excess of the extra costs incurred by the producer. This statement begs two questions: (1) What makes something valuable to buyers, and

(2) why does the producer incur extra costs? With regard to the first question, a firm can create value for buyers by raising buyer performance or by lowering buyer costs (in ways besides selling the product at a lower price). With regard to the second question, differentiation is usually inherently costly because uniqueness requires the producer to perform value chain activities better than competitors.

In order to achieve a differentiation advantage, strategists must be thoroughly familiar with the many discrete activities in their own value chain(s) and in the buyer's value chain and must have a passing knowledge of the value chains of competitors. Each discrete activity in the firm's value chain represents an opportunity for differentiating. The firm's impact on the buyer's value chain determines the value the firm can create through raising buyer performance or lowering buyer costs. Since competitive advantages are by definition relative, a firm's value chain must be compared to those of its competitors.

For each separate activity in the firm's value chain, there are *uniqueness drivers* analogous to the cost drivers described previously. The most important uniqueness driver is probably the set of policy choices managers make (regarding product features, services provided, technologies employed, quality of the raw materials, and so forth). Other uniqueness drivers, in approximate order of importance, are linkages within the value chain and with suppliers and distribution channels, timing, location, interrelationships, learning, vertical integration, scale, and institutional factors.

Buyers use two types of purchasing criteria: (1) *use criteria,* which reflect real value, and (2) *signaling criteria,* which reflect perceived value in advance of purchase and verification. Use criteria include product characteristics, delivery time, ready availability, and other factors that affect buyer value through raising buyer performance or lowering buyer costs. Signaling criteria include the producing firm's reputation and advertising, the product's packaging and advertising, and other factors through which the buyer can infer the probable value of the product before the real value can be known. Differentiators must identify buyer purchasing criteria; the buyer's value chain is the place to start.

Armed with an understanding of multiple value chains, uniqueness drivers, and buyer purchasing criteria, managers can pursue differentiation. There are four basic routes to a differentiation-based competitive advantage. One route is to enhance the sources of uniqueness, by proliferating the sources of differentiation in the value chain, for example. A second route is to make the cost of differentiation an advantage by exploiting sources of differentiation that are not costly, minimizing differentiation costs by controlling cost drivers, and/or reducing costs in activities that do not affect buyer value. Another route is to change the rules to create uniqueness, such as discovering unrecognized purchase criteria. The fourth route is to reconfigure the value chain to be unique in entirely new ways.

A differentiation-based competitive advantage will be sustainable only if buyers' needs and perceptions remain stable and competitors cannot imitate the uniqueness. The firm can strongly influence the buyer's perceptions by continuing to improve on use criteria and by reinforcing them with appropriate signals. The firm is, nevertheless, at risk that buyers' needs will shift, eliminating the value of a particular form of differentiation. The sustainability of differentiation against imitation by competitors depends on its sources, the drivers of uniqueness. The competitive advantage will be more sustainable if the uniqueness drivers involve barriers such as proprietary learning, linkages, interrelationships, and first-mover advantages; if the firm has low costs in differentiating; if there are multiple sources of differentiation; and/or if the firm can create switching costs for customers.

TECHNOLOGY AND COMPETITIVE ADVANTAGE

One of the most significant drivers of competition is technological change. Because technologies are embedded in every activity in the value chain as well as in the linkages among value chain activities, a firm can achieve and/or maintain low costs or differentiation through technology. The first step in using technology wisely is to identify the multitude of technologies in the value chain. Then, the astute manager must become aware of relevant technological improvements coming from competitors, other industries, and scientific breakthroughs.

A firm's technology strategy involves choices among new technologies, and choices about timing and licensing. Rather than pursuing technological improvements involving all value chain activities and linkages indiscriminately, managers should restrict their attention to technological changes that make a difference. New technologies are important if they can affect (1) the firm's particular competitive advantage, either directly or through its drivers, or (2) any of the five forces that drive competition in the industry. A firm's timing matters in technological changes because the technology leader will experience first-mover advantages (e.g., reputation as a pioneer, opportunity to define industry standards) as well as disadvantages (e.g., costs of educating buyers, demand uncertainty). Thus, the choice of whether to be a technology leader or follower should be made according to the sustainability of the technological lead. When a firm's competitive advantage rests on technology, licensing the technology to other firms is risky. Although there are conditions under which licensing may be warranted (to tap an otherwise inaccessible market, for example), often the firm inadvertently creates strong rivals and/or gives away a competitive advantage for a small royalty fee.

COMPETITOR SELECTION

A firm must be ever vigilant in pursuing and protecting its competitive advantage; however, there are dangers in relentlessly attacking all rivals. It is prudent to distinguish desirable competitors from undesirable ones. Desirable competitors may enable a firm to increase its competitive advantage (e.g., by absorbing demand fluctuations, or by providing a standard against which buyers compare costs or differentiation) or may improve industry structure (i.e., may weaken one or more of the five forces that collectively determine the intensity of competition in an industry). Characteristics of desirable competitors include realistic assumptions; clear, self-perceived weaknesses; enough credibility to be acceptable to customers; enough viability to deter new entrants; and enough strength to motivate the firm to continue to improve its competitive advantage. A smart industry leader will encourage some competitors and discourage others through tactics such as technology licensing and selective retaliation.

SCOPE AND COMPETITIVE ADVANTAGE

An industry consists of heterogeneous parts, or segments, due to differences in buyer behavior and differences in the economics of producing different products or services for these buyers. Therefore, the intensity of competition (i.e., the collective strength of the five competitive forces) varies among segments of the same industry. Moreover, because segments of the same industry have different value chains, the requirements for competitive advantage differ widely among industry segments. The existence of multiple industry segments forces a firm to decide on competitive scope, or where in the industry to compete. The attractiveness of any particular industry segment depends on the collective strength of the five competitive forces, the segment's size and growth rate, and the fit between a firm's abilities and the segment's needs. The firm may broadly target many segments or may use the generic strategy of focus to serve one or a few segments.

The competitive scope decision requires the manager to analyze all the current and potential industry segments. To identify product segments, all the product varieties in an industry must be examined for differences they can create in the five competitive forces and the value chain. The industry's products may differ in terms of features, technology or design, packaging, performance, services, and in many other ways. To identify buyer segments, all the different types of buyers in an industry must be examined for differences they can create in the five competitive forces and the value chain. Buyers can differ by type (e.g., several types of industrial buyers, several types of consumer buyers), distribution channel, and geographic location (according to weather zone, country stage of development, etc.).

When the value chains of different segments in the same industry are related at multiple points, a firm can share value-producing activities among segments. Such segment interrelationships encourage firms to use a broad-target strategy, unless the costs of coordination, compromise, and inflexibility in jointly accomplishing value-producing activities outweigh the benefits of sharing. Broad-target strategies often involve too many segments, thereby pushing coordination, compromise, and inflexibility costs too high and making the broadly targeted firm vulnerable to firms with good focus strategies.

Whereas broad-target strategies are based on similarities in the value chains among segments, focus strategies are based on differences between segments' value chains. A focuser can optimize the value chain for one or a few segments and achieve lower costs or better differentiation than broad-target firms because the focuser can avoid the costs of coordination, compromise, and inflexibility required for serving multiple segments. The sustainability of a focus strategy is determined by its sustainability against (1) broad-target competitors, (2) imitators, and (3) substitutes, the next topic of interest.

Both the industry's product or service and its substitutes perform the same generic function for the buyer (i.e., fill the same role in the buyer's value chain). The threat of substitution depends on (1) the relative value/price of the substitute compared to the industry's product, (2) the cost of switching to the substitute, and (3) the buyer's propensity to switch. The relative value/price compares the substitute to the industry's product in terms of usage rate, delivery and installation, direct and indirect costs of use, buyer performance, complementary products, uncertainty, etc. Switching costs include redesign costs, retraining costs, and risk of failure. Buyer propensity to substitute depends on resources available, risk profile, technological orientation, and the like. The threat of substitution often changes over time because of changes in relative price, relative value, switching costs, or propensity to substitute. To defend against substitutes, the focuser can reduce costs, improve the product, raise switching costs, improve complementary goods, etc.

CORPORATE STRATEGY AND COMPETITIVE ADVANTAGE

Whereas business-level strategy is concerned with the firm's course of actions within an individual industry, corporate-level strategy is generally concerned with the multi-industry firm's course of actions across industries. By exploiting interrelationships among its business units in distinct but related industries, the multi-industry corporation can increase its competitive advantage within one or more of those industries. Porter uses the term *horizontal strategy* to refer to a corporation's coordinated set of goals and policies that apply across its business units, and argues that horizontal strategy may be the most critical issue facing diversified firms today. It is through its horizontal strategy that a corporation achieves synergy.

There are three types of interrelationships among a multi-industry corporation's business units: tangible, intangible, and competitor induced. *Tangible interrelationships* occur when different business units have common elements in their value chains, such as the same buyers, technologies, or purchased inputs. These common elements create opportunities to share value chain activities among related business units. Sharing activities may lower costs or increase differentiation, thereby adding to competitive advantage. However, the benefits of sharing do not always exceed the costs of sharing. One cost of sharing is the need for more coordination in the shared value chain activities. Another cost is the need for compromise in the way shared value chain activities are performed; the compromise must be acceptable to both business units, but may be optimal for neither. A third cost of sharing is greater inflexibility in responding to changing environmental conditions.

A second type of interrelationship, *intangible interrelationships,* occurs when different business units can transfer general management know-how even though they have no common elements in their value chains. It is possible, though less likely, for intangible interrelationships to lead to competitive advantage. A third type of interrelationship, *competitor-induced interrelationships,* occurs when two diversified corporations compete against each other in more than one business unit. Such multipoint competition between two corporations means that any action in one line of business can affect the entire range of jointly contested industries. Therefore, for multipoint competitors, a competitive advantage in one line of business will have implications for all the linked industries.

Any diversified corporation will face impediments to exploiting interrelationships: The managers of business units that receive fewer benefits than they contribute will resist sharing; managers of all business units will tend to protect their turf; incentive systems may not appropriately measure and reward a business unit's contributions to other units; and so forth. Therefore, corporate-level executives must articulate an explicit horizontal strategy and organize to facilitate horizontal relations. Examples of organizational practices and mechanisms that are particularly helpful are horizontal structures (e.g., groupings of business units, interunit task forces), horizontal systems (e.g., interunit strategic planning systems and capital budgeting systems), horizontal human resource practices (e.g., cross-business job rotation and management forums), and horizontal conflict resolution processes.

A special case of interrelationships occurs when the industry's product is used or purchased with complementary products. Because the sale of one promotes the sale of the other, complementary products have the opposite effect of substitutes. Three types of decisions that a corporation must make regarding complementary products concern whether to control these products internally (as opposed to letting other firms supply them), whether to bundle them (i.e., sell complementary products together as a package), and whether to cross-subsidize them (i.e., price complementary products based on their interrelationships instead of their individual costs). All three types of decisions have repercussions for competitive advantage.

IMPLICATIONS FOR OFFENSIVE AND DEFENSIVE COMPETITIVE STRATEGY

The *industry scenario* is a planning tool that may be used to guide the formulation of competitive strategy in the face of major uncertainties about the future. Constructing industry scenarios involves identifying uncertainties that may affect the industry, determining the causal factors, making a range of plausible assumptions about each important causal factor, combining assumptions into internally consistent scenarios, analyzing the industry structure that would prevail under each scenario, identifying competitive advantages under each scenario, and predicting the behavior of competitors under each scenario. Managers may then design competitive strategies based on the most probable scenario, the most attractive scenario, hedging (protecting the firm against the worst-case scenario), or preserving flexibility.

Defensive strategy is intended to lower the probability of attack from a new entrant into the industry or an existing competitor seeking to reposition itself. The preferred defensive strategy is deterrence. The old saying about "the best offense is a good defense" holds here; a firm with a competitive advantage that continues to lower its costs or improve its differentiation is very difficult to beat. Nevertheless, when deterrence fails, the firm must respond to an attack underway. When a firm's position is being challenged, defensive tactics include raising structural barriers (e.g., blocking distribution channels, raising buyer switching costs) and increasing expected retaliation.

Sometimes attacking an industry leader makes sense. The most important rule in offensive strategy is never to attack a leader head-on with an imitation strategy. In order to attack an industry leader successfully, the challenger must have a sustainable competitive advantage, must be close to the leader in costs and differentiation, and must have some means to thwart leader retaliation. There are three primary avenues to attack a leader: (1) change the way individual value-producing activities are performed or reconfigure the entire value chain; (2) redefine the competitive scope compared to the leader; (3) pure spending on the part of the challenger. The leader is particularly vulnerable when the industry is undergoing significant changes, such as technological improvements, changes in the buyer's value chain, or the emergence of new distribution channels.

III

High- and Low-Performing Organizations

Most organizations don't want merely to survive; they want to be effective, or even excellent, at what they do. To do so requires a prior definition of success, and defining success often encourages the managers of an organization to examine the actions of their best competitors for comparative models (benchmarks). They assume that if they can identify the organizational characteristics that allow others to succeed, then these attributes can be transplanted (or adapted, or even improved upon) to facilitate their own success. Consequently, a wide variety of organizations and management groups have shown strong interest in what high-performing organizations actually do and what are their guiding principles. Effective work teams are often a key ingredient of the organization's success. By contrast, it is equally important to examine what causes high-performing firms to lose their edge and fail, and that topic is covered in the fourth reading in this part.

Marcus Buckingham is the author of *The One Thing You Need to Know.* In this book, Buckingham focuses on several themes, each of which envisions organizational success (i.e., high performance) as that which is achieved through the proper management of people. The author argues that the chief responsibility that great managers accept is to *find what is unique about each person and capitalize on it* instead of trying to remedy each individual's shortcomings. Turning the talents that a person brings to the organization into performance is more critical to organizational performance than trying to change (i.e., "fix") each employee. The chief responsibility of great leaders is to rally people to a better future.

Buckingham, a graduate of England's Cambridge University, worked for the Gallup organization for 17 years. During much of that time he conducted research focusing on the world's best managers, leaders, and workplaces. He is also the author of *First, Break all the Rules: What the World's Best Managers Do Differently, The Truth About You*, and *Now, Discover Your Strengths.*

In *Big Winners and Big Losers*, Alfred A. Marcus reports on his findings from a detailed review of the performance of the 1,000 largest corporations in the United States. Marcus reports that there is a consistent pattern that distinguishes the big winners from the big losers. Ranjay Gulati from the Kellogg School of Management at Northwestern University writes, "This book provides an excellent synthesis of the strategies that differentiate successful firms from the rest of the world," and Michael Cuscumano from MIT's Sloan School of Management notes that a central theme in Marcus's book is the idea that "successful companies . . . balance complementary and at times contradictory skills—the agility to find the right markets, focus on discipline to succeed, and the agility again to re-focus and adapt as markets change."

Marcus received his Ph.D. from Harvard University and currently holds the Edson Spencer Chair of Strategic Management and Technological Leadership in the Carlson School of Management at the Minneapolis campus of the University of Minnesota. He is the author or coeditor of 11 books (including *Strategic Foresight: A New Look at Scenarios*), and he has published numerous articles in such journals as the *Academy of Management Review, California Management Review*, and the *Strategic Management Journal.*

Beyond Teams lays out a simple premise based on research and case studies—that high-performing organizations stem from collaborative work systems. The authors (Beyerlein, McGee, Moran, and Freedman) identify 10 major principles that define collaborative organizations, including an emphasis on personal accountability, facilitation of dialog, managing trade-offs, and "exploiting the rhythm of divergence and convergence." They also demonstrate the applicability of the 10 principles across manufacturing, product development, service, and virtual office settings.

Michael Beyerlein is the author or editor of numerous books on collaboration. He is the director of the Center for the Study of Work Teams at the University of North Texas. Craig McGee is a principal with Solutions; Linda Moran works for Achieve Global; and Sue Freedman is president of Knowledge Work Associates.

Jim Collins is the author of two previous million-seller books—*Built to Last* and *Good to Great.* The former book was on *Business Week*'s best-seller list for several years. The latter book identifies five key factors common to sustained success, such as preserving core values, focusing on facts before making decisions, hiring the right people, and finding leaders who combine personal humility with strong professional intensity.

In *How the Mighty Fall*, Collins examines organizations such as Bank of America, Motorola, Circuit City, A & P, and Zenith to identify what made them slip into major decline (and sometimes total failure). Collins makes a strong eye-opening assertion: that *every institution is vulnerable to decline.* He identifies five stages of decline: hubris born of success, undisciplined pursuit of more, denial of risk and peril, grasping for salvation, and capitulation to irrelevance or death. Fortunately, he concludes, the pattern of decline can be avoided, detected, and reversed as seen by examples at Hewlett-Packard, Merck, IBM, Delta, and Nucor, which all emerged stronger than ever.

The One Thing You Need to Know

Marcus Buckingham

Summary Prepared by Kristie J. Loescher

Kristie J. Loescher is a Lecturer in the Management Department of the McCombs School of Business at the University of Texas at Austin, where she teaches management, leadership, and business communications. She has her doctorate in business administration from Nova Southeastern University, specializing in human resource management. Prior to her career in academia, Kristie worked in the health-care industry for 15 years in the areas of quality assurance, utilization management, and clinical research. Her academic publications focus on ethical education, organizational ethics, change management, and diversity management.

What *controlling insight* explains great managing, great leading, and high levels of individual success? Research conducted to identify the best explanation for each of these is based on examining greatness in each area. Greatness is not accomplished by avoiding what causes failure, or by doing the opposite of what causes failure, but by following a distinct set of behaviors that specifically define greatness. To be called *the one thing*, a controlling insight had to pass three research tests:

1. Be present with greatness in a variety of situations
2. Act as a multiplier, leading to high levels of sustained success when applied
3. Describe behaviors or actions

These tests are applied to both great organizational success stories (through evaluation of great managers and great leaders) and great individual success stories to identify *the one thing* you can do to achieve success yourself.

Marcus Buckingham. *The One Thing You Need to Know . . . About Great Managing, Great Leading, and Sustained Individual Success.* New York: Free Press, 2005.

GREAT ORGANIZATIONAL SUCCESS

This section presents behaviors that provide a foundation for both managerial and leadership success. Management and leadership are separate and distinct roles, and they require separate and distinct behaviors for success.

Great Managing

The controlling insight for management is to *capitalize on* **uniqueness**. Successful management begins with the individual employee and focuses on knowing that employee's skills and abilities, and then pointing that person in the direction of organizational goals. You must make understanding and serving the individual employee your first priority as a manager, so employees will believe you sincerely care about them and are invested in their success.

To be successful and enjoy the job of management requires an instinct for coaching and the ability to identify people's unique talents. You must enjoy watching people grow and succeed. Managers must also be talented at identifying an individual's skills, abilities, personality, and goals and at understanding how best to utilize these attributes for the benefit of both the employee and the organization. In addition to these two main talents, the following four skills are critical to successfully "capitalize on uniqueness":

1. Select the right people. Know the skills, abilities, and personality traits you need in each of your employees to reach organizational goals. Then use structured interviewing techniques to identify candidates that meet these needs.
2. Define clear behavior expectations. Provide a clear focus for your employees, so they understand the factors that define excellence for their job.
3. Motivate and shape behavior with praise. Once you define behaviors critical to job success, reinforce employees who exhibit these behaviors with frequent and sincere praise. Other employees will watch what gets praised, so set the bar high for excellence and praise the steps toward it and reward those who reach it.
4. Demonstrate your care and concern. Create strong bonds of trust and respect between yourself and each employee—only then can you expect them to forge similar bonds with each other and with customers. An employees' trust in you is built on a foundation of feeling understood and believing that you care about and are invested in his or her success.

As stated in the fourth point above, to gain employees' trust you must demonstrate that you understand them and their goals. Since each person is different and unique, the majority of a manager's time must be spent in the pursuit of understanding what is unique in each employee and devising how to use it in pursuit of both organizational and employee goals. The manager is an **intermediary** between the individual and the organization, and this job must be performed one-on-one. To the extent there is dissonance or disagreement between an employee's goals and those of the organization, the successful manager remains focused on the employee, which may mean changing the way the company operates or even helping the employees find a way to reach their goals at a different company. There are three unique characteristics, or *levers*, that a successful manager must know about each employee to "capitalize on uniqueness," and these include strengths and weaknesses, motivators, and learning style.

STRENGTHS AND WEAKNESSES   Focusing people on their strengths provides more payoff than trying to get them to improve on their weaknesses. A successful manager helps employees identify their key talents and use them in the pursuit of the organization's goals. Managers must also help employees identify whether their weaknesses are a result of a lack of training or a lack of ability. A lack of training can be fixed, but a lack of ability requires you to change the employee's job or help the employee find success elsewhere.

MOTIVATORS   Identifying what motivates employees and keeps them performing at their highest level is a key competency for managers. These motivators may be extrinsic (praise, recognition, rewards), intrinsic (opportunities for learning, advancement, empowerment, autonomy), or a combination of both. You need to know what fuels each employee's desire to give their best.

LEARNING STYLE   Understanding the best way for an employee to build new skills and learn new processes helps a manager maximize the potential of each employee. Effective learning approaches vary among individuals. Some employees learn by analyzing, others by doing, and some by imitating. Therefore, you will provide written instructions for the analyzer, allow the doer to use trial and error, and set up on-the-job training for the imitator.

If employee-focused management is good for the employee and satisfying for the manager, can it also be good for the organization? Indeed, focusing on individual employee strengths and goals creates four advantages for the manager and the company:

- **Saves time.** By using the talents of each employee and not expecting employees to be capable at everything, you save time correcting and disciplining employees, while increasing your opportunities to praise them.
- **Increases employee accountability.** People improve most in areas where they are already talented, rather than in areas where they are weak. Therefore, by focusing employees on their areas of greatest skill and ability, you can challenge them to deliver higher levels of performance. Recognizing they are being asked to do what they do best, they will be more likely to accept and meet your challenge.
- **Builds stronger team cohesion.** By focusing employees on their strengths, you create more interdependence between employees. In an environment with high interdependence, employees will recognize how much they need each other and will value those who have skills in other areas required to complete job tasks.
- **Creates healthy disruption.** Meeting each employee's unique needs challenges you as the manager to think creatively and to change systems and processes. In meeting the needs of your employees, you must continuously improve the match between employee skills and abilities and the organization. By doing so, you have the opportunity to discover new, more effective and efficient methods for meeting the organization's goals. In addition, by focusing employees on their talents, you open yourself and the organization up to the potential for benefiting from their exploration and discoveries.

Great Leadership

Successful leadership begins with a **vision** (a vivid mental image of a potential future for an organization) and focuses on making that vision clear and compelling for people to follow. The controlling insight for leadership is to *capitalize on the universal.* Despite each individual's unique qualities and outlook, the leader's job is to make each of us see and believe in the leader's vision by tapping into the basic needs we all have in common:

1. Need for security, driven by our fear of death
2. Need for community, driven by our fear of the outsider

3. Need for clarity, driven by our fear of the future and the unknown
4. Need for authority, driven by our fear of chaos and need for order
5. Need for respect, driven by our fear of insignificance

By showing us how their vision for the future meets one or more of these five needs, leaders are able to motivate and encourage us to follow them. However, *the most important of these needs for an effective leader to focus on is the need for clarity to alleviate our fear of the future.* To be effective, leaders must be optimists with the ability not only to see but also to clearly describe our bright prospects to us, thereby decreasing our fear and uncertainty about the future.

Providing goal clarity for followers, while allowing them room to design the path toward that goal, is the key balance point for effective leadership. Leaders must provide clarity in four areas:

- **Primary customers**—identifying who is the main audience
- **Focal asset**—specifying what they have/do that makes us special/different
- **Key measure**—clarifying how they know how well we're doing
- **Principal actions**—taking actions as a leader to reinforce their vision

Leaders maintain their ability to provide clarity and their creativity to provide direction through the disciplines of reflecting on the past and the future, selecting superior role models for themselves and their employees, and practicing the communication of their vision.

Primary characteristics of good leaders include *optimism* about the future, *dissatisfaction with the status quo*, and *self-assurance* in their ability to make their vision of the future a reality. Because these characteristics are so critical to successful leadership and tend to be wired into an individual's brain at birth, great leaders are, in essence, born rather than made.

SUSTAINED INDIVIDUAL SUCCESS

Maintaining *sustained success* means using your talents in work that you find rewarding and fulfilling over a long period of time. The controlling insight for sustained individual success, paradoxically, is "discover what you don't like doing and stop doing it." In researching highly successful, happy people, the main thing they have in common is the discipline to say no to activities that do not play to their strengths. They know their strengths in terms of their skills, abilities, and aptitudes, and they know their weaknesses. But instead of spending time improving their weaknesses, they spend their time focused on using and continuously growing their strengths. While you should always try new activities that utilize aptitudes you have not yet explored, pay attention to how you feel once you have learned the basics of any work activity or role. Stop doing those activities or roles that leave you feeling:

- **Bored**—tasks that are acutely uninteresting to you
- **Unfulfilled**—tasks that are inconsistent with your values and goals
- **Frustrated**—tasks that inhibit your strengths and/or force you to use your weaker skills and abilities
- **Drained**—tasks that are profoundly disagreeable, making you dread your work

By focusing on your strengths, you not only enjoy your work but also are able to perform at a higher level than you will ever achieve by focusing on your weaknesses. You will feel more confident and more enthusiastic about doing what you do well. The controlling insight speaks to what you should stop doing because the great challenge of sustained success occurs once you identify your strengths and begin to enjoy success. You will then tend to attract "opportunities" for promotion or for additional roles, and the discipline to say no to those offers that take you away from using your strengths or that force you to rely on your weaker skill sets will make the difference between achieving sustained success and hating your job. If you find yourself in a situation where you have accepted an opportunity that has begun to bore you, frustrate you, or leave you unfulfilled, you have three choices:

1. Quit the role
2. Change or refocus the role on your strengths
3. Find a partner who has strengths to complement your weaknesses to share the responsibilities

Conclusion

A key theme running through all three controlling insights is intentional imbalance. Great managers do not try to "do it all," but instead focus on their employees and what makes them unique contributors to the company. Likewise the great leader has an equally tight focus on communicating clarity and optimism about the future, while the individual looking for sustained success focuses on saying no to things that are not engaging their strengths. This type of focus requires discipline, commitment, and courage.

2

Big Winners
and Big Losers

Alfred A. Marcus

Summary Prepared by Allen Harmon

Allen Harmon *is President and General Manager of WDSE-TV, the community-licensed PBS member station serving Northeastern Minnesota and Northwestern Wisconsin. He also currently serves as an adjunct instructor in the Labovitz School of Business and Economics at the University of Minnesota Duluth, where he teaches Strategic Management. Before joining WDSE, Mr. Harmon held a series of senior management positions in a regional investor-owned electric utility. He earned an MBA from Indiana University's Kelly School of Business and has completed the University of Minnesota Carlson School of Management Executive Development Program.*

A natural parity prevails in most industries. Sustained competitive advantage is rare. Over the decade from 1992 to 2002, a scant 3 percent of the top 1,000 U.S. companies consistently delivered returns that bettered the average of their industry. Only 6 percent of the top 1,000 consistently underperformed industry averages. *What are the distinctive traits of the big winners that an organization should seek to emulate to reap the rewards of consistent winning? What traits should an organization eschew to avoid the punishment borne by the big losers?*

Winners occupy **sweet spots** in the market, which are attractive market positions characterized by a lack of direct competition that present incumbents with the opportunity to control the five classic industry forces. Winners move to those positions with agility, demonstrate the discipline to protect those positions by developing hard-to-imitate capabilities, and focus on fully exploiting the position's potential. Losers are disadvantaged by being positioned in industry **sour spots**, which are highly contested market positions affording incumbents little opportunity to control the five classic industry forces. Losers are hindered in moving from those positions by their own rigidity and are inept in developing the capabilities that would allow them to protect their positions. Losers' efforts to exploit desirable positions they might occupy are too diffuse to be effective.

Alfred A. Marcus. *Big Winners and Big Losers: The 4 Secrets of Long-Term Business Success and Failure.* Pennsylvania: Wharton School Publishing, 2006.

IDENTIFYING THE WINNERS AND LOSERS

Big winners and big losers were selected for study from the *Wall Street Journal*'s scorecard on the basis of stock market returns over the period from 1992 to 2002. A final screen was applied to determine whether the selected companies' performance during the turbulent first half of 2002 was consistent with results over the preceding 10 years. The *Wall Street Journal*'s industry designations were used; pairs of winners and losers in nine industry sectors were selected for study.

A separate analysis of the Fortune 1000 list with consideration for minor differences in timing and composition affirmed the selections of big winners and big losers. Use of accounting data in lieu of market data was considered and rejected; market data were favored for being forward looking and less susceptible to company manipulation.

Winning company performance met the following benchmarks:

- As of January 1, 2002, 10-, 5-, 3- and 1-year market returns exceeded their industry average.
- Five-year average market return was two or more times the industry average.
- Return for the period January 1, 2002, to June 1, 2002, exceeded the industry average.

Losing company performance was described by:

- As of January 1, 2002, 10-, 5-, 3-, and 1-year market returns were less than the industry average.
- Five-year average market return was half or less than half the industry average.
- Return for the period January 1, 2002, to June 1, 2002, was less than half the industry average.

The screening process identified nine pairs of companies:

Industry Sector	Company	5-Year Average Annual Market Return (%)
Technology	Amphenol	34.0
	LSI Logic	3.4
Manufacturing/Appliance	SPX	28.8
	Snap-On	1.7
Software	FiServ	31.2
	Parametric	−21.2
Food	Dreyers	22.4
	Campbell Soup	−2.8
Drugs/Chemicals	Forest Labs	58.5
	IMC Global	−18.7
Manufacturing/Industrial	Ball	23.9
	Goodyear	−11.5
Financial	Brown & Brown	48.7
	Safeco	−1.0
Retail	Family Dollar	36.1
	Gap	9.8
Entertainment/Toys	Activision	24.1
	Hasbro	−0.1

THE ANALYSIS

Over 500 experienced managers, each trained and competent in strategic management, participated in the effort to identify what differentiated the big winners from the big losers. Five teams of five or six manager/analysts were assigned each industry pair and participated in an iterative process of analysis and peer review that sought to answer:

- What external challenges did the company face?
- How did the company's internal strengths and weaknesses relate to those challenges?
- What moves did the company make?
- Why were the moves of one company more successful than those of the company it was paired with?

As the analysis progressed, patterns began to emerge. Winners tended to be smaller than losers—on average, winners in the sample generated $3.49 billion in annual revenue and employed 14,000; losers on average generated $10.66 billion in annual revenue and employed 48,000. Winners tended to be less well known than losers. Winners tended to have a broad customer base; losers found their customers more concentrated.

SWEET SPOTS VS. SOUR SPOTS

Perhaps most significant, big winners were found in industry "sweet spots" where they faced virtually no direct competition. Because they had come to offer something rare, valuable, and non-substitutable to their customers, big winners had achieved control over the five classic industry forces. Winners bring a combination of low cost and differentiation to their customers in striking packages. The net result is exceptional value.

In contrast, big losers were found in industry "sour spots" where they faced multiple competitors offering similar or equally good products or services. As their products offered customers nothing special, the losers had little leverage with which to control industry forces. Losers often found themselves disadvantaged by prices too high for customers to afford, prices too low to be profitable, and/or processes too complex to be managed effectively.

GAINING THE SWEET SPOT

Winners found sweet spots in their industries by achieving significant alignment with their customers. By successfully providing unique solutions to complex customer needs and by embedding themselves in customer processes and operations, winners were in a position to identify and exploit unique opportunities. This accomplishment took various forms—for Ball, it was providing a process for producing specialty packaging meeting customer needs; for Dreyers, it was managing the grocer's difficult-to-manage freezer space; for Family Dollar, it was geographic, embedding stores in underserved urban neighborhoods. In each case, achieving significant alignment with customers opened opportunities for the winners in uncontested markets and allowed them to grow under their competitors' radar.

Three Traits of Winners

Knowledge of customer needs gave winners a place to go; three traits shared by the winners—agility, discipline, and focus—gave them the ability to get there.

AGILITY   Each of the big winners knew exactly where they wanted to go. They also displayed the agility to get there and the capacity to regularly reinvent themselves. Whether through merger, acquisition, or internal growth, they added businesses that showed promise. They showed no reluctance to divest those businesses that did not show promise. Hallmarks of agility include:

- Responding quickly to changes in the market such as overcapacity and consolidations of competitors with new innovations
- Maintaining flexibility by controlling size, focusing on profitable growth, and building partnerships or outsourcing where others could contribute needed competencies
- Seeking growth in customers' changing needs, responding with products and services that become an intimate part of the customer's process
- Moving to markets that present specialized needs that only the company can satisfy, that are underserved, or that are perceived as unattractive and thus ignored by others
- Aggressively seeking acquisitions to exploit opportunities or to broaden and enhance product and service offerings
- Achieving sufficient diversification so that declines in one sector might be offset by improved performance in another

DISCIPLINE   Exercise of internal discipline allows big winners to protect their sweet spot positions by maintaining the scarce, hard-to-imitate capabilities that create best value propositions for customers. Evidence of organizational discipline is seen in:

- Effectively reducing costs and raising quality through applying technology, instituting process controls, achieving volume-driven efficiencies, and attaining best-in-class levels of service
- Controlling distribution through efforts ranging from employing aggressive globalization to serve new and existing markets efficiently and developing technology to track merchandise, to avoiding product deterioration in transit
- Smoothly integrating acquisitions, carefully selecting those targets that fit the organization's goals, quickly consolidating operations, and eliminating low- or no-profit components
- Creating a culture of employee involvement through selective hiring of skilled, aggressive individuals given the training, recognition, and respect that support their ability to make a difference to the company
- Monitoring and influencing regulatory changes—winners willingly comply with regulations, have good environmental records, and promote ethical behavior and integrity

FOCUS   Big winners do more than just defend their sweet spot positions; they are actively committed to growth by broadening and deepening the sweet spot. Risk of failure was reduced by focus on core competencies. Big winners demonstrated focus by:

- Concentrating on core strengths by spinning off noncore activities; avoiding activities with high risk of failure; allowing others to assume risks (such as R&D), consistent with their own competencies; and demonstrating total dedication to selected customer categories, developed brands, and related products
- Developing high-growth, application-specific products for growth markets, deepening relationships with customers to offer solutions driven by emerging customer needs rather than by a particular product or technology
- Extending reach globally, capitalizing on growth opportunities overseas through acquisition or internal development to extend the organization's global presence

While big winners demonstrated these three traits in a variety of ways, *all demonstrated consistent mastery of the one competence most difficult to replicate: balance.* A tension exists among the three key traits. In the extreme, focus and discipline can impair agility by closing off consideration of opportunities. The organization must at once defend and develop the space it holds while prospecting for new positions to occupy. Continual reinvention of the company produces stress between what the organization is and what it intends to become. The distinctive performance of the big winners is the result of achieving a unique balance of these attributes.

MIRED IN A SOUR SPOT

Losers found themselves competing in occupied sour spots in the market with products that were too expensive to be attractive to customers, products priced too low to be profitable, or business models that were too complex to execute effectively. They had, in short, lost contact with their customers and found themselves focused on products or internal processes rather than customer needs. Without the leverage provided by a unique value position, losers had little control over the classic industry forces.

Without the sense of direction that an intimate knowledge of their customers provided the big winners, when big losers moved (and they did), they moved in the wrong direction or at the wrong time. As a group, big losers demonstrated the traits of rigidity, ineptness, and diffuseness that prevented them from escaping their sour spots.

Rigidity—Like the big winners, losers sought movement. Their moves were often defensive and in reaction to a threat, however, rather than an offensive initiative to better align with customer needs. Their moves were characterized by a sense of rigidity that showed itself in:

- Exclusive reliance on expansion of core products for growth, sticking with the company's original business or current niche even as it lost potential, putting effort into expanding unprofitable businesses, and ignoring the prospects of noncore brands or holdings
- Reliance on commoditized products sold on the basis of price, or to concentrated buyers who because of that concentration hold pricing power
- Accumulating excess capacity at times of stagnant or declining demand; losers tended to expand too rapidly, buying weak or commodity businesses at inflated prices with debt that later became a burden
- Failing to mount a vigorous response such as new product development, capacity adjustments, or new market entrance to declines in the core business
- Failing to recognize and respond to changes in customer tastes or competitors' innovations
- Favoring size over agility and consequently becoming burdened with bureaucracy, losing the ability to anticipate and exploit changes in demand, profitable new niches, and competitors' blunders

Ineptness—Losers lacked the skills to create best-value propositions to offer their customers, finding themselves unable to defend what positions they did occupy from more adept competitors. Losers were unable to escape from the sour spots in part due to the following:

- Inability to provide best-in-class service or customized product offerings at low cost; losers exacerbated their disadvantages by failing to successfully correct even recognized inefficiencies or unwisely cutting the activities valued by customers in their efforts to reduce costs

- Failure to master their supply chain, alienating distributors and retailers of their products through ineffective performance and not developing the long-term relationships with customers that could be translated into leverage over suppliers
- Ineffective management of acquisition activities, resulting in overpayment, ineffective integration, and a failure to realize operational synergies
- Demoralizing employees by creating disarray and disruption when implementing new systems, developing an adversarial relationship with unions and ineffective (or nonexistent) incentive compensation plans
- Failure to maintain high ethical standards or to deal effectively with regulation, resulting in violations of environmental and accounting regulations.

Diffuseness—Without focus, loser's activities were ineffective in building competitive advantage that might have liberated them from their sour spots. The losing companies failed to reinforce the positions they occupied against attack from more competent competitors, failed to integrate disparate acquisitions to achieve common goals, and invested in R&D that was never destined to serve their customers. Evidence of the diffuseness infecting the big losers included the following:

- Lack of clear strategic direction meant that activities of both existing and newly acquired business units failed to coalesce around common goals or to exploit synergies among them; acquisitions were executed without a long-term plan, operations became needlessly complex or duplicative, and poorly executed attempts at vertical integration took one loser into value chain functions where it lacked competence
- Focusing internally on products and marketing existing, diverse brands caused losers to ignore promising opportunities presented by the market; out of touch with customers and the market, they failed to identify growth opportunities or to adequately support the rapidly growing product lines they did hold
- Looking to global markets as a fix for domestic problems only compounded losers' problems as they failed in the same ways in new markets: acquisitions failed, service levels fell short of customer requirements, local regulations were not dealt with effectively, and opportunities that did present themselves were not pursued aggressively

LOOKING FOR PATTERNS

Each of the big winners built competitive advantage through combinations of traits demonstrating agility, discipline, and focus; their performance resulted from building difficult-to-copy combinations of these contrasting traits. Multiple positive traits were interwoven to reinforce one another. In no case was success the product of a single positive trait.

Success, then, is not the result of building the strengths separately, but of combining strengths into a larger whole. Achieving that whole requires making nontrivial trade-offs in achieving a balance between agility and discipline and focus.

Conversely, the prolonged poor performance of the big losers was in no case the product of a single weakness. Multiple weaknesses in a pattern that reinforced each other condemned the losers to failure. Big losers had difficulty managing tension. Under stress, one negative trait simply piled on top of another negative trait.

TURNAROUNDS

Updating the selection process to include the most recent five-year period (1999–2004) shows that for the most part, big winners have continued to win and big losers have continued to lose. Of the 18 companies, only 2 have seen a reversal of fortunes.

Insurer Safeco went from loser to winner, beating the performance of the Dow Jones Industrial Average beginning in 2001. Safeco began its turnaround by embracing focus, cutting back on acquisitions while determining what kind of company it wanted to be and what it could do well. Divesting businesses that did not fit the new definition of the company reduced its size and increased its agility. Discipline—to increase accountability and aggressiveness, reduce costs, and raise quality—completed the groundwork for Safeco's turnaround.

Manufacturer SPX saw its performance deteriorate. While it did not fall behind big loser Snap-On during the period, the former winner did slide into mediocrity, barely besting the Dow Jones Industrial Average for the period. At the root of SPX's decline was diffuseness, as the company lost its strategic direction and spread itself too thin. Weakness then piled on weakness. Without clear strategic direction, diverse acquisitions quickly bloated the company and rigidity replaced agility. The unraveling continued as a loss of discipline led to inept ethical breaches in setting executive compensation.

The turnarounds at Safeco and SPX offer confirmation of the observation that *success results from building a reinforcing pattern of positive traits—agility, discipline, and focus—and managing the tensions inherent among them.* Failure is the product of a pattern of negative traits: diffuseness, rigidity, and ineptness.

3

How the Mighty Fall

By Jim Collins

Summary Prepared by Tanya Pietz

Tanya Pietz received her Bachelor of Business Administration degree from the University of Minnesota Duluth with majors in Human Resource Management and Marketing. She has worked extensively as a consultant in the health-care field and is currently coordinating the Physician Recruitment Program. She is also developing a systemwide employee engagement program with a focus on impacting bottom-line results at Riverwood Healthcare Center in Aitkin, Minnesota. Dedicated to the field of health care, she has spent the past 12 years in human resources, working with clients nationwide to build strong recruitment, employee engagement, and appreciation programs. She has a passion for training and continues to research and develop new strategies for increasing employee engagement within organizations.

INTRODUCTION

Why have some of the greatest companies in history fallen? What causes a great company to spiral toward demise? Do companies who fall from greatness have anything in common? Is there anything to be learned from researching these once successful organizations?

A research-based perspective of how some of the greatest companies in history succumb to decline and peril allows today's leaders the opportunity to avoid these same pitfalls and learn from these companies' mistakes.

By understanding and being aware of the typical stages of decline, leaders can equip their companies with tools and strategies for minimizing the chances of falling all the way to the bottom. One key conclusion from research is that *it is possible to avoid decline if you can catch it early.* Not all companies who enter the stages of decline are destined to fall and not all falls experience the exact same number of steps. A company may fall quickly through each stage or may have moments of recovery before again proceeding toward further decline.

James C. Collins. *How the Mighty Fall—And Why Some Companies Never Give In.* New York: HarperCollins, 2009.

FIVE STAGES OF DECLINE

Research has shown that there are typically five significant stages displayed in the decline of once-successful organizations. These stages are Hubris Born of Success, Undisciplined Pursuit of More, Decline of Risk and Peril, Grasping for Salvation, and Capitulation to Irrelevance or Death. Each stage will be discussed briefly.

Stage 1: Hubris Born of Success

In the first stage of decline, most companies in this category have no indication or suspicion they are starting on a path toward destruction—partially because of their past success. In contrast, leaders of organizations at this stage believe that all is going well, that they are on top of their game, and the company can do no wrong. They are guilty of the sin of **hubris** (excessive pride, pretentiousness, ambition, self-importance, or arrogance). This is the first assumption beginning the path to decline.

Common indicators of this stage may include:

- An attitude of arrogance
- Belief that success is an entitlement
- Assumption that past success will continue, no matter what the organization does
- Loss of inquisitiveness
- Loss of focus on learning and process improvement
- Neglect toward primary business line

In contrast, successful leaders maintain a learning curve as steep as when they first began their careers; they never stop learning. Successful companies also pay greater attention to improving and growing the core business, while not becoming overly distracted by the "latest and greatest" fad or product. Successful companies are able to find a balance between continuity and change.

Stage 2: Undisciplined Pursuit of More

The arrogant attitude demonstrated by companies in Stage 1 leads directly into Stage 2—The Undisciplined Pursuit of More. As leaders believe the company can accomplish anything, achieve anything, and be successful in anything, they embark down a path of pursuing more with disregard for strategic alignment with the core business values of the organization. We sometimes assume that companies fail because they become complacent, failing to make necessary changes and stay competitive in the market. While this can be the case, research indicates little evidence of complacency when companies experience decline. In contrast, *overreaching better explains how once indestructible companies self-destruct.*

Indicators of this stage may include:

- More scale, more growth sought at the risk of undermining long-term value
- Growth occurs beyond the ability of the organization to fill key positions with the right people
- Obsession with growth
- Confusion of being big with being great
- Taking undisciplined leaps of growth
- Trouble grooming and growing internal future leadership

Stage 3: Denial of Risk and Peril

As organizations enter this stage, warning signs begin to appear. However, external results still remain strong enough that leaders are able to justify and explain away the declining internal indicators as temporary, cyclical, or just an anomaly. Negative data are dealt with by adding a positive spin. In general, leaders remain in denial regarding any possible risk or potential peril.

Indicators of this stage may include:

- Warning signs begin appearing within the organization
- There is a disproportionate focus on positive data
- Big bets are made that pose too great a risk
- Restructuring becomes a primary business strategy to create a sense of doing *something*
- Team dynamics begin to weaken
- Blame is placed on external factors (i.e., economy, bad market, competitors)
- Leaders become detached from the daily life of the organization
- Excessive pride, presumption, or arrogance

Stage 4: Grasping for Salvation

As struggling organizations continue to deny the impending peril seen in Stage 3, they will inevitably find themselves in a steep decline, unable to be ignored and visible to those within, as well as external to the organization. Leaders confronted by this level of decline and peril will either return to the fundamentals and core business values that brought them to greatness or they will implement a strategy of grasping at any opportunity for salvation. In the 11 companies studied, 7 hired a CEO from outside the organization during their era of decline in a desperate effort to shake things up and save the company from certain demise. However, this action often comes too late to succeed.

Indicators of this stage may include:

- Grasping at silver bullets ("magical" solutions that will solve everything)
- Investing in an unproven technology, putting all hope in an untested strategy or a flashy new product
- Making a major acquisition that dramatically changes the focus of the company
- Seeking a "savior CEO"
- Exhibiting a desperation mentality
- Desiring quick solutions versus engaging in a slow, methodical process of rebuilding
- Making radical, revolutionary changes or initiating major transformations

Stage 5: Capitulation to Irrelevance or Death

There is a direct correlation between how long a company remains at Stage 4 (grasping for magic solutions) and the likelihood that they will spiral toward certain death or **capitulation** (ending all resistance; giving up; going along with or complying to irrelevance as an organization). The accumulation of failed strategies, flashy new products, desperate solutions, and attempts to save the organization erode financial strength and hope, causing many leaders to walk away or let the organization die.

Indicators of this stage may include:

- Failed strategies accumulate that erode financial strength
- Cash availability tightens
- Loss of the ability to make strategic choices
- Leaders are forced into implementing short-term survival decisions

Conclusion: Is There Hope?

In the midst of studying the causes of decline and stages of decline, one wonders if there is hope. Are there specific strategies to implement in order to avoid such demise? Perhaps learning from the struggles and challenges of companies facing decline offers us more information on how to avoid these pitfalls and remain a strong and viable company.

While a lack of discipline correlates with decline of an organization, a strong adherence to management discipline correlates with recovery and ascent. *Research shows those organizations that never give in, never give up on their core purpose, and never give up on the idea of building a great company have a much greater ability to maintain their greatness and strength.* Success is not as much about avoiding falling down, but the ability of a company to get up time after time after time.

Beyond Teams

Michael M. Beyerlein, Sue Freedman, Craig McGee, and Linda Moran

Summary Prepared by David L. Beal

David L. Beal *is a retired Operations Manager and Vice President of Manufacturing for Lake Superior Paper Industries and Consolidated Papers, Inc., in Duluth, Minnesota. Under his leadership, the all-salaried workforce was organized into a totally self-reliant team system using the principles of sociotechnical design to create a high-performance system. Dave teaches in the Labovitz School of Business and Economics at the University of Minnesota Duluth, where his areas of interest include designing and leading self-directed team-based organizations, teamwork, and production and operations management. He received his B.S. in Chemical Engineering from the University of Maine in Orono, Maine, with a fifth year in Pulp and Paper Sciences.*

INTRODUCTION

The challenges organizations face today continue to grow as a result of a rapidly changing environment, not the least of which includes the proliferation of new technology, a dynamic global marketplace, and (more recently) the threat of terrorism. Contemporary organizations must be structurally flexible, capable of adapting to changing markets, and able to compete and win on a national and frequently international scale. **Collaborative Work Systems** (CWS) provide the fundamental principles and means to meet these challenges. Collaboration and CWS are not new; they are simply the principles and practices that make organizations and teamwork succeed. There are 10 major principles for successful collaboration and a set of characteristics that collaborative organizations have that effectively apply these principles. Organizations that fail to embrace the CWS approach exhibit a contrasting set of defining characteristics.

Managers and employees at all levels working together can outperform individuals acting alone, especially when the outcome requires a variety of creative

Michael M. Beyerlein, Sue Freedman, Craig McGee, and Linda Moran. *Beyond Teams: Building the Collaborative Organization.* San Francisco, CA: Jossey-Bass/Pfeiffer, 2003.

abilities, multiple skills, careful judgments, and the knowledge and experience that different employees possess in achieving organizational goals. CWS are the means to achieve these goals and not an end in and of themselves.

RATIONALE FOR COLLABORATIVE WORK SYSTEMS

Collaborative work systems put into practice a disciplined principle-based system of collaboration necessary to be successful in a rapidly changing environment. All organizations collaborate to some extent in order to achieve their goals, including how the organization serves its customers and meets its financial objectives. CWS carry collaboration to a much higher level and therefore outperform organizations that do not consistently apply the principles of collaboration as a disciplined practice, or do not make collaboration the means to achieve business objectives and the goals of the organization.

Organizations that not only value collaborative practices, but consciously apply and nurture these practices with passion and conviction at all levels create a definite competitive advantage over organizations that simply assume collaborative practices will occur. Strategic direction and leadership at the top of the organization are paramount to achieving CWS. While team-based organizations and self-directed work systems depend on collaborative practices, these organizations may not go far enough in the degree or variety of collaboration to reach the full potential that CWS have.

Collaborative work systems are a key strategy for achieving superior business results. While employees create value through collaborative practices, their ability to perform and to be highly productive is often limited by the barriers the organization creates. These barriers stifle the collaborative practices employees are expected to have. Key employees at all levels solve problems, make and act on important decisions, invent new practices and improved methods of doing business, build relationships, and strategically plan for the future. The effectiveness of their processes and practices and the work system the employees are in determines the degree to which they reach their full potential. A high level of collaborative capacity will stimulate both formal and informal learning and enhance the effectiveness of work done at all levels.

When collaboration becomes both a strategy and competency for achieving business goals and a major part of the organizational culture, then:

- Organizational barriers to a collaborative work system are broken down.
- Employees at all levels know when and how to collaborate to achieve business results without wasting valuable time and resources.
- Managers and leaders in the organization create systems that are highly flexible, functionally adaptable, and fast to react to a changing environment.
- The waste that occurs within a functional silo and between functional silos diminishes and is replaced with a high level of cross-functional cooperation.
- Teams become accountable for their results and hold themselves to a high standard.
- The organization becomes a highly interdependent, interacting, and interconnected system of processes and functions that continuously performs at a high level.

Collaborative work systems do not require formal teams or a team-based system (i.e., an organizational arrangement where teams are the basic unit of organizational structure), but their collaborative capacity and competency are enhanced by the use of these structures. Since teams are frequently the most common form of business collaboration, the design, management, and work processes that make collaboration within and between teams successful are important features to discuss.

THE PRINCIPLES OF COLLABORATIVE ORGANIZATIONS

The 10 principles of collaborative work systems are as follows:

1. *Focus collaboration on achieving business results.* Collaboration is necessary to achieve the goals and strategies necessary for long-term success. It is not an end in itself, but a means to an end. This principle focuses the organization on a common goal where everyone understands their role in the broader context of achieving intermediate and overall corporate objectives. When collaboration is focused on achieving business results, everyone is focused on common goals and objectives and is in the business of getting results with very few self-serving obstacles. Employees know what needs to be done and can go about doing it in an efficient and effective manner. When collaborative efforts are not focused on business results, conflicts and disagreements will occur and employees may sub-optimize their own functional areas, sometimes at the expense of achieving overall organizational goals.

2. *Align organizational support systems to promote ownership.* This principle stems from an understanding that all systems of support must be congruent with the goals and principles of the organization. If a collaborative work system is a defined strategy to achieve the goals of the organization, then all systems must support the who, when, where, and why of collaborative practices. These systems include management systems, organizational design, performance management systems, and information and communication systems. Support systems that create a sense of ownership have a much greater chance of success in creating a competitive advantage. When these systems are aligned, employees are rewarded for acting in a predictable and consistent manner toward achieving individual, intermediate, and overall corporate goals and objectives. When it is not working, employees are sent mixed messages that collectively produce organizational chaos and poor performance.

3. *Articulate and enforce a few strict rules.* This principle applies to the policies, practices, and methods that drive decision making within organizations. Everyone needs to understand what needs to be done within a framework of a few highly understood rules. These rules must be consistently applied and individuals held accountable for their application. The application of this principle gives individuals and teams of individuals a common understanding of what needs to be done without limiting their ability to accomplish it. It also allows them to break down barriers and make and act on important decisions toward the accomplishment of the goals and objectives. Organizations with too many rules suffer from inaction and an unwillingness to take risks, whereas an organization with too few rules struggles from a lack of direction and consistency.

4. *Exploit the rhythm of divergence and convergence.* This principle provides a balance between creating new and exciting ways of getting the job done, and the discipline necessary to get the job done. Both of these are processes by which participants are allowed to diverge with their ideas and generate different ways of getting the job done, and also converge to a level of agreement necessary to move forward to get the job done. Managing the process of divergence and convergence is important to goal accomplishment. The process also has a rhythm that is recognizable. As collaboration within and between teams and individuals at different levels and across functional boundaries occurs, complex activities take

place toward the accomplishment of the stated goals and objectives. Each cycle accomplishes an intermediate objective that allows the next step or iterative cycle to occur. When the rhythm of divergence and convergence is effectively managed, new ideas and ways of getting the job done naturally occur, while the disciplined commitment to accomplish the objective in the expected time frame is achieved.

5. *Manage complex trade-offs on a timely basis.* Making timely and effective decisions requires the skills, knowledge, and a process for effective decision making. When the collaborative unit is faced with complex, interrelated, or interdependent decisions, trade-offs frequently have to be made between contradictory criteria or information. Managing these trade-offs for effective decision making sometimes requires specialized skills, knowledge, and information that the collaborative unit must recognize and acquire on a timely basis. When complex decisions are made on a timely basis, the collaborative unit can move forward with increased confidence.

6. *Create higher standards for discussion, dialogue, and information sharing.* Collaborative processes can be very complex and highly important to goal attainment. These processes must be well managed by leaders that recognize the need for good organization, coaching, and facilitation skills. Higher standards mean that participants have direct access to relevant information, expert opinions, and advice, new and improved capabilities for effective decision making, and a sense of excitement and commitment to be involved in CWS. When the collaborative capacity of an organization is not increased through coaching or training of the participants, decision making suffers, deadlines and expectations are more difficult to meet, and participants seek a safe haven by sticking to their own opinions and perspectives. Getting "out of the box" and taking a risk will become a rare event.

7. *Foster personal accountability.* When organization members are personally accountable for their own role and responsibilities in the collaborative process, the capability of the collaborative unit will improve. Accountability means that participants will build capability to achieve goals by breaking down the barriers to goal attainment, putting the goal ahead of self-serving considerations, and tackling the tasks of getting the job done with confidence, risk taking, and timeliness. Participants simply do what needs to be done and act in support of the collaborative process. When there is a lack of accountability, participants fail to acknowledge their responsibility or mistakes, and they will usually act in support of their own self-serving interests.

8. *Align authority, information, and decision making.* This principle means that teams and participants have all the tools, including the authority to make important decisions, the skills, knowledge, and information for effective decision making, and the resources and support to act and carry out the decisions they make for effective goal attainment. When these tools are present, decisions are timely and well executed, and participants are committed with a high degree of responsibility for their participation on the collaborative unit. When authority, information, and decision making are not aligned, participants experience a loss of both support and direction, a lack of ownership in the process, and chaos or confusion when decisions and plans have to be revisited.

9. *Treat collaboration as a disciplined process.* This principle means that CWS organizations must recognize and support the principles as a strategy for goal accomplishment. Making collaboration a disciplined process requires the skills, knowledge, and training of a critical mass of participants that can pass on their expertise in successfully conducting collaborative processes. When organizations are competent at collaboration, they are able to manage multiple interdependent and interacting processes at the same time. These organizations will

have good organization skills, the ability to quickly hurdle obstacles and break down barriers, easy access to relevant information, excellent communication skills, and the ability to make good decisions and act on those decisions in a timely manner. When collaboration is not treated as a disciplined process, meetings are not very productive or goal oriented, participants are frustrated by the lack of goal accomplishment, and managers with authority may try to micromanage the activities of the collaborative unit.

10. *Design and promote flexible organizations.* The successful organization today must be quick to respond to all sorts of changing business conditions and structurally flexible in its ability to get the work done and compete in a dynamic business environment. Flexible organizations respond with different structures, both formal and informal to maximize the speed and effectiveness of what needs to be done to be successful. The increasing complexity and dynamic nature of competing in a global marketplace requires that organizations react with different structures based on the situation. These organizations break down the barriers that traditional organizations have in a way that improves their ability to compete and respond to changing business conditions. Information and decision making are moved to those who have to take action, rather than those who control the action of others. Flexible organizations have leaders that decentralize decision making for maximum effectiveness and manage the organization with a high level of cross-functional capability. When organizations are structurally inflexible, their collaborative activities are less effective, they waste valuable resources, and decisions take a lot longer to make and implement.

APPLICATIONS OF THE PRINCIPLES

Manufacturing facilities produce tangible products from physical materials with the support of functionally based staff organizations. They have become flatter in organizational structure, more flexible in their ability to get the work done in many different ways, and faster to react to the marketplace and remain competitive. As manufacturing organizations integrate vertically and horizontally to achieve a competitive advantage, they have also integrated new work systems such as "team-based organizations," "high-performance systems," "self-reliant teams," and "sociotechnical systems." When properly applied, these principle-based systems can produce superior performance. All of these systems represent changes in how work is organized and how the empowerment of employees has moved leadership down to the productive process or shop floor. As organizations become flatter and more flexible, the opportunities to collaborate become more numerous. The leadership in organizations must make clear expectations of the "how" and "when" to formally and informally collaborate. The "when" occurs when more than one person is required to make a decision and when effective implementation requires the acceptance or the decision is executed by a group of employees.

Collaboration in service settings needs to occur when the skills, knowledge, and expertise needed reside in more than one employee, when the decisions or tasks are interdependent with other employees or parts of the organization, when decisions require the acceptance of a group of employees for effective implementation, and when multiple teams or areas need to share resources or have a common understanding for goal accomplishment. On the other hand, collaboration can be wasteful when there is not good direction or leadership for collaborative processes, when the practice of "command and control" of employees makes the empowerment of employees an abstract thought, and when management fails to share important information with employees or give employees direct access to information necessary to accomplish their tasks.

New product development creates unique and creative opportunities. Expertise in functional organizations is organized into silos as opposed to product or customer-based organizing structures. Another design is the team-based model, in which integration teams oversee the coordinated efforts and assignments of new product development teams. Global pressures, the threat of declining profit margins if new products are not developed, and the time to produce new products to preempt the competition are challenges these organizations face. The question is when, where, and who should collaborate to maximize the use of the valuable resources. It is also important to establish the training, expectations, and the time frame for effective collaboration.

The 10 principles can also be applied in "virtual work settings." **Virtual organizations** are "groups of individuals working on shared tasks while distributed across space, time and/or organizational boundaries." They are unique in that they traverse organizational and functional boundaries that exist at multiple national and sometimes international locations. The participants in virtual settings are not located at the same site, but it is still possible to apply the principles of CWS to virtual work settings.

Conclusion

Collaborative Work Systems are principle-based systems that are consciously designed and nurtured for high performance. CWS allow the creative capacities and talents of their employees to continuously increase through knowledge sharing and mutual support.

Individuals collaborating effectively in pursuit of common goals and objectives will consistently outperform individuals acting alone or in functional silos, especially when the task requires multiple skills, knowledge, different experiences, and creative abilities. As the work and the accomplishment of tasks become more complex, flexible organizational structures and collaborative practices must be carefully thought out and executed to meet the varied challenges the organization faces. When organizations apply the 10 principles of collaboration, employee ownership and involvement increases, decision making is more consistent and execution is more effective, positional power is replaced with knowledge and leadership, and employees learn and grow at a much faster rate. The organization is also quicker to respond to the business environment, more flexible in its ability to accomplish objectives in different ways, and flatter in an organizational structure that values cross-functional competencies.

IV

Organizational Strategy and Execution

Many of the authors in this book suggest that organizations can benefit by defining their own standard of effectiveness, especially after examining other successful firms. An organization's external environment has a powerful influence on organizational success and needs to be monitored for significant trends and influential forces. In addition, effective executives need to recognize when internal changes are necessary to adapt to the external environment.

The three readings in this section are designed to stimulate thinking about management through a focus on the management and leadership of the organization from its very top. Taken collectively, these readings suggest that organizations can (and should) proactively take control of their destinies. One way of doing this is by *articulating an engaging vision* that, along with effective strategies well executed, can systematically guide them into the future. In effect, managers are urged to have a master plan that defines their mission, identifies their unique environmental niche, builds on their strengths, and adapts to changing needs. This overall vision is then converted into operational goals by applying several very specific management practices.

Michael Raynor earned his doctorate in Business Administration from Harvard Business School and is an Adjunct Professor at the Richard Ivey School of Business in London, Canada, and a Distinguished Fellow with Deloitte Research in Boston. He is also the coauthor, with Clayton Christensen, of the best-selling *The Innovator's Solution*. His second book, *The Strategy Paradox*, was recognized by *BusinessWeek* as one of the 10 best business books of 2007.

The paradox presented by Raynor is simple—organizational strategies with the highest probability of succeeding also have the greatest chance of failure. Because the future is so uncertain and unpredictable, strategies that succeed are often the product of good luck more than anything else, while strategies that fail are often the victim of poor timing or unforeseeable forces. The key to success lies in strategic flexibility and a four-part approach—anticipating scenarios, formulating strategic options tailored to each scenario, accumulating data about the best options, and operating the actual portfolio of options.

William Joyce (professor of Strategy and Organization Theory at Dartmouth's Amos Tuck School of Business), Nitin Nohria (professor of Business Administration at the Harvard Business School), and Bruce Roberson (a partner with McKinsey & Company) combined to write *What (Really) Works*. A question driving this book is, "Why do some organizations consistently outperform their competitors? What do their managers know and do?"

To answer these two questions, the authors analyzed data from the Evergreen Project, a major field study analyzing more than 10 years of data from 160 companies and more than 200 different management practices. In *What (Really) Works*, the authors report their discovery of four primary (strategy, execution, culture, and structure) and four secondary management practices and four secondary areas (talent, leadership, innovation, and mergers) engaged in by all of the successful companies.

Corporate **downsizing**, sometimes euphemistically referred to as "rightsizing," has cost hundreds of thousands of employees their jobs in the past decade while organizations sought to reduce their costs, redirect their resources, and improve their stock price. Wayne Cascio, in *Responsible Restructuring*, reports on the results of an 18-year study of major firms that destroys many common myths about downsizing's presumably positive effects. By contrast, Cascio found that downsizing has a negative impact not only on the morale and commitment of the survivors, but also on key indicators of productivity, profits, and quality. He presents an alternative to layoffs—a step-by-step blueprint that revolves around treating employees as assets to be developed, and demonstrates how responsible restructuring has worked effectively at Compaq, Cisco, Motorola, and Southwest Airlines.

Wayne Cascio is a professor of Management at the University of Colorado—Denver, and also instructs in the Rotterdam School of Management. Cascio is a past chair of the Human Resources division of the Academy of Management and past president of the Society for Industrial and Organizational Psychology. A consultant and writer, he is the author of numerous other books, including *Investing in People*, *Applied Psychology in Human Resource Management*, *The Cost Factor*, *Costing Human Resources*, and *Managing Human Resources*.

1

The Strategy Paradox

Michael E. Raynor

Summary Prepared by Allen Harmon

Allen Harmon is President and General Manager of WDSE, the community-licensed PBS member station serving Northeastern Minnesota and Northwestern Wisconsin, where his job is to enable an extraordinary staff to do amazing work. He has also served as an adjunct instructor in the Labovitz School of Business and Economics at the University of Minnesota Duluth. Before joining WDSE, Mr. Harmon held a series of senior management positions in a regional investor-owned electric utility. He earned an MBA from Indiana University's Kelley School of Business and has completed the University of Minnesota Carlson School of Management Executive Development Program.

INTRODUCTION

The prerequisites of success are often the antecedents of failure. This illustrates the **strategy paradox**—*that the commitments required to achieve breakthrough success make it difficult to adapt when the future turns out differently than expected.* Resolving the strategy paradox requires a new approach to strategy, and to the uncertainty that shrouds the future. The two tools for implementing that approach are requisite uncertainty and strategic flexibility.

HIDING IN PLAIN SIGHT

That the strategy paradox has not been identified before now says more about the way business is studied than about the pervasiveness of the paradox. It is far easier to study success than it is to study the rubble of failure. Years after the fact, there is often little left of failures to study. Failures do not survive to become the subjects of long-term studies, so studies tend to compare successful companies with those whose performance is mediocre, not with those that have failed.

Michael E. Raynor. *The Strategy Paradox: Why Committing to Success Leads to Failure (And What to Do About It).* New York: Currency Books, 2007.

Successful companies, however, have more in common with those that suffer total collapse than with those that merely survive. Companies that realize breakthrough success and those that fail share the trait of commitment to an extreme strategy. Theirs is a different lot than that of companies that survive by avoiding the risks that attend commitment.

The Root of the Paradox: Commitment

Well-established theory, supported by empirical evidence, suggests that companies pursuing the most commitment-intensive strategies generate the highest returns—and suffer the highest mortality rates.

One of Michael Porter's most significant contributions to management thinking is the assertion that all strategies lie on a continuum between product differentiation and cost leadership. Companies with strategies at the extremes of the continuum are the most likely to develop an unassailable competitive advantage of either low cost or differentiation, advantages that are difficult for others to emulate. They are also the most likely to suffer rejection in the marketplace when their choice of strategy proves wrong for the competitive environment that they face.

Commitment to a strategy of low cost or differentiation is not costless; one of the costs is paid with a loss of flexibility. Good strategies are complex and difficult to redirect. A valuable competitive advantage is difficult to copy. So not surprisingly, it is difficult for a firm committed to an extreme product differentiation strategy to shift to a cost leadership strategy when the market favors cost leadership, and vice versa. *A commitment easily changed is no commitment at all.*

Despite the knowledge that extreme strategies are likely to produce the highest returns, a number of firms in any industry will cluster at the center of Porter's strategy continuum. While the competitive disadvantages of occupying this middle space are clear (lower potential returns, the prospect of flanking from both sides, and the difficulty of constantly managing competitive compromises), occupying the middle space is attractive as a rational reaction to uncertainty. Those firms in the middle might at least survive while avoiding the feast-or-famine choice that characterizes the extremes as the competitive environment shifts.

Adaptability Is Not the Answer

Recent studies have demonstrated that firms today are less likely to retain a position of market dominance than at any time in the past, suggesting that adaptability has become less valuable as the requisite response to environmental changes.

Environmental changes can occur at a range of different rates. Disruptive changes occur at rates too fast for any competitor to mount an adaptive response. The firms that survive these rapid changes will do so because unrelated experiences or strategic commitments made prior to the disruptive event have fortuitously positioned the firm to better serve redefined customer needs, not because of any adaptation in response to the environmental shift. Slow change also challenges organizations' adaptive capacity. Slow change can be characterized as a series of developments producing change that simmers for decades before exerting more pressure than existing institutions can withstand.

The record of America's largest industrial companies during the last quarter of the twentieth century demonstrates the pernicious effect of slow change. Over that period, while a few outstanding performers such as General Electric, 3M, and Johnson and Johnson were able to reinvent themselves and thrive, 81 of the Fortune 100 companies suffered protracted decline.

During good times, "adaptive" companies respond to slow change by making incremental innovations to existing systems, postponing the fundamental restructuring that will ultimately be needed. While these incremental improvements are enough to get by, when the bad times hit there are no resources available to effect the larger changes that could (and should) have been anticipated from the beginning.

For adaptability to be a valid response to strategic uncertainties, the organization must be able to match its rate of change to that of the environment. Seldom, however, will an organization need to respond to only a single environmental development. What organization can be so nimble as to respond with manifold adaptations at multiple rates? Even the most dexterous of companies will need additional capabilities to respond to the full range of strategic uncertainties.

Better Forecasting Won't Work

In *The Fortune Seekers*, William A. Sherden offers an evidence-based demonstration that forecasters routinely miss calling the major events and turning points that shape the world. Nonetheless, forecasting remains a keystone of modern strategic planning.

Two elements put accurate prediction of the variables relevant to strategic planning beyond reach: randomness and free will. Even orderly systems are subject to randomness of output when subject to the injection of exogenous shocks and randomness in the system's initial conditions. Exogenous shocks originate outside the boundaries considered in setting the forecast. The natural response to forecasting error caused by exogenous shocks is to extend the boundaries of the system. Unfortunately, there is no logical point at which to quit expanding the boundaries until one has built a full-scale model of reality—a 1:1 model that is no model at all.

Randomness also intrudes on a forecast of the behavior of an orderly system through the real randomness of the set of initial conditions. This form of randomness is captured in the metaphor of the "butterfly effect" description of chaos theory. While the rules governing a chaotic system are well understood and useful in making predictions of the system's behavior, the outputs are random because it is impossible to completely specify the set of initial conditions. It is impossible to accumulate all the information that is required to specify the initial conditions, nor can it be known before the event which are the "initial" conditions.

The work of Robert Lucas to explain the difficulty governments experience in affecting the economy demonstrates how free will can disrupt forecasting efforts. Lucas demonstrates that attempts to manipulate behavior will often result in individual and collective responses that offset the intended effect. Predicting the behavior of systems populated by contrarian individuals is difficult, but predicting the behavior of a system populated by "rational" companies is no more certain. Were an organization to always behave rationally, its behavior would be easy to predict—and to exploit. To preserve the option of presenting a credible threat in the future, companies may make decisions that are irrational and unpredictable in the short run. Again, free will disrupts the ability to forecast.

Even if it were possible to make an accurate forecast today, there is no way of knowing that it is, in fact, accurate. A forecast today should accurately represent the probability distribution function of the range of possible future outcomes. Between the "now" and the "then" of the forecast, a series of events, some contingent on others, will conspire to produce a single outcome. But whether the original forecast accurately represented the probability of that—or any—outcome at the time that it was made is still unknown. Unlike Las Vegas, where the rules are known and constant, we cannot restart the system for multiple trials. It is impossible to compare the forecast to the reality at the time the forecast is made. If adaptability and forecasting are inadequate, responding to the strategy paradox requires a new way of dealing with the strategic uncertainty that ties the possibility of great success to the possibility of abject failure.

ORGANIZING FOR SUCCESS

The works of organizational theorists Alfred Chandler and Jay Galbraith suggest that organizations should be structured around what matters most, as structure is an expression of priorities. In dealing with strategic uncertainty, what matters most is time. Time is central to uncertainty; the longer the relevant time horizon, the wider the range of likely outcomes. **Requisite uncertainty**, the principle of structuring the organization around strategic uncertainty, is a further development of **requisite organization**, the concept of structuring the organization around the time horizons of the players.

Canadian psychologist Elliot Jacques asserts that the most important characteristic in defining any job is the longest time horizon that the job must consider. Building on this observation, Jacques identifies seven time strata that correspond to hierarchical organizational levels and defines the requisite organization as one based on these time horizons.

Structuring the organization on the basis of requisite uncertainty shifts the organizing principle from Jacques' use of time to the uncertainty that attends it. *Requisite uncertainty structures the allocation of responsibility for managing uncertainty and for making good on past commitments.* In the organization structured on the principle of requisite uncertainty:

- Functional level managers worry little about uncertainty. They are charged with delivering the best results possible from the organizational commitments already made.
- Divisional managers deal with the uncertainties that may impact execution of the current strategy, working to avoid catastrophe if current assumptions prove incorrect.
- The Board and CEO deal with true strategic uncertainty, making certain that elements of the organization are positioned to succeed regardless of the future that develops.

Traditional hierarchies are appropriate for organizations structured under requisite uncertainty, but roles within the organization may require redefinition. For the CEO, the shift from choosing strategy and making commitments to positioning the organization to pursue potentially useful alternatives as a means of managing strategic uncertainty is profound. Managers who in traditional organizations are often called upon to deal with short-, mid- and long-term issues simultaneously will find their charge more focused. The role of the board evolves as well for organizations operating under requisite uncertainty. As the body dealing with the longest time horizon—*ad infinitum* for the going concern—the board's focus is not to define strategy. The board's role is to set the parameters of risk and opportunity within which management must operate, to determine whether the relevant uncertainties of strategies which management proposes have been identified and addressed, and to assure that management does not drift to the safe center of strategy continuum.

Microsoft demonstrates the potential of a strategy focused on managing uncertainty by pursuing a number of options with limited commitment until the prospects for each become clear. Implementing true strategic diversification requires a management that knows what risks to take, how much to invest, and when to cut investment off.

CREATING STRATEGIC FLEXIBILITY

Johnson and Johnson (J&J) provides an example of how "mere mortals" can achieve the **strategic flexibility** essential to overcoming the strategy paradox. J&J's 200-plus operating divisions require access to emerging technologies that potentially define their competitive future. Constraints imposed on the operating divisions with the intent of focusing attention on customers, markets, and the demand for returns, however, leave the operating units poorly positioned to deal with strategic uncertainty. Instead, the role of the corporate office is to focus on managing uncertainty; the task is assigned specifically to the corporate venture capital arm, J&J Development Company (JJDC).

JJDC President Dave Holveck has articulated the company's approach to creating strategic flexibility as a four-step process:

1. *Anticipate*—use scenarios to bound the relevant futures; doing so allows consideration of the future without having to guess right.
2. *Formulate*—and then decompose optimal strategies for each of the scenarios. Elements common to the optimal strategies are designated core elements, those found in only one, or a few of the optimal strategies are contingent elements.
3. *Accumulate*—pursue commitments to the core elements, invest in the contingent elements on an optimal basis.
4. *Operate*—monitor the environment, renew and refresh the scenarios, determine which optimal strategy is most appropriate, and exercise the options needed to complement the core elements. The operate phase calls upon the organization to create, preserve, exercise, and abandon options as required by shifts in the environment.

The Hallmarks of a Flexible Strategy

Scenarios *yield a working appreciation for the uncertainty the organization faces; options allow a calibrated response as the uncertainties become reality.* Scenario planning provides an alternative to the creation of the unreliable single-point predictions. At their best, scenarios are richly developed descriptions of alternative futures. As one incorporates more variables into each scenario, however, the number and complexity of the scenarios grow exponentially. The trade-off between detail and complexity can be dealt with by thinking of each scenario as a point in the probability space of the future. The scenarios of most interest are those that are "corner solutions," points on the relevant boundaries of all futures. Useful scenarios can be created by the following:

1. *Asking the right questions.* Appropriate questions are conceptually demanding, and demand consideration of strategic options over an extended time frame, not those that lend themselves to quantitative solution.
2. *Identifying the dimensions of uncertainty.* Recognize the uncertainties that define the probability space, perhaps by asking what uncertainties prevent the organization from making irrevocable commitments today.
3. *Determining the limits of uncertainty.* Actively seek credible, outlying assessments of the potential range of the relevant dimensions of uncertainty.
4. *Determining the final scenario set.* Reduce the number of scenarios to a manageable number by eliminating those with internal inconsistencies and combining those that differ only in degree.
5. *Determining relative probabilities.* Scenario planning drives the creation of options, and the probability assigned each scenario can indicate the probability that a particular option will be exercised.

The scenario set will drive different responses at each level of the organization. The board and executive management should be challenged to complete the process outlined by J&J (developing optimal strategies, identifying core and contingent elements, accumulating options, and operating the strategy). Operating divisions will build strategies from combinations of core and contingent elements, managers at the divisional level charged with executing those strategies can benefit from the scenario planning process as a means of identifying and hedging operating threats. Functional managers can gain insight into how to best execute the commitments the organization already has in place.

Structuring the firm's investments in a way that is reflective of the uncertainties explored in the scenario process and creates real, strategic options is the final step in achieving strategic flexibility. These real, **strategic options** differ from simple growth options. The exercise of strategic options will enable a strategic shift for the firm.

Scenarios provide a clear direction with respect to core elements; the decision of how to invest in contingent elements is more challenging. So-called "robust" strategies are a one-size-fits-all approach, in which all elements are considered to be core elements. Given the breadth of potential outcomes identified by the scenario process—and the resulting breadth of investments in core elements that a robust approach requires—it is unlikely that this approach will result in better-than-mediocre performance. Active management of options on contingent elements, however, will move the organization to the strategic equivalent of the efficient investment frontier.

The last two stages of the JJDC process (Accumulate and Operate) summarize the management of a portfolio of strategic options. Implementation of those stages requires the organization to:

1. *Create the portfolio.* While the deal making may be complex, the objective is simple: investing to secure the right, but not the obligation, to invest further in the contingent elements of alternative strategies identified in the scenario process. In creating the portfolio of strategic options, it is important to remember that the option being sought is not just an option on a particular business or technology but an option on a change in the organization's strategy. Valuing a strategic option is more complicated than pricing a purely financial option, and will ultimately rely more on judgment than on analytical rigor.

2. *Preserve the option.* Companies and interests acquired as strategic options will typically be allowed to operate autonomously, as to integrate them with existing operations is essentially the exercise of the option. Strategic options are, however, likely to require some level of engagement to maximize the value of exercising the option and to minimize the cost of abandoning it.

3. *Exercise the option.* Holding the option creates value indirectly by minimizing risk, just as a fire insurance policy represents value even if there is no fire. Exercise of the option can be initiated in response to the needs of an operating division (bottom–up), at the direction of corporate management (top–down), or by mutual agreement (split the difference).

4. *Abandon the option.* The ability to abandon an element is what makes it an option. Retreat from an option should be considered a sign of prudence, not weakness.

Conclusion

Reassessment of the plans built by organizations structured under requisite uncertainty to achieve strategic flexibility should be driven by the passage of events, not the passage of the calendar. Organizations that employ these tools effectively will be able to defeat the strategy paradox.

2

What (Really) Works

William Joyce, Nitin Nohria, and Bruce Roberson

Summary Prepared by Allen Harmon

Allen Harmon is President and General Manager of WDSE-TV, the community-licensed PBS member station serving Northeastern Minnesota and Northwestern Wisconsin. He also currently serves as an adjunct instructor in the Labovitz School of Business and Economics at the University of Minnesota Duluth. Before joining WDSE, Mr. Harmon held a series of senior management positions in a regional investor-owned electric utility. He earned an MBA from Indiana University and has completed the University of Minnesota Carlson School of Management Executive Development Program.

INTRODUCTION

The list of companies currently at the top of their game churns constantly. Management thinkers offer a seemingly endless supply of silver-bullet cures that are half-heartedly adopted, quickly fail, and are soon abandoned. Managers await the latest autobiographies of business legends only to find that the experiences described and suggestions offered by these luminaries fail to translate easily into their own situations. By contrast, the Evergreen Project—a search for the "evergreen" source of business success—was conceived to replace blind faith, luck, and guessing with statistically rigorous analysis of the results of previously effective organizations. The results of that study produced the 4 + 2 formula for corporate success.

THE STUDY

An initial study of several hundred companies confirmed that, despite the caprices of the market, total return to shareholders (TRS) is useful as a primary metric of organizational performance. Successful companies, as measured by TRS, were found to be winners by almost every other measure.

William Joyce, Nitin Nohria, and Bruce Roberson. *What (Really) Works: The 4 + 2 Formula for Sustained Business Success.* New York: Harper Collins, 2003.

From the initial group, 160 companies—4 companies in each of 40 industry groups—were selected for extensive study. The companies in each group were, at the start of the study in 1986, of comparable size, had achieved similar financial performance, and had similar prospects for the future. Failing companies and those conglomerates that defied classification were left out. Performance of the 160 companies was measured over two consecutive five-year periods, 1986–1990 and 1991–1995. Based on TRS performance, each company was labeled as a winner, climber, tumbler, or loser:

- **Winners:** Companies that outperformed their peers in both time periods
- **Climbers:** Companies that lagged their peers in the first period, but achieved performance better than their peers in the second
- **Tumblers:** Companies with better-than-peer performance in the first period, followed by underperformance in the second
- **Losers:** Companies that lagged behind their peers in both time periods. This grouping of the companies would provide insight into cause–effect relationships. Accounting for the differences in performance was the next step.

Three distinct methodologies were used to unlock the answer to what really works from the 10-year performance of the companies studied. First, all publicly available information on the 160 companies was scanned for references to 200 established management practices, and the companies were scored on each practice using a scale from 1 (poor relative to peers) to 5 (excellent relative to peers). Scores were independently verified through alternate sources, such as former executives. A second set of studies by academic experts identified connections among management practices. Analysis of hundreds of documents concerning each of the companies—analysts' reports, newspaper and magazine articles, business school case studies— confirmed the results of the first two studies.

WHAT DOESN'T WORK

Of the 200 management practices surveyed, four popular approaches stand out for having *no* demonstrated cause–effect relationship to sustained superior performance. Over the period of the study, no correlation was found between TRS and a company's investment in technology. Despite their popularity, neither corporate change programs nor purchase and supply chain management practices contributed to superior TRS. There was no evidence that attracting better outside directors, an effort promoted as a means of improving corporate governance, improved TRS. If anything, it is better performance that attracts more astute outside directors!

WHAT DOES WORK—THE 4 + 2 FORMULA

In fact, most of the 200 practices studied turned out to be largely irrelevant to corporate perform-ance. That is not to say that the vast majority of these practices are counterproductive, just that they are not essential to achieving superior performance. A compelling connection was found between sustainable high performance and just eight of the practices. *Four "primary" areas of management practice—designated in shorthand as strategy, execution, culture, and structure— proved essential to success.* Four "secondary" areas—talent, leadership, innovation, and mergers and partnerships—complete the set. Companies with high scores on each of the four primary areas and any two of the secondary areas had a better than 90 percent chance of being a Winner. This unique finding produced the *4 + 2 formula* in which four primary plus any two of the four secondary management practices are required for success.

THE FOUR PRIMARY MANAGEMENT PRACTICES

Strategy

Winning companies keep their attention and resources focused on growth of their core business through a *clear and focused strategy*. Positioning decisions, such as to be a product innovator, quality leader, or low-cost competitor, do not have a significant impact on whether the company will succeed or fail. Whether the planning process invited input from all levels of the organization or was the inspiration of the chief executive, whether long-range budgeting and planning were a part of the process or whether change was initiated in response to a takeover attempt or a change in management similarly had little effect.

What works well in the domain of strategy is:

1. Offering the customer a clear value proposition, rooted in an understanding of both the customer's needs and the company's capabilities.
2. Developing strategy from the outside in; what customers, partners, and investors say and do are more important considerations than relying on internal instincts.
3. Monitoring the marketplace and adapting the strategy to emerging trends; Winners have the ability to detect trends in their own and related businesses and to act on those that count.
4. Clearly communicating the strategy with both internal and external stakeholders, including customers; internal stakeholders give the strategy life, while communicating with customers encourages them to move from being "just" customers to true business partners.
5. Growing the core business; Winners achieve growth by focusing on their core business. When they do venture into other businesses, they do so before the growth potential of their core is exhausted.

Flawless Execution

Operational excellence—flawless execution in meeting the expectations of evermore demanding and sophisticated customers—can only be achieved through effort, study, and ingenuity. It will not, the Evergreen Project showed, be achieved through outsourcing operations; buying the latest enterprise resource planning (ERP), supply chain management, or customer relations management (CRM) software; or adopting a total quality management (TQM) program.

What *does* work in the pursuit of flawless execution?

1. Consistently meeting customer expectations. Winners need not deliver extraordinary products or services, but must *consistently meet their customers' expectations* in order to build trust.
2. Empowering employees on the front line of customer contact to respond to customer needs. This also requires keeping the organization's best employees in those frontline positions.
3. Eliminating waste and inefficiency and then focusing the effort on the processes most important to meeting customer expectations.

Culture

Winning requires that virtually everyone in the organization perform to the maximum of their capabilities. Evergreen Project Winners created a culture dedicated to performance and then serving the customer by:

1. *Inspiring high performance by creating and supporting a culture that holds all employees, not just managers, responsible for corporate success:* The ideal culture empowers employees to make independent decisions to improve company operations, while building loyalty to the employee's team and the company.
2. *Rewarding achievement through praise and pay, while constantly raising expectations:* Once a winning organization achieves "best in class" performance, it ratchets the goal up to "best in show."
3. *Creating an environment that is challenging, satisfying, and fun:* Winners stay on the right side of the fine line between a high-performance environment and a high-anxiety environment.
4. *Establishing clear company values, presenting them to employees, living them, and making them a part of every communication with employees:* Good ethical behavior promotes good business.

Structure

Bureaucracy may have its place, but the Evergreen Project found that Winners focus full-time efforts on eliminating unnecessary bureaucracy. How the elements of the organization are arranged—functionally, geographically, or by product—matters not. Neither does the extent to which profit and loss responsibility is delegated to subordinate units, nor does the level of autonomy granted subordinate units to select their own unique structure. The structural attributes that *do* matter are:

1. *Simplicity:* Winners work to eliminate redundant layers, bureaucracy, and the behaviors that create and sustain them.
2. *Cooperation and information sharing across the entire organization:* Winners devote resources to break down walls between organizational fiefdoms.
3. *Putting the frontline first:* Winners place the best employees in positions where their decisions can make a difference, and keep them there.

THE FOUR SECONDARY MANAGEMENT PRACTICES

Talent

About half of the Winners in the Evergreen Project dedicated significant human and financial resources to building an effective workforce and management team. It was not the resources dedicated to building the highest-quality human resources staff, maintaining a fast-track management development program, or implementing a 360-degree performance review system that made a difference. Instead, it was the effort devoted to the following that worked:

1. Promoting from within; filling mid- and upper-level positions with internal talent.
2. Offering top-quality training and education programs; committing resources to the programs that will develop candidates for internal promotion.

3. Designing jobs that challenge the best performers; decentralization and empowerment are tools for keeping people engaged.
4. Getting senior executives engaged in the competition for the best talent; recruiting isn't just for HR any more.

Leadership

The choice of a chief executive is crucial to the company's success. The Evergreen Project provides insight (contrary to many commonly held beliefs) into what leadership traits are consistent with becoming a Winner. The leader's decision-making style, be it independent or collaborative, is irrelevant. Personal characteristics—patient or impatient, visionary or detail oriented, secure or insecure—are irrelevant as well. Success is independent of whether senior managers make major decisions on the basis of qualitative or quantitative analysis. Instead, what does work in the domain of leadership is

1. Strengthening management's relationships with people at all levels of the organization; Winners see these relationships as the foundation of positive attitudes toward the company and its goals.
2. Focusing management on spotting opportunities and problems early; encouraging managers to anticipate change rather than dealing only with immediate difficulties.
3. Motivating the board to take an active role in governing the company by requiring a significant financial stake; when board members have their own money at risk, they tend to seek and retain stronger chief executives.
4. Pay for performance; stock price need not be the only factor considered, but executive compensation should reflect performance against preestablished goals.

Innovation

The Evergreen Project provides the evidence. Barely half of the Winners were able to excel in this challenging area of management practice. Yet the potential payoffs for success—greater efficiency, new products, and the opportunity to transform an industry—are difficult to ignore. Where new ideas come from makes no difference. For the companies that were successful, what worked was:

1. Introducing disruptive technologies and business models; success in innovation requires leading the industry and developing the innovative blockbusters that change the competitive landscape.
2. Using technological innovation both externally to produce new products and internally to improve efficiency.
3. Being willing to cannibalize existing products; Winners do eat their young in the battle to maintain their technological lead.

Mergers and Partnerships

In mergers and acquisitions analyzed by the Evergreen Project, 93 percent of the deals involving Winners created value, while only 9 percent of the Losers' deals did so. Why? Losers sought mergers and acquisitions to achieve diversification, or to fix a weakness in their primary practices. What worked for the Winners was:

1. Acquisition of new businesses to take advantage of existing customer relationships; making the most of both their own relationships with customers and the relationships that came with the acquired company.

2. Entering businesses that are complementary to existing strengths; picking companies with compatible cultures and strengths that extend or complete the value they offer the marketplace.

3. In creating partnerships, entering businesses that draw on both partners' strengths; successful partnerships provide benefits neither partner could have achieved alone.

4. Developing the capacity to successfully identify, screen, and close deals; successful merger management is a significant business activity in itself.

KEEPING SIX BALLS IN THE AIR

The seemingly simple 4 + 2 model challenges managers to attend to no fewer than six key elements of their business at once. The task is certainly more daunting than simply applying the panacea of the day, but the results provide significant motivation to do so. Over the 10 years of the Evergreen Project study, investors in the average Winner saw their investment grow nearly tenfold; the average loser eked out only a 62 percent gain for the entire decade. Follow-up evaluation of over 40 of the original study companies for 1997–2002 affirmed the earlier study's conclusions.

3

Responsible Restructuring

Wayne F. Cascio

Summary Prepared by Stephen Rubenfeld

Stephen Rubenfeld is Professor of Human Resource Management at the Labovitz School of Business and Economics at the University of Minnesota Duluth. He received his doctorate from the University of Wisconsin–Madison and was previously on the faculty of Texas Tech University. His professional publications and presentations have covered a wide range of human resource and labor relations topics, including job search behaviors, human resource policies and practices, job security, and staffing challenges. He has served as a consultant to private and public organizations and is a member of the Society for Human Resource Management, the Academy of Management, and the Industrial Relations Research Association.

A highly competitive business context carries with it both boundless opportunities and daunting challenges. On one hand, organizations are stimulated to become better at what they do by economizing, innovating, and honing their competitive advantage. But at the same time, the very existence of a business can be threatened by pricing pressures, declining profit margins, and burgeoning capital investment needs. This is not a situation that calls for "just getting by," mediocrity, or hoping that things will work themselves out. Intense competition is a call to action that tests the mettle of organizations and their leaders. It is a situation that demands thoughtful and aggressive actions. The pressures attributable to the global marketplace, pervasive technology, and more assertive consumers are not going to abate. Decisive steps are necessary to ensure that the critical elements of competitive success—price, quality, and customer service—are in place and fine-tuned to support continued organizational vitality.

The active pursuit of efficiencies, effective operations, and customer responsiveness are all subjects of much organizational rhetoric, but in practice it is the cost containment part of the equation that gets most of the attention. In fact, it is easier,

Wayne F. Cascio. *Responsible Restructuring: Creative and Profitable Alternatives to Layoffs.* San Francisco, CA: Berrett-Koehler, 2003.

faster, and more predictable to cut costs than it is to increase revenues or to fundamentally improve the organization's product or service. Whether driven by a current financial crisis or the desire to avoid future problems, actions directed at cutting or controlling costs, rooting out inefficiencies, and keeping prices in check have become almost universal. Unlike earlier times, this self-imposed pressure to focus on cost containment is not limited to organizations swimming in red ink; it has become a benchmark of good business practice.

Because employment costs are the most visible and frequently an organization's largest variable cost, downsizing along with wage and benefit containment are at the heart of most efforts to enhance competitiveness. Often characterized euphemistically as **organizational restructuring**, the logic of these efforts to control expenses by having fewer employees is compelling: Reducing costs will increase profit margins, which will produce immediate bottom-line results and help ensure future success. But the promised benefits of cost containment through reducing headcount often are elusive. Whether couched in the verbiage of *downsizing*, *rightsizing*, or other emotionless synonyms for reducing the number of employees, the benefits tend to be fleeting. By themselves these methods rarely offer a sustainable solution to the barriers to competitiveness. Likewise, wage freezes and benefits cuts may have an immediate and visible bottom-line impact, but the true savings are often reduced by diminished productivity along with undesired turnover or other employee withdrawal behaviors.

The net effect is that *restructuring that is built primarily on downsizing or containment of compensation costs will not have a positive effect on the areas where real competitiveness is built: innovation, quality, and customer service.* In the end, this approach to restructuring does not achieve the forecasted cost savings and does not help to improve long-term competitive vitality of the organization. If downsizing is not the solution, how can an organization succeed in a competitive marketplace?

IS RESTRUCTURING BAD?

Restructuring can be constructive and even essential when a company is struggling to regain or achieve economic success. Similarly, evolving technologies, nonperforming assets, or even aggressive moves by competitors can be a powerful impetus to restructure. It is obvious that job losses, layoffs, and sometimes radical changes to the jobs that remain are integral to most restructurings, but as is often the case, the devil is in the details. The issue is *how* these employment changes are made. Experience carries with it the lesson that across-the-board layoffs and hiring freezes, or similar *slash and burn* downsizing strategies, rarely achieve the promised benefits. The hidden costs and secondary impacts may even worsen the competitive crisis.

Many of the costs of downsizing are obvious and calculable. The decision to restructure typically carries with it a recognition that costs associated with severance pay, accrued vacations, benefit costs, outplacement, and additional administrative expense will be incurred. In contrast, there are many indirect costs that may be ignored or not even recognized. Even where acknowledged as potential problem areas, their severity is often underestimated. Although it may be difficult to accurately estimate their future costs and impacts, these costs are real and can have a dramatic negative impact on competitiveness. Examples of such hidden costs include:

- Reduced morale
- Risk-averse behaviors by surviving employees
- Loss of trust
- Costs of retraining continuing employees

- Legal challenges
- Reduced productivity
- Loss of institutional competencies and memory
- Survivor burnout

While these problems and costs may impede competitiveness efforts, restructuring is not inherently bad. Many businesses have successfully downsized and restructured to improve their productivity and financial success, but downsizing is not a panacea. Research conducted over the past 25 years indicates that *downsizing strategies for most organizations do not result in long-term payoffs that are significantly greater than those where there are stable employment patterns.*

MYTHS ABOUT DOWNSIZING

When confronted by the need to reduce costs, many employers (who self-righteously proclaim that "employees are our greatest asset") turn to layoffs first when responding to a competitive dilemma. This may be fueled by a number of myths and misunderstandings about downsizing. For example, the following six myths are refuted by research and experience (facts):

Myth 1: Downsizing increases profits.

Fact 1: Profitability does not necessarily improve.

Myth 2: Downsizing boosts productivity.

Fact 2: Productivity results are mixed.

Myth 3: Downsizing doesn't negatively affect quality.

Fact 3: Quality does not improve and may go down.

Myth 4: Downsizing is a one-time event.

Fact 4: The best predictor of future downsizing is past downsizing.

Myth 5: Downsizing has few effects on remaining employees.

Fact 5: Negative impacts on morale, stress, and commitment are common.

Myth 6: Downsizing is unlikely to lead to sabotage or other vengeful acts.

Fact 6: Such behaviors are not rare, and their consequences can be severe.

These findings should offer decision makers a note of caution about the potential consequences of restructuring efforts painted with a broad brush. An obvious conclusion is that restructuring should not be done blindly, and when restructuring does appear to be necessary, it should be approached strategically and responsibly.

RESPONSIBLE RESTRUCTURING

The approaches that employers take toward restructuring reflect significant differences in how they view their employees. Organizational decision makers can be thought of as falling into two camps concerning their view of employees—those that see employees as *costs to be cut* and those that see employees as *assets to be developed*. The *cost cutters* consider employees to be the source of the problem. They think of employees as commodities. Through the lens of the income statement they strive to achieve the minimum number of employees and the lowest possible labor expenditures needed to run the business successfully. In contrast, the *responsible restructurers* view employee expertise and contributions as central to any solution. They consider their employees as essential in fashioning and carrying forward sustainable answers to competitiveness challenges. The initial focus of the responsible restructurers is not on reducing headcount or shrinking the budget, but rather on enhancing effectiveness and empowering employees to overcome competitive challenges.

Responsible restructurers turn to broad-based layoffs and compensation cuts only as a last resort. Their initial and primary approach is to use a variety of developmental and effectiveness-oriented practices to achieve and maintain competitive viability. These organizations are likely to:

- Flatten their hierarchical structures.
- Create an empowered, team-oriented work environment.
- Seek labor–management partnerships.
- Share information.
- Make extensive use of training.
- Demonstrate a culture of continuous learning.
- Link compensation to performance and skills.

These employers do not advocate and use these responsible restructuring strategies primarily as acts of compassion or for other altruistic reasons. They truly believe that there are benefits that come from employment stability and that the best and most sustainable outcomes are achieved when employees are part of the solution.

These companies, which include in their ranks Southwest Airlines, SAS Institute, Cisco, Charles Schwab, Procter & Gamble, and 3M, share the following critical characteristics:

1. A clear vision of what they want to achieve and how to communicate this vision to stakeholders,
2. The ability to execute and develop employee-centered initiatives, and
3. Highly empowered employees who are committed to help the organization succeed.

These companies don't start with the premise that the minimal number of employees is the best number of employees. Rather, they ask how their employees can help them fashion a solution and meet the market challenge. They know that short-term downsizing does not solve long-term problems.

HOW DO WE MOVE FORWARD?

In addition to the basic elements of responsible restructuring already described, it is useful to keep these recommendations in mind as issues of competitiveness are confronted:

- Deal with the underlying competitive problem, not just the bottom line.
- Integrate staffing decisions with the strategic business plan and the drivers of success.
- Involve employees in shaping broad solutions as well as specific organizational responses.
- Consider the payoffs from employment stability.
- Communicate regularly, openly, effectively, and honestly.
- If layoffs are necessary, be logical, targeted, fair, and consistent.
- Give survivors a reason to stay and prospective employees a reason to join the organization.
- Empower survivors to succeed and encourage them to beware of burnout.

Conclusion

The ultimate payoff from successfully pursuing *responsible restructuring* rather than budget slashing in responding to competitive challenges is better and longer-lasting solutions. The organization also is more likely to reap the rewards of higher customer satisfaction, have the ability to respond more quickly and more successfully to future challenges, maintain a recruiting and retention advantage over its labor market competitors, and have committed employees who are not unduly risk averse. Remove the barriers to effective competition and financial success will follow.

V

Focusing on the Human Dimension

Traditionally, many employees were promoted to supervisory and managerial positions based on their prior success in technical fields of expertise, such as engineering, accounting/finance, or sales. Often, they were ill-prepared for the tremendous challenges of understanding the complexities of human behavior at work, and there was little information or training available to assist them.

Approximately a half century ago, the field of organizational behavior (OB) began to emerge, and its goal since then has been to establish an integrated field of knowledge based on a solid foundation of conceptual, theoretical, and research material. Borrowing initially from the fields of psychology, sociology, social psychology, and other domains, OB identifies the primary outcomes that organizations seek to obtain and the key causal factors that contribute to those outcomes. Although at one time focused on the academic preparation of future managers in college and university courses, several professors have become popular-press authors. Some of them have recently begun to share their insights and suggestions via substantive practitioner-oriented "best sellers." In this section, Professors Cameron, Lawler, and Csikszentmihalyi each offer their suggestions for humanizing the workplace.

Kim Cameron is the William Russell Kelly Professor of Management and Organization at the University of Michigan's Ross School of Business. He has conducted research on downsizing, corporate quality culture, leadership excellence, and virtuousness in organizations. His published books include *Making the Impossible Possible*, *Leading with Values*, and *Diagnosing and Changing Organizational Culture.*

Drawing on the fields of positive organizational scholarship and positive psychology, Cameron contends that *Positive Leadership* suggests three things—dramatically positive deviant performance; emphasis on strengths, optimism, and supportive communication; and facilitating the best of the human condition. Four associated leadership strategies are positive climates, relationships, communication, and meaning. This requires a diagnosis of current practices, careful role definitions, and measurement of progress toward positive leadership.

Edward E. Lawler III is widely acknowledged as one of the country's premier experts on management. He is a distinguished professor of management and organization in the Marshall School of Business and director of the Center for

Effective Organizations at the University of Southern California. Lawler received his Ph.D. from the University of California–Berkeley, was the recipient of a Lifetime Achievement Award from ASTD (the American Society for Training and Development), and has been named a Fellow of the Academy of Management. He has prepared over 30 books, including *Pay and Organizational Performance*, *Managerial Attitudes and Performance*, *The Ultimate Advantage*, and *High-Involvement Management*.

Lawler, in his book *Treat People Right!*, suggests that managing people correctly is a challenging task, with payoffs for both organizations and their members. He portrays a "virtuous spiral of success" that moves beyond simply providing adequate working conditions and fair pay to induce new levels of sustained peak performance. Specific practices include "branding" the firm as a place for high achievers, recruiting and selecting high performers, and institutionalizing a leadership style that supports and rewards desired levels of individual and organizational performance. This is achieved through the integration of job design, reward systems, training programs, and a host of other recommendations.

Mihaly Csikszentmihalyi, the author of *Good Business*, is the C.S. and D. J. Davidson Professor of Psychology at the Peter F. Drucker School of Management at Claremont Graduate University and the director of The Quality of Life Research Center. His research interests include positive psychology, creativity, socialization, and the study of intrinsically rewarding behavior in work and play settings. Csikszentmihalyi is the author of *Flow: The Psychology of Optimal Experience*, *The Evolving Self: A Psychology for the Third Millennium*, and *Finding Flow: The Psychology of Engagement with Everyday Life*. He is a recipient of BrainChannels' "Thinker of the Year" award.

Csikszentmihalyi argues that workplaces can be dismal places when they have destroyed employee trust, given workers no clear goals, failed to provide adequate feedback, and taken away any sense of control. He suggests that CEOs need to recognize that the total fulfillment of a person's potential is what usually generates true happiness, and this begins with a philosophy and belief that the company will be operating successfully 100 years from now. He articulates the eight central features underlying flow and suggests that managers can create the conditions for flow by making the workplace attractive, finding ways to imbue the job with meaning and value, and selecting and rewarding individuals who find satisfaction in their work.

1

Positive Leadership

Kim Cameron

Summary prepared by Jodi Nelson

Jodi Nelson is Chief Operating Officer for SISU Medical Solutions, LLC, in Duluth, Minnesota. SISU Medical Solutions, LLC, is an information technology organization with a focus on the information technology needs for health-care organizations. She concentrates her efforts in the areas of human resource management, organizational operations, and leadership. Prior to joining the SISU organization, Jodi worked in the human resource department at Miller-Dwan Medical Center in Duluth, Minnesota. Jodi has a bachelor's degree from the University of Minnesota Duluth in Business Administration, with a concentration in human resources.

INTRODUCTION

Leadership style within an organization can greatly impact the results that an organization strives for. While our society as a whole tends to focus on the negative outcomes of a given action, a person who is able to think outside of that box and provide a positive leadership style will be successful. Leadership in any organization can be a delicate balance of many outside forces. When dealing with decisions and adversity through use of a positive leadership style the organization will more likely reap the desired results.

POSITIVE LEADERSHIP

Three key belief systems underlie positive leadership:

- **Positively deviant performance**—the belief that results will exceed expectations and go above and beyond them.
- **Affirmation bias**—the belief that the focus should be on the positive assets and strengths of people.

Kim Cameron. *Positive Leadership: Strategies for Extraordinary Performance.* San Francisco, CA: Berrett-Koehler Publishers, 2008.

- **Facilitating the best of the human condition**—the belief that people are intrinsically good and simply need nurturing.

Organizations will improve themselves through the belief and practice of these three positive **leadership characteristics**.

FOUR POSITIVE LEADERSHIP STRATEGIES

For an organization to achieve positive leadership through a positive deviant performance, affirmation bias, and facilitating the best of the human condition, there are four leadership strategies to promote within an organization. Managers should focus on fostering the four positive leadership strategies that enable positive deviance. Those four strategies are positive climate, positive relationships, positive communication, and positive meaning.

Positive Climate

The positive climate in an organization is a direct reflection of the emotions of the employees working there. Leaders looking to achieve a positive deviance will embrace the concept of a positive climate or atmosphere and work to achieve it. This positive climate can be attained through consistent demonstration of compassion, forgiveness, and gratitude. Employee emotions within an organization will create the desired climate.

Positive Relationships

Positive relationships within an organization focus on both the relational value of the experiences among staff as well as extending to the more physical, mental, and emotional health of relationships within the organization. Ensuring that the organization fosters the relations of the individuals involved will enhance the strengths that each individual brings to the table as well as enhancing the physical and mental health of those individuals.

Positive Communication

Positive communication within an organization should be fostered to ensure positive deviance. Managers should focus on supportive communication and feedback. This is especially important during critical points within an organization's existence. Supportive communication is important to keep lines of communication open. Feedback must be provided whether it be of a negative or positive nature. Leaders within an organization who foster communication will ultimately help individuals as well as the organization to grow.

Positive Meaning

Managers should strive for positive meaning within an organization while looking for a balance between the work being done and the outcomes associated with that work. Work and meaningfulness come together when

1. The work has an important positive impact on the well-being of human beings.
2. The work is associated with an important virtue or personal value.

3. The work has an impact that extends beyond the immediate time frame or creates a ripple effect.
4. The work builds supportive relationships or a sense of community in people.

To ensure positive deviance within an organization, managers should recognize the importance of positive meaning.

IMPLEMENTING POSITIVE STRATEGIES

Providing positive leadership within any organization can be a delicate balance to ensure positive deviance. Initially, *managers should diagnose their current practices.* Before leaders can begin to instill a positive leadership style within an organization, it is mandatory that they understand where their leadership style has come from. After identifying current practices, leaders should plan for the implementation of change within their organization. A concerted effort needs to be made to ensure a positive leadership style is adopted by all.

As a portion of the implementation plan, managers should determine a strategy to build a positively deviant organization. To accomplish a positive leadership style within an organization, managers should pursue a Personal Management Interview (PMI) program. The first step in the PMI program is to define roles and responsibilities. Members within an organization must understand their role is to be successful and feel good about what it is that they do. Second, it is paramount that leaders revisit the individual role definitions and measure progress on a regular basis with their direct reports within the organization. Leaders need to communicate with all individuals and coach them as they move forward and grow.

Conclusion

Effective leaders inherently strive for greatness. Through the implementation of a positive leadership style and the achievement of a positively deviant organization leaders *will* succeed.

Treat People Right!

Edward E. Lawler III

Summary Prepared by Danielle DuBois Kerr

Danielle DuBois Kerr is a compensation practitioner at Uponor, Inc. A majority of her career has been spent focusing on organizations' compensation and benefits needs. Her areas of expertise include market pricing, salary surveys, job analysis, salary structure design, benefits administration, and compliance. Danielle attained her Professional in Human Resources (PHR) certification from the Society of Human Resources Management and has completed course work toward her Certified Compensation Professional Designation through WorldatWork. She received a Bachelor of Business Administration degree from the University of Minnesota Duluth, with majors in both Human Resource and Organizational Management. She is a member of the Twin Cities Human Resource Association, WorldatWork, and the Twin Cities Compensation Network.

In today's tough business environment, organizations and people can't succeed without the other. Organizations need to be successful so they can provide meaningful work and reward their people, but in order to be successful, organizations need high-performing people. Finding a mutually beneficial path that leads both parties to this joint definition of success seems difficult to find. However, there is a path that can lead both individuals and organizations to their goals. It is to "treat people right."

The challenge is to create organizational structures that provide employees with meaningful work and appropriate rewards, while motivating and satisfying them to behave in ways that help their organizations become effective and high performing. Both parties need to understand how the other operates in order to make informed decisions about the relationship. For example, an organization may treat its people right by investing in new training and development programs. However, for the training program to be successful, the individual must

Edward E. Lawler III. *Treat People Right! How Organizations and Individuals Can Propel Each Other into a Virtuous Spiral of Success.* San Francisco, CA: Jossey-Bass, 2003.

decide to take on additional responsibility for learning new skills and embrace the opportunity to manage his or her own career. Without a mutual commitment to the program, neither will succeed.

VIRTUOUS SPIRALS

Organizations that value and reward their people will motivate them to perform well, which in turn propels organizations to attain higher levels of accomplishment. When individuals and organizations achieve more and more of their goals, a virtuous spiral evolves. These spirals are the ultimate competitive advantage. They are win-win relationships that are hard-to-duplicate sources of positive momentum. The virtuous spiral begins with strategy, follows with organization design, and then proceeds through an iterative process of staffing–performance–rewards that continues onward.

Organizations that mishandle their human capital are susceptible to inverting this process, in turn creating a death spiral. During a **death spiral**, an organization will see both individual and organizational performance decline. These unwanted spirals can last for decades, or can be relatively fast and only last a few days.

How can a virtuous spiral be launched and a death spiral avoided? Simply being nice to people and treating them well are not enough. Organizations need to develop a wide array of human capital management practices that motivate people to excel and then follow through by rewarding them for high levels of performance. In turn, individuals need to make greater commitments to their own careers and organizations, at the same time becoming responsible for their own behaviors.

THE COMPONENTS OF AN EFFECTIVE ORGANIZATION

Before organizations can effectively establish human capital management practices, they need to lay the appropriate foundation for treating people right. The organization itself must be effective. This means that the organization must have alignment among four determinants of effectiveness:

1. Strategy: The master plan for the organization, which include its goals, purpose, products/services, and so on.
2. Organizational capabilities: The factors that allow an organization to coordinate and focus its behavior to produce levels of performance required by its strategy. One example is the ability to manage and develop new knowledge.
3. Core competencies: A combination of technology and production skills that help define and create an organization's products/services, such as an organization's ability to miniaturize its products.
4. Environment: The context in which the organization operates. Examples include the business climate, the state of the economy, and the political and physical environments.

The organization must have a clear understanding of these factors before it can cultivate its human capital, organizational structure, reward systems, and processes. Once the organization lays its foundation for effectiveness, it can take steps to treat people right. Implementing the seven principles to treating people right will give the organization the capability of launching a virtuous spiral.

SEVEN KEY PRINCIPLES FOR TREATING PEOPLE RIGHT

1. Attraction and Retention

"Organizations must create a value proposition that defines the type of workplace they want to be so that they can attract and retain the right people." Creating a value proposition communicates who the organization is, what it wants, and what is has to offer. This allows an organization to attract and employ individuals who are aligned with its values and goals. Each organization should consider having multiple value propositions to attract and retain a diverse workforce. For example, rewards that are designed to retain core employees probably focus on encouraging individual commitment to the organization. Rewards for this group of employees usually include a stake in the organization through some type of stock ownership. On the other hand, some employees may not be interested in ownership, so it would be wise to develop a separate value proposition for this group. Overall, the propositions should be well thought out and focus on what the organization has to offer in order to attract and retain the right people needed to achieve a high-performing organization. In turn, a virtuous spiral could evolve.

2. Hiring Practices

"Organizations must hire people who fit with their values, core competencies, and strategic goals." This requires a clear and disciplined process that allows the organization to properly assess the competencies, skills, knowledge, personality, and needs of applicants. Objective data should be collected through assessment tools such as personality tests or knowledge exams. Another valuable tool for collecting data is background checks, as past behavior has been demonstrated to be the best predictor of future behavior. An organization that does not have effective hiring practices will have a very hard time reaching a virtuous spiral.

3. Training and Development

"Organizations must continuously train employees to do their jobs and offer them opportunities to grow and develop." Commitment to an organization's training and development program reinforces the value an organization places on creating a virtuous spiral. By doing so, employees' skills are essentially increased and a virtuous spiral is reinforced. Overall, supporting a training and development program is not only valuable to the organization but also adds value to each employee as it helps ignite one's personal career spiral by providing the opportunity to learn, develop, and experience new things.

4. Work Design

"Organizations must design work so that it is meaningful for people and provides them with feedback, responsibility, and autonomy." Employee motivation, satisfaction, and performance are greatly influenced by this principle and can have a significant influence on the overall effectiveness of an organization. In order to influence these factors, organizations must make work involving, challenging, and rewarding for people. To do so, organizations must:

- Avoid simplified jobs.
- Design **enriched jobs** that allow one to experience meaningfulness, have responsibility for outcomes of his or her behavior, and receive feedback about his or her results.

Not all work can be enriched to the fullest extent, nor can all of the repetitive work in the world be eliminated. To combat this problem, an organization should consider making the work intrinsically satisfying, offer higher extrinsic rewards, or possibly outsource simplified, repetitive work to subcontractors. That said, paying attention to the way in which work is designed could have a significant impact on employees' motivation and satisfaction, which may in turn hinder or propel a virtuous spiral.

5. Mission, Strategies, and Goals

"Organizations must develop and adhere to a specific organizational mission, with strategies, goals, and values that employees can understand, support and believe in." Goals are a powerful motivator of behavior that can lead and direct an organization down a certain path. Accomplishment of goals gives people feelings of intrinsic satisfaction that cause them to reach for higher performance and to form a stronger commitment to the overall organizational mission and strategy. In turn, accomplishment sparks and carries the momentum of the virtuous spiral.

For the spiral to continue moving ahead, the established goals must be meaningful. Some may be noble and have a higher order mission, while others may be purely financial and performance driven. Both types have the ability to effectively influence individual and organizational results as long as there is a line of sight between the individual's behavior and the end result. For example, goals cannot be accomplished or even supported if they are hidden from the public eye. Employees must be committed to reaching goals and when they can see a direct connection between their behavior and the goal, attainment of the goal becomes more likely. In sum, when employees can understand, support, and believe in the developed mission and strategies, the potential for a virtuous spiral is greatly increased.

6. Reward Systems

"Organizations must devise and implement reward systems that reinforce their design, core values, and strategy." Reward systems are influential in obtaining a virtuous spiral. To be effective, the systems must reward performance; be properly aligned with the organization's design, core values, and strategy; and must motivate people to perform effectively. Several criteria should be considered when designing a reward system. First, the systems must have a clear line of sight between the desired outcomes and the individual behaviors needed to obtain those outcomes. Second, the size of the reward must be large enough to capture the attention of the employees and make a difference in their motivation. For example, average merit increases have been 3–4 percent over the past few years. If the reward were smaller than this, it might not capture their attention. However, a raise or a bonus of 10 percent is more likely to spark people's interest, in turn motivating certain behaviors. Third, if an organization has a pay-for-performance system in place, employees must possess the power, information, and knowledge they need to influence their performance. Finally, leadership must create credibility for their reward programs. This means being trustworthy and carrying out promises. If all criteria are designed properly, reward systems can be a powerful tool in becoming a high-performing organization.

7. Leadership

"Organizations must hire and develop leaders who can create commitment, trust, success, and a motivating work environment." Individual and organizational effectiveness can be greatly affected by leadership at all levels. So how can managers be most effective? The answer is simple: Set up win-win situations (in essence, virtuous spirals). Findings from the Ohio State University in the 1950s showed that the most **effective managers** focused on both organizational and individual results. Satisfying the wants and needs of both groups (managers and employees) can be a challenge; however, the responsibility should not reside on the shoulders of one person. The organization's leadership must be shared, including the responsibility for motivating employees and creating a vision.

CREATING A VIRTUOUS SPIRAL

Getting organizations to a point where they are ready to develop a virtuous spiral can be very challenging. It requires well-planned strategic actions to gain momentum. To start a virtuous spiral, a strategy must be developed by effective change leaders. Next, employees must be motivated to change and a vision should be created. Finally, all seven principles of treating people right need to be implemented. All steps must be set in place; one step simply cannot be omitted. Failure to do so leads to the risk of making all adopted principles dysfunctional. Once the spiral has begun, it needs regular checkups to make sure the organization is heading in the right direction. Depending upon changes within or outside the organization, changes may be needed to one or all of the steps used to initiate the spiral.

FALSE AND FRAUDULENT SPIRALS

As organizations develop their own spirals, false or fraudulent spirals can wreak havoc on the ability or potential to create a virtuous spiral of success. A **false spiral** occurs when an organization thinks a virtuous spiral has been initiated, when in fact the thought is simply an illusion. A good example of this was observed in the dot-com industry during the 1990s. In general, the market value of many dot-com organizations was greatly inflated. These companies believed they were in the midst of a virtuous spiral, when in fact their market values were too high. Eventually their stock prices collapsed, and the majority of these dot-coms fell into a death spiral. Fraudulent spirals are another type of spiral that can cause destruction. These spirals can be easily mistaken as virtuous although they are created by deceitful activities. These practices were uncovered at several large corporations such as Enron, WorldCom, and Adelphia. Once fraudulent behavior surfaces, the organization almost always falls into a death spiral. Organizations must steer clear of these two types of spirals and focus their efforts on successfully implementing the seven principles mentioned earlier.

THREATS TO A VIRTUOUS SPIRAL

Once a virtuous spiral has been initiated, there is no guarantee that it will stay intact. Many internal and external threats can quickly turn the spiral in the wrong direction. One important and increasingly prevalent threat is environmental changes, including new competitors or industry regulations. Environmental changes are serious threats, which may call for new organizational strategies. This threat is so critical that the virtuous spiral model presented earlier was revised to take this threat into consideration. The new model again starts with an initial sequence of strategy–organizational design–staffing–performance–rewards, but then includes strategy change, organizational design change, and performance change, all of which are based on the fact that organizations need to pay attention to the environment and may need to react to changes by altering their initial foundation. The model then proceeds onward to iterative cycles of rewards–staffing–performance.

Environmental changes occur in many different forms and in many different frequencies. Depending upon these factors, each organization needs individually to assess when to react to the environment. When the timing is right, an organization will have the capability to change by tweaking the seven principles of "treating people right."

Environmental changes are just one type of threat to an organization's virtuous spiral. Others include:

- Economic downturn within a country
- Industry-specific economic downturn
- Mistakes or self-inflicted threats
- Fads or fashions

Any one of these threats can devastate an organization's financial performance. However, threats do not and cannot automatically cause a death spiral. A well-thought-out response to any threat can actually save an organization and launch it into a new virtuous spiral by causing it to rethink its strategy and relay its foundation.

Conclusion

Virtuous spirals can flourish in organizations that perform well and treat people right. Despite the numerous threats to an organization, virtuous spirals can be rekindled and launched into new directions. It is important to consider and recognize that organizations serve multiple stakeholders. Meeting financial performance goals is important, but so is satisfying customers, employees, stockholders, and community members. It must be remembered that organizations are made of people, are created by people, and exist to serve people. If organizations do not treat people right, they should not (and often will not) exist.

Good Business

Mihaly Csikszentmihalyi

Summary Prepared by Kelly Nelson

Kelly Nelson *is a General Manager, Human Resources, with AK Steel Corporation, headquartered in Middletown, Ohio. She is responsible for the human resources programs of the organization's seven carbon, stainless, and specialty steel–producing facilities located in Pennsylvania, Kentucky, Ohio, and Indiana. In her position, she has daily opportunity to explore the "right" course of action and what framework provides the appropriate structure for the greater good not only of the organization but for all stakeholders. A believer in enhancing human well-being, she receives the greatest intrinsic rewards as a parent to her son John, as a daughter, as a sister, as an auntie, as well as an enthusiastic student of human behavior.*

INTRODUCTION

Business leaders who manage their businesses to enhance the happiness of human beings provide an environment in which individual workers flourish and reasonable profits are made. Leaders who manage their organizations with a moral obligation toward the greater good share characteristics that, if more widely adopted, will lead to businesses truly making life happier for all.

Business leaders today have become the leaders of society—much like the nobility of the past. As leaders of society, it is incumbent upon business leaders to enrich the lives of individuals in society. This obligation goes beyond the focus of the quarterly financial review. It reaches all aspects of life because the careers that everyone follows, and how they feel about those careers, affect how they feel about themselves as individuals, family members, community participants, and contributors to society.

Mihaly Csikszentmihalyi. *Good Business: Leadership, Flow, and the Making of Meaning.* New York: Penguin Putnam, 2003.

THE DUAL GOALS OF BUSINESS

As difficult as the balance is, today there are a number of CEOs who demonstrate that financially successful business enterprises can also contribute to human happiness. These individuals share common principles of good business and firmly believe that they have an obligation to society that is broader and has longer-term significance than success based solely on financial strength. These CEOs embrace the *hundred-year manager philosophy*, which dictates leading the business enterprise and making decisions based upon the belief that the company will be operating successfully 100 years from now.

The basis of human happiness is not universal, and this makes it more difficult to conduct a business in such a way that it ensures human happiness. It is generally agreed that happiness is, as Aristotle expressed it, the **summum bonum**, or the chief good. This philosophy holds that, while people desire other goods (such as money or power) because they believe those things will make them happy, they want happiness for its own sake. In fact, businesses are built on the premise that the goods and/or services produced will make people happy, so there will be a market for the products produced.

However, *the total fulfillment of a person's potential is what usually generates true happiness*. Total fulfillment depends upon the presence of two forces—differentiation and integration. The process of *differentiation* suggests that we are all unique individuals, responsible for ourselves, with the self-confidence to develop our uniqueness. *Integration* implies that, although we are unique individuals, we all are completely immersed in networks of relationships with other human beings, our environment, our culture, and our material possessions. A person who is fully differentiated and integrated becomes a *complex individual* and one most probable to develop true happiness.

The evolution of individual complexity changes throughout the stages of one's life. It culminates at the point where an individual has an appreciation for uniqueness and is in control of thoughts, actions, and feelings, while relishing dependence and interrelatedness to others, the environment, and the culture. Although the maturation of complexity is desired and necessary for ultimate happiness, businesses who work to support complexity work for not only financial success but also the ideal that the business exists for a greater good.

THE BASES OF FLOW

Individuals who have developed complexity have the capacity truly to enjoy the work that they do. The total immersion one feels when completing tasks with no distinction between thought and action, or self and environment, is an element of flow, and *flow is an individual's full involvement with life*. Although individuals may feel flow from different life activities, eight conditions determine flow.

1. *Goals are clear.* The clarity of the goal allows individuals to focus their attention and to appreciate the completion of each step along the way to the goal.
2. *Feedback is immediate.* The individual knows internally whether each step is completed with the level of excellence acceptable to the individual. This can be provided by external sources; however, an individual who has achieved flow is able through knowledge and past experience to trust his or her internal standards.
3. *A balance between opportunity and capacity exists.* When the challenges faced by the individual are high and equal to the individual's skills, flow is possible.

4. *Concentration deepens.* As an individual focuses on the task at hand, his or her concentration deepens to the point that "thinking" is no longer necessary. Instead, the individual is focused and the process feels effortless.

5. *The present is what matters.* Concentration on the events at hand allows other worries and thoughts to be eliminated. The individual escapes in a positive manner by using his or her skill to accomplish the task.

6. *Control is no problem.* Because flow allows the individual to control his or her own performance and disregard environmental elements, the individual is in control and feels the power of his or her own control.

7. *The sense of time is altered.* The speed at which time passes depends upon two elements—how focused the mind is on the task and whether the individual's "clock" speeds up or slows down. Occasions of flow can either cause time to fly by or to appear to be passing in slow motion.

8. *The loss of ego prevails.* The final condition of flow is the individual's loss of ego. As workers completely focus on the task at hand and their skills and activities to complete their tasks, there is no concentration left over to focus on themselves. The consumption of oneself allows one to be selfless.

The ability to enter flow, of course, does not guarantee that the individual is happy or contented. However, it provides the opportunity to grow. Individual growth, in turn, adds more happiness and accomplishment to the individual's life.

The ability to enter flow fluctuates during the day. Each individual's internal clock provides opportunities at different times. The activities faced in the individual's day also determine the propensity to enter flow, as a function of challenges (high or low) and personal skill level (high or low). If a person's challenges are high and the person's skills are high, flow is possible. This is most often achieved when the individual is involved in favorite activities. On the other hand, when challenges and skills are both low, the individual is more apt to feel apathy, such as when one is lonely or passively watching television.

As the individual's challenge level increases, but his or her skills do not increase, the individual first feels worried and then reaches anxiety. If, when at a high challenge period, the individual's skill level increases, the individual moves from anxiety to arousal. In the state of arousal, such as when learning a new skill, the individual is alert and focused. As the individual's skill level increases, it is possible to move from arousal to the state of flow.

When employees' challenges and skills are low, they feel apathetic. If their challenges do not increase but their skill level does, it leads to boredom. As skills increase, boredom turns to relaxation, which leads to control as challenges increase to meet the skill level. From the point of control, it is possible to increase both the challenges and skill level to enter flow.

Prospective leaders challenge themselves and develop their skill levels to increase the times in which they experience relaxation, control, arousal, and flow. As the proportion of time spent in these areas increases, the individual experiences more opportunities to grow in his or her complexity, leading to still more happiness and contentment in life.

Although flow is important for personal development, flow may or may not be a part of an individual's workday. Most jobs were created to get the most productivity out of individuals, but not necessarily to bring out the best in them. Managers should seek to provide career opportunities and motivational conditions that bring out the best in people. Motivation toward work is determined by three conditions: (1) the type of job available, (2) the value the culture assigns to the job, and (3) the attitude the individual has toward his or her job.

Managers who build an organization that brings out the best in workers have three options:

1. Make the objective conditions of the workplace as attractive as possible;
2. Find ways to imbue the job with meaning and value; and
3. Select and reward individuals who find satisfaction in their work.

Although there have been general improvements in the workplace over the years, there are several reasons that workers still lack the opportunity for flow in their jobs. First, the goals of individual jobs have become more obscure. Many times the individual worker does not understand either the short-term or long-term goals so although they may understand *what* they are doing, they do not understand *why*. It is difficult for workers to derive true satisfaction and accomplishment if they do not understand why they are doing what they are doing.

Second, *workers are rarely provided with clear, timely feedback.* The lack of feedback prevents employees from understanding that what they are doing is important and does matter to the organization. The skills of the worker are also not necessarily matched to the skills needed in the job, and this prevents the experience of flow. Also, workers feel a lack of control in not only setting the goals of the process but also determining the rhythm of the process. Managers who want to allow workers to achieve their best must redesign the workplace to eliminate barriers to flow.

BUILDING FLOW INTO ORGANIZATIONS

It is possible for managers to redesign the workplace to encourage the growth of individuals to allow more flow. It takes a complete commitment from top management to create an environment that will foster flow. Because the profitability of flow does not appear neatly on a spreadsheet, it requires strong leaders who have achieved complexity and who understand business's duty to increase human well-being to redesign the workplace to achieve it.

It takes a leap of faith by top management to believe that redesigning the workplace will eventually result in improved financial results. It is especially important that top management commits to and believes in the fact that greater good results from improving the well-being of the individual.

To create an environment conducive to well-being, it is imperative that the organization's mission is understood by all participants and that individuals are provided the flexibility to adjust their individual goals to match the organization's goals. Managers must also allow individuals to fail without responding too harshly. Calculated risk taking is important in challenging the individual and some risk-taking initiatives will result in either failure or lack of success. Individuals who are harshly criticized for risk taking will learn to avoid risks (and the challenges they offer) and will fail to achieve flow.

Managers can best ensure that their workers understand the organization's true commitment to redesigning the workplace by communicating at every opportunity and by ensuring that feedback is provided. After managers ensure individuals are placed in appropriate jobs, given clearly understandable goals, and provided with appropriate feedback, the work conditions must also include the eight properties conducive to achieving flow. The details of each person's properties may be different, and so these should be handled in the work area of the individuals, with input and creation of the properties left to the individual and supported by the direct manager.

THE SOUL OF BUSINESS

Creating a nurturing environment in which individuals are encouraged to achieve flow lays the groundwork to be an organization that improves human well-being; however, it does not ensure it. It is imperative that the organization has soul. *Soul is demonstrated by the organization when it devotes energy to purposes beyond itself.* The goals adopted by the organization for the greater good or to benefit others (without financial reward to itself) show the organization's base values. Often the concept of soul of the organization is similar to beliefs supported by religions—giving donations, assisting the poor, supporting community events, supporting volunteerism, and fighting for what is right.

Managers who believe their obligation is to improve human well-being share five common traits:

1. They are *optimistic* in both their feelings about people as well as their thoughts about the future.
2. They have *integrity,* or an unwavering adherence to principles on which mutual trust can be based.
3. They have a high level of *ambition* coupled with the perseverance necessary to overcome obstacles.
4. They also have *curiosity and a desire to learn.*
5. They possess *empathy* and have a basic respect for others.

Managers who possess these traits also possess the *self-confidence* to pursue their dreams and to support the dreams of others. These are the managers who supply the soul of business.

CREATING FLOW IN LIFE

Business leaders can only provide the environment that is conducive to achieving flow. Everyone possesses the ability to achieve that state of challenge and accomplishment. It is important for people to build on their strengths by creating challenges to hone their own skills. It is also important to identify weaknesses and to strengthen them. In order to build on strengths and minimize weaknesses, it is important that employees pay attention. By paying attention, people will learn not only what their strengths and weaknesses are but will also see what is necessary to optimize them. Focusing attention to detail provides the greatest opportunity for learning and growth. Paying attention requires an investment of time. Individuals who lead others to greatness hone their use of time, develop healthy and challenging habits, and invest energy in their consciousness.

THE FUTURE OF BUSINESS

In order for an organization to contribute to human well-being while also achieving reasonable profitability, the leaders of the organization must have a vision beyond the organization itself. They must envision the organization within the framework of its environment and the human environment. The leaders must also have the intrinsic need to do what is right in relation to human well-being that is based on trust and respect for others. This will allow the leaders to encourage the personal growth of the workers and to provide opportunities for flow in the workplace. Finally, it is imperative that organizations provide goods or services that truly enhance the well-being of people, and that they operate in an ethical, responsible manner.

The principles of good business have historically been gleaned from our religious beliefs and from the principles of our parents. The leaders of today's business who manage their business for improved human well-being will provide examples to be followed by future generations of business leaders.

VI

Motivation

A number of readings contained in this edition of *The Manager's Bookshelf* focus the manager's attention on the social-psychological side of the organization. New concepts and suggestions for proactive management call our attention to the importance of recognizing that all organizations have a natural (human) resource that, when appropriately motivated, can lead to dramatic performance effects.

This part has three readings, each of which takes a different but complementary path toward the same objective. In *The Enthusiastic Employee*, authors Sirota, Mischkind, and Meltzer describe ideal employees. Their unbridled enthusiasm helps them outperform others, strive to achieve the impossible, and rally each other to work hard and make unusual contributions. Unfortunately, unenlightened managers often *dampen* the enthusiasm of these stellar performers and *demotivate* them. The answer to this problem lies in a three-pronged approach involving equitable treatment, opportunities for achievement, and the experience of camaraderie.

David Sirota holds a doctorate in Social Psychology from the University of Michigan; Louis Mischkind received his Ph.D. in Organizational Psychology from New York University; and Michael Meltzer received his J.D. from Brooklyn Law School. All three are associated with Sirota Consulting, and they share background expertise in various aspects of opinion surveys, behavioral science research, and management assessments.

Fred Luthans, Carolyn Youssef, and Bruce Avolio are the authors of *Psychological Capital: Developing the Human Competitive Edge.* Luthans is Distinguished University Professor at the University of Nebraska, a former president of the Academy of Management, and a prolific author. With Bruce Avolio, he published *The High Impact Leader: Moments Matter in Authentic Leadership Development.* Carolyn Youssef holds a Ph.D. from the University of Nebraska and teaches at Bellevue University.

Psychological capital is the study of how to make healthy people happier at work. It draws upon positive organizational behavior (POB), whose attributes must be theory based, measurable, developmental, and positively related to work performance. The key attributes of positive organizational behavior are self-efficacy, hope, optimism, and resilience. The presence of psychological capital has been found to correlate with rated performance, objective performance, and employee satisfaction.

Based upon his observations of a large number of organizations (e.g., Southwest Airlines, the U.S. Marines, and General Motors), Jon R. Katzenbach, in *Why Pride Matters More than Money*, tackles the question, "How do I motivate my employees?"—the question most frequently asked by supervisors, managers, and leaders. While conventional wisdom, as practiced in most organizations, suggests that money and intimidation are the keys to sustained performance, Katzenbach asserts that the real answer is to be found in the word *pride*. He asserts that neither money nor intimidation contribute to the long-term sustainability of an organization. With regard to money, Katzenbach states that it is not a motivator and that pay-for-performance programs lead to self-serving behavior and ephemeral commitment to the organization. Instead, he notes that most employees are motivated by meaningful work, feelings of accomplishment, recognition/approval, and a sense of belonging and being a part of others in the work environment.

The author, Jon R. Katzenbach, was a senior partner and director of McKinsey and Company, a large U.S.-based consulting organization. He now directs his own firm, Katzenbach Partners, assisting organizations in such areas as workforce performance, team building, and leadership. Mr. Katzenbach is the author of several other books, including *Peak Performance, Teams at the Top, The Wisdom of Teams*, and *Real Change Leaders*. With Zhia Khan, Katzenbach published *The Informal Organization*.

Readers interested in exposing themselves to a contrarian view of motivation might be interested in examining Charles Jacobs' book, *Management Rewired*. Jacobs argues that many traditional approaches to motivation (rewards and punishment, criticism and praise) are blunt tools that are ineffective, and managers are better advised to use more subtle tactics.

The Enthusiastic Employee

David Sirota, Louis A. Mischkind, and Michael Irwin Meltzer

Summary Prepared by Shelley Ovrom

Shelley Ovrom is a human resources professional, having started her career in the private sector working as a recruiter for the Walt Disney Studios and Universal Studios. She then made the transition to the public sector, currently working as a human resource analyst for the City of Azusa in California. In her current position, she is responsible for risk management, recruitment, and workers' compensation, as well as daily support for city employees, department heads, and the public. She is passionate about the importance of human resources in an organization and is thrilled to be working in a capacity that benefits not only an employee population but also an entire community.

Most people begin a new job with a sense of enthusiasm. They are typically excited about their work and their organization, eager to be part of a productive team, and reasonable in how they expect to be treated. This is the case for approximately 95 percent of any employee population. The other 5 percent should never have been hired, and managers spend an inordinate amount of time with these difficult employees. However, an even bigger problem lies in the vast number of workers who are not openly troublesome; they are individuals who have become indifferent to the organization and its purpose. They have learned not to expect too much and not to give too much. The most significant decline in employee morale typically begins about six months after being hired and occurs in approximately 9 out of 10 companies.

There are various approaches and theories of how to best tackle this problem. However, a strong argument can be made that the first step is to determine what workers really want. *The key question is not how to motivate employees, but how to sustain—and prevent management from destroying—the motivation and enthusiasm employees naturally bring to their jobs.* **Employee enthusiasm**, a state of high

David Sirota, Louis A. Mischkind, and Michael Irwin Meltzer. *The Enthusiastic Employee: How Companies Profit by Giving Workers What They Want.* Philadelphia, PA: Wharton School Publishing, 2005.

employee morale that derives from satisfying the three key needs of workers, results in significant competitive advantages for companies with the strength of leadership and commitment to manage for true long-term results. A highly effective method of creating and maintaining high levels of long-term organizational performance is a **partnership relationship** in which employees work collaboratively, share common, long-term goals, and feel a genuine concern for other employees at work.

WORKER MOTIVATION, MORALE, AND PERFORMANCE

Many theories exist as to the differences in what employees want, explained by generational, racial, gender, or economic differences. Research indicates, however, that the percentage of people satisfied with their work is high for every group, with an average of 76 percent of all workers across all organizations generally enjoying the work they do.

Three-Factor Theory of Human Motivation in the Workplace

According to the **three-factor theory of motivation**, three primary sets of goals of people are at work:

EQUITY   Employees want to be treated justly—in comparison to others—in relation to the three basic conditions of employment. These conditions are unrelated to a position in the company or to performance. The three basic conditions are:

- Physiological—decent working conditions and working environment
- Economic—satisfactory compensation and benefits
- Psychological—respectful and consistent treatment by management

ACHIEVEMENT   Employees want to take pride in their achievements; they want to do things that matter and do them well; they desire to receive recognition for their accomplishments; they want to take pride in the organization's accomplishments. Statistical analysis shows there are six primary sources that contribute to a sense of achievement:

- Challenge of the work itself
- Acquisition of new skills
- Ability to perform
- Perceived importance of the job
- Recognition received for performance
- Feeling proud of their employer

CAMARADERIE   Members of the workforce wish to experience **camaraderie**—the feeling that they have warm, interesting, and cooperative relations with others on the job. This includes the extent to which an organization functions not only as a business entity but also as a community that satisfies the social and emotional needs of its employees. The impact that camaraderie can have on performance is often not recognized.

The overall relationship between morale and performance is reciprocal; each is both a cause and an effect of the other.

ENTHUSIASTIC WORKFORCES, MOTIVATED BY FAIR TREATMENT

Three important areas, as viewed by employees, define the issue of fair treatment:

- *Job security*—In general, 60 percent of workers are confident in the security of their jobs, but this ranges widely across organizations, from a high of 90 percent to a low of 6 percent. Many workers have experienced layoffs and typically do not view them as a prudent business decision, but rather as simply inequitable treatment. Many U.S. companies now seem to use downsizing as a strategic maneuver rather than as a last resort compelled by economic necessity. This "strategy" violates a fundamental need of workers and, in doing so, severely damages the sense of equity that is necessary for effective organizations.

  Companies genuinely committed to their employees adhere to five basic principles in doing their best to provide employees with stable employment:
  1. They exhaust all possible alternatives before laying people off.
  2. When layoffs cannot be avoided, they first ask for volunteers.
  3. When layoffs cannot be avoided and there are no more volunteers, they act generously and decently. From an organizational standpoint, they're not doing it just for those who are let go, but for those who will stay.
  4. They communicate honestly, fully, and regularly throughout the entire process.
  5. They recognize the impact of downsizings on the survivors and take steps to minimize the negative impact.

- *Compensation*—This factor is extraordinarily important for worker morale and performance. Pay provides the material wherewithal for life and is also a measure of respect, achievement, and the equitable distribution of the financial returns of the company. It is a satisfier of both the equity and achievement needs.

- *Respect*—This is the nonfinancial component of equity, with *equality* being at the heart of respect—the treatment of each individual as important and unique without regard to any other characteristics, such as gender, race, income, or even perceived performance or contribution to the organization. This is a fundamental human need that has enormous consequences for human behavior and the effectiveness of organizations. Three broad levels of respectful treatment in organizations can be distinguished:
  1. Humiliating treatment—This treatment is rare in most organizations at the present time. When it does occur, however, it can be devastating to people and their performance. This treatment comes in two forms: interpersonal, such as an employee's work being ridiculed by an immediate boss; and structural, such as formal organizational controls that allow workers absolutely no decision-making authority in the performance of their jobs. The consequences of this treatment show up most dramatically in labor conflict.
  2. Indifferent treatment—This treatment is more common than blatant humiliation and is often better termed *benign neglect*. It implies that workers are not worthy of management's time and attention, thereby making workers feel insignificant. Indifferent managers are solely focused on the bottom line. The response of workers to indifference is less anger than it is disappointment and withdrawal.
  3. Positive treatment—There are many factors that contribute to the positive treatment of employees, including physical working conditions, job autonomy, and communication. Ultimately, employees need to feel that they are not just being tolerated but are made to feel welcome and genuinely included.

ENTHUSIASTIC WORKFORCES, MOTIVATED BY ACHIEVEMENT

A critical condition for employee enthusiasm is a clear, credible, and inspiring organizational purpose. Research reveals a strong correlation between pride in the organization and the overall satisfaction of workers with that organization. The four main sources of pride, all of which reflect different facets of excellence, are:

- Excellence in the organization's financial performance,
- Excellence in the efficiency with which the work of the organization gets done,
- Excellence in the characteristics of the organization's products, and
- Excellence in the organization's moral character.

Success in this area consists of a combination of *purpose* (how an organization serves its customers) and *principles* (the moral character of the company). Any judgment about a company's principles must be based on its behavior in relation to *all* of its key constituencies.

One of the most important components of providing leadership is providing an organization with a purpose and principles of which employees can be proud, and to which they will willingly and enthusiastically devote their skills and energy. The basic points to keep in mind are:

- Purposes and principles must emanate from strongly held convictions of senior management.
- Statements of purposes and principles will be exercises in futility unless they are accompanied by a serious implementation plan.

In studies of group functioning, a useful distinction between three types of leadership exists: autocratic, laissez-faire, and participative. Of the three, research most strongly supports the participative method, which is an active style that stimulates employee involvement. A successful participative method is **self-managed teams (SMTs)**, which are teams of workers who, with their supervisors, are delegated various functions and the authority and resources needed to carry them out. The team operates like a small business whose members are highly involved in its management and in the sharing of its rewards. Effectiveness and job satisfaction are greatly enhanced by organizing teams, when possible, around identified customers and setting the primary goal of the teams to meet the needs of their customers.

External sources of satisfaction are feedback, recognition, and reward. Employees want to perform well, learn how to improve, and be recognized and rewarded for their achievements, which is among the most fundamental of human needs. There are four major means to recognize employees:

1. Compensation—differential compensation based on performance levels
2. Informal recognition—day-to-day recognition of performance
3. Honorifics—special awards for performance
4. Promotion—advancement to higher-level positions for superior performance

To be most effective, organizations must think of recognition as a cluster of components that need to be used consistently with each other and with the organization's goals and values in mind.

ENTHUSIASTIC WORKFORCES, MOTIVATED BY CAMARADERIE

The quality of social relationships in the workplace—its social capital—is of enormous importance, not only because of the general need people have for camaraderie but also because cooperative relationships are critical for effective performance and, therefore, for a sense of achievement in one's work. An employee's greatest sense of satisfaction and accomplishment can come from interacting as a team toward common performance goals. Teamwork is needed for just about every job at every level. This cooperation is the glue that binds together the different parts of the organization. Groups, when structured and managed correctly, allow for the emergence and consideration of different perspectives, which is vital to solve problems and make good business decisions.

BRINGING IT ALL TOGETHER: THE TOTAL ORGANIZATION

To create and implement a truly significant and lasting organizational change, the various components discussed cannot be thought of individually, but together as a system, one that is governed by an organization's culture. The essence of the system and culture discussed is a partnership relationship. Partnership has both a vertical dimension, which consists of the relationships between workers and management, and a horizontal dimension, which are the relationships between individuals and between work units. Essentially, a partnership is people working together toward common goals. The partnership method is a high-involvement model, with the successful hallmarks including:

- Win-win—all parties recognize they have key business goals in common and that the success of one depends on the success of the other
- Basic trust—intentions of all parties are trusted
- Excellence—high performance standards are set for all parties
- Competence—the parties have confidence in each other
- Joint decision making—key decisions are made jointly
- Open communications—parties communicate fully with each other
- Mutual influence—parties listen to and are influenced by each other
- Mutual assistance—parties help each other perform
- Recognition—contributions by each party are recognized
- Day-to-day treatment—parties routinely treat each other with consideration and respect
- Financial sharing—parties share equitably in results

Partnership is highly effective because it harnesses the natural motivation and enthusiasm that are characteristic of the overwhelming majority of workers. Although some conditions may make partnership inappropriate, such as extremely contrasting individual differences, there is no evidence that the approach does not work when it is applied to certain types of work or in certain cultures. Certain adaptations may obviously need to be made, but the fundamental concepts are applicable everywhere as long as the actions for a partnership organization begin with, and are sustained by, senior management.

Psychological Capital

Fred Luthans, Carolyn M. Youssef, and Bruce J. Avolio

Summary Prepared by Cathy A. Hanson

Cathy A. Hanson is the Director of Human Resources for the city of Manhattan Beach, California. She is responsible for all aspects of human resources within a dynamic city environment. A majority of her career has been spent in the human resources departments of Fortune 100 companies (Mars, Disney, and Kraft). Her areas of interest include high-performance work teams (both public and private sectors), change management, and team building. She received an M.B.A. from the University of Southern California and a B.A. in Business Administration from the University of Minnesota Duluth.

GAINING A COMPETITIVE EDGE THROUGH PSYCAP

In today's competitive work environment, employers need to find innovative and creative ways to gain and maintain a competitive advantage. One such way currently being explored is gaining a competitive advantage through human resources. This competitive edge has been termed **Psychological Capital (PsyCap)** and is defined as a positive psychological state that is characterized by a person displaying several key attributes.

The recent volatility in the economy has forced the corporate world to change dramatically through acquisitions, mergers, and business closures. It has left current and prospective employees with a generally lower level of commitment, loyalty, and feeling of ownership. In order for employers to maximize their competitive advantage now and in the future, they need to find ways to capitalize on "PsyCap." When done correctly, this can affect work performance and profitability.

An important prerequisite for PsyCap is the study of positive psychology—the study of how to help healthy people become happier. What separates positive

Fred Luthans, Carolyn M. Youssef, and Bruce J. Avolio. *Psychological Capital: Developing the Human Competitive Edge.* New York: Oxford University Press, 2007.

psychology from the latest trend or fad is that it bases its conclusions on science. From positive psychology two parallel and important movements have begun. These are:

1. **Positive organizational scholarship (POS)**, which focuses on the macro-organizational level and deals with attributes such as compassion. These traits may not be open to development or even relate to an individual's performance.
2. **Positive organizational behavior (POB)**, which focuses on the micro-individual level and deals with positive attributes that can be developed and directly relate to an individual's work performance.

Recent focus has been on POB in order to develop and maintain a competitive edge through human resources. For an attribute to be identified as a POB, the scientific research approach is used to ensure the attribute meets specific criteria. It must be:

- Theory based
- Measurable
- Developmental
- Positively related to work performance

FOUR ELEMENTS OF POB

Several positive attributes have been considered for inclusion in POB, but four have been identified that best meet the criteria. These are self-efficacy, hope, optimism, and resiliency. Each one not only impacts individual performance on its own but may work in concert for an even greater impact. Additionally, these attributes appear to improve with relatively short but focused training and development efforts, which is very appealing to most organizations.

Self-efficacy

This is the confidence that one will be successful given difficult circumstances. In addition to having various levels of confidence or "self-efficacy" in specific areas of one's life, an individual can have a generalized level as well. There are five key discoveries regarding efficacy:

1. It is area specific. For example, a manager may be very confident when giving positive feedback, but much less confident talking with one who is having performance issues.
2. Areas practiced and mastered lead to high levels of efficacy. Utilizing the example above, the manager may have given many positive performance evaluations and very few requiring giving constructive feedback.
3. It can be improved even within an area of high confidence.
4. It is influenced by others.
5. It can be variable, and influenced by things within and outside an individual's control. For example, by acquiring skills, abilities, and knowledge in a subject area, one's efficacy can be enhanced. On the other hand, a serious illness can detract from efficacy.

CHARACTERISTICS OF EMPLOYEES WITH EFFICACY   People with high levels of confidence or efficacy typically exhibit five distinct characteristics. They:

1. Set challenging goals that require themselves to grow, and they choose to participate in difficult tasks.
2. Consistently look for challenges.

3. Are highly self-motivated.
4. Put forth the necessary effort to reach goals.
5. Persevere despite difficult conditions and early failures.

COGNITIVE PROCESSES NECESSARY FOR EFFICACY   Five cognitive processes necessary for developing high levels of efficacy are as follows:

1. Ability to "see" the desired outcome ("symbolizing"), analyze how to get there, and use this knowledge for future interactions.
2. Ability to plan future actions based on the expected outcomes ("forethought").
3. Ability to learn from observing mentors in similar situations and internalize it for one's own use.
4. Ability to set goals and standards for oneself and to determine where one stands in relation to them.
5. Ability to reflect on past performance, successes, and failures and learn from them.

Research has shown that self-efficacy and work performance are strongly related. Of particular interest to organizations, self-efficacy can be developed through work experience, learning opportunities, social situations, feedback, day-to-day life experiences, and self-reflection. There have been four major identified sources of efficacy and ways in which they can be developed.

FOUR SOURCES OF SELF-EFFICACY DEVELOPMENT   Self-efficacy can be developed through:

1. Experiencing success on tasks important to the area in which one wants to build it. This can be accomplished through various training scenarios and/or on-the-job experiences.
2. Participating in vicarious learning through observing coworkers attaining success (or failure) in the desired area and reflecting and internalizing them.
3. Receiving positive feedback and individual recognition.
4. Having a positive emotional state and a generally positive sense of well-being.

In addition to developing an employee's level of self-confidence, an organization can look to build the organization's collective confidence through use of cross-functional teams, shared goals, and collaborative decision making.

Hope

This is the optimistic belief that challenging goals can be successfully achieved, and if one way doesn't work another one will. Early research supports a positive relationship between hope, work performance, and profitability. Hope can be developed through several approaches, including the following:

- Effective goal setting (joint goal setting where goals are internalized and the individual is allowed to determine the means to achieve them).
- Presence of goals that are realistically attainable but require the individual to "stretch" (go above and beyond).
- Breaking large goals down into manageable pieces ("stepping"). This allows employees to experience success and develop a belief that the larger goal can be reached.

- Involvement in decision making. By allowing employees to participate in decision making and giving them the freedom to determine *how* to achieve the organization's goals, they experience successes that can translate to other experiences.
- In addition, employees are likely to have a higher degree of hope if they believe that they have an appropriate reward system, have necessary resources available to them, are well matched to their jobs, and have training and development experiences available that focus on building employee strengths that can easily be applied to a variety of situations.

Optimism

This is the belief that positive events will happen now and in the future, and the reasons for those events are permanent and attributed to one's actions. An optimistic employee uses this belief system to explain why positive things happen and also believes negative events are caused externally, are temporary, and are situational. These employees believe they have the power and control to perform successfully despite the temporary setbacks.

On the other hand, pessimistic employees will attribute positive performance to factors outside their control and as the result of pure luck, and negative performance to the failure of other employees, or low expectations of supervisors. Pessimistic employees will continue to believe they have little power and control over positive events and believe these events are unlikely to happen in the future.

POTENTIAL DOWNSIDE OF OPTIMISM   At the extreme, using blind optimism to explain events can lead to undesirable consequences. These include:

- Exposing employees, coworkers, and organizations to higher risk.
- Underestimating the consequences of a risky action.
- Failing to learn from mistakes.

Additionally, extremely optimistic individuals may falsely believe they control the outcome of all events if they just work hard enough. At the extreme these individuals cannot correctly analyze negative events as external to themselves and will suffer both psychologically and physically.

In order to avoid these potential pitfalls, the employee needs to be able to use "flexible-optimism" and "realistic optimism" approaches where the individual analyzes the situation and appropriately utilizes the optimistic or pessimistic style to explain a given situation.

Optimistic employees welcome change and work toward maximizing that change for the good of the organization. Because they believe they greatly influence their performance, optimistic employees tend to be more flexible, adaptable, proactive, and independent.

Optimistic leaders are more effective than pessimistic ones by being more effective interpersonally, more able to utilize relevant information to make better decisions, and more flexible when faced with roadblocks. They are realistic and know what risks to take and when to take them. They can act independently and understand their strengths and vulnerabilities. They take responsibility for their actions and work hard to develop their subordinates to build their own realistic, flexible, optimistic approach.

DEVELOPING OPTIMISM   Optimism can be developed by either enhancing a currently optimistic style or altering a pessimistic style. For example, employees can learn to

1. Forgive the past.
2. Acknowledge or appreciate the present.
3. Recognize future opportunities.

Resiliency

This is the ability to bounce back and encourage/inspire others to bounce back in the face of extreme adversity or from positive occurrences such as quick business growth.

Several factors have been identified as contributing to or hindering the development of resiliency. These are as follows:

- Resiliency assets. These include "cognitive abilities, temperament, positive self-perceptions, faith, positive outlook, emotional stability, self-regulation, insight, independence, relationship initiative, creativity, humor and morality." When these are present, individuals and groups of individuals are more likely to develop and demonstrate resiliency when faced with adverse conditions.
- Resiliency risk factors. These are elements that cause an increased probability of an unwanted outcome. These risk factors can take several forms such as substance abuse, exposure to violence, stress, unemployment, and so on. Since each individual experiences these risk factors differently, the mere presence of them does not always lead to a lack of resiliency. By using the resiliency assets identified above these risks can be overcome and may actually allow an individual or group of individuals to identify potential that they didn't know they had. Resiliency assets and risk factors work together to determine overall resiliency.

DEVELOPING RESILIENCY   Several strategies have been identified to develop resiliency in the workplace. These include increasing the perceived and/or actual level of assets and resources to positively affect outcomes, looking for ways to prevent/reduce risk factors that lead to undesirable outcomes rather than avoiding them, and developing systems and processes that can adapt to the situation at hand and identifying the effective mix of assets in order to manage various risk factors.

RESILIENT LEADERS AND EMPLOYEES   Leaders play a key role helping their employees to become resilient. By utilizing transformational leadership skills, leaders can help their subordinates learn to view challenges as opportunities and can help them take charge of their future. Leaders do this by encouraging open communications, building trust, developing employees, and giving them the necessary independence to encourage them to feel they make an impact and their work has meaning.

RESILIENT ORGANIZATIONS   A resilient organization is able to bounce back from setbacks and extreme adversity. Similar to resilient individuals, the organization must utilize its assets, manage its risk, and have effective processes in place to determine the effective mix of assets to employ in order to manage these risks.

Other processes have been shown to affect/enhance organizational resiliency. These include developing a strategy (goals and objectives), aligning the strategy within the organization, and being aware of the corporate culture. Allowing employees to participate in decision making also enhances organizational resiliency as the employees feel they have a stake in the outcome.

POTENTIAL PSYCAPS

Recent research has identified four additional broadly defined categories as potential PsyCaps. While these do not meet all the criteria (theory based, measurable, developmental, and related to work performance) for inclusion as PsyCaps yet, they are worth mentioning. The four categories are cognitive processes (creativity and wisdom), affective/emotional (subjective well-being, flow, and humor), social (gratitude, forgiveness, emotional intelligence, and spirituality), and higher order (authenticity and courage).

Conclusion

With today's fierce competition between organizations and the high levels of volatility in the economy, organizations need to explore innovative ways to differentiate their businesses from those of the competition. While the PsyCaps of self-efficacy, hope, optimism, and resiliency best meet the scientific criteria for inclusion, several others are promising. Psychological capital appears to be a powerful and promising option for today's organizations.

Why Pride Matters More than Money

Jon R. Katzenbach

Summary Prepared by AnneMarie Kaul

AnneMarie Kaul is the Development Director for the North Central Chapter of the Arthritis Foundation in St. Paul, Minnesota. She previously served as the Donor Recruitment Manager for the North Central Blood Region of the American Red Cross in St. Paul, Minnesota. She also has several years of experience managing financial services operational departments. Her business expertise has been in the areas of leadership and customer service. She has a B.A. from the University of Minnesota Duluth and an M.B.A. from the University of St. Thomas in St. Paul, Minnesota.

Pride can be the key to unlocking the motivational spirit of any employee at any level and within virtually any enterprise. At the base of this building of pride is emotion. More specifically, it is critical to obtain the emotional commitment of associates, which in turn can lead to both positive and negative forms of motivation. The positive form of motivation is called institutional-building pride and the negative form is self-serving pride.

Companies that rely solely on monetary incentives to motivate employees will only realize short-term successes, because they are not taking advantage of the easily accessible building of pride that is a powerful motivating force. *Enterprises today must move beyond egos and monetary incentives to sustain not only employee satisfaction but also economic performance and long-term growth.*

WHY INSTITUTIONAL-BUILDING PRIDE WORKS

In the long run, a person who is allowed to pursue worthwhile goals and endeavors will be more motivated to work harder than a person only receiving monetary incentives. When associates take pride in their work, their job satisfaction increases, their productivity is higher, and the enterprise ultimately is more likely to succeed.

Jon R. Katzenbach. *Why Pride Matters More than Money: The Power of the World's Greatest Motivational Force.* New York: Crown Business, 2003.

One of the best reasons for using pride as a motivator is that it can be quickly learned and easily applied. Before leaders use pride to motivate, it is important that they understand the other reasons why instilling pride works so well to motivate others.

- The skills and knowledge for instilling pride are mostly teachable and can be readily learned.
- Pride begets pride; there is a closed loop of energy linking pride to work performance. The anticipation of higher performance feels good and generates the emotional commitment to obtain better results.
- The fundamental correlation between pride and performance can be found in any company that depends on humans.
- Leaders don't have to wait for real success before instilling pride in others. They can tap into past accomplishments as well as future expectations to trigger emotions.

DIFFERENCES BETWEEN SELF-SERVING PRIDE AND INSTITUTIONAL PRIDE

In companies that consistently perform better than their competition, pride is a primary driver of their higher performance. There is clear evidence indicating that in traditional larger companies, managers who instill pride also have better economic and market performance than their competitors.

Both categories of pride—self-serving and institutional building—can be a factor in the production of good and bad results, but typically self-serving pride only produces short-term success.

Self-Serving Pride

Self-serving pride is all about power and money. The individual's thought process goes something like this: "The more you can earn, the more visible you are, the more powerful and well-off you become." Power and control are believed to be all-important, so typically a person who is motivated by this type of influence will switch allegiances such that there is no loyalty or commitment to the company. However, there *are* some advantages of self-serving pride, especially in situations such as in individual sports. Monetary awards not only serve as indicators of talent and achievement but are also a simple way to distinguish between performers and nonperformers.

Institutional-Building Pride

This type of pride is based on the character and emotional commitment of associates. With institutional-building pride, people are motivated to help others and work for the good of the enterprise. They place their efforts on more basic performance factors such as customer satisfaction, peer and mentor approval, developmental opportunities, and quality of work. These in turn build self-worth, group cohesion, and personal developmental happiness—factors that lead to success.

When further comparing the two types of pride, it is important to note that institutional pride has real strength because it can work across different types of organizations, even in companies where money is not a realistic source of motivation. For example, organizations such as the U.S. Marine Corps and Kentucky Fried Chicken (KFC) have been very successful, because they have integrated institutional-building pride into the workplace. It has been demonstrated over and over again that money may attract and keep people, but it does not motivate them to excel. At the end of the day, it is the feeling of pride (self-serving or institutional building) that prompts employees to do well.

SOURCES OF INSTITUTIONAL PRIDE

Institutional pride can come from many sources. The primary origins fall into three main categories—work results, work processes, and coworkers/supervisors.

- **Pride in the results of one's work.** This is often exhibited when employees feel good about what they have accomplished. This can arise from the product or service delivered or the kind of work done.
- **Pride in how work is done.** Employees can take pride in "doing something right." This refers to the set of values, standards, work ethic, and commitment that is applied to one's job.
- **Pride in coworkers and supervisors.** The people that an employee works with—supervisors, subordinates, or peers—can all provide job satisfaction.

Given the fact that these sources of "good" pride can be easily directed and controlled by leaders within corporations (as opposed to money), institutional-building pride should be the primary source of pride for the broader base of employees. *It is important to remember that what motivates upper-level executives is very different from what motivates frontline employees, especially during difficult times.*

Why is this true? Top executives not only possess the business savvy in terms of schooling in business fundamentals, typically their individual goals are stated in terms of economic results and market share. As a result, their motivation is a function of performance logic and many rational factors. On the other hand, at lower levels, simple emotional factors from everyday occurrences are more important as a motivating source because on the front line, the performance statistics of the company are often less meaningful. The six most important nonfinancial elements of enterprise success that influence *all* associates are:

- Local company reputation
- Product/service attributes
- Customer satisfaction
- Work group composition
- Peer approval
- Competitive position

The good news is that these sources of pride result in the emotional commitment that motivates employees, leading to enterprise-wide success. Understanding the motivational differences between the top and the other levels of an organization is a critical challenge, but it can be learned. The enterprises that excel at engaging emotions, employ leaders who are masters at cultivating institutional-building pride.

THE FIVE PATHS TO HIGHER PERFORMANCE

There are five distinct applications or paths that motivate higher-performing groups in companies that have successfully developed emotional commitment.

- **Mission, Values, and Collective Pride (MVP)**—This is where companies use their rich histories of past accomplishments to instill pride.

- **Process and Metrics (P&M)**—Delivering value by measuring the right things and maintaining effective processes is a powerful source of pride.
- **Entrepreneurial Spirit (ES)**—High-risk/high-reward opportunities typically provide motivational direction on this path.
- **Individual Achievement (IA)**—Individual performance and personal advancement, rather than team performance, are the primary motivational sources.
- **Recognition and Celebration (R&C)**—Giving recognition and holding celebrations and special events are used to motivate others.

All of these paths lead to an emotionally committed workforce, which leads to a higher level of performance. Companies that desire to sustain an emotionally committed environment will be more successful if they integrate two of these paths, rather than concentrating on one. But what if you work for a company that does not appear to comprehend these concepts? What can a leader do as an individual to motivate the workforce?

IDEAS FOR INDIVIDUALS NOT IN AN INSTITUTIONAL-BUILDING COMPANY ENVIRONMENT

What if the company you work for is not a well-established enterprise—one whose size, market position, and growth prospects are not highly attractive? A manager in this situation can use the case study results of General Motors to identify successful key motivating features. The following three methods are not only useful but also easy to apply:

1. *Keep it simple.* Use one or two concentrated themes and place great significance on local sources of pride that employees can easily understand.
2. *Develop one's own unique pride-building formula.* Strong pride-influenced managers should connect to their employees in any way they can (e.g., by tapping into their pride in the community, pride in their families, and pride in a legacy).
3. *Make pride a priority.* Using pride on an everyday basis to motivate is the key to obtaining long-term results.

Pride-building people are aware that instilling pride along the way is the *only way* to gain long-term success from it. Therefore, it is more important for people to be proud of what they are doing every day than it is for them to be proud of accomplishing their goals and getting the wanted results. Good leaders appeal to emotions rather than rational compliance; that is why their internal compass is always pointing to pride.

Conclusion

The really good news is that a person does not have to work for a **peak performance** enterprise to experience pride and the motivation that comes with it. Institutional-building pride motivates people in almost any environment—from top-performing firms to traditional organizations to financially challenged companies.

The ability to instill pride can be learned and utilized, just like any basic performance management technique. What a manager must look out for, however, is trying to motivate employees solely by using sources that are more self-serving like monetary incentives and ego building. While money is economically necessary, it does not motivate one to excel in the long run. When a manager uses institutional-building pride sources, such as recognition, accomplishments, entrepreneurship, or team support, the general population of the workforce, especially people on the front line, is more likely to produce consistent and high-quality results.

At the base of pride-instilling motivation is emotional commitment. Employees want to feel connected to the cause, like providing the best customer service or not letting the team down. It is this connectedness to an overall objective that gives institutional-building pride its powerful force. *Managers must think beyond the compensation package.*

There are many peak-performing enterprises, such as KFC, General Motors, and the Marine Corps, that have clearly demonstrated that motivating by pride can lead to successful results. We should continue to look at these organizations for guidance. Pride is a powerful motivating force—one that has proven to result in improved success.

PART VII

Leadership

Leadership has been a popular and enduring theme in the twenty-first century. Notably in the recent U.S. presidential elections, voters seemed to be looking for the hero who can turn the country around, establish a new direction instill hope and create change, and pull us through tough times. Organizations, too, are searching for visionary leaders—people who by the strength of their personalities can bring about a major organizational transformation. We hear calls for charismatic, transformational, and visionary leadership. Innumerable individuals charge that the problems with the U.S. economy, declining organizational productivity, and lost ground in worldwide competitive markets are largely a function of the lack of good organizational leadership.

What do good leaders do? What do bad leaders do? What is the proper role for followers? What are the lessons provided by classic leaders such as Abraham Lincoln? These are some of the key questions addressed in the four readings in this section.

Leadership for Everyone, by Peter J. Dean, introduces the L.E.A.D.E.R.S. Method. This acronym reminds managers to Listen to learn, Empathize with emotions, Attend to aspirations, Diagnose and detail, Engage for good ends, Respond with respectfulness, and Speak with specificity. Dean suggests that leadership self-development is possible if individuals use their everyday opportunities to practice these seven skills. However, it requires personal courage, honesty, humility, and persistent commitment to make it work. Peter Dean holds the O. Alfred Granum Chair in Management at the American College. He is the recipient of numerous awards for teaching excellence, the author of several papers, and a consultant to many Fortune 500 companies.

Barbara Kellerman received her Ph.D. from Yale University and subsequently held professorships at Fordham, Tufts, Fairleigh Dickinson, and George Washington Universities. She is currently the James MacGregor Burns Lecturer in Public Leadership at Harvard University's John F. Kennedy School of Government. Before writing *Bad Leadership* and *Followership*, she published three previous books on leadership in the public sector.

Bad Leadership dispels the simplistic notion that all leadership is positive. Bad leaders can be either ineffective (inappropriate means or ends) or unethical (failure to distinguish right and wrong). Kellerman identifies seven types of bad leadership: incompetent, rigid, intemperate, callous, corrupt, insular, and evil. She proceeds to identify a wide variety of ways in which leaders can improve their behavior, and tactics for followers to engage in self-help. In short, bad leaders can still become good leaders if they are willing to attempt making personal changes.

In *Followership*, Kellerman suggests that we often fixate on leaders and believe that they have more power than they actually do. If followers are studied closely, we will discover that there are five major types arranged on a continuum of engagement: isolates, bystanders, participants, activists, and diehards. As with leaders, there are both bad followers and good followers. The latter can be agents of change, should always do something, can join with others to create change, and should support good leadership.

Doris Kearns Goodwin holds a doctorate from Harvard University, has taught courses on the American Presidency, and has served on the Board of Directors for Northwest Airlines. She won a Pulitzer Prize in 1995 for her book on Franklin and Eleanor Roosevelt, and she has also published biographies on the Kennedys and Lyndon Johnson.

Goodwin's newest book, *Team of Rivals*, has reportedly found its way onto President Obama's reading list. This book examines how President Lincoln skillfully soothed the egos of several former rivals by placing them on his cabinet. William Seward became his secretary of state, Salmon Chase was in charge of the treasury, and Edward Bates was named as the attorney general. Over time, these bitter losers grew to admire and respect Lincoln. The inexperienced president acknowledged and learned from his mistakes, let go of old grudges, and sought and accepted the wise counsel of his advisors. In short, he was inclusive, and this was essential to his success during the Civil War.

Leadership for Everyone

Peter J. Dean

Summary Prepared by Rebecca M. C. Boll

Rebecca M. C. Boll *is employed with Central Minnesota Federal Credit Union (CMFCU) as a Financial Analyst with responsibilities for asset–liability management, financial analysis, competitive analysis, and strategic analysis. Prior to joining CMFCU, Boll worked as an Equity Research Analyst at Piper Jaffray; during her tenure, she covered Medical Device & Diagnostic companies in the health-care sector. Ms. Boll received her B.B.A. in Organizational Management and Finance from the Labovitz School of Business and Economics (LSBE) at the University of Minnesota Duluth. During her undergraduate career, she participated in the LSBE Financial Markets Program and in the University's Undergraduate Research Opportunities Program, resulting in a paper entitled "Interorganizational Trust: Trust, Routines, & Institutionalization." For recreation, she enjoys spending time with friends and family, traveling, and participating in outdoor activities.*

HOW TO LEAD

Everyday interactions are opportunities to lead, and all members of an organization may establish themselves as leaders, teachers, and/or mentors. These leaders will then be viewed as proactive and effective contributors to any effort/team in which they participate. There are increased numbers of opportunities for individuals to practice leadership because organizations are changing from formal to cross-functional, there are fewer managerial ranks, and the percentage of knowledge workers has increased. Managers, or "everyday leaders," have the adaptability and flexibility to become forward-looking in order to put today's actions in a strategic context. By embracing self-development and responsiveness, everyday leaders put aside their personal and internal distractions in order to be receptive to others. Further, when they effectively manage their emotions and put their self-concept

Peter J. Dean. *Leadership for Everyone: How to Apply the Seven Essential Skills to Become a Great Motivator, Influencer, and Leader.* New York: McGraw-Hill, 2006.

aside in order to respond objectively, quiet leaders will emerge on an organization-wide basis. In order to become an everyday leader, managers should practice seven essential skills.

L.E.A.D.E.R.S. METHOD

Everyday leaders should practice the L.E.A.D.E.R.S. Method because it contains the skills necessary for them to become effective in today's organizational setting. It is an acronym for the seven critical leadership skills, including Listen to learn, Empathize with emotions, Attend to aspirations, Diagnose and detail, Engage for good ends, Respond with respectfulness, and Speak with specificity. On a daily basis and during typical interactions with others, everyday leaders should receive feedback, assess and analyze it, and then give feedback. Receiving feedback includes listening, empathizing, and attending to the aspirations of others. Assessing and analyzing the situation includes diagnosing and detailing, while giving feedback is comprised of engaging for good ends, responding with respectfulness, and speaking with specificity.

Receiving Feedback

To receive feedback efficiently and effectively, everyday leaders should listen to learn, empathize with emotions, and attend to aspirations. When these elements of feedback are practiced together, everyday leaders will interpret a situation realistically and strive for complete understanding. Receiving feedback using these three critical leadership skills sets the stage for the assessment and analysis process, which includes diagnosing the situation and detailing it prior to give constructive feedback.

LISTEN TO LEARN   Everyday leaders should first listen to learn in everyday interactions in order to capitalize on their opportunity to lead. By using active listening, managers will be leading in a collaborative and comprehensive style, increasing their own and their group's ability to engage in two-way learning. Active listening includes not only hearing what is said but also recognizing the other's tone, having an open mind, and avoiding distractions. In order to listen to learn, everyday leaders must acknowledge the following prerequisites:

- monitor self-awareness and practice self-regulation,
- become aware of their own and others' intellectual and emotional capacity,
- have the courage to hear conflict as creative energy,
- demonstrate a willingness to deal with problems, and
- indicate one has the ability to work toward a joint understanding.

Active listeners must learn the barriers to active listening so they do not jump to conclusions. This also allows them time to check for understanding. Barriers to active listening include lacking self-discipline or objectivity, becoming overemotional, missing tone, faking attention, and listening only for the next time one may speak. When putting these listening principles into action, everyday leaders will be demonstrating respect verbally, vocally, and visually, for they will be using eye contact, facing the speaker, assessing the whole message, minimizing interruptions, reducing filters, and using pauses effectively. Other actions everyday leaders may take in order to listen to learn include clarifying, restating, encouraging, justifying, and summarizing others' messages. Everyday leaders will be able to critically diagnose the situation and make an appropriate decision. Rewards for active listening include the following:

- learning extensively about the current situation,
- codifying thoughts,
- solving problems,
- making productive decisions, and
- gaining confidence in everyday leadership.

Once an everyday leader genuinely listens, he or she is one step closer to showing empathy, the next step in the L.E.A.D.E.R.S. Method.

EMPATHIZE WITH EMOTIONS   During their everyday interactions, everyday leaders should also empathize with others' emotions. Having listened to learn, everyday leaders will have gained an understanding that will allow them to empathize with the emotions of others and not judge them. Empathy includes considering others' needs, feelings, and emotions by aligning one's own feelings with the other person's, creating openness and acceptance. Everyday leaders also know that by offering empathy they are not showing sympathy, which implies a perception of helplessness. Everyday leaders, well versed in the four areas of emotional intelligence (self-awareness, self-management, empathy, and social/relationship management) and on the eight categories of emotions (anger, sadness, fear, enjoyment, love, surprise, disgust, and shame), are well equipped to use this skill. To empathize with emotions, everyday leaders should:

- recognize emotions by assessing verbal and nonverbal cues,
- reflect on the emotion in a nonthreatening way,
- show the other person that he or she is understood,
- move the conversation to address and resolve the emotion,
- tune out distractions,
- identify feelings you think the person is experiencing,
- probe the other person to reveal the cause of his or her feelings,
- respond with empathetic comments, and
- ask the other person to clarify if needed.

Once the everyday leader has empathized with the other's emotions by seeking to know the area of emotional distress and then learning, reflecting, and paraphrasing the emotion itself, he or she will be able to discuss the content that has become overshadowed by the emotion. This content will provide an opportunity for everyday leaders to attend to the person's aspirations.

ATTEND TO ASPIRATIONS   The final component of receiving feedback is attending to aspirations. Everyday leaders should cultivate a productive work environment by fostering people's natural tendency to grow. Limitations decrease productivity and creativity, leading people to leave the company if they feel their professional and personal growth is being hindered. People will feel secure and, therefore, more likely to increase their productivity if they are allowed to aspire within a conducive environment. In order to attend to aspirations, roadblocks that need to be overcome include the following:

- lack of clear vision, mission, or values in an organization,
- misalignment of employees' values with that of the organization, and
- misunderstanding others' levels of need.

Once these roadblocks have been overcome through listening to learn, empathizing with emotions, and attending to aspirations, everyday leaders attend to others as individuals because they understand that each person's needs and motivations may differ. Recalling Maslow's hierarchy of needs, we realize that many never reach self-actualization because they are too busy tending to their other needs such as food, drink, sex, safety, love, and esteem. Highly self-actualized people assimilate work into their self-identity, and everyday leaders can facilitate this process by aspiring toward goals of growth and development, increasing responsibility, and providing a conducive work environment for others to do the same. How exactly does an everyday leader attend to aspirations, so work is integrated into one's self-identity?

- Be conscious of individual people's ability, education, background, motivations, and goals.
- Allow members to participate in decision making and make suggestions through constructive feedback in order to set challenging work goals.
- Facilitate trust formation among organizational members.

A key part of attending to aspirations is giving and receiving feedback in order to engage in participative decision-making and goal setting. When giving feedback, everyday leaders avoid excess and blindness, which is presuming we know what's best for the other person. Guidelines everyday leaders live by when giving and receiving feedback include:

1. Giving feedback
   - accept self and others,
   - gauge the receiver's readiness and create immediacy,
   - be descriptive,
   - don't state the obvious,
   - give feedback on what can be changed and don't overload the receiver, and
   - share experiences with the receiver.
2. Receiving feedback
   - state what you want feedback on,
   - check what you heard,
   - share your reactions to what you heard,
   - utilize it to improve, and
   - discount destructive feedback.

Moreover, success is based on the commitment of everyday leaders who focus on the person and intrinsic rewards even if the organization structure focuses on extrinsic rewards. Their focus is on goal setting and constructive feedback in order to push forward.

Assessing and Analyzing

Now that an everyday leader has received a clear picture of the situation, he or she is ready to assess and analyze the **feedback** through diagnosing and detailing by shifting to a cognitive mode within the L.E.A.D.E.R.S. Method. Everyday leaders need to sort through the information they gathered during listening to learn, empathizing with emotions, and attending to aspirations in order to give constructive feedback.

DIAGNOSE AND DETAIL   Within the workplace, one key way everyday leaders apply the process of diagnosing and detailing is during performance improvement. They seek out knowledge to narrow the gap between existing and ideal performance by using diagnostic questions to uncover areas that need more detail. First, they will identify the accomplishment by determining if it is caused by a specific behavior and then by comparing it to the end purpose of the job. Once this has been completed, everyday leaders will apply the three criteria of an accomplishment. Questions they may ask during diagnosis include:

- Is the accomplishment a measurable quality, quantity, or cost?
- Is the accomplishment observable?
- Is the accomplishment reliable, whereby two or more observers come to the same conclusion?

Everyday leaders should also practice the following 10 subskills associated with detailing when sorting through the feedback they received:

- discern what is expected and what is observed;
- question without being threatening;
- reinforce what you want to have happen again;
- make sure you and the other person are ready, willing, and able to have the conversation;
- ensure the consequences are clearly understood;
- align yourself verbally, vocally, and visually to the message;
- make sure the person understands what needs to be done;
- probe for chronic problems;
- deflect sudden changes in emotion; and
- paraphrase complexity by addressing the emotion first and the complexity second.

By implementing these 10 detailing skills and applying the three criteria of an accomplishment during diagnosis, everyday leaders will determine the root causes of a situation, leading to joint understanding, participative decision making, and cooperative goal setting. Everyday leaders are now prepared to give feedback by engaging for good ends, responding with respectfulness, and speaking with specificity.

Giving Feedback

Giving constructive feedback begins with engaging for good ends, which includes ethical decision making. When everyday leaders respond with respectfulness, they create openness while maintaining consideration for the other person's rights. Finally, when responding with respectfulness, everyday leaders align their remarks verbally, vocally, and visually in order to speak with specificity.

ENGAGE FOR GOOD ENDS   Three enemies in the workplace include egoism, relativism, and lack of freedom of speech. Rejection of ethical egoism implies there is a nonegoistic foundation for judging right from wrong. Regarding relativism, certain universal principles transcend local customs. Everyday leaders challenge others by practicing freedom of speech, as well as by implementing ethics and professional integrity. They will also maintain motivation by applying policy consistently and practicing concern for others. Engaging for good ends includes everyday leaders maintaining and creating balance between standards of virtue such as integrity, productivity, and responsibility.

- Integrity involves fair play with a sense of justice and actions to establish long-term relationships.
- Productivity is prudent competence at work to achieve goals.
- Responsibility is characterized by the fortitude to practice courage and overcome fear in order to keep promises.

Everyday leaders must also internalize the universal rules and utilitarianism. Universal rules include the principle of universality (your action becomes universal law), principle of reversibility (treat others as you wish to be treated), and principle of respect for persons. Everyday leaders should also practice utilitarianism by considering which action produces the greatest good for whom. By examining consequences, resolving conflicts of interest, and recognizing primary stakeholders, everyday leaders maintain confidentiality, provide truth, use power correctly, and deny inappropriate requests. Further, everyday opportunities to apply this skill include cases involving employee rights, sexual harassment, whistle blowing, selection, termination, evaluations, safety, quality control, and environmental protection. Overall, engaging for good ends includes everyday leaders practicing ethical decision making by:

- listing the facts and defining the issues on all organizational levels,
- identifying all relevant stakeholders,
- determining possible alternatives,
- acknowledging implications for each alternative,
- considering practical constraints, and
- deciding which action should be taken.

RESPOND WITH RESPECTFULNESS   Once everyday leaders have engaged for good ends through ethical decision making, they will respond with respectfulness. When everyday leaders respond respectfully to others, they behave in ways that honor the other's intrinsic worth, are sensitive to power differences, resolve all conflicts honestly, create a good reputation for dependability, and practice courage in upholding these standards. Everyday leaders also minimize prejudice by speaking to increase the ethical and social contact among alien groups, by responding with a climate of equality, by vigilantly communicating to increase a positive attitude, and by practicing consciousness-raising techniques in all conversations. Individuals' behavioral responses can be categorized as people focused, task focused, control focused, or image focused. Everyday leaders strive to do the following at appropriate times:

- meet the human and social needs while providing an opportunity for personal growth (people focused),
- focus on continuous improvement and teamwork while thinking strategically (task focused),
- get results by taking control and being urgent while charging into action (control focused), and
- provide worth and seek acceptance while striving to please others (image focused).

Everyday leaders' self-concepts increase when they become aware of how to shift among the four major behavioral responses, maximizing respectfulness in their responses. Further details of each type of everyday leaders are provided in the following paragraphs.

People-focused everyday leaders are socially skillful and demonstrate patience; however, they may not use time well and may even lose sight of their own course. They need preservation of the *status quo*, and their key tools include preparing before change, taking shortcuts, and receiving reassurance. Task-focused everyday leaders thoroughly examine the situation and follow methods; however, they may feel the effects of paralysis by analysis and may get stuck in their old ways. They need precision and ready access to facts, and their key tools include opportunities created by others and a standard methodology.

Control-focused everyday leaders are impatient and desire change; however, they move too fast and may take control where they shouldn't. They need difficult assignments and the opportunity to explain why they do what they do, and their key tools include opportunity for advancement and freedom from supervision. Image-focused everyday leaders guide in their sphere of influence through statements of principle and fairness and are willing to hear other people's positions; however, they may accept unreasonable demands and may not act in fear of losing approval. They need objectivity and democracy, and their key tools include popularity and public recognition of their ability.

Each type of everyday leader solves problems in a different way, and if one can learn to identify which situations warrant which type of problem solving, their leadership will be far reaching. While people-focused leaders solve problems by observing, implementing, researching, and applying, task-focused leaders analyze, investigate, evaluate, plan, and critique. Control-focused leaders problem solve by being pragmatic, exercising efficiency, and reacting competitively and in a domineering manner. Last, image-focused leaders' problem solving can be characterized by supportiveness, experimentation, trust, and instinct. Moreover, by honing the ability to identify when each type of leadership is most applicable to the problem at hand, managers will be able to respond with respectfulness.

SPEAK WITH SPECIFICITY   While responding with respectfulness, everyday leaders should align their remarks verbally, vocally, and visually in order to speak with specificity. All three should be considered because the spoken word reveals leadership by indicating what we know and don't know. When the verbal, vocal, and visual aspects of speaking are aligned, understanding is enhanced and confidence and credibility are projected. Everyday leaders know that while the verbal element (words) leads, the vocal and visual elements trail behind. Considerations for the verbal element include word choice, meaning, pronunciation, sentence arrangement, vivid language, structured repetition of the residual message, and avoiding the use of jargon.

The vocal element is "how" one says words, and everyday leaders should use proper breath support to vary their tone, volume, pace, and pitch. Alignment of this element with the other two improves believability and articulation while eliminating a monotone sound and nonwords. Everyday leaders know they are the visual aid. The visual element includes utilizing facial expressions and eye contact, which enhances everyday leaders' credibility and shows sincerity. Gestures, when used properly, also amplify words while a nonslouching posture shows dignity. Physical movement, dress, and humor also establish a good first impression and help build rapport. These are some behaviors that everyday leaders use to hold a listener's attention:

- Begin with the conclusions, so the listener knows where you are coming from.
- Translate the benefits as soon as possible.
- Use examples to repeat your point, using specific conversations.
- Avoid too many details.
- Don't overestimate the other person's knowledge.
- Consider the many meanings a word can have.
- Don't forget to listen, because communication is a cooperative effort.

Conclusion

Everyday leadership is about individuals finding ways to become influencers, mentors, and teachers. Managers are encouraged to become everyday leaders by following the L.E.A.D.E.R.S. Method, which is a map for everyone to practice leadership everyday. Applying these seven leadership skills in order to receive feedback accurately, diagnose and detail the information, and give constructive feedback, managers have the building blocks for being an everyday leader. *Through self-development, individuals can seize the potential in everyday interactions to apply these seven leadership skills in order to put their actions into a strategic context, aligning themselves with their group and their organization as a whole.*

Bad Leadership

Barbara Kellerman

Summary Prepared by Warren Candy

Warren Candy *was Senior Vice President for Allete/Minnesota Power, a diversified electric services company headquartered in Duluth, Minnesota, where he was responsible for the electric, water, gas, and coal business units in Minnesota, Wisconsin, and North Dakota. His interests include high-performance organizational systems, sustainable organizational design, leadership development, and sociotechnical systems implementation. He received his diploma in Production Engineering from Swinburne Institute of Technology in Melbourne, Australia.*

INTRODUCTION TO BAD LEADERSHIP

What does bad leadership mean? Is bad leadership automatically immoral or unethical? Or does it mean leadership that is incompetent or ineffective? What is to be done to maximize good leadership and minimize bad leadership? Can we fully understand the impact and role of leadership within our organizations without acknowledging its dark side? What role do followers play in supporting and enabling bad leadership? Why do people hold idealized visions of their leaders and defer power and control to them? Why do competent people sometimes behave badly when leading? Finally, can there ever be any form of "leadership" without "followership"?

Over the past several decades a "leadership industry" has developed within the United States that is based on the proposition that leadership, as a body of knowledge, is a subject that can be studied and a skill that can be learned by any and all people. To support this industry, definitions of leadership have evolved to the point where they are always undeniably positive and always have leaders as people of competence and character.

For example, in 1978, James MacGregor Burns stated that leadership occurs when people use resources to attain goals by engaging their followers and satisfying

Barbara Kellerman. *Bad Leadership: What It Is, How It Happens, Why It Matters.* Boston, MA: Harvard Business School Press, 2004.

their needs. Warren Bennis, in 1989, suggested that a leader creates shared meaning through integrative goals, speaks in a distinctive voice so as to differentiate himself or herself, exhibits the capacity to adapt, and demonstrates his or her integrity. John Gardner noted that leadership is different from coercion. People who use coercion are judged as bad.

Therefore, all "leadership" has become synonymous with "good" leadership. This should not be surprising since there is a natural preference to want to go through life accentuating the positive and eliminating the negative in order to be as healthy and happy as possible. Recognizing and accepting the negatives of human nature goes against this tendency and is not something we naturally or easily acknowledge.

However, we need to think more broadly about the concept of leadership, not so much as a "thing" to be learned, but as an integral part of the human condition. It has not only a positive side but also a "dark side," or in the context used here, a bad side!

Leadership is a complex interaction that needs to be thought of in shades of gray and black and in terms of how people actually go about exercising power, authority, and influence.

Additionally, we need to understand that *leadership does not exist in isolation* or in the abstract. Without followers there is no leadership; leaders and followers are interdependent. There cannot be "good" leadership without "good" followers or, conversely, bad leadership without bad followers.

WHAT IS BAD LEADERSHIP?

Often leaders are assumed to be all powerful and independent. However, we must remember that leaders do not act alone. A leader chooses a particular course of action and then in some way gets others to go along, or, more subtly, encourages the led to "choose" the course that the group will follow. That followers matter is a presumption that is now widely shared.

There's something odd about the idea that somehow leadership can be distinguished from coercion, as if leadership and power were unrelated. There is no leadership without followership. Leaders cannot lead unless followers follow, either passively or actively.

Two fundamental categories of bad leadership exist—ineffective and unethical. *Ineffective leaders* are generally judged ineffective because of the inappropriate means they employ (or the appropriate means that they fail to employ) rather than the ends they pursue. *Unethical leadership* occurs when people fail to distinguish between right and wrong. Ethical leaders put their followers' needs before their own; unethical leaders do not. Ethical leaders exemplify private virtues such as courage and temperance; unethical leaders do not. Ethical leaders exercise leadership in the interest of the common good; unethical leaders do not. Most people are familiar with ineffective and unethical leaders. These leaders tend to disappoint us because they are inept or corrupt, and not because they are inherently evil.

Bad Leadership

Bad leadership is mainly a result of leaders behaving poorly because of who they are and what they want, and then acting in ways that do harm. This harm can be intentional or can occur as a result of carelessness or neglect. Seven types of bad leadership have become prevalent in today's organizations: incompetent, rigid, intemperate, callous, corrupt, insular, and evil.

- Incompetent leadership—the leader and at least some followers lack the will or skill (or both) to sustain effective action or to create positive change.

- Rigid leadership—the leader and at least some followers are inflexible and unyielding. Although they may be competent, they are unable or unwilling to adapt to new ideas, new information, or changing times.
- Intemperate leadership—the leader lacks self-control and is aided and abetted by followers who are unwilling or unable effectively to intervene.
- Callous leadership—the leader and at least some followers are uncaring or unkind. Ignored or discounted are the needs, wants, and wishes of most members of the group or organization, especially subordinates.
- Corrupt leadership—the leader and at least some followers lie, cheat, or steal. To a degree that exceeds the norm, they put self-interest ahead of the public interest.
- Insular leadership—the leader and at least some followers minimize or disregard the health and welfare of "the other"—that is, those outside the group or organization for which they are directly responsible.
- Evil leadership—the leader and at least some followers commit atrocities. They use pain as an instrument of power. The harm done to men, women, and children is severe rather than slight. The harm can be physical, psychological, or both.

WHAT IS BAD FOLLOWERSHIP?

To fully understand the role of leadership in organizations of today, we must understand leadership as two contradictory things: good and bad. Just as we have bad leaders, we also have bad followers; just as we have good leaders, we have good followers.

Bad followers commit themselves to bad leaders. They do so knowingly and deliberately, and generally mirror bad leaders for a variety of complex reasons.

Good followers are true partners with leaders. They think independently, engage in self-direction and self-control, follow through on their own, and fulfill their responsibilities willingly.

Individual vs. Group Needs

People do not exist in organizations in isolation, so they are driven to satisfy a wide variety of both individual and group needs and expectations. Among the most compelling explanations for the willingness of followers to obey authority is the need that people have to *keep things simple.* Even bad leaders often satisfy the most basic human needs, in particular safety, simplicity, and certainty. Leaders, even bad ones, can provide a sense of order and certainty in a disordered and uncertain world. The construct of the leader itself is a manifestation of our preference for simple as opposed to complex explanations.

Groups also go along with bad leaders to gain important benefits for themselves collectively. Leaders maintain order, provide cohesion and identity, and do the collective work. Hierarchy, it turns out, is the natural order of things since as societies increase in size, they become even more dependent on leaders to order, organize, and carry out their collective activities. There will always be leaders, and there will always be those tasked with getting the group's work done.

For reasons that are now quite clear, followers have good and sound reasons for following, even when their leaders are bad. To meet their needs as individuals and a member of groups, followers usually conclude that it's in their interests to go with the flow.

FROM BAD TO BETTER, HOW LEADERS AND FOLLOWERS CAN IMPROVE

We cannot stop, slow, or change bad leadership by attempting to change human nature. Exhortations to do good works are often ineffective. And we cannot expect to reduce the number of bad leaders until we reduce the number of bad followers.

Leaders and followers will change only when they decide that it is in their best interest to do so. When the cost/benefit ratio of bad leadership tips in favor of good leadership, then change will occur!

From the research and analysis of many real-life examples of bad leadership specific actions have been identified that can be used by leaders and followers alike to limit, correct for, and prevent bad leadership and followership.

Ideas for Leadership Self-Help

- Share power and work with others collaboratively in meaningful ways.
- Don't believe your own hype: "For leaders, to buy their own publicity is the kiss of death."
- Get real, stay real, and stay in touch with reality.
- Compensate for your blind spots by acquiring in-depth knowledge, or support, in areas of weakness.
- Stay balanced, because balanced leaders develop healthier organizations, and make more thoughtful and effective decisions.
- Remember the mission, your reason for existence, and use it as your compass during difficult times.
- Stay healthy; physical and mental health are critical.
- Be reflective and develop self-knowledge, self-control, and good habits through quiet contemplation.
- Establish a culture of openness in which diversity and dissent are encouraged.
- Bring in advisers who are both strong and independent.
- Avoid groupthink, encourage healthy dissent, minimize excessive cohesiveness, and strive for frank and open discussions to realistically appraise alternative courses of action.
- Get reliable and complete information, and then disseminate it.
- Establish a system of checks and balances. For example, limit the tenure of leaders, rotate responsibilities, hold regular performance reviews, and use multiple metrics.
- Strive for stakeholder balance by connecting with all constituencies and not just a chosen few.

Ideas for Follower Self-Help

- Empower yourself to take action and don't merely "go along."
- Be loyal to the whole, and not to any single individual.
- Be skeptical, realizing that leaders are not gods and are subject to errors and omissions that need to be highlighted and discussed.
- Take a stand.

- Pay attention; do not contribute to bad leadership through deliberate or inadvertent inattention.
- Find allies, since there is always strength in numbers when working with other like-minded individuals.
- Develop your own sources of information to verify correct and complete information, remembering always that the interests of leaders and followers do not always coincide.
- Take collective action.
- Be a watchdog; do not abdicate responsibility for oversight and for minding the store.
- Hold leaders accountable to all stakeholders through transparency, open discussions, and meaningful participation.

Followership

Barbara Kellerman

Summary Prepared by Claudia PlauntMartin

Claudia PlauntMartin *has devoted much of her life to a career in education. She is currently the coordinator of the Tutoring Center at the University of Minnesota Duluth and is a fervent and a long-time proponent of education and its personal and far-reaching benefits. She has specific interest in human resources and the relationship between employee and customer satisfaction, and enjoys administering and analyzing divisional staff satisfaction surveys. She takes great pleasure in the fact that her children have inherited her love of education, as they have pursued formal education and careers in business, mathematics, and education.*

INTRODUCTION

Much energy, research, and resources have been devoted to the study of leaders and leadership. Even though the word "leader" assumes one or more followers, and the word "leadership" implies a relationship with those who would follow, *little effort has been put into exploring the characteristics of followers.* In part, the leader-centric approach, which has dominated thinking about the leader–follower connection, has contributed to the inferior image evoked by the word "follower."

All of us are both followers and leaders, sometimes simultaneously, and depending on the situation. It's no surprise that the line separating them is often blurred and that good leaders and good followers have many of the same characteristics. Followers can, however, be distinguished from leaders by examining their subordinate *rank* and understanding different degrees of their compliant *behavior.* This requires two key definitions:

Followers are subordinates who have less power, authority, and influence than do their superiors and who therefore usually, but not invariably, fall into line.

Barbara Kellerman. *Followership: How Followers Are Creating Change and Changing Leaders.* Boston, MA: Harvard Business Press, 2008.

Followership implies a relationship (rank) between subordinates and superiors, and a response (behavior) of the former to the latter.

SEEING FOLLOWERS

There are several reasons followers have been overlooked, resulting in an unclear picture of followers and what motivates them.

- The prevailing leader-centric view has its roots in the Revolutionary War, which gave birth to a stubborn individualism that emerged as the American ideal, and played perfectly to the economic allure of capitalism.
- The derogatory connotations that associate "follower" with passivity and dependence created a *fear of following*, which dissuaded those in the leadership field from fully exploring followership.
- Humans have a skewed view of leadership. The *great man theory* accounts for our tendency to believe that leaders alone dictate the course of human history.
- The finite capacity of the human brain causes us to simplify thoughts by *compartmentalizing*: we fixate on leaders because leaders help us order our world.
- The **leader attribution error** leads us to believe that leaders have more power to achieve results than they actually do and accounts for how successes and failures have been attributed to leaders throughout history without mention of the followers who carried out their orders.
- Leadership literature continues to focus on how leaders can produce an impact on followers without considering the reverse. By committing this *sin of omission*, researchers contribute to the conventional wisdom, which suggests leaders matter and followers do not.

Pressures from within and outside the field have shaped the study of leadership. Early leadership literature focused on traditional organizational hierarchies and dismissed followers. The focus began to shift after the holocaust of the World War II, when it became evident that those who obey orders play an equally important role as those who issue them. The new focus on followers prompted the first serious studies into the psychology of followers and why they follow.

The academic leadership field has begun to move away from the ancient hierarchical models, which assumed command and control, but it is still primarily leader-centric. Outside the field, however, there are indications that the balance of power and influence is shifting. Two significant changes during the last half century began to level the playing field between those with power, authority, and influence and those without.

1. *The World the Sixties Made*—The sociopolitical turmoil caused by the cultural revolution of the 1960s challenged authority and created irreversible changes to the existing order.
2. *The Information Revolution*—Knowledge is power; the information revolution built on the generational changes of the 1960s to disperse power away from leaders to followers. Its factors include:
   - The Internet, which promotes the idea that the many are smarter than the few.
   - Bloggers, who have become the reputational conduit of our time.
   - E-mail, which can be used as a "new force" to mobilize consumers and group members.
   - The Web, which puts small companies on equal footing with large competitors.
   - The Global Technology Phenomena, which spans countries and cultures without regard for traditional boundaries of any kind.

Even though followers have begun to assert themselves, power holders are generally unwilling to share, so power redistribution becomes a process in which *those with less power must persuade those with more to surrender some.*

- In the business world, vocal shareholders have taken up where labor unions left off and become the new bane of CEOs. Technological innovations have enabled activist shareholders to communicate, connect, and track vital information.
- A newfound sense that all people have the right to be heard has led those without obvious sources of power to demand change from their governments around the world.
- Leadership literature has begun to broaden its scope as leadership research considers followers.
- Leaders are paying more attention to followers in both defensive and proactive ways.

As followers move to the forefront by demanding and getting more power from their leaders, it is important to maintain perspective on the need for followers to follow. It is impossible for people in large numbers to govern themselves without structure (groups need a leader), just as it is impossible for everyone to be a leader (leaders need a group). The symbiotic leader–follower relationship is an arrangement that provides benefits to both. Obvious leader rewards include power, influence, status, and access to resources. In turn, individual followers are able to satisfy their need for social order, stability, security, and community. Leaders serve groups of followers by providing them with professional or personal satisfaction, structure, goals, and instruments of goal achievement.

As followers have become more visible, researchers have become more interested in defining who they are. A handful of writings by authors like Abraham Zaleznik, Robert Kelley, and Ira Chaleff identified different types of followers and categorized followership styles by plotting them on two-dimensional grids with various axes. While each author brings different perspectives to the issue of followership, the underlying concept of each view balances dominance on the one hand against deference on the other.

A less-cumbersome follower model presumes subordinate rank and some type of behavior. Five different types of followers are arranged on a *level of engagement* continuum that ranges from being completely disconnected on one end to being totally involved on the other. The following table identifies the five types of followers and categorizes them by their level of engagement, characteristics, potential consequences of their behavior (or lack of), and gives examples of each.

Type	Engagement	Characteristics	Consequence(s)	Example(s)
Isolates	Completely disengaged	Disinterested. Indifferent. Consciously opt out. Unmotivated.	Cede power to leaders. Their silence causes them to be ignored.	Eligible voters who never vote.
Bystanders	Conscious decision to disengage	Observe but don't participate. Neutral	Give tacit support to the *status quo.*	People who "look the other way" (German people during WWII).

(Continued)

Type	Engagement	Characteristics	Consequence(s)	Example(s)
Participants	Clearly engaged	Clearly in favor of, or opposed to group. Have desire and ability to make an impact.	Inexpert leaders of knowledge workers must monitor them more closely.	Engaged knowledge workers whose expertise give them power (Merck employees who worked on Vioxx).
Activists	Eagerly engaged	Feel strongly about their leaders (pro or con). Heavily invested in people and process. Work hard on behalf of, or to undermine, leaders.	Have great capacity to create change.	People who have clear feelings about their leaders and have the energy and support to act accordingly (Laity during the Catholic priest sexual abuse scandal).
Diehards	Deeply engaged	Deeply devoted, or fiercely opposed, to leaders. Prepared to die for cause.	Most likely type of followers to morph into leaders.	Suicide bombers; whistle-blowers; soldiers.

BEING A FOLLOWER

It is important to understand the art of following, since *all of us follow some of the time.* Suggesting a follower typology creates an order that has been largely lacking, and it presents a new perspective that views the leader–follower relationship from the bottom–up instead of from the traditional top–down. Five types of followers include

- *Isolates These are actually unfollowers.* They fulfill the criterion of subordinate rank, but they exhibit no useful behavior. They are completely detached, have no interest in their leaders, and do not respond to them in any way.
- *Bystanders* These are the followers that give other followers a bad name. They are aware of the situation around them, but *they make a conscious decision to do nothing.* Edmund Burke talked about this type of follower when he said "All that is necessary for the triumph of evil is for good men to do nothing." The somber lessons learned from the results of standing by during Adolf Hitler's control of Germany are:
  1. Abnegated personal responsibility at an individual level seeps upward to the group level.
  2. An established habit of standing by and doing nothing is difficult to break.
  3. Standing by cedes more power to those who already have it.
  4. Followers matter even when they do nothing.

- ***Participants*** *All leaders want followers who are participants,* because they are in sync with the dynamics of the group and have the desire and ability to effect change. Since *participants* often have experience or expertise that grants them high levels of power and influence, which in turn enables them to have great impact on the process, leaders of *participant* followers should maintain a high level of involvement with these subordinates. On the other hand, *participant* followers need effective leaders.
- ***Activists*** These persons *are determined to create change and are willing to invest their own resources to do it.* They care deeply about their leader (pro or con), other followers, and the whole of which they are a part. What they may lack in traditional sources of power, authority, and influence they make up for with zeal and the ability to mobilize other followers.
- ***Diehards*** These are the rarest of the five types, *extremely dedicated to their cause*, and also the most likely to become leaders themselves. The dedication of diehards is so great that they are willing to die, or sustain lethal damage to their careers, for their cause.

FUTURE FOLLOWERS

Leaders absolutely depend on engaged followers to support them. Followers become engaged for many reasons including, but not limited to, dissatisfaction with the *status quo*, strong feelings about an issue on which their leaders are silent, or inspiration from other followers. However, *willingness to engage is not of itself good.* Generally, good followers can be separated from bad followers based on their level of engagement, motivation, and reaction to their leaders, suggesting the following five axioms of followership:

- Bad followers do nothing (*isolates* and *bystanders*).
- Bad followers oppose good (effective and ethical) leaders.
- Bad followers support bad (ineffective and/or unethical) leaders.
- Good followers oppose bad (ineffective and/or unethical) leaders.
- Good followers support good (effective and ethical) leaders.

While the historic view of the leader–follower relationship has been leader-centric, subconsciously we have always known that the idea of a leader cannot exist without at least one follower. As natural progression widens the focus to include both leadership and followership, successful creation of a synthesized hybrid will require consciousness raising to consider followers as an independent force, along with followership education as a part of leadership education.

Followers are more important to leaders than leaders are to followers. Therefore, promoting good followership doesn't suggest changing follower rank, but rather changing followers' response to their rank, to their superiors, and to the situation at hand. Programs focused on developing followers can make the following assumptions:

- Followers constitute a group that has *members with interests in common.*
- Followers, by definition, lack authority but they *don't lack power and influence.*
- Followers can be *agents of change.*
- Followers should *support good* leadership and *oppose bad* leadership.
- Followers who do *something* are generally preferred to those who do *nothing.*
- Followers can circumvent leaders and *create change by joining with other followers.*

New leadership models reflect the prevailing *trend toward more equality between superiors and subordinates in the workplace.* While supporting good leaders is easy, there can be negative effects of followership when bad leadership is involved. Standing up to superiors often involves risk, and followers are cautioned to carefully consider timing, preparation, allies, strategy, other approaches, and documentation. "Managing up," a strategy employed by smart followers to deal with difficult superiors, has been receiving more attention. For example:

- Subordinate issues are being presented in new ways in leadership literature.
- It is more widely understood that leaders are also followers.
- There is a new spotlight on what subordinates have the right to expect from superiors.
- 360-degree evaluations have gained in usage and respect.
- We now realize that CEOs can't change companies on their own.

Conclusion

Followers have always mattered. Even though followers lack authority due to their subordinate rank, they do possess power and influence, and are able to impact the course of events irrespective of their level of engagement. While followers have previously been dismissed and overlooked, there has been an increase in the level of attention leveled at followers. The leader-centric view of leadership, which prevailed in the past, has broadened to include followers as the balance of power has shifted away from leaders and toward followers. This is an important trend to consider since we are all followers some of the time.

Team of Rivals

Doris Kearns Goodwin

Leadership Lessons from Abraham Lincoln: A Conversation with
Historian Doris Kearns Goodwin by Diane Coutu*

In January 2008, CBS anchor Katie Couric asked Barack Obama which one book
he would take with him to the White House, apart from the Bible. The eventual
winner of the presidential election singled out *Team of Rivals*, Doris Kearns
Goodwin's 2005 best-selling account of President Abraham Lincoln's leadership
during the Civil War.

In the months following his election victory, President Obama has made it
clear that he is modeling his leadership on the style of his presidential predeces-
sor from Illinois. By bringing heavyweight politicians who are themselves past
and future presidential contenders into his cabinet, Obama has reprised
Lincoln's strategy of creating a team composed of his most able rivals, people
who are unafraid to take issue with him and are confident of their own leadership abilities.

If the new U.S. president can learn from Abraham Lincoln, so too can business leaders who are grappling now with similar questions of how to lead in turbulent times. To find out what the lessons from Lincoln are, *Harvard Business
Review*'s senior editor Diane Coutu interviewed *Team of Rivals* author Goodwin, a
Pulitzer Prize–winning historian whose other books include *No Ordinary Time*
(about Franklin and Eleanor Roosevelt and their era), *The Fitzgeralds and the
Kennedys,* and *Lyndon Johnson and the American Dream.*

In the course of a wide-ranging, two-hour conversation, Goodwin described
the qualities that made it possible for Lincoln to "bring disgruntled opponents
together to create the most unusual cabinet in history," offered some advice to the
new president as he confronts the current economic crisis, and expressed her belief
that the United States will weather this storm as it has weathered worse before.
What follows is an abridged and edited version of the interview.

Doris K. Goodwin. *Team of Rivals: The Political Genius of Abraham Lincoln.* New York: Simon &
Schuster, 2005.
*Reprinted by permission of *Harvard Business Review.* From "Leadership Lessons from Abraham
Lincoln: A Conversation with Historian Doris Kearns Goodwin" by Diane Coutu, April 2009.
Copyright © 2009 by the Harvard Business School Publishing Corporation; all rights reserved.

What lessons can President Barack Obama and other leaders take away from studying Abraham Lincoln's presidency?

There are several, but the first one President Obama focused on in discussions during the election campaign concerns the way Lincoln surrounded himself with people, including his rivals, who had strong egos and high ambitions; who felt free to question his authority; and who were unafraid to argue with him.

For example, Lincoln brought Salmon Chase into his cabinet as treasury secretary and kept him there for three years, knowing full well that Chase craved the presidency with every fiber of his being and knowing that Chase was undermining him all the time with cabinet members, Congress, and the rest of the country. So long as he was doing a good job at his post, that was more important than personal feelings. Obama is obviously trying to do the same thing by choosing his chief rival, Hillary Clinton, to be secretary of state; by picking rival Joe Biden as his vice president; and by including powerful Republicans in his cabinet like Robert Gates and Ray LaHood.

But you have to remember, the idea is not just to put your rivals in power—the point is that you must choose the best and most able people in the country, for the good of the country. Lincoln came to power when the nation was in peril, and he had the intelligence, and the self-confidence, to know that he needed the best people by his side, people who were leaders in their own right and who were very aware of their own strengths. That's an important insight whether you're the leader of a country or the CEO of a company.

What's the downside of creating a team of rivals?

If you are as inclusive a leader as Lincoln was, or as President Obama seems to be, then the danger is that you're constantly talking and arguing about things late into the night without reaching a consensus. It can be paralyzing. So you have to be prepared to vote on decisions, and if a vote results in a stalemate, then you have to make the decision yourself and be ready to tell the team, "Like it or not, here's what we're doing."

For example, for months Lincoln let his cabinet debate about if and when slavery should be abolished. Finally, though, he made up his mind to issue his historic Emancipation Proclamation to free the slaves. He brought the cabinet together and told them he no longer needed their thoughts on the main issue—but that he would listen to their suggestions about how best to implement his decision and its timing. So even though some members still did not support Lincoln's decision, they felt they'd been heard. And they had been. When one cabinet member suggested that Lincoln wait for a victory on the field to issue the proclamation, Lincoln took his advice.

You've written biographies of three other American presidents. What, in your opinion, are the essential qualities of a successful leader?

I can't emphasize strongly enough the fact that you've got to surround yourself with people who can argue with you and question your assumptions. It particularly helps if you can bring in people whose temperaments differ from your own.

When Lincoln brought Edwin Stanton into the cabinet in 1862 as secretary of war, for example, Stanton was much tougher, much more secretive, than Lincoln, who was often too kind to subordinates and at times too open. Their opposite temperaments balanced each other out. Where Lincoln was too lenient, issuing pardons for soldiers who had run away from battle to the point of hurting military discipline, Stanton was relentless in his desire to punish cowardice. By working together, pardons were issued, but not in the numbers they had been under Lincoln alone.

You also have to be able to figure out how to share credit for your success with your inner team so that they feel a part of a mission. Basically, you want to create a reservoir of good feeling, and that involves not only acknowledging your errors but even shouldering the blame for the failures of some of your subordinates. Again and again, Lincoln took responsibility for what he did, and he shared responsibility for the mistakes of others, and so people became very loyal to him.

History also shows that it's essential to know how to connect to the larger public, whether that's through radio, in the case of Franklin Roosevelt, or in Lincoln's case, through speeches that were filled with such poetry and clarity that people felt they were watching him think and that he was telling them the truth.

I would add here that one more success factor is key for great leadership, be it in business or politics, and it's one that's usually overlooked. As a leader you need to know how to relax so that you can replenish your energies for the struggles facing you tomorrow.

Lincoln went to the theater about a hundred times while he was in Washington. And although he suffered from a certain melancholy, he had a tremendous sense of humor and would entertain people long into the night with his stories. Franklin Roosevelt was the same way. He had this cocktail hour every evening during World War II when you just couldn't talk about the war. He needed to remain free from thinking about the bad things for a few hours. Or he would play with his stamps. This ability to recharge your batteries in the midst of great stress and crisis is crucial for successful leadership.

More books have been written on Lincoln than on any other American president. What does Lincoln's magic as a leader really come down to?

Well, it wasn't anything so immediately felt as charisma. In fact, it took the country some time to warm to Lincoln; his popularity almost came from the inside out. His cabinet was the first to see something unusual about him.

Take William Seward, who originally was a rival. Some eight weeks after becoming secretary of state, Seward wrote to his wife that Lincoln was unlike anyone he'd ever known. Other members of the cabinet came to think so, too. One after another, they came to power thinking Lincoln was rather unexceptional and ended up believing that he was as near a perfect man as anyone they'd ever met.

What Lincoln had, it seems to me, was an extraordinary amount of emotional intelligence. He was able to acknowledge his errors and learn from his mistakes to a remarkable degree. He was careful to put past hurts behind him and never allowed wounds to fester. The rare example I could find of Lincoln's being unable to forgive someone was his father. Lincoln never visited his father when he was dying, which suggests that he could not let go of the anger he felt toward the man who considered the future president's fierce desire to learn a sign of laziness.

He had flaws, of course; every leader has flaws. Lincoln's greatest flaw came out of his strength, which was generally liking people and not wanting to hurt them. He always wanted to give somebody a second or even a third chance. This weakness proved disastrous with George McClellan, who was head of the Union Army for some months near the beginning of the war. Lincoln should have fired McClellan within weeks of seeing how narcissistic and insubordinate he was. In part, Lincoln didn't because at that time he didn't have enough confidence in his own understanding of military affairs. He was still learning about how to wage war by going to the Library of Congress and reading books on military strategy. But in the end it was his inability to hurt people that made Lincoln keep McClellan on far too long. As a result, battles were lost, and thousands of soldiers died who might have lived had Lincoln fired McClellan earlier. So it wasn't just a small flaw.

In your biography of Lincoln, you rely heavily on the intimate letters between wives and husbands. What will historians do without such letters in the future?

It's a big issue for historians—and for leaders who are trying to learn from history—because traditionally it's in people's private correspondence that you get the emotional understanding of what leaders are really feeling and doing as history is being made.

Unfortunately, Lincoln left few personal letters, but Seward would write to his wife daily to tell her what Lincoln did that day or about some of the arguments that went on in the cabinet, and those letters provide a unique insight into what Lincoln thought and felt as great decisions were being made.

Looking back, the thing that's really impressive is that here were these leaders running the Civil War, and people like Seward still had time to meditate on the day's events and to write these long letters to his wife at night. These were the days of no television. Leaders weren't worried about cable news or their BlackBerrys. They weren't multitasking; they had time to reflect. It's a luxury many leaders just don't have today, and that's a real loss.

For historians, the biggest loss is going to be the time between the rise of the telephone in the 1940s and the advent of e-mail in the 1990s. There's a 50-year period that is almost completely gone from history, unless, like Richard Nixon and Lyndon Johnson, you taped conversations. Today, at least we have e-mails, which are in some way reviving the art of letter writing. I don't know whether or not, 200 years from now, we'll be able to retrieve e-mails found on old computers. But I think—or at least I hope—that if people send a long e-mail to somebody now, and they know it's something important, they will have the foresight to print it out.

Obama took your book with him to the Oval Office. What else would you recommend he read?

Obama does seem to have a sense of history, and were I to speak with him again, I would suggest that he read about other presidents going through difficult times. I would certainly recommend Roosevelt's fireside chats, where he explains in such simple language terribly complicated problems like the banking crisis, the economic crisis, and the war. And since Obama is interested in the moments in history when people come together to produce change from the bottom up, he also might want to look at the Progressive movement at the turn of the twentieth century—which led to curbs on the giant trusts, pure-food-and-drug legislation, railroad regulation, and conservation measures—or the civil rights movement, to learn how it created the pressure that allowed the voting rights and desegregation acts to pass.

I find it interesting, though, that Lincoln didn't read biographies—at least you don't hear about him reading of Washington or Jefferson, the people you would imagine he'd be very interested in. He was more impressed by their words. It's the documents of American history—the Constitution and the Declaration of Independence—that became his inspiration. He said himself that he never had a thought that didn't come from the Declaration of Independence. If Lincoln is Obama's role model, then he might want to go back to those documents and study them in great detail. I think that appreciating them and their great promise is what makes you understand what hope is all about.

Do you really have such hope when everything seems to be crashing down around us?

Yes, I really do. In times of crisis, things become possible that wouldn't be possible in ordinary times. The way the U.S. government is set up, with so many checks and balances, means that it almost takes a deep crisis to move forward. So there are only certain moments in history when great change can take place. FDR had this opportunity in the Depression; Lincoln did during the Civil War. Obama has that same great opportunity now. The challenges Americans are now facing give him a chance to pull the country together in new ways, working across party lines.

Also, history is a great reminder that, however bad things look today, they've been worse before, and Americans still pulled through. Today's crisis is not as bad as the Great Depression, let alone the Civil War that Lincoln confronted. One of my favorite FDR speeches is one he made in 1942 that was very similar to Obama's victory speech in Chicago. FDR warned his listeners that there would be many failures before the country won World War II. But he reminded them that America had faced disasters before and had come out the other side. Despite the cruel winter at Valley Forge, for example, Americans still won independence. FDR's speech was so successful that thousands of affirming telegrams flooded into the White House.

Obviously there's a fine line between optimism that's simply not credible and a sense of real confidence that there's something about the United States and its people and its system that's going to make the country pull together and get out of this hole. Roosevelt once said something like, "The most efficient dictatorship could never compete with the free energies of a free people in a democratic system." I think that's right—and not just for the United States but for democracies around the world.

Of all the politicians you've written about—the Kennedys and the Fitzgeralds, FDR, LBJ, Lincoln, and now Theodore Roosevelt—whom would you choose to spend an evening with?

Lincoln, without question. It took me 10 years to write his biography, and he was a very amiable companion all those years.

If I did get to meet him, though, I wouldn't ask him what I, as a historian, know I'm supposed to ask him—about what he would have done to bring the country together after the Civil War, had he lived. I'd ask him to tell me stories. Everyone remarked upon his extraordinary sense of humor, and he was widely admired as a storyteller. He said himself that a good story is better than a drop of whiskey. I'd just sit at the kitchen table with him and have him tell me one story after another, for then he would truly come to life again.

VIII

Organizational Change

A Greek philosopher (Heraclitus of Ephesus) once noted that a person never steps into the same river twice, for the flowing current is always changing (as well as the person). Contemporary organizations have their own "river"—a turbulent environment around them. Consequently, managers of today's organizations are being called on to integrate their operations with a rapidly changing external (e.g., social, economic, and ecological) environment. To bring about this integration, they must often adapt their organization's internal structure, processes, and strategies to meet these environmental challenges. The ability to manage change effectively is far different from the ability to manage and cope with the ongoing and routine operational side of the organization.

Experts frequently advise American managers to invest in research and development (R&D) to keep their product mix current. Some companies (e.g., 3M) derive as much as 25 percent of their revenues from products introduced in the past five years. Nevertheless, many critics charge that one of the reasons for the decline in the competitiveness of U.S. industry revolves around its failure to innovate at sufficiently high levels. Clearly, organizations need to manage change, stimulate renewal, and develop organizational cultures in which change can thrive.

Robert E. Quinn is the M. E. Tracy Collegiate Professor of Organization Behavior and Human Resource Management at the University of Michigan, and also the cofounder of the Center for Positive Organizational Scholarship. He has written a trilogy of books that focus on the positive tensions associated with excellent performance—*Deep Change, Change the World*, and *Building the Bridge as You Walk on It.*

Dr. Quinn believes that understanding change is the foundation for building a better world. He suggests that each of us faces a core dilemma: Make deep and significant changes within ourselves, or face a slow but certain death. The solution to this dilemma lies in practicing the "fundamental state of leadership," which involves eight practices of increasing integrity—reflective action, authentic engagement, appreciative inquiry, grounded vision, adaptive confidence, detached interdependence, responsible freedom, and tough love. To effect change, Quinn says, requires that leaders become results centered, internally driven, other focused, and externally open.

Clayton M. Christensen, professor of Business Administration at the Harvard Business School, and Michael E. Raynor, a director at Deloitte Research (the research arm of Deloitte Consulting), teamed up to write *The Innovator's Solution*, which is a sequel to *The Innovator's Dilemma*, authored by Dr. Christensen. In this later book, Christensen and Raynor explore how managers become blinded by "disruptive innovations" because of their preoccupation with their existing businesses and most profitable customers. In *The Innovator's Solution*, the authors reveal how organizations that are capable of sustaining growth get beyond this crippling dilemma. These organizations have managed to create a "disruptive growth engine." By drawing upon organizational examples, Christensen and Raynor identify and discuss the forces that cause managers to make bad decisions and suggest how to make disruptions succeed.

The third reading in this part focuses on the work of Edward E. Lawler III and Christopher Worley. Dr. Lawler is on the faculty at the University of Southern California and director of the Center for Effective Organizations. He has a Ph.D. from the University of California, Berkeley, and has held faculty appointments at Yale and the University of Michigan. Dr. Lawler has a long and distinguished scholarly career contributing extensively to the organizational sciences. He is the author or coauthor of several other popular management books, including *Rewarding Excellence, The Ultimate Advantage,* and *The New American Workplace.* Chris Worley holds a Ph.D. from the University of Southern California and is a research scientist for the Center for Effective Organizations. He has previously published *Integrated Strategic Change* and *Organization Development and Change.*

The authors of *Built to Change* argue that contemporary [built-to-change (B2change)] organizations need to be designed and structured so as to stimulate change in the context of today's global economy. Specifically, B2change firms should maintain a close connection to their environments, reward employee experimentation with new ideas, search out and learn about new practices and technologies, make a strong and vocal commitment to the improvement of performance, and do "whatever it takes" (ethically) to gain competitive advantages. Two major strategies for accomplishing continual change are the commitment to development and the travel light approaches.

John P. Kotter is the Konosuke Matsushita Professor of Leadership Emeritus at Harvard Business School and author of 17 books on leadership and change, including *The Heart of Change, Leading Change,* and *Our Iceberg Is Melting.* Collectively, his books have sold over two million copies and have been printed in 120 languages.

A Sense of Urgency argues that the real nemesis of change is complacency, but an even more insidious threat is a *false* sense of urgency that drives frenetic activity. Instead, it is imperative that managers stir feelings and emotions powerful enough to drive employees to overcome obstacles to change. Four key tactics for creating true urgency are described—bring the outside (various stakeholders) in through questions and listening, behave with urgency every day, find opportunity in crises, and deal promptly and firmly with perpetual naysayers.

Building the Bridge
as You Walk on It

Robert E. Quinn

Summary Prepared by Peter Stark

> *Peter Stark teaches Strategy, Managing Change, Entrepreneurship, and International Marketing courses in the Labovitz School of Business and Economics at the University of Minnesota Duluth. Peter is an ABD doctoral student in organizational change at Pepperdine University. He has previously taught at several institutions in the United States, Mexico, and China, and is a frequent visiting instructor with the Helsinki School of Economics in Finland. He is an international consultant working with many global companies. His research interests include the application of systems theory and chaos theory to the process of understanding and dealing with the embedded ontological archetypes that inhibit culture change in organizations.*

THE BASIC IDEA AND CONCEPT PATH

Leadership, rather than being a set of tool-like behavioral patterns to be enacted through emulation, is best portrayed as a state of *being* ("who we are") rather than a means of *doing* ("what we do"). Many people spend most of their time in the "normal life state." They tend to be comfort centered, externally driven, self-focused, and internally closed. As a consequence, many organizations reflect the embedded selfishness, insecurity, and lack of courage inherent in this state of being. Fortunately, anyone can transform their state of being and enter the extraordinary **fundamental state of leadership** in which they become results centered, internally directed, other focused, and externally open. These individuals become role models for others to emulate, and hence they stimulate positive organizing approaches and more productive social systems.

There is a strong link between an individual's personal transformation to the fundamental state of leadership and subsequent organizational transformation. *Anyone who aspires to leadership must engage in a continuous and, perhaps most*

Robert E. Quinn. *Building the Bridge as You Walk on It: A Guide for Leading Change.* San Francisco, CA: Jossey-Bass, 2004.

importantly, courageously and consciously intended learning journey. This requires that they wed their individual ability to let go of ego needs-based control and venture into uncharted territory with their capacity for inspired, authentic leadership. Leaders who undertake this journey of self-transformation enable the positive creation of a more productive community capable of creating, leveraging, and enduring change.

Five major conclusions about leadership can be offered:

1. Extraordinarily positive organizations (productive, flourishing communities) are reflections of (and are brought about by) extraordinary states of being among their members; they are consequently capable of creating, leveraging, and enduring great change. Without such states of being present among an organization's leaders, organizations will entropy (decline).

2. Leadership has nothing to do with position and power. It is about your fundamental "state of being" (who you are), not what you do or what you have. Leadership is realized not in what the leader does but in what others do as a consequence of the leader's state of being.

3. The normal state of being for most individuals is comfort centered, externally driven, self-focused, and internally closed. Leadership in the "normal state" isn't really leadership at all—it is a self-interested rationalization in support of socially normed organizational coping strategies. The fundamental state of leadership is results centered, internally directed, other focused, and externally open.

4. Entering the "fundamental state of leadership" requires those who aspire to leadership to experience deep, revitalizing personal change in which they challenge and change many, if not all, of their basic beliefs and assumptions in pursuit of greater awareness and authenticity.

5. Organizations change only when the leaders among its members change. The creation of extraordinarily positive organizations/productive communities is contingent upon a leader's acceptance of and engagement in a process of deep personal change.

How, then, should one fundamentally "be" in the context of a catalytic and systemic organizational process? It must be noted that human beings are complex paradoxes of qualities, attributes, and behaviors. Leadership, then, is the effect on others that emerges from the confluence of these creatively tense paradoxes. Positive traits and tensions tend to exist and operate as part of a larger, more complex, reciprocal system. Integrating the oppositions of eight polarities of being (spontaneous/self-disciplined, compassionate/assertive, mindful/energetic, principled/engaged, realistic/optimistic, grounded/visionary, confident/flexible, and independent/open) suggests eight creatively tense states from which a more dynamic and more accurately representative view of the state of leadership emerges. These practices serve as "guard rails" on the path and are both realistic and idealistic in conception and application. In *striving* for the integrated path, one is in the fundamental state of leadership.

PRACTICES FOR ENTERING THE FUNDAMENTAL STATE OF LEADERSHIP

The eight integrated but creatively tense and seemingly paradoxical practices individuals can engage in for entering the fundamental state of leadership are as follows:

- *Reflective action*—the practice of integrating the realm of personal identity (who we are) with the realm of action (what we are doing). This person acts and learns simultaneously.

- *Authentic engagement*—the practice of increasing our integrity by engaging the world of action with genuine love for what we are doing. This person is authentically engaged (ethical, while also highly involved).
- *Appreciative inquiry*—the practice of gaining the capacity to see the best in the world and what is possible. These persons are optimistic, constructive, realistic, and questioning, which allow them to help others surface possibilities that previously have been less recognized.
- *Grounded vision*—the practice of integrating the present with an image of a positive future. Such leaders are grounded, factual, hopeful, and visionary.
- *Adaptive confidence*—the practice of letting go of control and moving into a state of action learning. The adaptively confident person is concurrently flexible, confident, secure, experimental, and open to feedback.
- *Detached interdependence*—the practice of considering one's relationships from a very high level of maturity. This leader combines independence, a strong sense of purpose, and strength with humility and openness.
- *Responsible freedom*—the practice of being aware of and acting in regard to the intimate connections between freedom and responsibility. The practitioner of responsible freedom is spontaneous, expressive, self-structuring, self-disciplined, empowering to others, and responsible.
- *Tough love*—the practice of living in the balance of being both simultaneously compassionate/ concerned and assertive/bold. The **tough love** practitioner is assertive, challenging, bold, compassionate, and concerned.

DEVELOPING LEADERS

Leaders are developed through a two-step process: changing ourselves and choosing to enter the fundamental state of leadership. In the first step, all change requires and begins with self-change and requires making a personal choice to change. The second step is helping others to do the same. Leadership development similarly involves these interdependent, mutually reinforcing phenomena. Developing leaders is not just imparting a set of concepts or teaching a toolkit of strategies and behaviors; *it is encouraging people to engage in the process of deep change in themselves and then inviting others to do the same.*

Self-change can be viewed as a nine-stage path or spiral:

- Precontemplation: increasing information about one's self—one's own problems (self-deceptions), negative routines, and self-defeating behaviors. This involves consciousness raising (becoming aware that we don't know what we don't know).
- Social liberation: increasing social alternatives for behaviors that are not problematic.
- Emotional arousal: experiencing and expressing feelings about one's problems and solutions.
- Self-reevaluation: assessing feelings and thoughts about one's self with respect to a problem.
- Commitment: choosing and committing to act; belief in one's own ability to change.
- Countering: substituting new and positive alternatives for problem behaviors.
- Environment control: avoiding stimuli that elicit problem behaviors.
- Reward: rewarding one's self, or being rewarded by others, for making appropriate and positive changes.
- Helping relationships: enlisting the help and support of someone who cares to aid in preventing you from relapsing.

The fundamental state of leadership has significant implications. First, it redefines what leadership means. It is not authority and not a set of easily imitated attributes or skill sets. It is, instead, a state—a way of being that has the ability to profoundly change the systems that it is a part of. Second, it redefines what it means to develop leaders. Leadership development is first and foremost self-change, which requires an understanding of the stages and strategies inherent in this process as well as the ability to support others as they go through them.

There really is no way to teach what it means to be in a fundamental state of leadership. The best way is simply to be what you wish to evoke from others. However, the fundamental state of leadership is an inherently fragile and episodic phenomenon; it is difficult to get into and difficult to stay in.

We attract others into the fundamental state of leadership, then, by our own change process in pursuit of our own uniqueness and ever-increasing integrity. *It is one's courage to engage in the process and not one's success in mastering it that attracts others.*

The Innovator's Solution

Clayton M. Christensen, Michael E. Raynor, and Scott D. Anthony

Summary Prepared by Warren L. Candy

Warren L. Candy is a Senior Vice President at Allete Minnesota Power, a diversified electric utility located in Duluth, Minnesota, where he is responsible for generation, transmission, distribution, mining, and customer operations in Minnesota, Wisconsin, and North Dakota. His interests include sustainable organizational design, leadership excellence, and sociotechnical systems. He received his Bachelor of Science degree in Production Engineering from Swinburne Institute of Technology in Melbourne, Australia.

SUSTAINING CORPORATE GROWTH

Research and observation of hundreds of both successful and unsuccessful growth-oriented businesses have resulted in the identification of a number of key theories and practical responses for creating and sustaining new growth in business. Growth is important to all management teams because companies create shareholder value through profitable growth. However, approximately 1 company in 10 is able to sustain the kind of growth that translates into above-average increases in shareholder returns for more than a few years at a time. It's hard to know how to grow, but pursuing growth the wrong way can be worse than no growth at all.

As the core business approaches maturity, investors demand new growth, and executives develop seemingly sensible strategies to generate it. Although they often invest aggressively, many times their plans still fail to create the needed growth fast enough. Probably the most daunting challenge in delivering growth is that once you fail to deliver it, the odds of ever regaining past levels of success are very low. It has been shown that of all the companies whose growth has stalled, only 4 percent are able to successfully reignite their growth, even to a rate of 1 percent above GNP!

Clayton M. Christensen, Michael E. Raynor, and Scott D. Anthony. *The Innovator's Solution: Creating and Sustaining Successful Growth.* Boston, MA: Harvard Business School Press, 2003.

What *can* make the process of innovation more predictable comes from an understanding of the forces that act upon those individuals and the management teams building the business. When comprehended and properly applied, these forces can powerfully influence what managers can choose to do, and what they cannot choose to do.

A dearth of good ideas is rarely the core problem in a company that struggles to launch exciting new-growth businesses. The problem is in the shaping process itself. The major obstacle for growth-seeking managers is that the exciting growth markets of tomorrow are most likely small and off the radar screen today. Managers who understand these forces, and learn to harness them in making key decisions, will develop successful new-growth businesses much more consistently than historically seemed possible.

FUNDAMENTAL ISSUES AND PRINCIPLES

The following set of issues highlights some of the most important decisions that need to be addressed by managers. The answers to the underlying questions, and the essential principles supporting them, can guide managers as they successfully grow new and profitable businesses.

Outperforming Your Competition

A key management question is always "What could our competition do to outperform us?" A natural follow-up question becomes "What courses of action could actually give *us* the upper hand?" A new market entrant is more likely to beat the incumbent with disruptive innovations, rather than with sustaining innovations. **Disruptive innovations** occur where the challenge is to commercialize a simpler, more convenient product that sells for less money, a product that appeals to a new or unattractive customer set. This compares to **sustaining innovations**, where the goal is to deliver a better product that is sold for more money to an already attractive set of customers.

Disruptive innovations don't attempt to bring better products to established customers in established markets. Rather, they disruptively redefine the market by introducing products and services that are not as good as the currently available products, but instead offer other benefits such as being simpler, more convenient, less expensive, and more appealing to a new, or less-demanding, customer group.

This distinction is important for innovators seeking to create new-growth businesses. Whereas the current leaders of the industry will almost always triumph in battles of sustaining innovation, successful disruptions are most likely to be launched by the new entrant companies.

Identifying Desired Products

Managers appropriately ask the questions, "What products should we be developing?" "Which improvements will our customers want?" and "Which new products will be rejected out of hand?" Managers need to rethink their perceptions and opinions of why customers actually use or don't use their products and services. In reality, customers "hire" products to do specific jobs that regularly arise in their lives and that need to get done under specific circumstances. Companies that target their products at the circumstances in which customers find themselves, rather than the customers themselves, can launch predictably successful products.

Identifying Best Customers

As managers create new business ventures, they must ask themselves "Which initial customers will constitute the most viable foundation upon which to build a successful business?" The first step is to find the ideal customers for **low-end disruptions**. They are the current users of the mainstream products who seem disinterested in offers to sell them improved performance products. They may be willing to accept improved products, but they are often unwilling to pay for them.

A **new-market disruption** is an innovation that enables a large population of people who previously lacked the money or skill to now begin buying and using a product, and doing the job for themselves. However, a product that purports to help nonconsumers do something that they weren't already prioritizing in their lives is unlikely to succeed.

Internal Vs. External Activity

A key decision for the long-term sustainability of any organization revolves around the activities required to design, produce, sell, and distribute products and services—Which ones should be done internally? Which ones should be done externally by partners and suppliers?

Traditionally this decision has been made around the organization's core competency model, which suggests that if something fits your core competency, then you should do it inside the organization. If it is not a core competency and another firm can do it better, then you should rely on them to do it. The problem with this approach is that what might seem to be a noncore activity today might become an absolutely critical competence to have mastered in a proprietary way in the future, and vice versa. The real question to be asked, and the decision to be made, is "What do we need to master today, and what will we need to master in the future, in order to excel on the path of improvement that customers will define as important to them?"

Core competence is a dangerously inwardly looking notion. Competitiveness is far more about doing what *customers* value than it is about doing what you think you are good at. Staying competitive as the competition shifts requires a willingness and an ability to learn new things rather than to hold onto what has been successful in the past.

Avoiding the Commoditization of Products

As organizations grow, they need to maintain strong competitive advantage and attractive profits within a marketplace that, over time, is trending toward commoditization. **Commoditization** is a natural and inescapable process that occurs as new markets coalesce around proprietary products that become increasingly difficult to differentiate from the competition. Attractive future profits can often be found elsewhere in the value chain, in different stages or layers of value added, usually in the places where previously profit was hard to attain.

Considering Disruptive Growth

One ongoing responsibility for all management teams is to ensure that the optimal organizational design and structure is in place to facilitate ongoing business growth. Many potentially successful innovations fail not because of market forces but because the management of the organization is not up to the task. Those capabilities that were assets in sustaining circumstances become liabilities when disruption is needed. To be confident that managers can handle the new challenges placed before them, executives need to examine in detail the types of actual problems that they have had to deal with in the past, and diminish their emphasis on broad leadership attributes that are believed to be inherently important (e.g., good communicator; results oriented). By focusing on a person's ability to learn and adapt, managers can avoid the trap of assuming that the skills that are important today are those that will still be required in the future. In many ways this results in a paradox: *The managers that corporate executives have come to trust most today because they have consistently delivered the needed results in the core business cannot be trusted to shepherd the creation of new business ventures tomorrow.*

Establishing a Strategy that Works

Most questions that are raised about strategy focus on its substance. However, the crucial question really relates to the *process* of strategy formulation, that is, using the right process in the right circumstances. Although senior management can become obsessed with finding the right strategy, they can actually wield greater leverage by managing the processes used to develop the strategy, and by making sure that the right process is used under the right circumstances.

Within organizations there are essentially two types of strategies: deliberate and emergent. **Deliberate strategies** are the product of a conscious and analytical plan based on rigorous analysis of data. *Emergent strategies* are responses to unanticipated opportunities, problems, and successes that were unforeseen in the deliberate strategy-making process. The emergent process should dominate in circumstances where the future is hard to read and in which it is not clear what the right strategy should be. Alternatively, the deliberate process should dominate once a winning strategy has become clear and effective implementation is crucial.

PREFERRED SOURCES OF CAPITAL

As companies seek to grow and expand, three key issues emerge for senior management to consider. These focus on (1) identifying whose investment capital will help the firm succeed, (2) determining whose capital might be the "kiss of death," and (3) exploring what sources of money will help the firm most at different stages of its development. The best resource for facilitating success in a growth-oriented business is money that is "patient for growth but impatient for profit." By contrast, money should be impatient for growth in later stage, deliberate-strategy circumstances after a winning strategy has emerged.

THE ROLE OF SENIOR EXECUTIVES

One reason that many soaring hot-product companies flame out is that the key initial resource, the founding team, fails to institute the processes or the values that will help the company continue to develop and initiate disruptive products and services. The CEOs of all companies play a critical role in sustaining the growth of the business.

Senior executives have three roles to play in ensuring repeated disruptive growth in their organizations. First, they must stand astride and manage the interface between the disruptive growth businesses and the mainstream businesses. Second, these executives must shepherd the internal processes that repeatedly create new organizational growth. Third, they must sense when circumstances are changing and respond appropriately.

The larger and more complex a company becomes, the more important it is for senior managers to train employees at every level to act autonomously. Doing so will help them make prioritized decisions that are consistent with the strategic direction and business model of the organization. Senior management's role is to decide when to keep their hands off the new business, and when to get involved.

Conclusion

Managers need to know how to use a key number of theories and principles to create and sustain continuous organizational growth. An integrated body of theory derived from the successes and failures of hundreds of different companies has been developed, and each of these address a different aspect of the "innovator's dilemma."

Built to Change

Edward E. Lawler III and Christopher G. Worley

Summary Prepared by Martha Golden

Martha Golden is a graduate of the Labovitz School of Business and Economics at the University of Minnesota Duluth, where she double majored in Organizational Management and Human Resource Management. Martha is currently a manager at Wintergreen Northern Wear, a handmade clothing manufacturer in Minnesota. She looks forward to starting her professional career with a progressive change-oriented organization. Martha currently lives in Duluth and enjoys proximity to the North Shore of Lake Superior.

INTRODUCTION

Change is everywhere and occurs more rapidly every day. Every organization needs to pay attention to change in order to survive. Organizations continue to struggle with change because they traditionally have been encouraged to be stable, constant, and methodical. Most organizations view change as a necessary, or in some cases unnecessary, evil. Change is seen as difficult, disruptive, and too often ineffective. Today's organizations need to adopt a group of short-term competitive advantages in their organizational design that assumes change is a normal activity and become *B2change* (built to change) *organizations*.

LEADERSHIP

Effective leadership is critical when organizations experience change. The larger and more significant the change the greater need there is for a leader who can guide the organization through the change. B2change organizations employ *shared leadership* for three reasons. It can replace rigid hierarchies and spread decision making across many people; it can help an organization build a large pool of leaders at all levels to draw from; and it supports more effective change management. Being an

---

Edward E. Lawler III and Christopher G. Worley. *Built to Change: How to Achieve Sustained Organizational Effectiveness.* San Francisco, CA: Jossey-Bass, 2003.

effective manager and an effective leader is attractive to B2change organizations because managers with shared leadership skills can switch between roles as needed as they react to the organization's changing environment.

HUMAN CAPITAL MANAGEMENT

Globalization has raised the level of competition and opened new markets, which challenges organizations to deal with a global consumer base. Being able to change rapidly and react to their environments means that firms need to invest a significant amount in their human capital. The way a firm is organized, and the quality of its management, staff, and employees, can prove to be a significant competitive advantage. B2change organizations begin to compete, in part, on the basis of intangible assets and their staff, instead of tangible goods.

How individuals react to change is a major barrier that organizations encounter when considering change initiatives. People need a reason to change, and most organizational structures have been designed around stability, which is a natural resister to change. Past efforts have shown that large-scale change operations are usually unsuccessful and ultimately have little effect. However, competitive pressures dictate that an organization must change. If it does not, it will likely become extinct. *The best **competitive advantage** an organization can have is the ability and willingness to change.* Every part of an organization's design, every department, every policy, and every employee needs to be committed to change and the implementation of the change strategy. B2change organizations are so reliant on their human capital that it should command as much as or more attention than the organization's financial or other physical assets. Recruiting individuals who already possess the ability and willingness to change is critical.

Two key human resource strategies are employed by B2change organizations. The *Commitment to Development* strategy involves hiring individuals who are skilled, but who are willing and able to change and develop regardless of where the organization goes. This strategy avoids the high cost of turnover, yet it is expensive to maintain and may even slow down change while people learn new skills. The other option is the *Travel Light* strategy, which allows companies to obtain new talent when needed and discard it when the need ends. This allows for a flexible workforce that can shift core competencies quickly. Unfortunately the organization may not be able to find the exact talent it needs or find it when it needs it, and this tends to lead to a disloyal workforce short in leadership and management. The approach that works best depends on the rate of change in the organization's environment.

Effective decision making is a challenging process to manage for many organizations, and even more so for B2change organizations. It is most effective to allow decisions involving operations and existing processes to be made at the level the processes are centered on, and managed with input from employees. By contrast, strategic decisions that concern the entire organization ultimately need to be made at the top, but B2change organizations seek input from all levels. All decisions need to be communicated to everyone they will affect as soon as possible to reduce confusion and create accountability.

REWARD SYSTEMS

Once an organization has decided whether it is a travel light or commitment to develop organization and has identified its core employees, it needs to define the reward system. Quantity and mix are the key factors in a successful reward system. For B2change organizations, designing a reward system that will attract and retain the type of individuals they need is an important part of human capital management. Along with an appropriate reward system, B2change organizations need to have a complex performance management system in place so that they can quickly determine if they have the correct mix of employee skills to match their current and near-future environment. An organizational reward system should motivate its employees to perform in ways that support the strategic intent and requirements. B2change organizations need to offer the rewards that employees value highly, so that they will be willing to do what is asked of them. A clear connection has to be established between the reward and the behavior required to obtain it; this is called a line-of-sight approach, or *organizational transparency*. As B2change organizations change, their reward systems will change and employees need to be able to see that what they are told about the changes will actually appear. It also creates a level of accountability. B2change reward systems need to be tied to individual, team, business unit, or organizational performance in order to motivate performance so that they maintain the core competencies and capabilities.

B2change organizations stay away from seniority-based reward systems and base their reward structure on bonuses. Giving bonuses enables them to reward individual or team performance and can result in the retention of highly effective people. Bonus systems can even be tied into change goals that the organization sets for itself and its employees. They also provide the clearest line of sight between what the employees are doing and what they are being rewarded for. Profit sharing and stock ownership are two bonus reward programs that companies can use. B2change organizations can also implement a person-based pay reward system. People are rewarded for their skills and knowledge, not just their job. This leads to the further development of the labor force as employees work to improve their capabilities. This can lead to high levels of motivation and the ability of the organization to develop and improve employee competencies and capabilities quickly and efficiently.

THE BUILT-TO-CHANGE MODEL

The B2change model consists of three primary organizational processes that revolve around an organization's *identity*, which is the core values, beliefs, and behaviors that an organization will try to keep constant. It originates in the company's culture and describes the way a company does business. An organization's identity reacts to *environmental scenarios* that represent a variety of possible future business conditions. The processes of *strategizing, creating value*, and *designing* are the main contributors to an organization's effectiveness. These processes help an organization to decide how to react to the changing environment.

Strategizing, in the B2change model, describes the way an organization decides where to focus in respect to product, service, and market. The organization's **strategic intent** is its guide to creating value and overall design. Ironically, a B2change organization needs to have a stable identity—but one that is committed to change. Five elements of strategic intent help to identify what an organization needs to do to accomplish its objectives:

1. The breadth of an organization's activities
2. The aggressiveness of its operations
3. The way it orchestrates change
4. The differentiated features of its products and services
5. The logic for making profits

Orchestration is the most important of these five, as it describes how all the rest fit together. It is the most challenging for organizations to implement, but the most critical investment if a company wants to become a B2change organization. Only through tremendous orchestration will a company be able to embrace a strategic change. When an organization's strategic intent describes a path that is proximate to both its environment and its identity, the organization achieves *critical configuration.* **Critical configuration** refers to the importance of specifying the relationships between an organization's environment, identity, and strategic intent, all of which determine performance.

The strategizing process a B2change organization should follow has three phases. Phase 1 is the strategic review, consisting of an identification of the causes of an organization's current performance and an analysis of the current strategy's appropriateness for the future. Phase 2 is the strategic choice. This phase works with the information developed in the strategic review and decides whether a change is necessary. Phase 3 is the strategic change. If the organization decides that its strategy does need to change, then this phase is the reconfiguration point. If a strategic change is necessary, it is essential to inform all members of the organization so that they are as involved as possible, so that they, too, are committed to the change. Again, the orchestration step emerges as a critical capability for a B2change organization.

Finding the best approach to creating value is the major consideration when designing and structuring an organization. The top designs put as many employees as possible in contact with the external environment to ensure the powerful feedback from customers that can be a source of motivation for change. This approach to organizational design leaves no room for rigid, fixed job descriptions. B2change organizations are in an environment of continuous change, and having their employees unable to change with them because of their confining job descriptions is costly and inefficient. Individuals and teams who are known by what they *can* do instead of being known for their *job* encourage employees to be flexible and more adaptable to change initiatives. B2change organizations utilize temporary teams to build relationships and to help employees develop skills they may not already have. Virtual teams, business units, matrices, and front–back structures are some types of team-based relationships that B2change organizations can use. All have their advantages and disadvantages and can be utilized effectively for B2change companies.

Creating value is a critical part of the B2change model because it details how an organization creates competencies and capabilities. **Core competencies** are defined as the combination of technology and production skills that underlie the product lines and services of an organization. They are based in science, technology, and engineering and can be found in an organization's staff. **Capabilities** are the clearly identifiable and measurable value-adding activities that describe what the organization can do. Processes, routines, behaviors, and systems constitute the major part of capabilities and can be found anywhere in the organization. By constantly improving competencies and capabilities, they can be leveraged to result in a competitive advantage for the B2change organization.

The last process of the B2change model is designing. To perform effectively, an organization designs processes and structures that allow it to create the appropriate competencies and capabilities it needs. It is a constant process that modifies and adjusts all parts of an organization. **Dynamic alignment** exists when all of the pieces in the designing and creating value process are evolving in the same direction and in support of the strategic intent. There are three questions at the foundation of an effective dynamic alignment that must be considered at the beginning of the design process. They are:

1. What kind of information do you collect and how do you communicate it?
2. How do you measure individuals, units, and the organization as a whole?
3. Who should be involved in making decisions?

Information on how the business operates, the organization's environment, and how it is currently performing are the three most important kinds of information that an organization needs to collect. Communicating the information to everyone in the organization will connect the employees to their environment, which will help bring about the changes needed. B2change organizations concentrate on measuring predictors of performance. Measuring individuals, teams, business units, the total organization, and key processes is a difficult task. B2change organizations look at all of these parts and determine if what they are doing presently will continue to allow them to perform effectively in the future. There are many different options that the B2change organization can employ to measure these organizational parts.

CREATING A VIRTUOUS SPIRAL

Creating a **virtuous spiral** is the goal of B2change organizations. This state exists when everything comes together in such a way that critical configuration and dynamic alignment equally coexist for extended periods of time. They are very unusual and almost impossible to duplicate. IBM, Nike, Microsoft, Procter & Gamble, and GE are organizations that have found the virtuous spiral path and have continued on it for many years. Unfortunately, a rapidly changing environment is the biggest hazard for virtuous spirals and sustained effectiveness. It is for this reason that successful B2change organizations are difficult to maintain. Creating a B2change organization is a daunting prospect, but it is becoming more and more important in today's increasingly competitive business environment. Using a B2change model can help organizations adapt to their surroundings and give them the competitive edge they need to gain or sustain organizational effectiveness.

A Sense of Urgency

John P. Kotter

Summary Prepared by David L. Beal

David Beal is a retired Operations Manager for Stora Enso, formerly Consolidated Papers, Inc., and Vice President of Manufacturing for Lake Superior Paper Industries in Duluth, Minnesota. Under his leadership, an all-salaried high-performance work system was organized into a totally self-reliant team system using the principles of sociotechnical design (STS). Dave teaches in the Labovitz School of Business and Economics at the University of Minnesota Duluth, and his areas of interest include designing and leading self-directed team-based organizations, teamwork, organizational studies, and production and operations management. He received his B.S. in Chemical Engineering from the University of Maine in Orono, Maine, with a fifth year in Pulp and Paper Sciences.

INTRODUCTION

Managers need to understand the psychology of creating a true sense of urgency in organizations to solve problems and address issues that will achieve strategic and financial objectives. If they focus on capturing the hearts and then the minds of a critical mass of employees, that will create this "true" **sense of urgency** necessary to succeed in a fast-moving, turbulent environment. When true urgency is not present, either complacency or a false sense of urgency gives people enough sense of security to believe that the organization will survive and be able to address any real threat.

Complacency exists to a certain extent in all organizations and is much more common than we believe. **Complacency** is often not seen or recognized by the employees involved because it is the product of success or perceived success. Unfortunately, it can still be part of the culture long after great success has disappeared.

The perception of success does not have to be accurate nor do the complacent rarely believe they are complacent. *The fear of what change might do to the organization or their involvement can drive irrational behavior.* The complacent

John P. Kotter. *A Sense of Urgency.* Boston, MA: Harvard Business Press, 2008.

are satisfied with the *status quo* and want predictability as they have known it more than anything else. Because of this, they pay more attention to what is happening internally than externally and ignore real competitive threats to the organization. While the opposite of urgency is complacency, an even more insidious threat is a **false sense of urgency**—thinking that frenzied activity alone can produce success. However, that type of activity is not likely to address real issues or threats occurring outside the organization. This false sense of urgency is as prevalent today as complacency, and it is dangerous because employees believe that the activities that occur are moving the organization into the future when in fact the opposite may be true. False urgency comes from a belief that there is a real threat to the organization when past experience has failed to achieve intended results or from others in the organization applying extreme pressure on the group. Employees with a false sense of urgency think the situation is a mess, and their frantic attempt to deal with it makes them angry, frustrated, and exhausted.

The issues of complacency and having a false sense of urgency are easily illustrated by some examples of organizations that have both succeeded and failed. Learning from these and many other case studies combined with decades of studying organizations, a strategy has emerged for increasing a true sense of urgency that is exceptionally alert, inclusive of the external environment, and relentlessly aimed at achieving success by making incremental progress each and every day. This strategy includes getting rid of seemingly important activities that do not win over the heart for change and instill a compulsive determination to act now. The actions that really matter are about *creating feelings essential for the change process to succeed.* When it comes to changing the behaviors of people, feelings are more powerful than thoughts. Feelings will motivate people to achieve more ambitious objectives despite seemingly insurmountable obstacles. Feelings will create timely actions that move the organization forward and do so every day.

THE STRATEGY FOR INCREASING TRUE URGENCY

The primary way to develop a true sense of urgency is to aim at the heart first. This can be done by creating thoughtful human experiences, such as bringing in a customer that has a passion for quality and performance, or visiting a successful competitor's place of business. Managers need to rely on all the senses to make the experience move people to address real issues and threats. Not all experiences create the desired emotional reaction. Effective experiences should move people from their day-to-day comfort zone to actions that address real problems and issues that do not have to be explained. These experiences do need to be carefully crafted so they develop a true sense of urgency that will embrace strategic goals and model desirable and observable behaviors. Strategies should be designed to empower employees by giving them access to important information and the ability to decide and act on critical issues. In short, strategies need to be created that address real issues and problems by winning, by making continuous progress every day, and by appealing to the heart as well as the mind.

THE FOUR TACTICS FOR CREATING A TRUE SENSE OF URGENCY

There are four tactics for creating a true sense of urgency. They are:

1. Bring the outside in
2. Behave with urgency every day
3. Find opportunity in crises
4. Deal with the NoNos

Bring the Outside In

Success creates an inward focus and a false sense of security that diminishes the critical influence and reality of serious threats from the outside. To **bring the outside in** to the organization, top management needs to listen to those employees who have regular contact with customers, suppliers, and the business community. More and more enterprises need to listen to the valuable information that frontline employees bring into the organization. This requires establishing a trusting relationship that values their input and ability to understand the customer in a changing environment. Asking the right questions, closely listening to the responses, and appropriately acting on the information will become increasing valuable. When important data become available, it should not be shielded from employees, especially if it is troubling. Data made available to those who have the ability to make important decisions and act in service of their customers will address critical issues and problems if a true sense of urgency is instilled in the culture.

The initiative to act starts at the top when management sees an opportunity and not just a problem. The primary objective is to transition from complacency to urgency without creating a flurry of activity that makes people anxious and angry. Information should be freely disseminated and direct access given to those who have the ability to act. Successful management clearly reinforces the importance of bringing the outside in to strengthen the organization. As top managers act with confidence, they make it clear that the focus is on urgency for creating the future and not blaming employees for the past. Managers need to predict how the organization will react so that fear and anger will be defused by a conviction that a sense of true urgency will produce future success.

Behave with Urgency Every Day

The information revolution and proliferation of electronic communications have added to the often-unrelated busy activities that fail to address real threats and bring the outside into the organization. Adding more hours in the day or working harder simply adds to fatigue and clutters the mind with pressure and activities that add little or no value in achieving true urgency. So why would anyone behave in a way that is contrary to their belief that they are modeling a true sense of urgency? The answer is usually complex, with a combination of forces at work. These forces may include being pushed in the wrong direction by the organization's culture; being unapproachable by peers and subordinates; not seeing the problem because of complacency; or being trapped in a set of behaviors that created past successes.

In order to **behave with urgency** every day it is important to

- Free uptime by eliminating low-priority activities and busy appointment books that prevent acting with a true sense of urgency every time the opportunity arises.
- Delegate by empowering employees with the ability to make and act on decisions that increase a true sense of urgency. Hold employees accountable and do not allow them to delegate up.
- Leave enough free time during the day to respond immediately to high-priority issues, and bring closure to conversations and meetings by clarifying the next steps with a true sense of urgency.
- Leave at least one hour each day to talk to subordinates with feeling and passion about the importance of having a true sense of urgency and what it means to the success of the organization. Listen, listen, listen, and respond with true urgency by identifying the strategic issues and activities that will move the organization into the future.

- Make sure you "Walk the Talk" by modeling behaviors that are supportive of the passion you have for a true sense of urgency. Bring the outside world into your actions in various ways that appeal to the multiple senses that people have.
- Be as open and visible as possible, using your personal strengths effectively.

Find Opportunity in Crises

Managers can often **find opportunities in crises** if the situation is used effectively to create a true sense of urgency. The following principles will guide the effectiveness of using crises productively:

- Look for potential solutions that turn crises into opportunities. A crisis can be a valuable opportunity for change that appeals to the heart and reinforces supportive behaviors.
- Recognize that crises do not by themselves reduce complacency. They must be used as opportunities to create the kind of behaviors that address real business problems and demonstrate a true sense of urgency for everyone to see.
- When using crises to reduce complacency, predict how people will react so that specific plans will be timely and effective.
- If the organization is highly complacent and hurting deeply, never depend on a crisis to create a true sense of urgency. The issue needs to be addressed with paramount importance by bringing the outside in and developing critical urgent behaviors that address real issues every day.
- Great care should be taken in creating a crisis because of the backlash others might have if they feel manipulated or less secure. Their reactions will not be supportive.
- If you are in the middle of the organization and see a looming crisis that others do not see, try to work open mindedly and communicate that information with someone who is in a position of power and influence.

Deal with NoNos (Perpetual Naysayers)

NoNos are those few individuals in the organization who are against change in any form. They are far more dangerous than we want to believe, and frequently their negative behavior is not fully seen by their superiors. Their peers and subordinates know who they are and by using a nonthreatening questioning approach, their identity can be revealed. NoNos are highly effective urgency killers who will do almost anything to discredit others who are trying to create a sense of urgency. Their negative impact by undermining the efforts of others can have a damaging, even disastrous effect on the organization. They must be dealt with effectively and with a true sense of urgency.

There are three strategies that work and two that are rarely successful. The three strategies that are most successful are as follows:

1. Keep the NoNos fully occupied with value-added responsibilities and activities that do not allow them to have a negative effect on the change process;
2. Eliminate NoNos from the organization and give them an appropriate severance package;
3. Expose their negative behaviors and allow the force of peer pressure to reduce or eliminate their effectiveness.

The two strategies that usually do not work are making a NoNo part of the change process that will move the organization forward with the hope that the NoNo will change and support a sense of urgency and isolating the NoNos from the change process. This latter strategy almost never works because the NoNo can create a great deal of damage behind the scenes that may not be observable to top management.

Conclusion

Organizations today need a true—not a false—sense of urgency to survive and prosper. Fortunately, there are strategies available for creating this, but managers must focus on the hearts of employees to stimulate them to buy into that passion. Four techniques—bringing the outside in, behaving with urgency, finding opportunity in crises, and dealing strongly with naysayers—are vital to the success of programs for change.

IX

"Undiscussable" Issues at Work

Organizational culture is all about the relationships that exist among organizational members, and how people connect and interact with one another as they carry out their organizational roles. However, there is an intended culture and an actual culture in many cases—and the two can be vastly different. In this section, three book summaries (*Workplace Survival*, *The No Asshole Rule*, and *It's All Politics*) are presented, with each one providing insight into what are often and unfortunately the negative and harmful internal and interpersonal workings of people in organizations.

Three dysfunctional elements in any organization can lead to its downfall: bad bosses, bad employees/colleagues, and bad jobs. Bad bosses, according to Ella and David Van Fleet, use heavy-handed threats to abuse their power, show favoritism, micromanage, are insecure and/or incompetent, and cannot accept criticism. Bad employees don't carry their own weight and may bully, harass, threaten, or sabotage others. Bad jobs create an unpleasant or unsafe workplace. Any of these factors can cause workplace turmoil, dissatisfaction, or even violence.

Dr. Ella Van Fleet is Founder and President of Professional Business Associates and has been an educator, trainer, and consultant for over a quarter century. Dr. David Van Fleet has been a faculty member, Fellow of the Academy of Management, and editor of prestigious business journals. He has published several previous books, including *Contemporary Management*, *Behavior in Organizations*, and *Organizational Behavior*.

Dr. Robert Sutton holds a Ph.D. in Organizational Psychology from the University of Michigan and serves on the faculty in the Stanford Engineering School. He is an award-winning writer, the former editor of *Administrative Science Quarterly*, and a member of the *Academy of Management Journal*'s Hall of Fame. His previous books include *Weird Ideas That Work* and *Hard Facts, Dangerous Half-Truths, and Total Nonsense*.

Sutton confronts a previously taboo topic—the ubiquitous and persistent presence of mean-spirited jerks who are bullies and tyrants that make other people miserable and fearful. He provides two key tests for whether an individual qualifies as an asshole—whether the target of the abuse feels belittled and humiliated (via insults, shaming, rudeness, and sarcasm), and whether there is a power differential between the two parties. Sutton proposes a simple solution—the banning of assholes via strict policies, careful monitoring, constructive confrontation, and saying "good riddance" to incorrigible jerks.

In *It's All Politics*, Kathleen Kelley Reardon notes that hard work and potential are not the only keys for an individual's movement upward and ultimately to the top of the organizational hierarchy. Those who make it—the winners—and those who don't—the losers—differ from one another in terms of their political skills and the use of those skills. Those who make it upward successfully manage their relationships with those who are capable of rewarding them with key organizational moves.

Kathleen Kelley Reardon is a professor of management and organization in the Marshall School of Business at the University of Southern California. She holds a Ph.D. in Communications from the University of Massachusetts in Amherst and is an expert in the areas of persuasion, negotiations, and politics. Dr. Reardon is also the author of *The Secret Handshake*.

Workplace Survival

Ella W. Van Fleet and David D. Van Fleet

Summary Prepared by Kelly L. Nelson

Kelly L. Nelson earned her Bachelor of Business Administration from the University of Minnesota Duluth and her MBA from Xavier University. She is currently General Manager, Human Resources, with AK Steel Corporation. Kelly strives to avoid being known as a bad boss or a bad coworker by following the guidance provided in Workplace Survival: Dealing with Bad Bosses, Bad Workers, Bad Jobs.

BAD BOSSES

Three key elements in the workplace have a profound effect on everyone: bosses, workers, and the tasks that make the job. Bosses in particular, through the course of their duties, have a significant effect—for better or worse—on employees in the workplace. Bad bosses can demonstrate their effects in a number of ways:

- Abusing their power. Threats can include any number of subjects, but some common threats include threatening to give a difficult (or distasteful) assignment to keep employees in line, threatening to fire employees if even a minor mistake is made, threatening to withhold raises unless the employee follows questionable directions, and so on. Bosses can also abuse their power by defending actions "because I am the boss," and setting poor examples by requiring employees to follow rules that the supervisor doesn't feel he or she needs to follow. Bad bosses take the power they have over workers to exploit them.

  Furthermore, insecure bosses can attempt to withhold promotions from competent employees whom they feel may pose a threat to their own job security/promotional opportunities, treat employees as their own personal servants, abuse employees in order to force them to resign, act inappropriately or illegally, and lie or exaggerate. In short, bosses who abuse their power rely

Ella W. Van Fleet and David D. Van Fleet. *Workplace Survival: Dealing with Bad Bosses, Bad Workers, Bad Jobs.* Baltimore, MD: Publish America, 2007.

on using a "whip" instead of a "carrot" and subsequently cause misery for those who report to them.

- Failing to control their anger. Most people have worked for a "screamer" at one point in their career. Bosses who yell provide public embarrassment to the subject of their rant, and this flies in the face of the good management axiom to "praise in public; correct in private." As a part of their responsibilities, supervisors should display maturity and level-headedness. However, bad bosses don't control their behavior; instead, they fly off the handle and react emotionally over business-related issues.

  Bad bosses who fail to control their anger often use foul language habitually, curse at bearers of bad news, and use snide remarks to intimidate workers. This offensive language creates an unprofessional workplace and unhappy, unproductive workers. Foul language may be considered degrading behavior, but it is not the only method. Nor is degrading behavior always done in person. It can be accomplished through e-mails or by talking about someone when they are not present. Furthermore, behavior that belittles others can be done under the guise of teasing or intimidating an employee due to race, gender, or cultural differences. Behavior that demeans is done to instill fear in employees and "to keep them in line."

- Exhibiting poor management skills. Nothing screams "bad boss" as loudly as the insecure manager who micromanages, focuses on activity instead of results, or constantly checks on his or her employees to ensure they are staying on task. Poor management skills are also demonstrated by providing poorly done, unconstructive, and/or inaccurate performance appraisals. Inaccurate appraisals can be used in the future to "prove" the employee is a poor employee, even when the appraisal is not an accurate depiction of the employee's true contribution to the organization. Finally, bosses who fail to let others do their job and fail to provide strategic leadership to the organization are content to have a rudderless ship.

- Being insecure and/or incompetent. Bad bosses often try to cover up their incompetence by refusing to participate in the work to be done, relying on the reason "because I'm the boss," and, in extreme instances, deliberately sabotaging operations in order to be the hero by providing the solution to the problem. Incompetent or insecure bosses often show their lack of ability by failing to manage the employees who work for them. They ignore problems that exist, fail to solve even simple problems, and act like a friend instead of a boss. Insecure bosses show their stripes when they are unable to accept criticism, surround themselves with only those who agree with them, and refuse to accept any blame when problems occur. They often use their employees for scapegoats and spread the blame to everyone but themselves.

- Being backed by weak/poor upper management. Higher levels of management play a crucial role in the behavior of bad bosses. The problem can be exacerbated when upper management either ignores the bad behavior or, worse yet, affirmatively supports the bad behavior. They can also cause the bad boss behavior by failing to train bosses, criticizing the boss but doing nothing to correct the behavior, or rewarding the wrong behavior from the boss. Bad bosses have the ability to affect the work life of their employees, but they are not necessarily the only "bad" element that can impact others' work lives.

BAD EMPLOYEES

Bad employees (coworkers) can also make others miserable. They may

- Lack interpersonal skills. Not only can a coworker's bad attitude be difficult to endure, it can also shape the attitude of workers around him or her, spreading the poor morale.

However, employees don't have to have a bad attitude to affect others; they can also be so self-focused that they are actually inconsiderate to coworkers, and this can directly affect team outcomes. Finally, appearance or hygiene problems can be a nightmare. Who wants to work next to an employee who thinks toothpaste and deodorant are not necessary?

- Take or subject others to unnecessary risks. Taken to the extreme, an employee who subjects others to risks may actually cause the death of a coworker. At the very least, this risky behavior can damage assets and decrease productivity. In addition, the bad worker can also be a danger to himself or herself, leading to injuries, or worse.
- Manipulate, threaten, harass, bully, or sabotage others. Similar to the bad boss who uses threats and manipulation to accomplish goals, coworkers can do the same. They may lie, deliberately undercut others' work, or threaten coworkers to make themselves feel like successes on the job—at the expense of all of the others around them.
- Don't carry their own weight. Not only do coworkers depend upon their fellow workers to be at work when expected, they also need for them to do their fair share of the work. Some good workers actually perform more than their fair share in order to make the operation successful; however, others' performance can be negatively affected when they feel they are expected to make up for the bad employee's lack of productivity, particularly when the bad worker's behavior is not corrected because there is a bad boss in the picture.

BAD JOBS

As if bad bosses and bad workers weren't enough of a problem, there is a third element that can make the workplace miserable—the bad job. A number of factors can make a job a "bad" job:

- Unpleasant or unsafe workplaces. Not only can unsafe or physically demanding work take its toll on workers, the environment can be uncomfortable and inconvenient. In addition to the environment, the tasks themselves can be changed or unexpected, leading to disappointment for the workers.
- Low rewards and poor security. Workers and bosses both may suffer from insecurity caused by unstable employment prospects and lack of compensation. It is difficult for employees to perform at their highest level when plagued by doubts about the organization's survival or haunted by their own ability to make ends meet with their current level of compensation.
- Bad customers. As if bad bosses, bad coworkers, and bad jobs aren't bad enough, the employee may also need to deal with unpleasant or "bad" customers, which makes the job even more difficult on which to function.
- Poor organizational culture/climate. If the organization is filled with bad workers and bad bosses, the probability is high that the organizational culture actively or passively supports this behavior. Some organizations are so "bad" that they create a threatening environment throughout all levels of the organization.

WHAT CAN BOSSES AND WORKERS DO TO BECOME "GOOD"?

Bosses should make a determined effort to not abuse their power, control their anger, learn new management skills, refuse to micromanage employees, provide timely performance feedback, not show favoritism, be an effective role model (and find one for themselves), use meetings appropriately, become competent and secure, learn to make good decisions, learn to accept criticism, hire and keep the right employees, and communicate effectively.

At the same time, workers should analyze their own job performance, seek constructive criticism from coworkers, analyze and address their personal problems, obtain others' perceptions of their boss, and choose to exercise one or more of these options:

Option #1: Talk with your boss (prepare by listing your complaints, ask others for their inputs, consider your boss's lack of experience, assess your boss's personality, narrow your list of complaints, schedule a meeting, and meet with the boss to resolve issues.)

Option #2: Report the situation.

Option #3: Get another job.

HOW CAN JOB SEEKERS AVOID JOINING AN ORGANIZATION WITH BAD BOSSES AND BAD COWORKERS?

First, job seekers need to find out as much as possible about the organization, its people, and the job in advance of the interview and certainly before accepting the job. Talk to people who work in the organization or live in the area. Search for relevant information on the Internet—both from the employer and from observers and commentators.

Second, take advantage of the job interview. Use it to evaluate everything you see and hear. Analyze the questions you are asked. Ask questions yourself that probe the issues you might be concerned about.

If you are given the opportunity to talk with people other than the person who will be your boss, find out how well the supervisor communicates, and ask about the supervisor's interpersonal style.

Finally, follow up. While the details are fresh in your mind, write them down, including impressions of interactions, the "feel" of the workplace, and the apparent culture of the organization.

WHAT CAN BOSSES DO TO AVOID HAVING BAD WORKERS?

1. Hire the right employees (know what skills you need, recruit the right people, and evaluate applicants to gather maximum information).
2. Be aware of employees' behavior through direct observation and second-hand reports.
3. Reinforce your expectations consistently.
4. Take action with bad workers promptly.
5. Provide feedback to employees.
6. Provide remedial training.
7. If the employee doesn't correct the unacceptable behavior, assist the exit.

WHAT CAN COWORKERS DO ABOUT BAD WORKERS?

Resolve to be polite and professional, but don't ignore the problem. Identify your values so that it will be easier to determine what is acceptable and what is not. Practice avoidance behaviors so as to not become irritated. Focus on your life off the job. Carefully try to change the person, but pick your battles carefully. Identify the bad behavior, and analyze your feelings about it before deciding what you want. Talk with the coworker, and assertively specify how the bad behavior impacts you. Most critically, avoid potentially violent coworkers, and report your assessment of their behavior to several other persons.

WHAT CAN BOSSES DO ABOUT BAD JOBS?

1. Improve undesirable workplaces, by asking employees for suggestions.
2. Ensure employees' safety is your top priority all of the time. Implement rules to keep employees safe, and hold employees accountable to follow the rules. Engineer out safety problems. Keep employees safe from criminal behavior. Eliminate workplace violence. Ensure employees are properly trained for job tasks. Do not tolerate unsafe behavior.
3. Try to modify a dysfunctional organizational culture.
4. Select better workers and outside contacts.
5. Explore increasing pay, job security, and advancement opportunities.
6. Redesign jobs to make them more desirable.

WHAT CAN WORKERS DO ABOUT BAD JOBS?

1. Change or adapt to the workplace.
2. Try to deal with the organizational culture.
3. Change or adapt to bad bosses, coworkers, and outside contacts.
4. Reevaluate your career.

Conclusion

There are many challenges to developing and living a satisfying career; however, it is not impossible. Success begins with the attitude of the individual and maintaining a positive outlook, no matter what the circumstances. Bosses, workers, and job seekers all have choices to make. Each individual should commit to avoid the characteristics that make people "bad" at their jobs and should make positive steps to improve shortcomings. Furthermore, each person should be proactive enough to provide suggestions to make the job better, more efficient, and more satisfying. However, if an employee realizes that he or she is faced with challenges that are not within one's control and that will prevent him or her from having a satisfactory career, the employee must accept the reality that not every job (and not every boss) is going to be a good match for every worker, and decide to move on. After all, *life is too short to work in an atmosphere filled with bad bosses, bad workers, and bad jobs.*

2

The No Asshole Rule: Building a Civilized Workplace and Surviving One that Isn't

Robert I. Sutton

Summary Prepared by Stephen Rubenfeld

Stephen Rubenfeld is Professor of Human Resource Management in the Labovitz School of Business and Economics at the University of Minnesota Duluth. He received his doctorate from the University of Wisconsin-Madison and was previously on the faculty of Texas Tech University. His professional publications and presentations have covered a wide range of human resource and labor relations topics, including workplace accommodations, compensation, human resource policies and practices, job security, and staffing challenges. He has served as a consultant to private and public organizations and is a member of the Society for Human Resource Management and the Academy of Management.

INTRODUCTION

"Who hired this jerk?" is a frequently asked question. *Unfortunately, almost all organizations have some mean-spirited employees who are bullies, tormentors, tyrants, egomaniacs, and weasels—bluntly speaking, assholes—who make our lives miserable.* In many cases, however, formal policy prohibitions and informal or unwritten codes of civilized interactions serve as *no asshole rules* to make offensive

Robert I. Sutton. *The No Asshole Rule: Building a Civilized Workplace and Surviving One That Isn't.* New York: Business Plus, 2007.

behaviors unacceptable in the employment setting. Nevertheless, these antisocial interactions exist and flourish. This is not a culture-bound phenomenon: they are found across the globe. Likewise, they are not unique to particular industries or cultures. The problem is ubiquitous and persistent. Organizations and their denizens seem to overlook and forgive, and, at times, even encourage abusive and boorish behaviors.

WHY ARE THERE SO MANY OF THEM?

The terminology is used widely and frequently, perhaps indiscriminately, and without an agreed-upon definition. We know one when we see one. People that annoy us, that cross us, and even those that show us up are often tagged with the label of *asshole*. While researchers have explored the nature of conflict, hostility, and psychological abuse, most of us assign this label to a guilty party spontaneously, emotionally, and vindictively. But to better understand the implications for organizations and how to cope with (and hopefully reform) these social misfits, there must be some metric to operationalize this construct. Answers to the following questions are a start:

1. Does the *target* of the abuse feel oppressed, humiliated, de-energized, or belittled by the person?
2. Is the venom directed at people who are *less powerful* rather that at those with greater stature and hierarchical power?

Affirmative responses to both questions provide a strong indication that we are dealing with an *asshole* (jerk). If we are completely honest, every one of us has the potential to act in ways that might earn us the title when we are placed in high-stress situations, are blindsided, are dealing with people who are socially inept, or immersed in a culture that encourages and reinforces such behaviors. We might temporarily regress and commit a social *faux pas*, but the *certified asshole* demonstrates ongoing and persistent patterns of behaviors that are overt and hurtful.

There are strategies and techniques that are frequently found in the quiver of everyday actions that such individuals use. They include the following:

- Personal insults
- Sarcastic teasing
- Two-faced attacks
- Humiliation
- Public shaming
- Threats
- Intimidation
- Rude interruptions
- Treating people as if they are invisible

These are but a few of the tools used to accomplish their inhumane deeds—particularly when dealing with subordinates and other who are less powerful in the work setting.

The answer is not to ban people who are forceful and driven to accomplish valued outcomes. Hiring only sycophants cannot be the answer. Tension, pressure, and high expectations can be constructive and perhaps essential to achieving excellence. Strong-willed, forceful, and even argumentative people can contribute to **constructive confrontation** (using evidence and logic to deal with problems) but not at the expense of engaging in character assassination and abusive personal conflicts. Research on bullying, workplace incivility, and psychological abuse tells us that there are many—way too many—occurrences in the workplaces of today. The preponderance of issues arise in dealings with subordinates and others seen as lower in the organizational pecking order. Doctors and their treatment of nurses, CEOs and their interactions with administrative assistants, and senior professors and their untenured colleagues are frequently cited situations of destructive work relationships.

EVERY WORKPLACE NEEDS *THE RULE*

All organizations need a no asshole rule to offset the harm caused by mean-spirited and abusive people. These jerks cause damage to the targets of their venom as well as to bystanders and colleagues, and their actions are detrimental to the success of the organization and to themselves.

The **victims** of this abusive treatment suffer psychologically, physiologically, and through damage to their careers. Demeaning, hostile, and overly aggressive treatment by abusive supervisors lead victims to exhibit less commitment to the organization and its goals, suffer burnout, and possibly to quit or withdraw. Likewise, the ramifications go beyond the employee's work life. Overall life satisfaction diminishes, people develop sleep problems, issues of mental health and depression may arise, and marital relations may be affected as well. As one office administrator reported, he "dies a little" with every meeting with his boss. These insensitive and demeaning interactions are damaging and pervasive. Too many of the perpetrators are oblivious to the disproportionate impact that negative interactions have on employees.

Innocent **battered bystanders** also are affected by the acts of these misguided managers and colleagues. Coworkers who cringe in fear of future interactions based on what they have observed or heard second hand are also less likely to take prudent risks and follow unproven paths. They, too, may question the wisdom of investing so much of themselves in the organization and therefore be more receptive to opportunities to escape. But the ripple effects felt by the *innocent*s are not necessarily limited to work colleagues; spouses, children, and friends also pay a price.

The direct and indirect effects (and costs) to organizational performance can be enormous, although not always obvious. The costs of increased turnover, absenteeism, lowered commitment, distraction, and reduced individual contributions can be quite substantial. Other risks including the increased probability of litigation involving harassment and other violations of employment law are lurking behind each boorish act and are greatest for organizations that ignore or cover up the inappropriate actions of their managers. Likewise, protective behaviors and revenge can have a tremendously negative impact. Protecting oneself becomes a priority and may push aside efforts directed toward organizational improvement. Human nature may lead victims to get even and achieve equity in a bad situation, which rarely works to the advantage of the employer. The risks are tremendous.

Finally, the *assholes* themselves may suffer as victims of their own abuses. While they are unlikely to get much sympathy from victims and bystanders, they often do pay a real price. They suffer career setbacks and, eventually, humiliation and ridicule. While our vindictive human nature may lead us to gloat when an abuser falls, there are elements of a Greek tragedy in this story line. Moreover, the perpetrators also may take some innocent bystanders down with them.

The effects are many, and the total costs can be tremendous. Some are obvious and others nearly invisible. Some are felt directly and immediately, while others are indirect and felt over the long haul. Some are easily quantifiable, while others are well below our budgetary radar. Some of the less obvious effects on organizations are as follows:

- Low levels of innovation and quality improvement
- Reduced cooperation
- Lower individual contributions "at the margin"
- Impaired ability to recruit high-caliber employees
- Higher health insurance costs
- Time spent appeasing, calming, and counseling
- Cultural changes that detract from performance

IMPLEMENTING AND KEEPING ALIVE *THE RULE*

If an employee is extremely successful, our societal norm is to overlook *little* imperfections in conduct and the lack of cultural fit. But even organizations that seem to relish (or at the very least tolerate) having some arrogant jerks in their midst do have limits. Some organizations have tightly enforced zero tolerance policies, but most have a combination of rules, policies, and cultural norms that provide guidance but allow discretion and *wiggle room*. Most large organizations have behavioral conduct policies that capture the spirit of the *no asshole rule*. However structured, successful rules share a number of characteristics and implementation guidelines:

1. **Make it public:** Having official policies buried in handbooks, sentiments posted in the hallways, and intranet reminders are necessary but not sufficient. What you say and what you do—consistently—are what really matters.
2. **Integrate the *Rule* into hiring:** Left to their own devices, people making hiring decisions will hire people similar to themselves. The potential for bad outcomes is obvious when we hire our clones. To escape this dilemma, references are essential, especially those that go beyond technical competence. Likewise, interviews and other face-to-face elements of the selection process should focus on human qualities. All job candidates should be interviewed by people who will work with and be subordinates of the new hire.
3. **Apply the *Rule* to customers and clients:** Organizations that really care about their employees expect their customers and clients to uphold comparably high standards of behavior.
4. **Status and rank shouldn't matter:** Rules are not just for mortals—the powerful and the high producers must be held to the same standards.
5. **Enforce the rules and walk the talk:**
   - Write it down and use it.
   - Recognize that *assholes are incompetent*, so just get rid of them.
   - Be aware that power breeds nastiness.
   - Manage moments; don't simply engage in policy enforcement.
   - Legitimize constructive confrontation.

HOW TO SURVIVE NASTY PEOPLE

Don't become one of the jerks; recognize that *assholes are contagious*. Anyone can catch the disease, so don't let your **inner jerk** (innate ability to be caustic and cruel) surface. But even if you keep yourself pure, you *will* come in direct contact with jerks in all facets of your life. You have to find ways to **reframe**, or change your mindset regarding what is happening to you. Here's how:

1. Hope for the best, but expect the worst.
2. Develop indifference and emotional detachment.
3. Look for small wins; you're not going to change the world.
4. Limit your contact and risk.
5. Develop a support network.

Even if you *can* endure abusive behavior, the question remains, should you? This is a personal decision, but the reality is that we can't (and probably shouldn't) go on the attack or pick up and run every time adversity rears its head.

DO *ASSHOLES* HAVE ANY VIRTUES?

Much to the annoyance of their peers and subordinates, jerks often are successful—sometimes, very successful. They gain personal power, intimidate their rivals, and motivate fear-driven performance. Even the good guys may find it useful to temporarily use jerklike strategies. Some people are so clueless or lazy that a tantrum and a little noise might help to bring them to their senses. Despite the sometime successes and the selective usefulness of out-of-character behaviors, most defenses of being an asshole are misguided. Many jerks assume their successes are driven by their abusive ways, when in fact it is just as likely to be despite the way they treat others. *Most assholes suffer from delusions of effectiveness.*

THE RULE AS A WAY OF LIFE

The lessons shown below will not cure the ills of the world or suddenly turn jerks into model citizens. They are, however, constructive steps to achieve incremental improvement and help victims cope with bad situations. The seven key lessons are as follows:

1. A few jerks can overwhelm the good of a large number of civilized people.
2. Policies and rules are a start, but successes are built on day-to-day actions.
3. The *Rule* lives or dies by dealing with problems immediately and directly.
4. A few bad people, if managed properly, can be helpful in demonstrating how *not* to behave.
5. Enforcing the *no asshole rule* is *not* just management's job; everyone should step up to the plate and support the goal of eliminating unacceptable behavior.
6. Embarrassment can be a powerful learning tool, so jerks must be put on the spot.
7. Remember, there are times when WE are the *assholes*.

Conclusion

It would be nice if we never had to deal with people who treat us like second-class citizens and offend our sensibilities. But since this isn't the case, we must continuously strive to create a civilized, jerk-free workplace.

3

It's All Politics

Kathleen Kelley Reardon

Summary Prepared by AnneMarie Kaul

AnneMarie Kaul is the Development Director of the North Central Chapter of the Arthritis Foundation. Previously, she served as the Donor Resources Manager for the St. Paul Blood Center of the American Red Cross. She also has several years of experience managing financial services departments at Securian Financial, Inc. Her business expertise has been in the areas of leadership and customer service. She has a B.B.A. degree from the University of Minnesota Duluth and an M.B.A. from the University of St. Thomas in St. Paul, Minnesota.

POLITICS: IS IT REALLY A BAD THING?

Most people consider workplace politics as a necessary evil. The words themselves are usually associated with negative feelings, such as anger, anxiety, and fear. Moreover, people usually attribute politics to a whole host of problems including missed promotional opportunities, terminations, and even smaller decisions such as who gets the best office. In fact, many people sling around the word *politics* as if it was mud. But truth be told, it is a well-known fact that politics, in general, is a part of life and those who can overcome their fear and learn how to be more politically astute have a higher rate of success and satisfaction. The downside is that, even though politics plays an important role in one's life, rarely do we see a college class focused on learning how to become politically skilled. However, the good news is that we can learn how to enhance our political competencies on our own. Politics can be a positive influence in our lives; we just need to observe and practice it.

Kathleen Kelley Reardon. *It's All Politics: Winning in a World Where Hard Work and Talent Aren't Enough.* New York: Broadway Business (Crown), 2005.

THE DEFINITION OF POLITICS

Quite simply, politics is the positioning of ideas in a favorable light by knowing what to say, and how, when, and to whom to say it. There are five key areas of political development: intuition, insight, persuasion, power, and courage. To increase one's political acumen, developing and strengthening skills in these five areas is essential.

Letting Intuition Be the Guide

People who are born with natural intuition are a very rare breed. The good news, however, is that anyone without natural instincts can develop them just by observing those who are intuitive and then replicating certain behaviors. Therefore, it is important to be able to identify these general characteristics of an intuitive person.

A person using intuition is constantly *unpredictable* and does not work on the premise of going with the *status quo*. For example, instead of the typical greeting, "Hi, how are you?" an intuitive person would more likely quickly assess the social level of the passing individual and customize a more appropriate response. If the other person is more reserved, a simple head nod would suffice. An intuitive person will make others feel comfortable, yet keep them guessing by varying his or her behavior.

Another trait of an intuitive person is the ability to use **gut feelings** to make quick decisions. This person acts on a hunch or a feeling versus analyzing the facts. The trouble with pure intellect is that it allows us to take in only a small portion of the relevant information. On the other hand, intuitive people tend to multitrack, which means taking in information from gestures, tone of voice, and other nonverbal cues in addition to the words. They process the message at a deeper level, resulting in more effective communication.

In addition to unpredictability and the use of feelings, being empathetic is another key ingredient to enhance political intuition. **Empathy** is being sensitive to the changing feelings of another person. Getting connected to people and how they think will place a person in a better position to guide future outcomes of almost any interaction.

Here are some common, straightforward guidelines to improve your intuition skills:

- Ask a lot of questions.
- Don't make assumptions.
- Learn how things are normally done.
- Read between the lines.
- Look for differences between verbal and nonverbal communication.

Political Insight: It's About Thinking

Another component of politics is knowing what to do after you predict what is about to happen. This is called **political insight**. Political insight is typically 99 percent perspiration and 1 percent inspiration. Essentially, it is using creativity to respond to typical situations. Insightful people demonstrate the following behaviors:

- Being patient
- Looking at problems from all angles (using the **mind-mapping** technique)
- Choosing the best option after considering the positives and negatives
- Considering possible **choice points** or reactions of others
- Using the concept of framing to position ideas in an appealing manner to others
- Not making assumptions

More specifically, it is important to develop political insight *before* and *during* inter-actions with others. Advance work primarily involves managing the perception of others and being prepared for different reactions. Some tactics to include in this prep work are as follows:

- Getting to know people and forming alliances
- Testing an idea or concept on a select audience
- Preparing a response prior to negative reactions
- Possessing a solid track record in your field of work

During an interaction, thinking on your feet helps to glean political insight. Responding in the moment is critical, but many people feel inadequate in this area of political interaction. In the context of political strategies, responding properly to problems, personal attacks, and hidden agendas holds the key to creating a favorable outcome. The following guiding principles can be used to defuse negative conversations:

- Know when to confront, when to back off, and when to ask for support.
- Recognize when to apologize.
- Give credit to others.
- Divert attention away from sensitive or unresolvable issues.
- Paraphrase what was said in a favorable context.

Understanding how to proceed in a politically charged environment by doing up-front homework can virtually save a person's job and, at a minimum, a person's credibility and reputation.

Understanding Persuasion

Political influence can be more important to bring about change in the workplace than the standard methods of authority, culture, or expertise. **Persuasion**, one of the most important components of influence, is the ability to position ideas in an appealing manner so others will accept them. Interestingly, whether specifically at work or generally in life, many people con-sider persuasion as the "high road" of manipulation, which is actually a form of deception. To be an astute student of politics, both persuasion and manipulation techniques should be well understood.

Listening to really understand the actual meaning of a message and taking time to formu-late thoughts *before* responding wields great power and influence. Knowing when the content of a message is relevant, called **conversational coherence**, and how to introduce a new topic, called **topicality shift**, are also necessary skills to enhance persuasive ability.

These preparation steps are critical to enhance political persuasion:

- Understanding what motivates the other person so as to connect the message to those interests
- Determining how much should be said and the way it should be said
- Ensuring that the information is reliable and relevant

Common Persuasion Strategies

There are many methods and approaches to persuade others. The approach that is most effective will depend on each person and situation. Typically, however, the three more commonly used strategies are reciprocity, scarcity, and authority.

Reciprocity is doing a favor for someone *now* in order to have it returned *later.* Skilled politicians are very good at giving help up front to get things accomplished in the future. **Scarcity** is the ability to create a high demand by providing scarce resources. People want what they can't have. An example of this strategy was the Tyco Beanie Baby craze of the late 1990s. **Authority** is becoming an expert in a certain field, preferably in a field that is inadequately filled. Thus, a person becomes a "niche" player.

Whether a person's strategy encompasses any of the three just described or a combination of others, it is helpful to keep the following suggestions in mind:

- Keep your work visible to the right people.
- Be in a position to be noticed.
- Make sure the project goals are in line with the company's goals.

How Does Political Power Work?

In order to get ahead in the workplace it is paramount to understand how political power works and to learn how to gain this power. Accomplishments alone are not enough; selling yourself is the key.

Power can easily be gained and lost, so cultivating and maintaining it should be a continual process. During this process, it is important to keep in mind that it is the *perceptions* of others that essentially create and sustain the somewhat nebulous power. In other words, if a person feels powerless, it is because that person has allowed someone else's perception to influence how he or she thinks, feels, and behaves. Fortunately, by following the power strategies listed below, people can improve and maintain their power base.

- Maintain appearances, including attire, office décor, handshaking, gestures, and so on.
- Maintain relationships by getting to know the people who can help you (be charming and humorous).
- Enhance communication by listening and then adapting one's style to fit another's style.
- Assess the power of your position within the hierarchy of the organization.
- Seek out advisors.
- Be sure to thank people who help you and remember to help them, too.
- Increase knowledge by learning about the company's culture and real goals.
- Manage your reputation by acquiring the skills to do the job well, and ensuring that others know about it.

Political Power: Courage Vs. Suicide

Most people would agree that in order to increase power, a person must take risks and not be afraid to make misjudgments or mistakes. *But the question is: When does political courage become political suicide?* The answer lies in one's intentions. If a person is taking a stand based on true beliefs and feelings, then showing courage by speaking out is the smart and necessary option. On the other hand, if the intent is artificial or self-centered, eventually these actions will lead to career suicide. Of course there are varying degrees between doing what is best for the company and what is best for the person. Political courage should not lead to self-destruction or the destruction of others. *One must assess the real risks and rewards before moving too quickly, keeping in mind that achieving the goal is not always as important as the way it is reached.*

Before jumping into a politically charged situation, the following questions should be evaluated and answered honestly:

- Do I have the needed support?
- Is my track record sufficiently developed?
- Am I up for the challenge right now?
- What are the win-win and no-win options?

Ultimately, having the strength and stamina to proceed with caution is the key. It is up to each individual to personally reconcile his or her motives with the risks and rewards to make this type of decision.

POLITICAL BOUNDARIES

To some extent, all organizations mold and shape their political direction by the nature of their culture. A company's political environment should be carefully analyzed prior to employment whenever possible. By doing this up-front work, a person will be in a better position to react when faced with political choice points. It is good practice to establish a personal "comfort zone" when dealing with politics, since many individuals who do not do so end up confused and misunderstood.

From a corporate culture perspective, smart organizations will intentionally influence their political direction. Good organizations encourage positive politics. They develop and communicate a set of values that can be adopted at every level—from the mailroom clerk to the CEO. Two examples of politically smart companies are Mars and Nokia. Both of these firms put a high priority on rewarding associates who demonstrate a strong work ethic. They also support workplace principles such as responsibility, mutuality, and freedom of expression.

THE POLITICAL GAME

Staying on top of the political game can make all the difference between hiding out on the bench (frightened to take risks) and getting out on the field to score the necessary points to stay ahead. The good news is that anyone can nurture and strengthen their political savvy to actually win the game. The process to improve political know-how requires only two simple actions: observing and practicing. Equipped with enhanced intuition and persuasion skills, a not-so-politically adept person can take more control over his or her life and make some highly astute political decisions and useful connections. Moreover, having the knowledge of the political culture in the workplace and the courage to abide by personal political boundaries will provide the necessary strength to face and overcome political adversity. The opponent is no longer a threat but an adversary.

X

The Managerial Brain

Managers at all levels of organizations make decisions. Some of these are relatively trivial and some are powerfully significant. Some managers make decisions frequently, and others engage in the process more infrequently. Some managers make decisions intuitively (e.g., using gut feelings or their "adaptive unconscious") and others follow a more systematic process. Nevertheless, from a systems perspective, all decisions eventually affect the success of the enterprise. It is critical to discover useful frameworks for how managers should approach the decision process so as to avoid common errors and increase the probability of success. This becomes increasingly true for decisions with large potential payoffs or when managers are faced with crisis situations.

Gerd Gigerenzer has been both Professor of Psychology (University of Chicago) and Visiting Professor in the School of Law (University of Virginia). He is currently a director at the Max Planck Institute for Human Development in Berlin. His published books include *Calculated Risks*, *Bounded Rationality*, and *Rationality for Mortals*.

Gigerenzer contends, in *Gut Feelings*, that decision makers might consider discarding their propensity to acquire more and more data. Instead, he proposes that they seek to use their intuition, hunches, and unconscious intelligence. Rules of thumb (heuristics) are useful aids; these rely on trust, identification, deception, wishful thinking, and cooperation. The operating definition of a gut feeling is one that arises spontaneously, is not fully understood, and yet is strong enough to be acted upon. (Note that Dan Ariely's popular book, *Predictably Irrational*, shares a similarity with *Gut Feelings* in the argument that human behavior is often irrational. Whereas Ariely may see this as a flaw, Gigerenzer views this as an asset to be capitalized upon via intuition.)

Howard Gardner is the John H. and Elisabeth A. Hobbs Professor of Cognition and Education at the Harvard Graduate School of Education. His 20 books include well-known publications such as *Leading Minds*, *Changing Minds*, *Extraordinary Minds*, and *The Disciplined Mind*. He has extensively studied "GoodWork," which is defined by the three criteria of being socially responsible, excellent in quality, and personally meaningful.

Gardner contends that it is limiting to think of intelligence as a single phenomenon. Instead, it may be useful to conceptualize it as a composite of five minds that can better respond collectively to the fast-paced changes of the future. These five minds are disciplined, synthesizing, creating, respectful, and ethical. Unfortunately, resistance to embracing this new structure will take various forms—conservatism, fear of faddism, concern about hidden risks and costs, and lack of knowledge about how to acquire them.

Malcolm Gladwell, a staff writer for *The New Yorker*, has a remarkable record in his book publishing career. He has written two popular books that have each sold over a million copies. The first, *The Tipping Point*, explained how simple ideas and trends can snowball into veritable social epidemics that have tremendous positive inertia to them. The second book, *Blink!*, suggests that on-the-spot decision makers can be extremely successful at identifying familiar patterns based on very limited information (in the blink of an eye). They do this by using their "adaptive unconscious" to zero in on a few highly salient details and by using the process of "thin-slicing" to find patterns in situations based on narrow samplings of information. As a result, Gladwell suggests that managers should learn to trust their intuitive decisions, while also controlling their snap judgments. Fans of Gladwell might wish to take a look at a newer book of his—a collection of essays in *What the Dog Saw*.

Gut Feelings: The Intelligence of the Unconscious

Gerd Gigerenzer

Summary Prepared by Rebecca M. C. Boll

Rebecca M. C. Boll is employed with Central Minnesota Federal Credit Union (CMFCU) as a Financial Analyst with responsibilities for asset–liability management, financial analysis, competitive analysis, and strategic analysis. Prior to joining CMFCU, Boll worked as an Equity Research Analyst at Piper Jaffray; during her tenure, she covered Medical Device & Diagnostic companies in the healthcare sector. Ms. Boll received her B.B.A. in Organizational Management and Finance from the Labovitz School of Business and Economics (LSBE) at the University of Minnesota Duluth. During her undergraduate career, she participated in the LSBE Financial Markets Program and in the University's Undergraduate Research Opportunities Program, resulting in a paper entitled "Interorganizational Trust: Trust, Routines, & Institutionalization." For recreation, she enjoys spending time with friends and family, traveling, and participating in outdoor activities.

INTRODUCTION

A driver slows her car as she approaches the four-way stop at the upcoming intersection. She does not use deliberate calculation in order to react, nor does she weigh the pros and cons of continuing through the intersection; instead, she relies upon an automated response based on evolved capacities in order to slow, stop, and offer the right-of-way to the oncoming driver. Her driving accuracy is guided by her unconscious intelligence, since there is not enough time for her to safely conduct complex calculations for every decision she makes on her drive to work.

Gerd Gigerenzer. *Gut Feelings: The Intelligence of the Unconscious.* New York: Viking Press (Penguin), 2007.

UNCONSCIOUS INTELLIGENCE

Intelligence is often thought of as deliberate and guided by the ideas of logic, but it is also based on gut feelings and intuition. Managers traditionally consider intelligence as conducting complex calculations, weighing pros and cons, and analyzing before acting. However, the mind also relies upon **unconscious intelligence**—rules of thumb and evolved capacities in order to save time while making accurate decisions. In order to fully understand total intelligence, managers should learn how employees, teams, and organizations utilize both conscious intelligence and unconscious intelligence to solve problems, determine strategy, and execute business decisions in dynamic environments. Managers should acquire many mind tools, including both logic and gut feelings. Gaining a solid understanding of both types of intelligence is necessary for managers to become effective in today's organizational setting.

Gut Feelings and Intuition

Gut feelings (hunches or intuition) are judgments that appear quickly in consciousness and are strong enough to act on them, although the individual may not be aware of the underlying reasons for doing so. Gut feelings steer people in life because intelligence is not solely based on deliberate reasoning. Managers should recognize that the question is not *if* they should trust their gut, but the question is *when* they should trust their gut.

Good intuitions ignore nonapplicable information and manifest gut feelings from rules of thumb that extract only a few pieces of information from a complex world. In order to understand and best utilize both types of intelligence, managers should

- explore rules of thumb underlying intuition,
- pinpoint when these rules will succeed or fail, and
- acquire many mind tools, including logic and gut feelings.

Simple rules of thumb, also known as heuristics, take advantage of **evolved capacities** of the brain, which are a function of both genetics and the learning environment one has encountered and drawn from. Nature (genetics) gives people capability, practice turns it into a capacity, and the rule of thumb solves the problem. The recognition heuristic is one example of a simple rule of thumb. It indicates that what one recognizes is the right decision. An example of this is traveling to the supermarket in order to pick up peanut butter and laundry detergent. In both cases, people purchase what they recognize, or what they know.

Less is (Sometimes) More

The concept of "less is more" stems from the benefits of forgetting, the importance of starting small, and the speed-accuracy tradeoff. The benefits of forgetting prevent detail from slowing people down; in a dynamic world, remembering all details would weigh them down. When a manager is training a new employee, the importance of starting small prevails just as it does when a parent is teaching a child to speak. Finally, the speed-accuracy tradeoff suggests that the faster a task is completed, the less accurate it becomes. However, this depends on one's evolved capacities and ability to know when to use gut feelings. If experts take too long to complete a task, they'll perform worse than if given a time limit because their expertise is executed by unconscious intelligence. However, if a novice lacks instruction, he/she will not perform optimally.

Managers should internalize that less is more under these conditions:

- a beneficial degree of ignorance exists,
- unconscious motor skills are at play (trained experts' gut feelings outperform overdeliberation),
- cognitive limitations exist, and
- the freedom of choice paradox occurs.

In addition, the costs associated with information often make "having less" a better choice, while the benefits of simplicity indicate that simple rules of thumb may be better predictors of successful decisions than complex rules in an uncertain world.

How Intuition Works

Unconscious inferences combine sensory information and depend on prior knowledge that is accumulated about the world. Intuition allows people to focus on a few pieces of information and ignore the rest. It is based on an adaptive toolbox, mentioned previously as rules of thumb. Moreover, minds fill in missing information based on the information that is available; in other words, they make perceptual bets. *Specifically, intuition occurs when a manager experiences a rule of thumb move from unconscious to conscious.* Evolved capacities are the building blocks of rules of thumb, and rules of thumb produce gut feelings while the environment helps determine whether a rule of thumb will succeed. Furthermore, gut feelings help apply the correct rule of thumb under the most appropriate circumstances. Managers should remember the three parts of an intuition, which suggest that intuition is

- strong enough to act upon,
- inflexible, and
- triggered automatically by external stimuli.

Evolved Brains

Brains are a function of their genes and learning points from the environment. Important business decisions often rely on more than complex calculation of pros and cons; managers often also rely on a "gut check," which is based on evolved capacities from prior experiences. Additionally, managers should be forward thinkers by reflecting on their experiences to further build their evolved capacities and sharpen their gut feelings.

Adapted Minds

Managers should accept the fact that gut feelings help shape an organization's culture. In their jobs, employees develop rules of thumb to aid decision making, which ultimately expedites workflow and saves precious organizational resources. These rules of thumb are absorbed into the organization's bloodstream and are sometimes adopted or possibly forgotten. In either case, an organization's culture may shift. Therefore, organizational leaders should think carefully about the values their rules communicate and realize how these rules shape the organization. Periodically, managers should conduct an inventory of conscious and unconscious intelligence demonstrated by employees, teams, and the organization as a whole. They can then use this information to align rewards with rules of thumb that shape the desired team or organizational culture.

Adapted minds are necessary for navigating uncertainty as an organization executes its strategies. Complex calculation often relies too heavily on historical information, and only portions of this information are suitable predictors of the future. In a dynamic operating environment, organizations will ignore some information and base strategic initiatives on one good reason because even if problems are well defined, ideal solutions may not be obtainable. Hence, *good rules of thumb become irreplaceable.*

Why Good Intuitions Shouldn't Be Logical

Rigid logical norms ignore volatility in the environment, whereas unconscious intelligence goes beyond the information given and makes reasonable guesses. People often frame logical information in different ways, yet people decipher information often overlooked by logic. For example, when a man is told by his doctor that there is a 90 percent chance of survival associated with a surgery, he acknowledges this statistic but also considers the 10 percent chance that complications or death may occur. Therefore, managers should recognize that intuition is richer than logic and often helps solve a problem.

GUT FEELINGS IN ACTION

American culture has embraced the belief that more information is better and more choices are best; however, managers also should study gut feelings, which include recognition, recall, "one good reason" decision making, moral behavior, and social instincts. These gut feeling applications also belong in a manager's intelligence toolbox because they save time, prevent information overload, and predict well while operating under uncertainty. The next section analyzes these gut feelings individually.

Ever Heard Of . . . ?

Recognition memory is the ability to tell the novel from the previously experienced, or to decipher the old from the new. It is an evolved capacity that the recognition heuristic utilizes. Recognition shapes intuitions and emotions in everyday living. It reinforces reciprocity by aiding recognition of names and faces. This evolved capacity leads people to rules of thumb that generate gut feelings about which brand of a product should be purchased and which business partner has been fair and is likely to continue to be fair.

Managers should discover that the recognition heuristic is one simple tool in the adaptive toolbox; it guides intuitive judgments, including both inferences and personal choices. If one object is recognized but the other is not, people infer that the recognized object has higher value. Furthermore, this heuristic is impacted by quality, publicity, and validity. High-quality products are mentioned more often, those mentioned more often are recognized more frequently, and those recognized more often are thought to have higher quality. Therefore, by measuring the impact of quality and publicity, managers can predict in which situations recognition is informative versus misleading.

Effective use of the recognition heuristic depends on recognition and automatic evaluation. It is important for managers to note that evaluation is absent in automatic rules of thumb; however, scientists have studied the human brain and have discovered that specific neural activity is observed when unconscious intelligence, or automatic evaluation, occurs. People follow the recognition heuristic intuitively when it is valid.

One Good Reason is Enough

Recall memory takes recognition memory one step further by recalling episodes, facts, reasons, cues, and/or signals to assist with decision making. Sequential decision making is part of recall memory, whereby cue after cue is considered until a decision can be made. There are three fundamentals behind this heuristic, and they include:

- a search rule, where reasons are looked up in order of importance;
- a stopping rule, which stops a search as soon as alternatives differ; and
- a decision rule, which chooses the alternative that this reason suggests.

The "take the best" heuristic is efficient and accurate since less information and computation is needed. The intuition underlying this heuristic is exemplified when two friends are viewing a football game and are trying to predict the winner: "If the Minnesota Vikings won last season, they will win this season too. If this is not the case, then bet on the team leading at half time." Another sequential decision was discussed in the introduction; weighing the pros and cons in heavy traffic could be unsafe. When one is leaving a crowded stadium after a football game, he/she obeys the police officer directing traffic rather than the stop light. This person's unconscious intelligence tells him/her not to question the police officer but to follow his/her instructions instead of the stop light when the police officer is present. Continually making conscious tradeoffs would turn the world into a risky place; decisions would be made too slowly.

LESS IS MORE IN THE REAL WORLD Physicians' judgments are usually based on the highest expected utility, statistical aids, or intuition. Simple rules of thumb can be faster, less costly, and more accurate than computer-driven strategies, but oftentimes the fear of litigation drives physicians to make deliberate and complex calculations. Fast and frugal trees should be used by managers when solving a problem of classifying one object into two or more categories.

A "fast and frugal" decision tree asks a few "yes" or "no" questions, places the most important factor on top, and is transferable from managers to employees. A real-world example of this is found in the emergency room where physicians are trying to determine whether a patient's severe chest pain is related to cardiac problems or another health problem. If the former is determined, that patient should be taken to the coronary care unit, and if the latter is found, he/she should be taken to the general hospital ward. In this case, a fast and frugal tree has been devised to focus on what is important and to improve decision making, thereby freeing up scarce and costly emergency room resources.

MORAL BEHAVIOR Managers should also study the three principles of moral intuition, as follows:

- *Lack of awareness* symbolizes that gut feelings appear quickly and are strong enough to act upon.
- *Roots and rules* suggest that intuition is attached to the individual, family, or community and to an emotional goal described by a rule of thumb.
- *Moral behavior* is also contingent upon the social environment, which triggers a rule of thumb. Putting these principles together, moral intuitions are based on rules of thumb and rely on one-reason decision making.

To use an example of organ donation, people utilize a *default rule of thumb* (versus stable preferences) as a basis for their decision. In countries where people have to consciously "opt in" (i.e., choose to become organ donors) few are donors; in countries where people must "opt out," many more are donors. Default rules of thumb are often viewed as the reasonable recommendation.

Managers should recognize that defaults set by their companies have considerable impact on economic and moral behavior. When managers know both the unconscious and conscious mechanisms underlying moral behavior as well as environmental triggers, they will prevent or reduce moral dilemmas and increase ethical behavior within the organizational setting.

SOCIAL INSTINCTS   Special gut feelings lead to social interaction and include family and community instincts that are based on trust and reciprocity. Imitation is another gut feeling that lends itself to social instincts; for example, each generation does not begin from scratch; it learns from the previous generation and adapts. Imitation of the majority therefore satisfies the community instinct. However, when the world changes too quickly, imitation can be inferior to individual learning. Since organizational systems are continuously changing, managers should rely on unconscious intelligence, or the ability to know without thinking which rule to rely on and in what situation it applies.

Conclusion

Unconscious Intelligence is about gut feelings taking advantage of evolved capacities, which are based on rules of thumb. They enable people to act fast while maintaining accuracy. Meanwhile, the quality of intuition lies in the intelligence of the unconscious, that is, knowing without thinking which rule to rely on and what situations are appropriate. Managers are encouraged to study and apply gut feelings since they can be faster than and equally as accurate as deliberate reasoning and complex computation. From screening patients with chronic chest pain to branding and marketing peanut butter in supermarkets, managers should realize the importance of understanding unconscious intelligence and recognize there are good reasons to trust their own guts on occasion.

Five Minds
for the Future

Howard Gardner

Summary Prepared by Meghan Keil

Meghan Keil *obtained her bachelor's degree in Human Resource Management from the Labovitz School of Business and Economics at the University of Minnesota Duluth in 2008. She is currently working as an Executive Team Leader of Human Resources at Target Cooperation in Minneapolis, Minnesota.*

INTRODUCTION

How and why the human mind works the way it does has been pondered by both psychologists and scientists alike for decades. Most of the research, however, has focused on the typical *operation* of the human brain using ideas of cognitive science and neuroscience and less on the type of "minds" that people may need to develop in order to succeed in their ever-evolving world today. In other words, we have focused on a description of why the mind does what it does, instead of evaluating the type of minds, as a society, we *should* work to develop. The latter approach represents more of an intentional prescription of the type of minds that will best allow us to thrive in years to come.

THE FIVE MINDS

The identification of "minds" that will allow our species not only to be well prepared for the expected but also the unexpected are drawn from a variety of perspectives ranging from scientific research to humanistic disciplines such as history and anthropology. The current economic and political direction of our society was also taken into consideration when narrowing down a broad range of possibilities into five key minds for the future.

Each of the following minds can be (and more likely should be) nurtured across learners of all ages and at different points in their lives. The minds are global and should be developed by scholars, corporate leaders, and professionals

Howard Gardner. *Five Minds for the Future.* Boston, MA: Harvard Business Press, 2008.

alike. Each of the five minds should be considered to be of equal importance. There is no reason why one should focus on one mind at the expense of another. However, as with any practical matter, there may be trade-offs as individuals work to develop each of these minds.

Disciplined Mind

The meaning of the word discipline revolves around the ability to perfect a certain skill. Therefore a **disciplined mind**, as presented, has the ability to master at least one way of thinking about the world. The idea of a disciplined mind, however, is not to be confused with learning and understanding simple *subject matter.* Learning subject matter as we do in most schools today constitutes committing to memory a variety of facts, formulas, dates, key works, and figures to name a few categories. While working to memorize the subject matter alone does not create a disciplined mind, the process of finding connections and correlations between the subject matter as well as the answers to the underlying questions is very important in the development of a disciplined mind. The process of learning to think in a disciplined manner begins before adolescence and should continue throughout life; it should be intuitively obvious that *everyone* should be a continuous learner. Once one has a good understanding of what a disciplined mind is, the next obvious question becomes how does one go about disciplining their mind? The answer to this question is found in the following four essential steps. It's also important to note that the four steps are the same regardless of which discipline one has in mind of mastering.

1. *Identify truly important topics or concepts within the discipline.* This will vary depending on the discipline; some topics may be content related (i.e., the law of supply and demand), while other concepts may be methodological (i.e., how to set up a scientific experiment.)
2. *Spend a significant amount of time on the topic.* Mastering one discipline can take up to 10 years. Any topic worth spending this much time on is worth studying deeply.
3. *Approach the topic in a number of different ways.* This step takes advantage of the multiple ways individuals learn. It should be noted that any topic is more likely to be fully understood when approached from a variety of different ways—video, stories, and role play to name a few examples.
4. Most importantly, *set up "performances of understanding."* The only way to truly test if understanding, not just good memory, has been achieved is to pose a new question and see how the individual fares. This step explains why most standardized measures of learning in today's education system are of little use. They do not set up "performances of understanding" and therefore do not test whether or not a student can actually use the information they've recently learned outside the classroom (or in another context).

The process of developing a disciplined mind is intentional and takes time. It should be pursued because one finds pleasure in doing so and not because it has become an obsession. Along with this, one must realize that no topic can be fully mastered from only one disciplined perspective and that it is important to make connections, or synthesize knowledge, across several disciplines. This brings us to the second mind—the synthesizing mind.

Synthesizing Mind

The rate at which we are able to accumulate knowledge compared to generations that immediately followed the biblical era is astronomically different. In recent history, the amount of knowledge accumulated by human beings is reportedly doubling every two to three years.

Because of this, the ability to synthesize knowledge is crucial in today's world. The **synthesizing mind** takes information or knowledge from a variety of sources, seeks to understand and evaluate the information impartially, and then puts it together in order to make sense of the information. The task of synthesizing can seem daunting, especially after looking at how long and how much effort it can take to master a discipline. Now, not only does one need to master a number of different perspectives but also needs to piece them together into a useful "illustration" that can be understood by many.

Ironically, individuals often use synthesis without even knowing it. For example, many common ways to synthesize include (but are not limited to) narratives, taxonomies, metaphors, images, theories, and metatheories. Achieving an understandable synthesis like the ones listed above entails the use of four minimum components:

1. A goal. The synthesizer must have an idea of what they are ultimately trying to achieve as an end result.
2. A starting point. An idea, image, or any previous work on which to build.
3. Selection of strategy, method, and approach. At this point in synthesis, one must use their disciplinary training to choose the format of synthesis. With that said, there is no guarantee that the first format chosen will best fit the ultimate goal. The synthesizer must understand that their chosen tool is always subject to change.
4. Drafts and feedback. At some point, the synthesizer needs to begin to actually "synthesize" the information by creating a draft and then asking those around them for feedback on it. While the initial draft may not be perfect, it will often contain the critical elements of the final version.

Just as developing a disciplined mind is intentional, so, too, is the ability to synthesize and then present information in a way that is understood by the masses. While in the past a comprehensive synthesizing mind seemed well within reach, today's world offers many challenges for those attempting to achieve synthesis. Perhaps two interventions offer hope for the future: (1) The training of individuals so that they can participate effectively in interdisciplinary groups and (2) the creation of educational programs directed specifically at certain individuals of promise. In order to be most effective, two conditions must come from, and/or with, the above interventions. We need synthesizing role models—individuals who are already good at synthesizing themselves—to teach others. Secondly, we need to develop criteria that differentiate excellent from inappropriate integrations. The development of the synthesizing mind is both simple and complicated at the same time. However, when faced with a difficult synthesizing task, one should look to a creative solution. This leads to the next mind of the future—the creating mind.

Creative Mind

While the creative mind may be thought of as a "mind of the future," in today's world, creative individuals have not always been thought of as an asset to society. Instead, they were often ridiculed and discouraged for their foolish ideas. In more recent history, however, creativity, or what has been coined by Edward de Bono as *lateral thinking*, has been embraced and encouraged by companies and institutions looking to gain a competitive advantage. **Lateral thinking** is defined as the capacity to shift frameworks, wear different hats, and/or come up with a plethora of ingenious solutions to a nagging dilemma.

The development of the creative mind begins at an early age, even before the age of formal schooling, but a truly creative mind comes after at least partial mastery of both the disciplined and synthesizing minds. The creative mind goes beyond existing knowledge and synthesis to pose new questions and offer new solutions to existing problems. However, creativity is never the lone achievement of one individual but rather an outcome of three independent elements working together:

1. The individual who has mastered at least one discipline or area of expertise.
2. The cultural domain in which the individual is working.
3. The social field in which the individual gains relevant opportunities and educational experiences.

Together, these three elements play a large role in the development of the creative mind that seeks to stay at least one step ahead of today's every advancing technology. As stated earlier, the creating mind not only needs to build on an already established discipline, but the ability to appropriately synthesize information also plays a role. There have been many examples of creative achievements that emerged from an attempt at synthesizing information that has gone wrong. While the use of these minds together may ultimately achieve the same goal, they each have very different objectives to begin with. A synthesizer's goal is to place already-understood information into a useful form, much different from a creator's goal of *extending* knowledge beyond what is already known. Simply stated, the creative mind will continue to compete with artificial intelligence and computer software, but for this reason, it is important that as a society we understand the importance of "testing the limits" and never settle on the first answer when fulfilling our obligation as a world citizen. With that said, both moral and ethical considerations come with a task like this.

The Respectful and Ethical Minds

The first three minds focus primarily on cognitive forms, while the last two, respect and ethical, focus on our relationships with other human beings. The mind of respect is much more specific and tangible for the human brain to comprehend. The ethical mind, on the other hand, still relates to other persons, but in a more abstract way.

In a world composed of so many diverse individuals and groups it is imperative that people must learn how to reside in neighboring places without hating one another. This is often referred to as tolerance, but the concept of respect often fits even better. It can seem unreasonable to expect human beings to completely ignore differences among individuals, but they should learn to accept them and learn to live with them. Just as the creative mind begins to develop at a young age, the **respectful mind** starts at birth if a supportive environment is present. Then the schools, work, the media, and role models must continue to nurture this mind.

An ethical orientation also begins at home. Children often learn about what is "good" or "bad" by listening to what their parents say or watching what their parents do. Therefore, ethics becomes somewhat of an **abstract attitude**—the capacity to reflect explicitly on the ways in which one does, or does not, fulfill a certain role.

How does one go about cultivating these two minds? Clearly, the schools play a role. Young people spend more time in school than in any other institution until nearly the third decade of their life. While parents, the media, churches, and many other institutions also play a role, formal education plays a key (if not *the* key) role in determining whether or not our youth are on the road to good work and good citizenship. For this reason, it is pivotal that students understand *why* they are learning the topics that they are and how they can be used away from the classroom to improve our current quality of life. A student must leave our schools and become a citizen of good work. Then the job of the workplace and society is to support and sustain this idea. Good work can be evaluated using three facets: (1) excellence in quality (meaning highly disciplined), (2) responsible (meaning it takes into account the implications on the wider community), and (3) engaging and meaningful (because it adds value even under challenging conditions).

A truly respectful individual gives the benefit of the doubt to all human beings regardless of their differences. It should saturate one's life. In addition, an **ethical mind** questions the nature of one's work as well as the needs of the society in which they live. It moves beyond self-interest and instead ponders how it can work unselfishly to improve society as a whole. These latter two minds go hand in hand because it is difficult to imagine an ethical person who does not respect others, or a respectful person who does not strive to become an ethical worker and responsible citizen. Good work may begin with an individual, but ultimately it must extend beyond the person to the workplace, the community, the nation, and the world in order to be well equipped to deal with what the future has in store for the human species.

Conclusion

The five minds presented here may sound like an idealistic way of looking at the future. However, the best workers and the best citizens do not let the difficulty of a daunting task keep them from putting forth their best efforts to make big achievements. The five minds should be considered from two perspectives: first, the younger generation and those that are being educated in our schools today and, second, those already in today's workplace. Regardless, the five minds described are the ones that people will need and should strive to develop if we are to thrive, as a species and society, in eras to come. Here are some final reminders of why each mind is essential for our future:

- Individuals without one or more disciplines will not succeed in a demanding workplace and instead be restricted to redundant unskilled tasks.

- Without synthesizing abilities, individuals will be overwhelmed by the amount of information available and therefore unable to make sensible decisions.
- Robots and computers will replace individuals who are unable to think creatively.
- Those that do not respect others will not be worthy of respect themselves.
- Individuals without ethics will create a world that lacks decent human beings and responsible citizens.

Positive human potential depends on the five minds described here. They can and should be intertwined into our education and professional systems today in order for our species to survive and thrive in the impending future.

3

Blink!

Malcolm Gladwell

Summary Prepared by Cheri Stine

Cheri Stine *holds a bachelor's degree in Human Resource Management from the University of Minnesota Duluth. First and foremost, Cheri is a wife to her husband Dan and a mother to her two young children Kayla and Carter. She has owned and operated her own distributorship for an internationally known paper-crafting products company called Stampin' Up!® for over five years. She provides training for new distributors, markets her business locally, and teaches her customers to use the products that she offers to tap into their creativity and to touch people's lives in a meaningful way.*

INTRODUCTION

In today's society, we are instinctively skeptical of quickly made decisions. We consider them to be reckless and not well thought out. The quality of a decision is believed to have a direct relationship with the amount of time and effort we spent making the decision. In fact, for this reason, decision makers in all walks of life spend countless hours, days, weeks, and even years trying to reach decisions that they could have reached in two or three seconds if they had trusted their instincts. *Despite common belief, decisions made very quickly can be every bit as good as decisions made cautiously and deliberately.* In fact, in many situations they can be better.

HOW WE PROCESS INFORMATION

In life and in business, we are constantly faced with situations in which we have to make sense of a large amount of new and confusing information in a short amount of time. *Therefore, our brains have developed two separate and very different ways to process information and render decisions, each of which is valuable under different circumstances.* These two forms of decision making are conscious and unconscious.

Malcolm Gladwell. *Blink!: The Power of Thinking Without Thinking.* New York: Little, Brown, 2005.

Conscious Decision Making

Processing information and rendering decisions on a conscious level is intentional. It is typically a slow process and entails gathering information, employing logic, and coming up with a definitive answer to a problem, with the action following the decision. It is used in situations where a person knows that a problem exists or an answer is needed. Examples of processing information in this conscious way include when businesses gather market information and analyze it to make strategic decisions, or when people explore their choices among health-care providers. In each of these situations, some quantity of information is gathered and analyzed, and a decision is made based on the result of that analysis. This way of making decisions requires substantial time. However, in situations where more time is available and when good information is available, we can reach well-thought-out and appropriate decisions if we don't fall prey to the following problem areas:

- Inundation with irrelevant information
- Overanalysis of pertinent information
- Overlooking a critical piece of information

Conscious research and analysis is a commonly used and useful tool for decision makers everywhere. However, it is not appropriate for every situation nor should it be used in every situation. Our brains make unconscious decisions all the time that change our lives and businesses without doing formal research, and those decisions are just as good if used appropriately.

Unconscious Decision Making

In situations where conscious decisions are being made, some degree of unconscious decision making is also taking place. *However, making unconscious decisions, also known as rapid cognition, is very different from conscious decision making.* The biggest difference is that the thought process is not intentional. The individuals making decisions on this level, more often than not, don't even know that they are doing it. Decision makers may feel their heart race, or their palms begin to sweat . . . but may not know why it is happening or what it means. Nevertheless, even before the first piece of relevant information is gathered or analyzed, decision makers may have a "gut feeling" about what they should do. This gut feeling is the result of their unconscious analysis of the situation, which is made by tapping into their experiences, skills, knowledge, and other such factors that are readily accessible but not easily communicated.

This gut instinct can be a highly useful tool in making decisions, especially in situations where decisions need to be made quickly and no time is available to conduct research. However, many are skeptical of this quick decision-making process and don't trust decisions reached through snap judgments or gut feelings because they are deemed hasty. In the world of business, this could be a serious handicap. By not being able to respond quickly, many strategic business opportunities could be missed due to a company being bogged down in extensive research and analysis rather than taking advantage of a timely opportunity based on "a gut instinct." Often decision makers will have a "feeling about a decision" and will still spend days, weeks, months, or even years researching the situation, only to come up with what their initial instincts had already told them so long ago. However, a word of caution should be heeded in trusting your instincts. Although often accurate, there are some inherent problems associated with decisions of this type:

- Relevant information may be difficult to decipher quickly.
- Individuals may be slow to react due to interpretation problems.
- Snap judgments can overlook important information.

Despite these problems, our brains are capable of rapidly gathering information deemed valuable in assessing a situation and then quickly sending the analysis of that information to the rest of the body so that it can react appropriately. In addition, processing information in this way typically allows the brain to reach conclusions and begin to react to a situation before we are even aware that a problem exists. Our brain's ability to unconsciously process information allows us to react far sooner than we would be able to if we relied solely on our conscious ability to make assessments and reach conclusions. Other examples of situations in which our brains engage in rapid cognition include carrying on a conversation with another person, reacting in an emergency situation, and breathing.

ADAPTIVE UNCONSCIOUS

The part of our brain that reaches these conclusions very quickly is called the *adaptive unconscious*. This portion of our brain operates like a supercomputer that efficiently processes lots of data that are needed to keep us functioning on a daily basis. It allows us to make judgments quickly without requiring a lot of additional information and to respond quickly to varying situations. Some functions of the adaptive unconscious are:

- Warning us of danger
- Setting goals
- Initiating action in a sophisticated and efficient manner

During our daily life it is common for us to switch back and forth between conscious and unconscious decision making depending on the situation. An example of conscious decision making is when you decide to invite a coworker for dinner. You think about it, you decide that it would be fun, and then you invite the individual to join you. There is a deliberate thought process involved in making the decision to extend the invitation to the coworker. This process may take a few moments or many weeks, but the invitation does not occur until after the decision is reached. The very next moment, however, you could get into an argument with that same coworker, which would be an example of unconscious decision making. Most likely you did not walk into the coworker's workspace with the intention of arguing. Nevertheless, through the process of communicating with that person, your unconscious mind perceives a "problem" and causes you to react to something that was said or done, and an argument ensues. You reach the decision to argue unconsciously; therefore you often are not aware that you are arguing, or why, until after the situation is over. The decision to argue is made by the adaptive unconscious portion of your brain and happens very quickly, even before you are aware that something has happened to cause you to respond.

Thin-Slicing

In order to have a better understanding of how rapid cognition works, we need to recognize that a little information goes a long way and our brains are extremely adept at picking up on the minute details in any situation. This concept is called *thin-slicing*. Thin-slicing refers to the ability of our unconscious mind to find patterns in situations and behavior based on very narrow slices of experience. The color of a label on a product, the slight raising of a person's eyebrow, and many other thin slices of information all play a part in our decision-making process. The way in which we make decisions to buy a certain product or talk to a person is determined by information that is both gathered by and stored in our brains. Body language, stereotypes, skills, and experiences are just a few of the things that the brain uses to analyze a situation and make snap decisions. The ability that our brain has to thin-slice situations is amazing. During this process, our brain will observe and dissect a concept, idea, interaction, or experience into its smallest parts in as little as a matter of seconds. In doing so, it has the ability to recognize patterns or overriding themes that are then used to make a prediction or decision based on minimal information. Thin-slicing is a necessary component to rapid cognition because it is essential for the brain to be able to process information quickly. That can happen only when it takes that information in small ("bite-sized") pieces.

Problems with Rapid Cognition

Rapid cognition is often an accurate and useful tool for decision makers. *However, errors in snap judgments do occur for three common reasons:*

1. Ideas, experiences, and attitudes cause altered perceptions.
2. Too much information clouds the ability to thin-slice.
3. Too little information can make it difficult to see the big picture.

By having an awareness of these common errors, decision makers will be better equipped to avoid them and improve the quality and speed of their decisions.

Conclusion

By taking steps to understand and educate the unconscious mind, we can and will improve our ability to make faster and more useful judgments. Although snap judgments take place in a matter of seconds, they can be just as useful, if not more so than those we reach through lengthy analysis and research if we allow them to do their job. However, the key to successful decision making lies in knowing when to rely on rapid cognition—and when additional information or research is needed. Decision makers, businesses, and individuals can become more responsive and adaptable by becoming more comfortable with trusting their gut instincts rather than relying on extensive analysis every time a decision-making opportunity presents itself. The quicker response time will allow them to be more able to take advantage of time-sensitive situations by being responsive and flexible in situations that would have ordinarily led them to conduct time-consuming research and analysis and miss out on opportunities that require quick responses.

XI

Ethics, Values, and Spirituality

Almost daily, newspaper and television reports appear that document unethical activities engaged in by organizations, their executives, and their employees. The corporate world has been rocked by reports of scandal and corruption. Simultaneously, the past several years have seen an increase in the number of schools of business that have introduced ethics courses into their curricula. A large number of organizations are actively discussing ethical behavior, developing codes of conduct or codes of ethics, and making statements about the core values of their organizations.

A number of books have explored the ethical dilemmas that managers face, the core principles that guide ethical decision making, and the need for linking corporate strategy and ethical reasoning. However, questions still surround which values ethical leaders should hold and how those values could be conveyed to their employees. The four books in this part address the need for managers to be ethical, credible, and spiritual.

In *Moral Intelligence*, Doug Lennick and Fred Kiel, two leadership experts with an international audience, introduce and define the essence of moral intelligence. The authors illustrate how the best-performing organizations have leaders with a strong moral compass. Throughout their book they illuminate ways that managers can build moral skills such as integrity, responsibility, compassion, and forgiveness. Included in their book is an inventory that can be used to assess where you and your organization currently stand with regard to its own level of moral intelligence.

Moral Intelligence is a coauthored book. Doug Lennick worked for and still serves as an advisor to American Express Financial Advisors' CEO, focusing on workforce culture. Today he is a managing partner of the Lennick Aberman Group. Fred Kiel, Ph.D., is a cofounder of KRW International. He consults with senior executives of several Fortune 500 firms, focusing on leadership excellence.

Rushworth Kidder obtained a Ph.D. from Columbia University, taught at Wichita State University, founded the Institute for Global Ethics, and has served as a columnist for *The Christian Science Monitor*. His previous books include *Shared Values for a Troubled World, How Good People Make Tough Choices*, and *Moral Courage*.

The Ethics Recession, Kidder's newest book, is a collection of approximately 30 columns written for *Ethics Newsline®*, the Web-based weekly news publication from the Institute for Global Ethics, whose subscribers include readers in over 140 countries. He argues that most writers have focused on the recession's financial and power implications and underpinnings, ignoring the key issue of integrity. He believes that there is a severe and widespread lack of ethics that has increased dramatically as the economy worsened. He pleads for a "world-class culture of integrity" and offers a set of ten approaches for getting to that point.

Authentic Leadership is the third reading in this section on ethics, values, and spirituality. Drawing upon his 20-year leadership position at Medtronics, a world-leading medical technology company, Bill George offers lessons on leading with heart and compassion—a guide for character-based leadership. He identifies what he believes to be five essential dimensions of authentic leadership—purpose, values, heart, relationships, and self-discipline—and discusses how they can be developed.

Bill George is the former chairman and CEO of Medtronic. The Academy of Management recognized Mr. George as Executive of the Year, and the National Association of Corporate Directors and *Business Week* recognized him as Director of the Year. Currently, he serves as a professor of Management at Harvard Business School and has sat on the boards of ExxonMobil, Goldman Sachs, Novartis, and Target, as well as several nonprofit organizations. The author of *True North* and *Finding Your True North*, his newest book is *7 Lessons for Leading in Crisis*.

Ken Blanchard and Phil Hodges have collaborated on several books, including *Leadership by the Book*, *The Most Loving Place in Town*, and *The Servant Leader*. Blanchard is the cofounder and Chief Spiritual Officer of the Ken Blanchard Companies, a visiting lecturer at Cornell University (where he earned his doctorate), an instructor at the University of San Diego, and a widely known speaker and consultant. He has been honored by the National Speakers Association and Toastmasters International and inducted into the HRD Hall of Fame. His numerous books, which have collectively sold millions of copies and made him one of the top 25 best-selling authors of all time, earned him induction into Amazon.com Hall of Fame.

Lead Like Jesus asks readers to answer several key questions: Whose servant are you? Who do you want to be? Are you willing to emulate Jesus as your leadership role model? If so, how would you lead like Jesus? Blanchard and Johnson discuss the learning stages on the road to leadership and the obstacles to success. They encourage leaders to make their heart, head, hands, and habits mirror Jesus' leadership examples, and suggest that leaders will find spiritual, practical, and leadership benefits from doing so.

Moral Intelligence

Doug Lennick and Fred Kiel

Summary Prepared by Adam Surma

Adam Surma is a store manager with Target Corporation. Adam has held several positions with Target overseeing guest service and logistics operations in three Minneapolis Target stores. Primary management responsibilities include team development, corrective action, and store process execution. Adam received a Bachelor of Business Administration degree from the University of Minnesota Duluth with a major in Organizational Management. He belongs to the honorary business fraternity of Beta Gamma Sigma and spends much of his free time volunteering with the Southwest Metro Animal Rescue Adoption Society.

INTRODUCTION

Today's high-profile accounting scandals, corporate misconduct, and well-publicized accounts of abuses of executive power have left organizations as a whole facing a serious crisis of employee and stakeholder lack of confidence. In addition to a solid business model, efficient production, and world-class marketing, organizations in today's market need a strong grasp of the concept of moral intelligence to attract and maintain high-performing employees and build stakeholder confidence. Though organizations have known for years the importance of vision statements, corporate value credos, and emotional intelligence, morality as such has only recently been added to the mix of essential management paradigms and practices that define a successful and high-performing organization.

Moral intelligence is the mental capacity to determine how universal human principles should be applied to our values, goals, and actions. This capacity is similar to a person's cognitive, creative, or emotional capacity in that it is a sliding scale, as everyone sits somewhere along the continuum exhibiting different degrees of moral intelligence. Though many cultures and religions stress different behavioral and mental characteristics as being important or virtuous, all cultures share a

Doug Lennick and Fred Kiel. *Moral Intelligence: Enhancing Business Performance and Leadership Success.* Pennsylvania: Wharton School Publishing, 2005.

simple set of universal human principles on which moral intelligence is based. The knowledge that killing another human is wrong, treating others as one would like to be treated, and commitment to something greater than one's own self are all principles that numerous studies have confirmed to be common among humanity at large. *Aligning the values, goals, and actions of one's self and organization to consistently deliver morally "right" decisions strengthens worker loyalty, increases job satisfaction, and ultimately leads to increased long-term performance.*

THE COMPONENTS OF MORAL INTELLIGENCE

Moral intelligence as a mental capacity develops in every person from their earliest days as an infant. Although each person's individual life experience growing up plays a factor in their moral development, the overwhelming source of information for their internal moral compass is hard-wired from birth. Nature, not nurture, is our primary guide; studies have shown that as a species, humanity has used social groups as a survival mechanism, relying on our "moral nature" to help each other find food, shelter, and comfort. This is the basis for a set of universal human principles that we all share.

In studying the many skill sets and other factors that go into moral intelligence, four principles were found to relate most strongly to high performance both personally and organizationally when examined under the lens of morality: integrity, responsibility, compassion, and forgiveness. Each of these principles is made up of **moral competencies** that are the actionable components of each skill set, which, if followed, lead to a more morally intelligent person or organization. These skill sets of competencies, more than any other, were found to build trust, respect, and a highly effective group of individuals. They include the following:

- Integrity. This principle is the cornerstone of any moral character. It involves doing what you said you would do and following through on promises even when they are difficult. In business, integrity is what builds strong partnerships and convinces subordinates to entrust their confidences within a leader. The behavioral competencies involved in this skill set that can be practiced and honed to increase proficiency are keeping promises, standing up for what is right, telling the truth, and acting consistently within your own principles.
- Responsibility. This skill set also plays a large role in being morally intelligent. Taking on power as a leader necessarily means taking on responsibility. Accepting responsibility for personal choices, embracing those choices as you serve others, and admitting mistakes and failures are part of this principle.
- Compassion. Actively caring about others as a leader and organization may be the trendy thing to promote in modern organizations, but there are also real results to be reaped from doing this in a morally intelligent manner. Showing employees that you care builds fierce loyalty, even when the organization as a whole may be going through hard times. It is one of the few intangible assets of an organization that will keep workers feeling good about their jobs, even when losing them may be an option.
- Forgiveness. Forgiving may be the hardest thing for many to do in the demanding world of perfect results. It encompasses not only forgiving others for their mistakes but also focusing on the morality of letting one's own mistakes go. Mastering this skill will help develop an organizational culture that encourages risk and new ideas as people know that possible failures will be forgiven.

LIVING IN ALIGNMENT

Although everyone has a hardwired sense of universal human principles, this does not mean everyone always acts on them in a positive and morally correct manner. Having a foundation of the four principles of moral intelligence is just the first step; it is our moral compass pointing us in the direction that we know deep down is correct and true. To complete our sense of well-being and moral consistency we have to align our moral compass with both our goals and behavior. When our actions and behavior lead to obtaining our goals in a morally constant manner, we have stayed true to the principle of moral intelligence and consequently increased our own sense of worth by building trust and respect among the people around us.

Developing and maintaining a large group of moral competencies in the four principles allows for more control of your alignment between what you believe (moral compass), what you would like to accomplish (goals), and what you actually do (behavior). Moral intelligence moderates the relationship between how we set our goals (based on what we know is right) and how we behave (based on our goals).

MISALIGNMENT

Sometimes knowing what is right and what needs to be done to accomplish this is not enough. Emotions play a role in determining if the person or group of people is strong enough to make the moral decision. Two types of variables must be guarded against if moral intelligence is to be observed.

- Moral Viruses. Moral viruses are negative beliefs that develop that conflict with the universal human principles that make up the foundation of our moral compass. These viruses infect the moral compass such that goals form that are not normally allowed under moral intelligence. Common viruses include beliefs such as "I'm not worth much," "Might makes right," and "Most people can't be trusted."
- Destructive Emotions. A more common yet still dangerous variable that prevents us from acting in a manner consistent with our goals is *destructive emotions*. This phrase is a catchall for negative emotions that cloud our judgment and mask our sense of morality; greed, racism, jealousy, and fear can turn even the most morally intelligent person from alignment.

With such dire consequences for both leaders and organizations who fall prey to these two negative factors, we must constantly monitor and realign our moral compass with the goals and behaviors we wish to adopt. Both actively inquiring and physically creating lists and documents stating and comparing beliefs, goals, and actions help to keep us true to our universal human principles. The alternative is a dissatisfied, confused, and ultimately underperforming workforce.

Conclusion

Moral intelligence is based on universal human principles of right and wrong, and these are largely hardwired into each of us at birth. It is the guidance for our moral compass, which in turn helps us set our goals and guide our behavior to be consistent with our goals. Though the alignment model shows us how to form and act upon a fundamental moral foundation, atrocities and misdeeds occur on a daily basis. This straying from the moral path is found in varying degrees of alignment decay brought about through moral viruses and destructive emotions. These negative factors can be long term and severe enough to take years to correct.

A structured approach to identifying goals and determining behavior is the best way to develop and maintain a moral culture. Frequent review and challenging of actions, goals, and beliefs leads to open dialogue and quicker identification of possible moral viruses that may have crept into the concept of living in alignment unnoticed.

Moral intelligence is a concept that leaders and organizations alike can no longer ignore. It is a vital part of an organization's culture, and when paired with a solid business model it can produce real long-term results in terms of increased job satisfaction, higher worker productivity, and stronger stakeholder confidence in knowing what the organization is doing is "right."

2

The Ethics Recession

Rushworth M. Kidder

Summary Prepared by Linda Hefferin

Linda Hefferin has been a full-time business professor at Elgin Community College, in Elgin, Illinois, for the past 20 years, where she teaches Business Ethics and Management courses. Hefferin completed her master's and doctoral degree in business at Northern Illinois University. As a founding member of the Multicultural and Global Initiatives Committee (MAGIC), Hefferin is a firm supporter of global ethics and social responsibility.

COUNTERCYCLICAL ETHICS?

Economists say that people buy more chocolate during times of economic decline. Chocolate may be seen as an inexpensive "treat." Maybe it is seen as a cheap escape mechanism. Or perhaps chocolate is thought to be a low-cost pick-me-up when money is tight. Whatever the reason, sales of chocolate appear to be **countercyclical** (moving in the opposite direction) to the economy. When the economy slows down, chocolate sales increase. Seems strange? Not really, if you stop to think about it.

Do ethics violations also run countercyclical to the economy? Stated alternatively, is there a link between moral decline and financial downturns? It is likely that that *people around the world are more likely to engage in unethical and illegal activities during times of economic recession.* Consequently, a strong argument can be made that we do not just need a *financial* bailout; we need an *ethics* bailout. Clearly, the time has come for an *integrity revolution.* Any solution-oriented approach to the current economic crisis must also address the ethics recession.

Rushworth M. Kidder. *The Ethics Recession: Reflections on the Moral Underpinnings of the Current Economic Crisis.* Rockland, ME: Institute for Global Ethics, 2009.

EVIDENCE OF THE ETHICS RECESSION

This new variety of recession is evident in numerous examples of moral irresponsibility. The media provides daily stories of ethical downfalls as financial numbers plummet. Basic values seem to have diminished to an unprecedented level. **Ponzi schemes** (a type of illegal pyramid scheme, often involving soliciting new money from investors to pay off earlier investors until the situation collapses), unscrupulous mortgage lending practices, Wall Street excesses, and regulatory inattention all played a part in the financial recession. Like individuals, corporations can develop **cultures** (internal patterns of commonly held beliefs) of greed, fraud, and deceit. Many corporations have developed entire cultures of immorality based on the motto of *"If it ain't illegal, it must be ethical."*

Fannie Mae and Freddie Mac, the two institutions guaranteeing home mortgages in the United States, exaggerated potential homeowners' levels of income and overlooked uncreditworthy backgrounds. The corporate culture ultimately led to declines of tens of billions of dollars in the value of their portfolios. Ted Stevens, the most senior U.S. Senate Republican in history, was indicted for filing false financial statements that hid hundreds of thousands of dollars in gifts and services he had received from friends. The former accountant of electronics giant Siemens, A. G., Reinhard Siekaczek, was convicted by a German court of maintaining a **slush fund** (a special financial account used for illegal activities) of $40–50 million used to pay bribes to corrupt government officials around the world. Ehud Olmert resigned as prime minister of Israel amid six separate investigations of corruption involving taking hundreds of thousands of dollars in bribes. These examples are only a sampling of the countless news headlines involving ethics. How harmful is this **global ethical recession**? The World Bank estimates the cost of ethical corruption at *trillions* of dollars annually.

Take the example of Boeing Corporation, which lost a $40 billion contract from the U.S. Air Force in 2008, after several ethical missteps. Problems first surfaced at Boeing in the late 1990s, when employees were accused of stealing proprietary documents from competitor Lockheed. In 2002, Boeing was charged with winning Pentagon contracts in return for promised jobs. As a result, two key Boeing employees were charged with conflict of interest and fired, fined, and jailed. CEO Phillip Condit resigned in late 2003, while Boeing underwent a federal investigation for ethics violations. A conservative and respected former CEO, Harry Stonecipher was brought out of retirement to replace Condit. Mr. Stonecipher was charged to change the ethical culture at Boeing by strengthening its code of conduct. Criminal charges against Boeing were dropped, but a $615 million fine was levied, which is the largest penalty ever for a military contractor. A month later, the married 68-year-old Stonecipher was investigated for having an affair with a young female Boeing employee, thus breaking ethics rules he himself created for the company. Finally, in 2004, the Pentagon pulled $1 billion in rocket contracts from Boeing, and the aerospace company was hit with a 20-month suspension of its bidding rights.

HOW DO WE END THIS ETHICAL CRISIS?

As a result of catastrophic economic failures, renewed public concern over moral stagnation has surfaced. The only long-lasting solution to the ethical crisis lies in creating authentic cultures of integrity and decision making within organizations, thus making ethics the responsibility of everyone in the institution. An expectation of integrity must permeate organizations from the top down, reaching every crevice and corner. Leaders must possess the courage to state, *We don't do things like that around here*, instead of thinking that ethics is merely an option when everything is going well.

During his 2009 inaugural address, U.S. President Barack Obama pleaded for "a new era of responsibility." President Obama called on Americans to embrace a new culture of transparency and responsibility in both the public and private sectors. In this time of financial and ethical crisis, ethical progress must shift from an **evolutionary** (gradual) to a **revolutionary** (quick; dramatic) process. That process must include not just creating more ethical leaders but rather building more ethical cultures. Time will tell if President Obama is successful in bringing together financial geniuses who can stimulate global economic growth with ethical wizards who can create a world-class culture of integrity.

Research indicates that world-class cultures of integrity result when organizations implement the following actions:

1. Embed ethics in every action strategy and policy. Everyone from the CEO down to the last person in the organization is responsible for bringing the stated culture into alignment with the practiced culture.
2. Define ethics not simply as right versus wrong but as right versus right. Recognize that many decisions are not just black and white; they involve ethical complexity. Often the choice involves two sides of opposing moral arguments.
3. Engage moral reasoning to shape future decisions. Developing early detection warning systems helps address **ethical dilemmas** (complex situations involving equally undesirable alternatives) before they surface.
4. Focus on intrinsic rather than instrumental values. Emphasize basic values (such as respect, fairness, and truth) for their ability to achieve good rather than instrumental values used as a means to achieve good.
5. Emphasize moral principle over legal compliance. Rather than simply following legally enforceable rules, moral principle relies on adherence to the unenforceable.
6. Expand people's moral perimeter to include global concerns. Engage in ethical inclusiveness.
7. Focus on relationship building, not just deal making. Important relations are values based. The "bottom line" must include not just financial but social, environmental, and ethical success.
8. Cherish and repeat fireside stories of moral traditions. Educate new employees about moral traditions through narratives about taking courageous stands.
9. Build and maintain deep reserves of **moral courage** (mindset of adhering to one's values). Cultures of integrity depend on, and require, large amounts of courage in everyday decision making.
10. Keep the ethics flame alive collectively. Cultures of integrity depend on creating an entire community of honor.

Conclusion

Creating a culture-of-integrity movement will not be an easy task, but it can be accomplished. A 2008 study conducted by the Ethics Resource Center reported dismaying results—*only 9 percent of U.S. companies view themselves as possessing strong ethical cultures*. If all organizations in the world strived for a culture of ethics at every level, the only question left to be asked would be, "How could a financial crisis like the one we have recently experienced ever happen again?" Yet deliberately building cultures of integrity may be the best, and only, hope to survive the economic recession. Let the Ethics Revolution begin.

Authentic Leadership

Bill George

Summary Prepared by Randy Skalberg

Randy Skalberg is an assistant professor of taxation and business law at the University of Minnesota Duluth where he has taught courses in Corporate and Individual Tax, Business Law, and Corporate Ethics. He holds a B.S.B. in Accounting from the Carlson School of Management at the University of Minnesota, a J.D. from the University of Minnesota Law School, and an L.L.M. in Taxation from Case Western Reserve University in Cleveland, Ohio. He has served as an in-house tax counsel to Fortune 500 corporations including Metris Companies and The Sherwin-Williams Company, and also served in the tax department at Ernst & Young's Minneapolis office. He is admitted to practice law in Minnesota, as well as before the U.S. Tax Court.

AUTHENTIC LEADERSHIP

Authentic leadership involves those actions taken by people of high integrity who are committed to building enduring organizations relying on morality and character. It means being your own person as a leader. A leader's authenticity is based not only on differentiating right and wrong (the classic "moral compass") but also on a leadership style that follows qualities of your heart and mind (passion and compassion) as well as by your intellectual capacity. All too often, society has glorified leaders based on high-style and high-ego personalities instead of personal qualities that provide for true quality leadership.

DIMENSIONS OF A LEADER

An authentic leader practices the five dimensions of leadership: purpose, values, heart, relationships, and self-discipline. *Purpose* focuses on the real reasons people choose to become leaders—not the trappings of power, the glamour, or

---

Bill George. *Authentic Leadership: Rediscovering the Secrets to Creating Lasting Value.* San Francisco, CA: Jossey-Bass, 2003.

the financial rewards that go with leadership. *Values* provide the "true north" of a leader's moral compass. Failure of leadership values lies behind the failure of Enron, but more importantly, leadership values have been critical in the growth of virtually all of America's long-term corporate success stories. An example of *Heart* in leadership is provided by Marilyn Nelson, CEO of Carlson Companies. She took over an organization bordering on crisis from previous years of "hard-nosed" management and created a program called "Carlson Cares," which has resulted in both corporate growth and an improved bottom line. The *Relationship* dimension debunks the myth that a great leader needs to be distant and aloof to prevent the relationship from interfering with "hard" decisions. An authentic leader creates close relationships as part of leadership. The existence and fostering of such relationships is actually a sign of strength in leadership, not an indicator of weakness. Consistency is the hallmark of *Self-Discipline* in a leader. Consistency enables employees who work with the leader to know where he or she stands on important issues and to rely on even the most difficult decisions the leader has made.

LEADING A BALANCED LIFE

One of the key characteristics of authentic leadership is the focus on the journey rather than the destination. The leader must recognize that a career is rarely a straight-line path to success (and most likely should not be), but rather it is a journey wherein all of the leader's experiences contribute to overall success.

This concept of success implies not merely financial or professional success, but the overall success that comes from leading a **balanced life**—one that recognizes the importance of work, family, friends, faith, and community service, with none of them excluding any of the others. Leaders who subordinate everything else in life to their work do not develop organizations as well as those who live a more balanced life. Living such a life and allowing their employees to do so as well creates higher levels of commitment to the organization and, in turn, improves the organization's bottom line. *Balancing work, family, social, and spiritual aspects of your life and providing a meaningful amount of time to each provides the leader with richness in life* that is unavailable to someone who chooses an 80-hour week and is simply a "company person." The balance between work and family life is a substantial challenge, especially in today's two-career families. One of the challenges every leader will face is the impact of increased time demands from the organization on his or her family. The "delicate balance" between work and family life continues to be very difficult to achieve.

In addition to work/family balance, friendships are important. True friendships offer a place to share your emotions outside your family and without workplace involvement. This sharing process is an important part of the process of personal development. Equally important is the mentoring process. Contrary to the traditional view of mentoring, where an older person provides one-way advice to a younger person, true mentoring is a two-way process where both parties learn from each other. This two-way process acknowledges that mentoring is not merely the older generation telling "war stories," but a process where younger employees and students can provide insight into the questions that young leaders have about the business world. Finally, community service is an essential part of authentic leadership. Through community service, leaders have an opportunity to work with people of lesser economic means. *Getting in touch with people helps develop both the heart of a leader and sensitivity for the difficulties of the lives of others.*

ORGANIZATIONAL MISSION AS MOTIVATION

A common phrase in today's business world (some would say almost a mantra) is "maximizing shareholder value." While that might be an appropriate goal for a company seeking a white knight in a takeover battle, it is fundamentally flawed as a long-term business model. The best way to create real long-term value for a company's shareholders is to be a **mission-driven organization**—one that utilizes its mission statement as an integral part of managing the organization, not merely a plaque that hangs on the CEO's wall. The best organizations have a corporate mission that inspires creative employees to develop innovative products and provide superior service to the customer. This strategy creates a self-sustaining business cycle. In Medtronic's case, this mission is to "alleviate pain, restore health, and extend life" of the patient consumer, which creates demand from physicians who are the immediate customers.

CUSTOMER FOCUS

Every company's purpose boils down to serving its customers well. If it does this better than any of its competitors, and does it over the long term, it will ultimately create more shareholder value than its competitors. **Customer-focused quality** relies for its success on measurements that focus externally on customers and uses customer feedback as the ultimate measurement of quality. The role model for customer focus must be senior management. If senior management is focused on internal operations instead of on customer service, the company will eventually fail to an environment that empowers and rewards employees who provide high-quality sales and service to the customer.

TEAM-FOCUSED MANAGEMENT

CEOs are given credit when companies succeed, but it is largely a myth that the CEO is primarily responsible for the success of a company. Many of the great corporate success stories of the past 25 years—Intel, Nokia, Hewlett-Packard, Microsoft, Coca-Cola, and Pepsi—have all been managed by a team at the top, not merely by a single high-powered CEO. Upon being named CEO of Medtronic, Bill George immediately proposed a partnership (as opposed to a traditional boss–subordinate relationship) with Vice Chair Glen Nelson. This was critical to Medtronic's success. Nelson, an M.D., brought a critical perspective on the relationship of the practice of medicine and technology to the management team, while George brought experience in high technology management from his previous employer, Honeywell.

PITFALLS TO GROWTH

There are seven key pitfalls to sustainable corporate growth: lack of mission, underestimation of core business, single-product dependence, failure to spot change, changing strategy with changing culture, ignoring core competencies, and overreliance on growth through acquisition. Avoiding each of these pitfalls requires disciplined leadership to recognize the problem and aggressively solve it without immediately retreating into a dangerous cost-cutting mode. This type of leadership in the face of inevitable criticism from securities analysts and the media will provide inspiration to the organization and rejuvenate its growth.

OVERCOMING OBSTACLES

A key obstacle for Medtronic involved litigation in the implantable defibrillator market. A former Medtronic employee held patent rights to the first implantable defibrillator and went to work for Eli Lilly, a Medtronic competitor. Lilly used the patents to prevent Medtronic from developing its own defibrillator, a product that was critical to its core pacemaker business. Medtronic and Lilly litigated this patent claim to the U.S. Supreme Court, where Medtronic won the right to develop its implantable defibrillator. Even after this victory though, Medtronic still had to negotiate a cross-licensing agreement with Lilly, clear FDA approval, and face the challenge of another competitor (Guidant) that reached the market with a dual-chamber defibrillator prior to Medtronic. This 15-year struggle proved worthwhile, however, since Medtronic now enjoys greater than 50 percent market share in the implantable defibrillator market.

ETHICAL DILEMMAS

Socially responsible organizations need to confront directly the issue of ethical standards in international business. Medtronic discovered shortly after acquiring the Italian distributor of Medtronic's Dutch pacemakers that the distributor was depositing large sums in a Swiss bank account, presumably to pay off Italian physicians who were Medtronic customers. George confronted the recently hired president of Medtronic Europe about the account and terminated him for violating Medtronic's corporate values. The termination caused uproar within Medtronic Europe, but in the 12 years since this incident, the Dutch pacemaker subsidiary has responded with outstanding performance.

A second crisis arose in Japan, where two Medtronic-Japan managers were arrested and put in jail for giving airline tickets to a physician so that he could give speeches at two international transplant conferences. The arrests were part of a series of arrests of executives of foreign pacemaker manufacturers apparently based on the Ministry of Health's frustration at its inability to force the manufacturers to reduce prices in the Japanese market. The two managers were eventually released from jail following a guilty plea and returned to work. But George took the critical step in visiting Japan to reestablish confidence in Medtronic-Japan's employees and meet with officials from the Ministry of Health. This visit led to the creation of an industry-wide code of conduct approved by the Ministry of Health. Medtronic continues to be a leader in the medical device industry in Japan and has not agreed to mandated price concessions.

GROWTH BY ACQUISITION

In the fall of 1998, Medtronic engaged in a series of acquisitions costing a total of $9 billion. Medtronic's growth had been in sharp decline, so George decided to make a series of bold moves. These included the acquisition of Physio-Control, a manufacturer of manual defibrillators used in hospitals. George had to overcome internal resistance to the Physio-Control deal, as well as others, based on a poor history of acquisition integration at Medtronic. After overcoming that resistance in the Physio-Control deal, the groundwork was set for two more acquisitions in 1998 and 1999—Sofamor Danek, the world's leading spinal surgery company, and AVE, the leader in the U.S. stent business.

By late January 1999, Medtronic had completed five acquisitions at a total cost of $9 billion. Next Medtronic faced the more difficult task of integration. Most acquisitions that fail do so not from financial issues or lack of strategic vision, but rather from cultural clashes within the newly merged entities. Medtronic took a proactive approach to integration focusing on four key issues: leadership of the business, financial leadership, business integration, and cultural integration. George formed integration teams for each company led by a Medtronic executive and including Medtronic employees and employees from the acquired company.

SHAREHOLDERS COME THIRD

George's executive philosophy was described in an article in *Worth Magazine*, quoting him as saying, "Shareholders come third." George expected some backlash from the article, but surprisingly received none. The theory is simple. Customers are first, employees are second, and shareholders come third. Only by truly meeting the needs of the first two stakeholder groups does the successful company have any chance of satisfying the shareholders. *The key to meeting shareholder expectations is transparency.* Medtronic is completely transparent about every corporate event inside the company with respect to shareholders, a policy that can be contrasted with the Kozlowski-led Tyco, which hid major corporate expenditures from its own board of directors, much less the shareholders.

CORPORATE GOVERNANCE

The key to improved corporate governance is to restore power to boards of directors to govern corporations. The board should play an important role as a check on the company's executives and a means of ensuring long-term as opposed to short-term focus. One key to creating this type of board is to have a majority (perhaps two-thirds) of truly independent board members that have no business relationship to either the corporation or the executives. This will ensure that the directors can truly act independently of the CEO, not merely as "inside" directors who serve at the pleasure of the CEO.

PUBLIC POLICY AND RISK TAKING

Medtronic found itself cast in a leadership role in the reform of the U.S. Food and Drug Administration. The key issue in the reform movement was the steadily increasing approval time for new drugs. Drugs that were already in use in foreign countries were taking months, and in many cases years, to be approved in the United States and American patients were dying without access to life-saving medications. George presented his ideas about the need for reform at the Food & Drug Law Institute in Washington, D.C., and went on to work with the late Senator Paul Wellstone to generate bipartisan support for the Food and Drug Modernization Act of 1996. Today, new drugs are approved in less than 6 months, as opposed to 29 months at the height of the FDA's delay problems.

SUCCESSION PLANNING FOR THE CEO

One of the most critical and often overlooked steps in a CEO's career is succession. Almost as many CEO succession processes fail as succeed. If the board working with the incumbent CEO fails to identify a qualified and appropriate internal candidate, they are often forced to look outside the organization for a "star" CEO, a process that more often than not fails, as happened at Xerox and Maytag. One of the key factors is a lack of clarity on the CEO's part about how and when he or she will step aside. The CEO should identify a retirement date well in advance (Bill George announced his retirement date one year in advance), develop a succession plan, and make the transition as seamless as possible. This transition method is critical not only to employees and shareholders who desire consistent leadership but also to the new CEO who knows when he or she will take over. This prevents the new CEO from being forced to choose between waiting around and moving on to other opportunities.

Lead Like Jesus: Lessons from the Greatest Leadership Role Model of all Time

Ken Blanchard and Phil Hodges

Summary Prepared by Kevin Wold

Kevin Wold, SPHR, is a human resources professional with management experience in government services, business services, and retail industries. He is the Human Resources Manager at a consultant engineering firm in Minneapolis, Minnesota. Kevin volunteers as a worship leader and treasurer at his church and has served on the state board of directors for a campus ministry organization. He continues to be amazed by God's mercy and blessings in his life.

INTRODUCTION

The world is in dire need of a different leadership role model. Many leaders today are motivated by self-promotion (caused by pride) and self-protection (caused by fear). They elevate themselves above the team they lead, take credit for successes, and place blame on others when situations go awry. This is often true for both traditional organizational leaders in businesses, civic groups, and churches and leaders in life situations with families, friends, neighbors, and as a volunteer.

Jesus is the only perfect leadership role model. His leadership examples in the Bible teach us to live and lead by a standard at odds with today's norms. Matthew 20: 25–28 says:

> Jesus called them together and said, "You know that the rulers of the Gentiles lord it over them, and their high officials exercise authority

Ken Blanchard and Phil Hodges. *Lead Like Jesus: Lessons from the Greatest Leadership Role Model of All Time.* Nashville, TN: W Publishing Group, 2005.

over them. Not so with you. Instead, whoever wants to become great among you must be your servant, and whoever wants to be first must be your slave—just as the Son of Man did not come to be served, but to serve, and to give his life as a ransom for many."(*The Holy Bible*, New International Version)

You can follow Jesus' mandate by taking God from your private life into the leadership roles in your public life. This not a one-time act, but rather a life-long journey to lead in a different manner. *When your heart, head, hands, and habits mirror Jesus' leadership examples, it will have a dramatic impact on your personal life, your relationships, your leadership, and your legacy.*

A SERVANT LEADER'S HEART

However, in order to lead like Jesus, you must first examine your **heart** and discover your motivations and intentions. The biggest hurdle you will face to lead like Jesus is a self-serving heart. What is your heart's **EGO**? (Does your heart want to Edge God Out or Exalt God Only?) There are three heart exams you can perform to determine if you are a self-serving leader or a servant leader. Ask yourself these questions:

1. *How do you handle feedback?* As a self-serving leader, you view negative feedback as an attack on your self-worth and a challenge to your leadership role. As a servant leader, you view negative feedback as a gift you can use to improve your leadership.
2. *How do you handle succession planning?* As a self-serving leader, you view developing your successor as a burden or even as a threat to your own leadership role and often fail to develop your replacement. As a servant leader, you view your time in a leadership role as a season and a well-developed successor as leaving a leadership legacy.
3. *Who leads and who follows?* As a self-serving leader, you think you should lead and everyone else should follow. As a servant leader, you seek to respect the wishes of those you lead and to guide them down the right path.

Leaders who Edge God Out replace God or trust something other than God and often react to situations with little thought and much emotion. They are full of pride and/or fear and are controlling and avoid conflict. They are seldom seen when difficulties arise. They divide people, compare themselves to others, and distort the truth to protect their own interests.

Leaders who Exalt God Only worship and depend on God. They respond to situations with deliberate thoughts, words, and actions, are rooted in humility, and confident in their God-given leadership role.

You must shift your focus from yourself to Jesus in order to be a leader who Exalts God Only. As a result, your relationships will grow deeper, you will be content with who you are, and you will seek the truth in your decision-making process. Once you are focused on Jesus, you will have a servant leader's heart and make leadership decisions with an eternal perspective grounded in forgiveness and grace.

A SERVANT LEADER'S HEAD

Once you have a servant leader's heart, the next step to lead like Jesus is to examine your **head**, which is your belief system and point of view on leadership. Effective servant leadership starts with setting a clear vision and a way to implement that vision.

In Matthew 28:19–20, known as The Great Commission, Jesus gave His disciples a clear vision, a method to implement the vision and a view of His leadership legacy:

> Vision "Therefore go and make disciples of all nations," Method "baptizing them in the name of the Father and of the Son and of the Holy Spirit, and teaching them to obey everything I have commanded you." Legacy "And surely I am with you always, to the very end of the age."

A successful servant leader will also define, prioritize, and live out clear values that support the vision. Jesus defined and prioritized His two top values in Matthew 22:36–40:

> "Teacher, which is the greatest commandment in the Law?" Jesus replied: " 'Love the Lord your God with all your heart and with all your soul and with all your mind.' This is the first and greatest commandment. And the second is like it: 'Love your neighbor as yourself.' All the Law and the Prophets hang on these two commandments."

While nearly all organizations have a vision and goals, many fail to effectively implement them. A servant leader can help engrain the vision and goals of an organization by consistently living out the organizational values, and helping others to do the same. Vision, goals, and values that are embedded in an organization will survive beyond an individual leader's season of influence and will be carried forward by future servant leaders.

A SERVANT LEADER'S HANDS

A servant leader's **hands**, or actions and behaviors, are primarily demonstrated by serving as a performance coach. A coach can't win unless the members of the team win. Three steps an effective performance coach must take to ensure the team wins are establishing a performance plan, being a daily coach, and evaluating performance.

Establishing a performance plan is accomplished through goal setting and providing direction to achieve the goals. This focuses performance on specific outcomes or objectives and draws a road map to the destination. Without this step, it is impossible to be an effective performance coach.

A servant leader must be a daily coach who observes performance, rewards progress, and refocuses efforts. Being a daily coach is the most important thing a servant leader can do to help people achieve their goals.

Evaluating performance is easy for those who lead like Jesus. Clear goals have been established, and there has been day-to-day communication on progress toward achieving the goals. Be focused on the future, and use this opportunity to establish new goals. There are no performance appraisal surprises for people following someone who leads like Jesus.

A Servant Leader's Habits

Jesus demonstrated five **habits** for persevering on His mission: spend time in solitude, spend time in prayer, spend time in scripture, trust and demonstrate God's unconditional love, and develop small-group intimacy.

- *Spend Time in Solitude*—Many people find spending time in solitude, to spend time alone with God without human interactions or outside distractions, to be nearly impossible. Yet Jesus often spent time alone with God either before or after major events in His life.
- *Spend Time in Prayer*—Jesus also frequently spent time in prayer. A servant leader's prayers should not merely be to bless a meal or be reserved for times of deep struggle, but should follow Jesus' examples. Jesus frequently sought God in prayer—often in solitude. He poured out His heart when He prayed and sought God's will for His life, not a quick answer to today's dilemma.
- *Spend Time in Scripture*—Jesus often drew upon His knowledge and understanding of scripture. Three common ways to learn any subject, including scripture, are by listening, reading, and studying. Memorization and meditation are two additional ways to internalize scripture.
- *Trust and Demonstrate God's Unconditional Love*—As a servant leader, you must trust in and demonstrate God's unconditional love. You must both love Jesus and love like Jesus if you wish to lead like Jesus. If you do not love Jesus, your ego will seek to Edge God Out rather than to Exalt God Only.
- *Small-Group Intimacy*—Jesus demonstrated small-group intimacy. He chose a group of 12 to disciple, but there were 3 with whom he was especially close. To lead like Jesus, you must have a small group of trusted individuals with whom you can share your struggles, who will give you honest feedback, and who will hold you accountable for your actions.

WHY SHOULD YOU LEAD LIKE JESUS?

There are three legacy benefits to leading like Jesus.

Spiritual Benefits

You fulfill The Great Commission and bring glory to God by leading like Jesus. You also honor His command to "love your neighbor as yourself," put Jesus' love into action, and model Jesus to others.

Practical Benefits

Leadership is about results and relationships. There is no leadership model that will produce better results and deeper, more authentic relationships than the leadership example of Jesus. Your competitors can duplicate everything about your company except the relationships you have with your coworkers and the relationships you and your coworkers have with your customers. You provide better leadership through humility and self-esteem as a servant leader. You are more likely to admit weaknesses, ask for help, and avoid unethical behavior.

Leadership Legacy Benefits

You will leave a better leadership legacy if you lead like Jesus. Your season of influence is short, but the impact you leave is long. A life that Exalts God Only, is rooted in humility, abundant in integrity, and lived in submission to the will of God leaves a long-lasting, positive legacy.

Conclusion

Leading like Jesus begins by changing your own thoughts, actions, and behaviors. You can't attempt to change other leaders before you are consistently leading like Jesus. It is a daily decision, not a one-time event. Each day will present opportunities and challenges that can be met when your life is lived in submission to God and you are committed to lead like Jesus.

XII

Emotions at Work

Topics of interest to managers encompass a wide array of themes, and these are constantly changing and evolving. This part includes a sampling of topics that have received substantial attention in recent years, all focusing on employee emotions, feelings, and attitudes. The topics in this part include employee mindfulness, compassion, toxic experiences at work, and the need for employees to find meaning in their (work) lives. These readings are designed to raise issues, provide an opportunity for reflection on oneself, and stimulate conversations regarding the balance between emphasis on corporate profits and employee (and personal) needs.

Resonant leaders recognize the importance of the "soft" side of management. Their stresses and sacrifices place them at risk of a downward spiral into dissonance. Resonant leaders, however, rely on three major ingredients—mindfulness, hope, and compassion—to overcome the negative effects of stress in their own work lives while also stimulating continuous renewal throughout their organizations. In effect, they recognize that their leadership role includes an astute management of both their own emotions and the emotions of others.

Resonant Leadership was written by Boyatzis and McKee. Richard Boyatzis is a professor with joint appointments in the departments of Organizational Behavior and Psychology at Case Western Reserve. Annie McKee is the cochair of the Teleos Leadership Institute, and also teaches at the University of Pittsburgh's Graduate School of Education. They, along with Daniel Goleman, are the authors of the best seller *Primal Leadership*.

Toxic bosses and organizational cultures exist in many workplaces even in this enlightened era, and their impact is often compounded by the presence of combative customers, impossible deadlines, and unexpected tragedies. The results of this insidious organizational toxicity include lower productivity, job stress, workplace sabotage, and labor–management disputes. *Toxic Emotions at Work* by Peter J. Frost provides a description of the positive roles that toxin handlers can engage in to reduce and even minimize the adverse impacts of toxic pain. They can listen with compassion, facilitate the discussion of emotions, intercede on behalf of colleagues, and reframe painful situations. Frost concludes his book with a three-stage model for managing toxicity that identifies strategies for prevention, intervention, and restoration.

Peter J. Frost received his Ph.D. from the University of Minnesota and served as the Edgar F. Kaiser Professor of Organizational Behaviour on the Faculty of Commerce of the University of British Columbia. In addition to *Toxic Emotions at Work*, he is the coauthor of many other books, such as *HRM Reality, Doing Exemplary Research, Organizational Reality*, and *Reframing Organizational Culture.* In 2003, Peter Frost received the George R. Terry Book Award from the Academy of Management for *Toxic Emotions at Work.*

Viktor Frankl is one of the world's best-known survivors of the Holocaust's Nazi concentration camps in World War II. He attributed his survival under horrifying conditions to a driving search for meaning in a seemingly hopeless situation and reported his lessons learned in his book *Man's Search for Meaning* (named by the Library of Congress as one of the 10 most influential books of the twentieth century). Alex Pattakos, in *Prisoners of Our Thoughts*, has distilled Frankl's 30 books down into seven core principles: choose your attitude, commit to meaningful goals, find meaning wherever you are, recognize how you work to defeat yourself, search for insight and perspective while laughing at yourself, learn to shift your focus of attention, and make a difference in the world. Pattakos shows us how to connect with others so as to create and experience meaning in our lives.

Alex Pattakos is the founder of the Center for Personal Meaning in Santa Fe and also a principal of the Innovation Group. He is a speaker, writer, facilitator, and consultant to corporate clients on the Fortune 500. He is a strong advocate of "community building" in a wide range of settings, an adjunct professor at Penn State University, and author of the books *Intuition at Work* and *Rediscovering the Soul of Business.*

Resonant Leadership

Richard E. Boyatzis and Annie McKee

Summary Prepared by Beverly Frahm

Beverly Frahm is founder and principal of Frahm Consulting located in Danville, California. She specializes in human resource management and organization and leadership development. Her previous internal management positions and her work with consulting and coaching clients have given her the opportunity to work with and learn from leaders at all levels. She has done research on leadership, executive coaching, and emotional intelligence, exploring the unique experiences of individual research participants as leaders and coaches. Her life is enriched by her relationships with family, friends, nature, and the great outdoors.

INTRODUCTION

Leadership is often an emotional roller-coaster ride. It can be exciting, stressful, powerful, consuming, energizing, lonely, frustrating, rewarding, influential, overwhelming, and exhausting. The personal sacrifice that comes with the leadership role can be overwhelming and destructive.

While leadership has never been easy, the ride is intensified by our ever-changing and uncertain world of challenges and dangers and by organizations that are becoming more global, complex, and confusing yet leaner. Leaders today face new and greater challenges and higher levels of stress and pressure.

Organizations are realizing that greater results are achieved through **resonant leaders**, those who create and sustain resonance and effectiveness. **Dissonant leaders** who are emotionally unaware, volatile, and reactive do not fit into those organizations.

Now, a new kind of leadership is required—resonant leadership.

Richard E. Boyatzis and Annie McKee. *Resonant Leadership: Renewing Yourself and Connecting with Others Through Mindfulness, Hope, and Compassion.* Boston, MA: Harvard Business School Press, 2005.

GREAT LEADERS ARE RESONANT LEADERS

Resonant leaders are great to work with and get the desired results. They give of themselves *and* care for themselves. They have a personal vision for their lives, work, future, and who they want to be. They have an agenda for learning and a process for continuous renewal. They focus on the future, lead with mental clarity, and inspire others with a clear and meaningful vision.

They are awake and aware of themselves, others, and their surroundings. They are compassionate, empathetic, mindful, hopeful, and optimistic. They manage their own attitudes, behaviors, and impulses and recognize, understand, and manage their own emotions and the emotions of others. They establish positive relationships, bring out the best in others, and encourage fun, reflection, and self-care. They build trust, create excitement about the present, and stimulate hope for the future. In essence, they have developed emotional intelligence.

THE SACRIFICE SYNDROME—A SLIPPERY SLOPE

Over time, the burdens of leadership and its associated exhaustion take their toll. *Those who give too much of themselves and receive too little for too long become victims of the **Sacrifice Syndrome**.* They fall into *dissonance* and lose their effectiveness.

Some of the same factors that contribute to their effectiveness can lead them down the slippery slope of the Sacrifice Syndrome. It starts as leaders are striving to achieve, putting their work and organization ahead of their own best interests. They have little or no time for friends or family.

Once in the Syndrome, leaders become its victim and go into a downward spiral. Their judgment is impaired and they lose emotional intelligence. They numb out. They close off from others, shut down, and become difficult to deal with. They misuse power, inflict stress on others, and create dissonance and suffering. They become ineffective—mindless and clueless about what is going on around them and with them. They miss real goals. Life may lose its meaning. Their high state of constant alert and stress weakens the nervous and immune systems. Eventually their career, relationships, and physical and mental health are negatively impacted.

Leaders set themselves up to fall into the spiral trap when they do not take care of themselves. They have a personal and professional responsibility to manage the pressures of their role so they can prevent the Sacrifice Syndrome. They must learn and develop skills and practices so they can counter the effects of stress and personal sacrifice and build and sustain resonance and effectiveness.

There are organizations that encourage individual self-sacrifice, and train and reward people to achieve results at any cost. They overvalue achievement, undervalue interpersonal skills, and tolerate dissonance and bad behavior. Their environments are full of tension. Their leaders create dissonance and the spiral continues. Especially then, individual leaders must be able to maintain themselves and make choices that are in their own best interests.

DISSONANCE

*When leaders do not create and sustain resonance, they fall into **dissonance**.* It happens as a result of **power stress**, a type of stress that is sometimes blinding and often chronic, that goes along with being a leader. This stress is exacerbated by loneliness at the top, continuous self-sacrifice, and failure to allow time for recovery. Even though they may sense something is going wrong, they ignore it and keep going.

Even the most effective leaders can become dissonant, especially during difficult and trying times. They lose their patience and become nervous and driven, often overworking and undervaluing themselves and others. Their behavior causes others to feel threatened and frustrated. Dissonant leaders behave in ways that may threaten and frustrate others. They create a dissonant climate in which people become less effective and helpless; complaints and infighting increase.

When in dissonance, it takes more energy to focus; decision making is more difficult, confidence levels decrease, relationships become less fulfilling and ignored, values fall by the wayside, and spiritual and emotional lives diminish. The dissonant leader disconnects from self and others.

People sink into dissonance and remain there because of the following:

- The Sacrifice Syndrome—unchecked power stress and personal sacrifice
- Defensive routines—bad habits that keep them in denial
- Organizations—tense environments that encourage dissonant behaviors

THE CYCLE OF SACRIFICE AND RENEWAL

Leaders must be able to recognize their destructive patterns and take steps to renew themselves holistically so they do not go into the spiral of the Sacrifice Syndrome. They must regulate their own cycle of sacrifice and renewal, countering the effects of power stress and personal sacrifice.

Those who have fallen into the Sacrifice Syndrome can break out of it. For some, however, it may take one or more wake-up calls, such as a medical illness, loss of a significant relationship, being passed over for a promotion, or loss of their job, in order for them to do so. They must then begin a process of renewal and intentional change.

KEYS TO RENEWAL

Renewal is an ongoing process, a way of life that requires conscious daily efforts and practices. Three key elements of renewal are mindfulness, hope, and compassion. Renewal begins with mindfulness.

Mindfulness is a conscious awareness of self, others, and the way in which we work and live. Mindful people are awake and tending to themselves, their lives, and their environment. They are aware of their thoughts, emotions, and bodily sensations. They listen to their inner voice as it tells them when something is right or wrong. They are able to recognize and respond to power stress early on.

Mindfulness must be learned and practiced. Without practice it can decline slowly without our noticing it, leaving us unaware, clueless, and shut off from others. We become mindless leaders, left out of meetings or excluded from membership on the management team because of it. Mindlessness can derail careers and destroy marriages, families, and other important relationships, leaving the individual more alone and empty.

The capacity for mindfulness can be developed through reflection, practice, and supportive relationships.

Reflection involves taking time to stop, quiet the mind, and pay attention to what is going on inside our mind, body, heart, and spirit. It may include practices such as meditation, mental imagery, nature walks, and journaling.

Supportive relations and connections with others provide another source of reflection that helps leaders learn and counter the stress and loneliness of leadership. The leader must, however, make the effort and take time to develop and nourish the relationships and maintain the practices.

Slipping into Mindlessness

Even successful leaders at the peak of their careers can lose touch. Over the years, their drive and ambitions overpower them; they develop irritating patterns and behaviors that alienate others. They become more self-protective and self-centered, losing sight of organizational goals. Getting caught in the Sacrifice Syndrome, they shut themselves off from others. They slip into *mindlessness*. Some reasons for this are tunnel vision and multitasking, shoulds, fragile self-esteem, and the imposter syndrome.

TUNNEL VISION AND MULTITASKING   Although the ability to focus and multitask are considered strengths, when carried to the extreme they lead to exhaustion, unpredictable emotional responses, and mindlessness. Subtle patterns, early warning signs, and new opportunities are missed. Eventually, the ability to focus and multitask declines.

SHOULDS LEAD TO COMPROMISES AND MINDLESSNESS   When people get on a track of doing what they think they should do to become what they want to be, they can get stuck there; *they become the role and lose touch with themselves and what really matters to them.* They get lost and lose their sense of fulfillment about their work and home life. They deny that they are having problems; they become defensive, angry, and go into fight or freeze mode. Their emotions paralyze them and mindlessness sets in.

FRAGILE SELF-ESTEEM AND THE IMPOSTER SYNDROME   When leaders possess fragile levels of self-esteem, they feel insecure and afraid. They fall into the *imposter syndrome* and become defensive and disconnected; they focus on overachieving, proving their worth, shutting down, and hiding so they are not found out as being less than what they want to project. Their battle results in bad behavior.

Hope is an emotional state that enables us to believe in ourselves and our visions. It is cultivated by developing an attainable vision and a dream one believes is feasible. Hope inspires leaders to move toward goals and dreams and inspires others to go with them. It also inspires leaders to face their situation, correct their mistakes, and make a fresh start. Hope arouses compassion.

While hope inspires, it also hurts when used by leaders to create an illusion of hope and to manipulate others.

Compassion implies understanding other people and their wants, and feeling motivated to act on our feelings about them. Listening leads to understanding, which in turn sparks compassion. Compassionate leaders create a positive work environment wherein the leader and his or her people are able to sustain effectiveness longer. Compassion is contagious, and as it spreads it positively impacts the organization.

Leaders who have slid into dissonance must reignite their own compassion. However, they also need to draw on the compassion of others in order for renewal to occur. During their decline into dissonance, others may have given up on them and walked away. They need to reach out and reconnect with those who are still willing and able to support them.

INTENTIONAL CHANGE

In order to create and sustain effectiveness, leaders must engage in intentional change and continuous self renewal. *Intentional and sustainable change involves a process of deep personal discovery and the creation of a learning and development plan.* The process requires mindfulness, compassion, and hope.

Coaching and Intentional Change

Personal transformation is essential. In order for transformation to occur, leaders have to recognize the need for change and have the inspiration and courage necessary to do the work. They must be honest with themselves and admit to and face their shortcomings. They must recognize and be accountable for their contributions to the situation, develop a plan for change, and focus on making the necessary changes. They need to develop more constructive habits, attitudes, and behaviors.

While transformation is a personal process, it needs the connection and support of others. Relationships are essential, and friends, bosses, peers, spouses, and coaches can be helpful. Many leaders appreciate and benefit by the safe and confidential environment, guidance, honest feedback, and confrontation that a coach can provide. In turn, the leader learns to coach.

Coaching others and being coached help leaders stay connected with others instead of being lonely and isolated. Being a compassionate coach helps leaders on the path of renewal.

LEADERSHIP CHOICES

Leadership is more than planning, organizing, and controlling. It is also about the body, mind, spirit, and heart. Along with the new kind of leadership necessary for today's world, there is a new language along with concepts and skills that must be learned, integrated, and managed. They are mindfulness, hope, compassion, resonance and renewal, intentional change, and emotional intelligence. The impacts of power stress and the Sacrifice Syndrome must be acknowledged and managed.

Leaders can *choose* to be great leaders. They can become great by learning from others, engaging in a personal transformation process, renewing themselves, and sustaining resonance.

2

Toxic Emotions at Work

Peter J. Frost

Summary Prepared by Gary J. Colpaert

Gary J. Colpaert *received a B.A. in Business Administration from the University of Minnesota Duluth and a master's degree in Health Care Administration from the University of Wisconsin in Madison. He worked for the U.S.S. Great Lakes Fleet, with his responsibilities there including marketing, sales, and running the day-to-day operations of the commercial fleet. After leaving Duluth, Gary held the position of Vice President of Clinical and Support Systems at the Children's Hospital of Wisconsin and then became the Executive Vice President of the Blood Center of Southeast Wisconsin. Gary is currently the Administrative Director of the Eye Institute in Milwaukee. He has developed and implemented internal coaching programs, a Winning at Work program, and a Leadership Intensive Program. He leads a men's group whose members are interested in leading an authentic life of leadership and service and also has a meditation practice that includes a yearly 10-day period of silence.*

OVERVIEW

Work organizations and their leaders sometimes take actions—intentional and unintentional—that cause emotional pain to their employees. That pain can become toxic and thus have a negative effect on the organization. Alternatively, there is a meaningful role for compassion in an organization, and managers face the task of handling toxic emotions and their consequences for those people who experience pain in the workplace. In short, *compassionate companies can improve their toxin-handling practices.*

Organizations by their very nature create a regular supply of emotional pain. New bosses, mergers, layoffs, stifling or confusing policies, salary decisions, and

---

Peter J. Frost. *Toxic Emotions at Work: How Compassionate Managers Handle Pain and Conflict.* Boston, MA: Harvard Business School Press, 2003.

even the way that changes are communicated can all be sources of emotional pain felt by all organizational members. If the pain cannot be dissipated, it will, at a minimum, become a source of decreased productivity and a toxic condition that renders significant negative consequences for the organization and its staff.

Most organizational leaders lack the awareness to encounter and neutralize toxins, and therefore an informal structure of toxin handlers emerges that takes on the difficult (often unsupported) work of maintaining emotional homeostasis. The large amount of emotional pain caused by organizations, the unrecognized value of engaging this pain, and the already heavy workload of toxin handlers put the organization at risk for not having the capacity to deal with the emotional pain it creates.

SPECIFIC SKILLS NEEDED BY AN EFFICIENT TOXIN HANDLER

A Gallup poll of two million employees revealed the value of compassionate managers, finding that most people value having a caring boss higher than money or the fringe benefits they receive. It takes some basic skills to be an effective toxin handler.

- Reading emotional cues of others and themselves
- Keeping people connected and in communication
- Acting to alleviate the suffering of others
- Mobilizing people to deal with their pain and get back to a stable state
- Building a team environment that rewards compassionate action

The impact of using these skills to diminish the emotional pain of even one person in the organization can have a significant positive impact on the whole organization.

USEFUL PRACTICES

Compassionate organizations promote a healthy, productive culture through a set of policies, procedures, and belief systems that produce generative responses from people at all levels of the organization. Useful compassionate practices include the following:

- Identifying a link between the emotional health of the organization and the bottom line;
- Recognizing and rewarding managers who are good at handling emotional pain;
- Using hiring practices that emphasize attitude as well as technical skill;
- Maintaining fair-minded practices consistent with loyalty, responsibility, and the fostering of community in the workplace;
- Implementing intervention strategies during times of distress and initiating rehab strategies to ensure long-term vitality; and
- Building a culture that values compassion.

Studies reveal a direct correlation between harmony in the workplace (as a result of these compassionate practices) and company profits. For example, there is a 20 percent increase in survival probability for firms that are one standard deviation above the mean as compared to organizations one standard deviation below the mean on the dimension of valuing human resources.

TOXIN HANDLERS

The work of the toxin handler is to respond compassionately to pain in the organization, reduce its impact, and enable people to return to constructive behaviors. Toxin handlers have complex profiles. They are caregivers, leaders, social architects, and builders of productive systems of relationships. Their work reflects five major themes:

- **Listening**—providing moments of human compassion by giving attention and consideration to the pain of others;
- **Holding space for healing**—providing support and time needed for healing;
- **Buffering pain—reframing** communications, using political capital, building relationships, displaying personal courage;
- **Extricating others from painful situations**—making the decision to get people out of the situation causing the pain; and
- **Transforming pain**—framing pain in constructive ways by changing the view of painful experiences and coaching.

BURNOUT CAN OCCUR

The potential toll on toxin handlers is, not surprisingly, burnout. Without support and the ability to "decompress," the toxin handler can suffer psychological, physical, and professional setbacks. Often anger and guilt are the first symptoms of problems developing within the toxin handler. It is imperative for a toxin handler to manage negative emotions because the effects of stress last a significant period of time. Stress impairs the immune system and has been shown to influence the brain's neurological pathways.

Paying attention to others more than themselves has its costs, and the potential for becoming addicted to helping others is real. A trap that toxin handlers may frequently fall into is having an agenda for the person being helped. Another particular problem that handlers often face is that they may not know how to handle their own pain. If they overidentify with the role, they may have the incorrect perception that there is no one else they can count on for help. It may be difficult to maintain their perspective or manage their time when results of this type of work are ambiguous. Adding to the potential for burnout is that all of this work is in addition to the stress and strain of their life experience outside of work.

PROVIDING ASSISTANCE

Healing the handlers is possible when there is a clear personal vision of why they are helping someone, when they are provided with the tools and skills to protect themselves, and when conversations are held that recognize and bring into consciousness the intention to not get overly involved emotionally with the people in pain.

A game plan for self-protection that includes options for action is critical for long-term success. World-class athletes, for example, overcome stress through methods including hydration, physical movement, mental change of channels, balanced eating programs, and emotionally changing channels. It is also necessary to build up one's reserves in advance, and this can be fostered by:

- **Increasing one's physical strength**—keeping fit; getting a massage.
- **Boosting one's emotional capacity**—staying positive; not taking things personally; accepting what you can't change.

- **Regenerating mental capacity**—refocusing the mind; creating personal space; developing mental sanctuaries; learning to say no.
- **Building spiritual capacity**—being clear on values; revering one's life balance.

AIDING AND SUPPORTING TOXIN HANDLERS

What handlers and their organizations can do at the interface between the handler, the organization, and the person in pain is to generate an increased level of organizational understanding, respect, and language for the role and work of toxin handling. This results in the toxin handler's feeling connected and less isolated. There is power in naming this work as a positive, contributing factor in the organization's success. The way in which this work is spoken about is a critical factor in building a compassionate organization. For example, the question "What did you do at work today?" is typically difficult for a toxin handler to answer. A positive way for the toxin handler to answer this question is to acknowledge that there is a lot of pain in the office and to express feeling that progress is being made toward shifting the situation. Other positive actions for the handlers to systematically manage and diffuse the emotional pain in organizational life include the following:

- Acknowledging the dynamic, by naming the work, giving it legitimacy, and creating a forum to talk about it.
- Offering support, by encouraging toxin handlers to meet with professionals/experts for assistance.
- Assigning handlers to **safe zones**, by sending toxin handlers to an outside conference.
- Modeling healthy behavior, by having top leaders demonstrate and reinforce the behaviors.
- Creating a supportive culture, by allowing them to learn from each other.

WHAT DO COMPASSIONATE LEADERS DO?

Leaders sometimes create painful messes by themselves. When this happens, they need a repertoire of personal pain-handling skills. Compassionate leaders

- Pay attention, because there is always pain in the room.
- Put people first, so as to keep the feelings and the well-being of staff in mind when decisions are made.
- Practice **professional intimacy** by empathizing without clouded judgment or overidentification.
- Plant seeds, by thinking long term and noticing the power of leadership's compassionate actions.
- Push back, by addressing the toxic sources whether they be people or systems.

Leaders must be willing to place responsibility where it belongs (with whomever is accountable for the toxicity) and then sharpen the practices listed above so that the organization is responsive to pain.

THREE MAJOR STRATEGIES

The compassionate company is more than just the leaders and gifted people who excel at handling toxic situations. The institutional venues and structures necessary to create healthy and productive workplaces can be compared to a biological system. Toxins are natural by-products in a biological system. Using the metaphor, three sets of strategies become apparent for use before, during, and after the toxic situation.

1. *Prevention* can be accomplished by choosing new people wisely, developing existing staff, being fair minded, and setting a healthful tone.
2. *Intervention* can be implemented by dealing with downturns, dealing with acute trauma, being visible, creating meaning for the pain, and providing a context to talk about the pain.
3. *Restoration and recovery* occur when managers demonstrate patience and trust, provide guidance, acknowledge pain, and then focus on constructive actions for resolving it.

ORGANIZATIONAL AND INDIVIDUAL CAPACITY FOR HANDLING TOXIC SITUATIONS

The following list of questions can help the organization make an assessment of its organizational capacity and individual capacity for compassionate response(s).

For *organizational* capacity, consider the following:

- What is the breadth of resources that can be provided to the people in need—money, work flexibility, or physical aid as well as others' time and attention?
- What is the volume of resources (time and attention) required by the people who are suffering?
- How quickly can a response to the suffering be delivered?
- How specialized is the need in the organization?

For *individual* capacity, consider the following:

- Can you listen and be aware of grief and maintain awareness of your own and others' response to it?
- Do you know how to support initiatives that come from subordinates that may be outside of organizational norms?
- Have you expressed sympathy to others in the past and can you imagine doing that in the context of your work life?
- Can you deal with fast-moving changes in circumstances that have an emotional focus?

Conclusion

Paying attention to these kinds of questions and pondering how the person or the organization would answer them is an effective initial response. This can lead to a greater acknowledgment of the emotional toxicity and pain, broader self-awareness in the organization, and (hopefully) utilization of the strategies for increasing the capacity for compassionate responses within the organization.

3

Prisoners of
Our Thoughts

Alex Pattakos

Summary Prepared by Gary P. Olson

Gary P. Olson is CEO of the Center for Alcohol and Drug Treatment, Duluth, Minnesota. He is responsible for the overall direction of this regional not-for-profit corporation. He received his MBA from the University of Minnesota Duluth.

INTRODUCTION

How many of us have worked at jobs we didn't really like? Perhaps we were happy to be making a living, but were unfulfilled by the work itself. We found ourselves asking, "Isn't there more to life than this?"

Sometimes we are frustrated when we seem to have little control over our work situation and feel that there is little we can do to change our circumstances. These common experiences often lead us to ask ourselves fundamental questions about the way we live, work, and play.

Viktor Frankl, the world-renowned psychiatrist and Nazi concentration camp survivor, saw these questions as part of a fundamental human drive he called "man's search for meaning." Frankl believed that *the meaning of a person's life can only be determined by your own life, not the circumstances you find yourself in.* Dr. Frankl's theory was put to the test during his incarceration by the Germans during World War II at the Auschwitz and Dachau death camps. He survived these horrific conditions with his humanity intact and the certainty that his ideas had universal application.

The following principles use Dr. Frankl's work to guide our search for meaning no matter what job or situation we are in, and to connect our work with the meaning in other parts of our lives. These principles are as follows:

1. Choose your own attitude.
2. Commit to meaningful values.
3. Find meaning in the moment.

Alex Pattakos. *Prisoners of Our Thoughts: Viktor Frankl's Principles at Work.* San Francisco, CA: Berrett-Koehler, 2004.

4. Don't work against yourself.
5. Practice self-detachment.
6. Use creative distraction.
7. Transcend your personal interests.

MEANINGFUL WORK

The basic principle of Viktor Frankl's work is that *we are entirely free at all times to choose our response to the circumstances of our lives.* Frankl's **logotherapy** was a method by which the therapist helped the client become fully aware of this freedom of choice. Frankl believed in the unconditional meaningfulness of life and the intrinsic dignity of every person. He also believed every person had the capacity to search for meaning under any conditions. In other words, no one is off the hook.

When we search for meaning, we are looking for that which is meaningful for ourselves in relation to our own core values. Situations that may "try our souls" can become opportunities to help us clarify our own values. The way we accept the things we cannot control can lead to a deeper sense of personal meaning.

If we view our jobs as somehow apart from our "real" lives, we shut ourselves off from a large portion of our life experience. This often happens when we fall into the habit of constantly complaining about our work, our bosses, and our coworkers. When we choose to search for meaning and acknowledge our freedom to choose our responses, work becomes a rich opportunity.

CHOOSE YOUR OWN ATTITUDE

The freedom to choose is not always easy to exercise in practice. Our personal ability to cope and adapt is often tested. In order to effectively exercise this freedom, we must be able to look at a situation differently, even if this leads us to choose a path that is at odds with other people's expectations of how someone in our position normally responds.

No one can choose our attitude for us. Everyone knows someone who relentlessly complains about his or her working conditions, but does nothing to change them. It is when we take responsibility for exercising our freedom to choose our attitude that we move from being part of the problem to becoming part of the solution.

When we choose our attitude, we

- can choose to bring a positive attitude to the situation
- adopt a creative approach to imagining what is possible
- unlock the passion or enthusiasm that makes the possible actual

When we abstain from the responsibility for choosing consciously, we are choosing instead to remain locked in habits of thought that may no longer serve our search for meaning. We have the freedom, but we must make a conscious decision to exercise it. Out freedom is limited by conditions, but we *can* take a stand.

COMMIT TO MEANINGFUL VALUES

Frankl described the **will to meaning** as the authentic commitment to meaningful values and goals that only we as individuals can actualize. He believed *the will to meaning is a basic human drive.* Other drives may be more externally apparent, such as the will to power (or superiority) and the will to pleasure. Frankl believed these "drives" were actually efforts to mask a void of meaning that exists in many people's lives.

It is not difficult to find examples of what Frankl meant. It is obvious that no amount of power or pleasure can fill such a void when it exists. If it did, the most powerful and pampered among us should be the most fulfilled and satisfied, but this is not the case. Only the sustained search for meaning can lead to the sense of fulfillment that most of us desire from our work and our lives.

Values that are primarily related to power and pleasure are not those values that lead us to meaning in our lives. The will to power, for example, is always contingent on external conditions. Power relies on a cooperative set of subjects and circumstances to be meaningful at all, and since change is the only constant, power tends to dissipate over time despite our efforts to sustain it. The will to meaning, on the contrary, comes entirely from within us. Only we can discover and realize it.

Some modern, progressive companies attempt to create the illusion of freedom in the workplace, but fail to connect with the emotional, intellectual, and spiritual values of their employees, customers, or communities. Yet business and economics are connected with all aspects of our lives, communities, and planet. The inability to honor meaning at the top of any organization often leads to demoralization, dissatisfaction, and, ultimately, decreased productivity.

FIND MEANING IN THE MOMENT

If we could live life over for a second time, would we make different choices? Although meaning may exist in every second, we have to make an effort to find it. Meaningful moments often slip by without notice only to be realized months or even years later. Meaning does not exist within our own minds, and it is not created; it is discovered in the world around us. *The search for meaning requires a conscious effort.*

The pace of modern life and work conspires against the search for meaning. Unless we stop to consider why we are doing what we are doing and what our lives and work mean to us and to examine the reasons we do what we do, we cannot expect to find meaning. This requires time for serious reflection, time without a cell phone to our ear or a list of e-mails to check. Technology, which is designed to make life easier, can instead become a relentless, demanding set of obligations. It may take a serious effort to disconnect from these tools long enough to find time to reflect.

Finding meaning in our lives and work is our personal responsibility and rests on our ability to achieve a certain level of awareness or mindfulness. To be aware means to stop and consider our situation and discover what life lessons it may hold. When we become aware of the many possibilities open to us, we become open to meaning. We can be creators or complainers, for example, for both of these potentials exist within us. Which potential is realized depends on our decisions, not our external conditions.

DON'T WORK AGAINST YOURSELF

How satisfied can we be if we achieve a lofty goal at the expense of a friendship, loss of respect, or our own health? Meaning exists in appreciation of the moment, the present, or the process—not in a particular outcome!

Sometimes our efforts to create meaning, particularly in our work, can lead us away from meaning. This is because the meaning and value in our work are acquired not simply through our own performance, but in the way our work contributes to society. We do not work in a vacuum. Our bosses, coworkers, and customers have their own agendas that may be at odds with our own. Like the football coach whose plan went awry because the opponent did not follow it, we can't ignore the others on the field.

Our jobs are never just *our* jobs. We work within a fabric of relationships that extends far beyond our immediate workspace. These relationships have meaning individually and collectively. Becoming too focused on ultimate outcomes and results can cause us to overlook the meaning that exists moment to moment. Our anxiety about a successful outcome can actually undermine our ability to "get it right." Instead, we need to focus on the meaning in the process.

Our good intentions can become the cause of failure. This happens when we overlook and neglect the relationships that are integral to the process of accomplishing a larger goal or project. Ignoring the opportunity to experience meaningful moments with others at work undermines the chance for success because business issues and people issues are usually intertwined. Even a desired promotion at work can, in the end, depend more on your relationship with your coworkers than it does on pleasing the boss. Your boss may understand that *your ability to relate in a meaningful and positive way with coworkers is a key indicator of your ability to lead.* Your knowledge of what your coworkers value and care about can be a more important asset in leadership than your job knowledge. The more meaning we experience in the process, the more satisfied we will feel *irrespective* of the outcome.

PRACTICE SELF-DETACHMENT

Humor is an excellent way of distancing ourselves from something—even our own predicament. It can be a form of self-detachment. Our ability to laugh at ourselves can make a serious situation more bearable, not just for us, but for those around us. When we can laugh at mistakes, we can own up to them, learn from them, and move on.

Even in a concentration camp, Frankl was able to find humor, and he believed it was an important weapon in the fight for self-preservation. Nevertheless, it is important to distinguish between detachment and denial. *Detachment* is a conscious choice to create psychological distance that opens the door to action, learning, and growth. *Denial* of our experience involves disconnecting from ourselves and others who may share an experience with us. Detachment permits us to acknowledge a mistake, a poor decision, or even fear, but not be paralyzed into inaction.

USE CREATIVE DISTRACTION

Thinking itself can become an obsession, particularly when it is focused on negativity and complaint. Venting frustration can become a habit of blaming and complaining that saps our energy and ultimately leads nowhere. There are times when we need to shift our focus and distract ourselves from something we don't like in order to see the possibilities in a situation. This is the principle of creative distraction.

When we are too focused on something—a demanding boss, a boring task, an unproductive coworker—we can lose sight of the meaning in our lives. The principle of creative distraction allows us to ignore some aspect of our lives that *should* be ignored. In doing so, we may perceive our situation in an entirely new way. We can then transcend the limits in our condition, avoid becoming self-absorbed, and direct our attention toward discovering new meaning in our lives.

TRANSCEND YOUR PERSONAL INTERESTS

Real success, like happiness, is not a goal or a target. It is a by-product of a dedication to a cause or purpose greater than one's self. When we reach beyond the satisfaction of our own limited needs, we enter the realm of ultimate meaning.

This personal transcendence is for some a religious or spiritual relationship. For others it is our connection with a greater good or with the human spirit. It is sometimes experienced when we are part of a team—doing and being with others. On a team with "team spirit," for example, the greatest reward is being part of the team, part of the process, and not necessarily contingent on the final result of our efforts.

No matter who we are or where we work, the opportunity to go beyond our own interests is almost always present. Companies that can look beyond the bottom line and bring meaning to the business at hand also bring meaning to everyone who works there. It takes more than good intentions to grow meaning in a corporation. For one thing, corporations are not in business to grow meaning! It requires courage and a deep commitment to meaningful personal values on the part of corporate leaders to place meaning before quarterly profits.

LIVING AND WORKING WITH MEANING

The opposite of meaning is despair—a condition brought on by the apparent meaninglessness of life. Each of us has the freedom and responsibility to place ourselves somewhere along a continuum that connects the two. Success or failure in the eyes of others has no bearing at all on where we stand with regard to meaning. A low-profile, low-paying job in a setting filled with meaningful purpose or one where we are able to fully realize our personal values in relationship to our work can fill us with a sense of meaning and purpose. It can truly make life worth living.

When we connect with ourselves, our coworkers, or to the task at hand, we experience meaning. When we continuously adjust our attitudes and reflect on the choices and possibilities open to us, we will be led to discover meaning. No matter what our job or our personal situation is, we can transform it with meaning.

PART XIII

Emerging Dimensions of Organizational Environments

Two powerful and pervasive trends affecting employers have dramatically emerged in the twenty-first century: the increasing emphasis on being "green" and the geometric growth in the use of social technologies. These are in addition to the previous and still-dominant factors of information technology development and the globalization of business. The idea of "greening" the corporation actually began in the 1980s and 1990s and has grown stronger as corporations have focused on renewable energy resources, energy conservation, prevention of pollution, and the practice of sustainable development.

Tom Friedman is the foreign affairs columnist for the *New York Times*. He has won the Pulitzer Prize three times for his outstanding and informed journalism. In addition to his regular editorials in the *New York Times*, Friedman is the author of several previous books, including *From Beirut to Jerusalem*, *The Lexus and Olive Tree: Understanding Globalization*, *Longitudes and Attitudes: Exploring the World After September 11*, and his best seller, *The World is Flat: A Brief History of the 21st Century.*

In his book *Hot, Flat, and Crowded*, Friedman contends that three powerful forces are affecting the earth in important ways: global warming, global population growth, and global flattening. These have produced disruptive climate change, energy differentials across countries, a huge transfer of wealth to oil-producing countries, an increasing demand for natural resources, and biodiversity loss. America, Friedman suggests, needs to become the leader in creating the greenest country in the world, which will result in achieving the twin goals of national security and economic prosperity.

Josh Bernoff and Charlene Li are the authors of *Groundswell*. Bernoff is senior vice president for idea development at Forrester Research, where he created an approach to classifying customers according to how they approach technology. He has written for the *New York Times*, *Wall Street Journal*, and *Advertising Age*. Charlene Li was Vice President and Principal Analyst at Forrester Research and has served as a consultant with Monitor Group in Boston and Amsterdam. Her ideas on interactive media, social technologies, and marketing appear in her blog, The Altimeter.

In *Groundswell*, Li and Bernoff identify three key trends—emerging interactive technologies, a strong desire among people to connect with each other, and online economics (through online advertising) that combine to produce an unprecedented opportunity for businesses. The dominant groundswell is "a social trend in which people use a variety of technologies to get what they need from each other." These technologies include those used in MySpace, Facebook, YouTube, Wikipedia, eBay, Craigslist, LinkedIn, blogs, and Twitter. Bernoff and Li advocate using one or more of five progressive approaches to engage the groundswell: listening, talking, energizing, supporting, or embracing.

Hot, Flat, and Crowded

Thomas Friedman

Summary Prepared by Bob Stine

Bob Stine is Associate Dean in the College of Continuing Education at the University of Minnesota, and he is responsible for academic programs. He was formerly Associate Dean in the College of Natural Resources. His interests include leadership, organizational management, adult education, and natural resources and the environment. He earned his Ph.D. in Forest Policy from the University of Minnesota, M.S. from Oregon State University, and bachelor's degree from Indiana University.

THREE CHARACTERISTICS OF THE WORLD

The world is hot, flat, and crowded. It's hot because of global warming, it's flat as a result of a growing middle class with instant connectivity around the globe, and it's crowded due to rapid population growth. The result is a planet that is dangerously unstable. Indicators include tightening energy supplies, deepening energy poverty, strong dictatorships in oil-producing countries (**petrodictatorships**), and accelerating climate change. The conditions and their symptoms are tightly intertwined, and how they are addressed will greatly determine the quality of life on earth in the future.

America will play a key role in the response to these issues, much as it has done for nearly every key global issue in the past. *America needs to become the greenest country in the world, not as a selfless act of charity, but as a core of national security and economic prosperity.* The United States cannot do this alone, but if it leads the way, others will most assuredly follow.

As of now, America (along with the rest of the world) is entering the **energy-climate era**, where energy and climate change issues will dominate. There are five key problems that define this era: growing demand for ever-scarcer energy supplies and natural resources; a massive transfer of wealth to oil-rich nations; disruptive

---

Thomas Friedman. *Hot, Flat, and Crowded: Why We Need a Green Revolution—and How It Can Renew America.* New York: Farrar, Straus, and Giroux, 2008.

climate change; energy poverty (large populations without access to dependable electricity); and rapidly accelerating biodiversity loss.

We arrived at this new era primarily because the parts of the world with rapidly growing populations want to mimic the lifestyle and energy consumption of Americans. While total energy consumption is growing faster in these areas, per capita consumption in the United States is still dramatically higher (9–30 times) than in China and India. Efforts to produce the same per capita amount of energy for billions more people around the world is creating negative effects, and in the end, is simply not sustainable.

PETRO POLITICS

U.S. dependence on foreign oil is causing negative consequences in four primary ways. First, we are helping support an intolerant, antimodern, anti-Western, anti–women's rights strain of Islam practiced in Saudi Arabia. Second, we are helping finance reversals of democratic trends in Russia, Latin America, and elsewhere. Generally, as the price of oil goes up, the pace of freedom goes down. Third, we are causing a global energy scramble, where repression, human rights, and religious freedom take a backseat to the need for oil. Finally, by purchasing foreign oil, the United States ends up funding both sides of the war on terror—our military on one hand and terrorists funded by nation-states from whom we purchase the oil on the other.

Of particular concern is the relationship between the price of oil and the pace of freedom within "petrolist" nations (defined as authoritarian states that are highly dependent on oil production for the bulk of their exports and government income). Among notable countries on that list are Angola, Nigeria, Iran, Russia, Egypt, Kuwait, Indonesia, Venezuela, Qatar, United Arab Emirates, Syria, Sudan, and Saudi Arabia. In several measures of "freedom" (e.g., open elections, invasion of other countries, nationalization of industries, coups, and independent newspapers), the price of oil and the pace of freedom or democratization are inversely related. Not one of the 23 nations that derive a clear majority of their export income from oil and gas is a democracy.

One cause of this phenomenon is the "taxation effect." Countries with high oil income need few, if any, taxes from their citizens, and therefore feel little need for their citizens to be represented in government (in a twist, the phrase becomes "no representation without taxation"). A second cause is the "spending effect," where large oil income allows patronage spending, dampening the pressure for democratization. This also tends to translate into less education and less innovation, since the government can provide everything needed for daily life. Governments can also use their oil profits to prevent the formation of groups that might challenge them in a number of ways.

ENERGY POVERTY

The World Bank estimates that one-quarter of the earth's inhabitants (many of them living in sub-Saharan Africa) do not have regular access to an electricity grid. The 47 countries in this region (excluding South Africa) only add about 1 gigawatt of electricity annually, which is about the same amount added *every two weeks* in China.

A general rule among all energy-poor countries is that they don't have functioning utilities that are able to raise the financing needed to build and operate power plants and transmission lines. This is the result of persistent misgovernance and/or civil war. The lack of reliable energy results in negative impacts on nearly every other aspect of life (e.g., access to food and clean water, quality education, manufacturing, and health care). There is little chance these countries will rise out of financial poverty and health crises without eliminating their **energy poverty**.

CLEAN ENERGY

Simply providing reliable energy to everyone who currently doesn't have it by burning more fossil fuels is not tenable. The impacts on pollution and climate would be catastrophic. Instead, *the world (with the United States preferably leading) needs to move toward the creation and deployment of "abundant, clean, reliable, and cheap electrons."* Companies that invent and deploy clean power technologies most effectively will have a dominant place in the future economy. Countries that develop integrative systems to take advantage of such clean energy will be stronger and freer in the future.

In this new system, everything must be interconnected—production, distribution, and use. Individual components of the system can be optimized to a point, but only the creation and operation of an entirely new system will make a significant difference. In order to get there, innovation needs to be stimulated. Some of that will happen naturally, but it should also be stimulated by tax and regulatory incentives, renewable energy mandates, and other market-shaping mechanisms that create durable demand for the technologies. Advancement can also be stimulated by increasing government-funded research, which leads to both steady progress on existing technologies and "eureka" breakthroughs in new technologies.

At the same time, we need to focus on efficiency to reduce the demand for energy production. Clean and inexpensive energy solutions may be years down the road, but reducing energy consumption starts lowering CO_2 emissions immediately. Using available energy more efficiently has the same effect.

MOVING FORWARD

The United States has yet to seriously embrace a "green" economy. Most efforts to date have simply been tweaking on the margins. *To keep from doubling the amount of CO_2 in the atmosphere by mid-century, eight of the following types of actions need to occur:*

- double fuel efficiency of two billion cars from 30 mpg to 60 mpg;
- raise efficiency at 1,600 coal-fired electric plans from 40 to 60 percent;
- replace 1,400 coal-fired electric plants with natural gas–powered plants;
- install carbon capture and sequestration capacity at 800 large coal-fired plants;
- add twice today's current global nuclear capacity to replace coal-based electricity;
- increase wind power 40-fold to displace all coal-fired power;
- halt all cutting and burning of forests;
- cut electricity use in homes, offices, and stores by 25 percent

Accomplishing one of these would be a miracle. Accomplishing eight seems nearly impossible. But this is the scale at which change in energy production and consumption must occur to slow and then start reversing the level of CO_2 in the atmosphere.

A SMART ELECTRICITY GRID

One proactive approach would be development of a "smart" energy grid. Existing electric utilities across the country grew in a haphazard manner, with little or no integration between them, and little ability to alter real-time pricing to reflect supply and demand. Imagine instead an electric grid that would include integrated large production facilities (e.g., clean coal plants, wind farms, and nuclear facilities) and many small distributed production facilities (e.g., solar panels on roofs and individual wind mills). Then imagine vehicles and appliances that are able to communicate with the grid, running (or charging) and buying electricity when prices are low (middle of the night), and at times selling it back when prices are high (peak demand times during the day). All this would happen on an **Energy Internet** and be controlled by programmable chips in every vehicle and appliance.

As an example, your dishwasher would wait to run till the middle of the night, when electricity prices drop to a predetermined price. Your car would charge itself at night (using the same strategy), and sell some back to the grid during the day when prices are higher, making sure to leave enough stored in the battery to get you home. Not only would your costs be reduced (by buying low and selling high), but the need to produce excess electricity to meet peak demand would also be reduced, because vehicles and other items containing batteries would serve as storage units, available for meeting peak demand. This would be a smart grid.

WHERE TO START

Homes, business, and factories would be a good place to start the smart grid. They account for 40 percent of electricity use in the country, and therefore 40 percent of CO_2 emissions. A smart grid would be more efficient, thus reducing emissions. A second key component would be to electrify most of the transportation sector. This sector accounts for 30 percent of CO_2 emissions, and making it part of the smart grid would also reduce emissions. It is estimated that 73 percent of cars, trucks, and SUVs could be replaced with plug-in hybrids without any need to build new generating capacity because they would be recharged at night with off-peak electricity.

To get to this future will require a combination of policies, regulations, standards, innovation, market incentives (and disincentives), and breakthrough technologies, all coordinated in an intelligent system that moves us rapidly from high CO_2-producing energy sources to clean energy production and efficient use of the energy that is produced. Businesses need to learn to view these policies, regulations, and incentives not as a barrier to their success but as a way to differentiate themselves from their competitors.

BARRIERS

What is in the way of moving in this direction rapidly? Primarily it is the continuing legacy of the "Dirty Fuels System": auto companies, coal companies, some unenlightened utilities, and oil and gas companies. Their influence in political decisions remains significant across the country. Second, the country as a whole really has no sense of urgency about energy conservation or clean energy research. "Green" is still viewed more as an option than a necessity.

Conclusion: Getting Started

Moving forward, we need leaders who can shape issues about energy, climate change, and global connectedness so they are viewed and understood as opportunities, not threats. We also need to be successful not only in the United States but also around the globe. Thinking globally, these changes will be successful only if China, India, and other areas with rapidly growing populations and standards of living also follow a path to clean energy production and efficient use. Is all of this possible? Yes. Do we have enough time to do it? Yes, we have exactly enough time—but only if we start doing so *now*.

Groundswell

Charlene Li and Josh Bernoff

Summary Prepared by Amber Christian

Amber Christian is consulting partner at Phoenix Endeavors, LLC. She assists clients in implementing and enhancing financial systems processes. She received her M.B.A. from the University of Minnesota Carlson School of Management and undergraduate degrees in Management Information Sciences and Organizational Management from the University of Minnesota Duluth.

INTRODUCTION

As online technologies evolve, it is easier than ever for individuals to connect with each other. This trend began simply with e-commerce and grew as more people gained Internet access and comfort levels. Critical mass was reached as the majority of North America and Europe began using the Internet. The transformation of technologies has now created a world where a consumer can be online virtually anywhere, at any time. Today the consumer also has the ability to obtain information without relying on traditional sources, and increasingly makes purchasing decisions without input from the seller of the goods and services. This has far-reaching implications for companies today and into the future.

Groundswell represents the major trends in online technologies and shifting consumer behavior that are forcing companies to reexamine their traditional marketing and customer interaction models. As these new models emerge, it is easy for a company to place their focus on any one online technology as the answer to interact with the customer. The technologies enabling the groundswell are viewed by many businesses as a problem to be solved. However, they are really only intended to be the medium used to reach customers in order to build relationships. Horror stories abound of bad public relations generated from dissatisfied customers in the online community. The inability to completely control

Charlene Li and Josh Bernoff. *Groundswell: Winning in a World Transformed by Social Technologies.* Boston, MA: Harvard University Press, 2008.

a message about a brand or a company makes many businesses nervous, as significant time and money have been expended to build brands and reputations. It is difficult to understand how to engage this groundswell, but a description of the major online trends and recommendations for addressing the online community can help substantially. Each trend identified is supported with case studies to demonstrate how companies can be successful when engaging their customers.

SOCIAL TECHNOGRAPHICS PROFILE

Who is participating in the groundswell? Why do they participate? These are the first two fundamental questions to answer. *Understanding why your customers participate provides direction on how to engage them to participate with you.* The **Social Technographics profile** was created with the central idea that not all participants in the groundswell will participate in the same way. This profile groups participants into six different types: creators, critics, collectors, joiners, spectators, and inactives. *Creators* are the most active participants and typically generate original content. This group includes people who post articles, write blogs, and upload their own videos to YouTube. As a much larger group than creators, *critics* generate content through responding to the content generated online by others. Critics participate in online forums, respond to blogs and articles, and write product or service reviews. *Collectors* aggregate information to centralize in one place. They typically use services such as **Really Simple Syndication (RSS) feeds**—a technological process that allows readers to subscribe to areas of content interest and automatically receive updates in a standardized form from a site when new content is published. *Joiners* participate in social networking. They are found on Facebook, MySpace, LinkedIn, and other social networking sites. Joiners are a large group with continued growth trends. However, the largest online group is *spectators*. This group reviews the content generated by others, reads blogs and product reviews, and watches online media. Finally, the last group are nonparticipants. These *inactives* include both those customers that are online and offline. This group does not participate in the groundswell and is served through traditional marketing.

A company can align each of the types with different age groups and genders to provide a mechanism to refine the classification of their customers. This helps explain why customers participate in a particular way. These classifications help direct the focus of marketing efforts to reach customers. Marketing budgets typically include online and more traditional sources, and expenditures must be prioritized. There are a variety of options when moving to online sources, depending upon the available budget. The process to begin engaging the groundswell does not have to be expensive. Monitoring customer feedback through existing channels is one inexpensive way to begin the process. Other efforts such as creating an online community will require significantly more time and money and must be prioritized against other marketing objectives.

TAPPING THE GROUNDSWELL

It is very easy to become trapped in the "me, too" phenomenon where anything a competitor does online must be responded to equally and immediately. This is often done regardless of whether the strategy and logic behind the competitor's actions are well understood or should even be replicated. Instead of simply copying a competitor's strategy, a four-step process called the POST method can be used to plan a groundswell strategy. This process consists of the following steps:

- *People.* What is the Social Technographics profile of my customers? Do they even participate in the groundswell? Are they more likely to create content, or respond to content? This profile will provide both the motivation behind a customer's actions and ideas on the features and functionality required in the technology that is used to address them.
- *Objectives.* What is our company's purpose in participating? Are we going to energize our customers to drive sales, gain insights to help market our products, or simply listen to what our customers say about us and our products? The objectives clarify goals against which to measure progress.
- *Strategy.* How do we want to interact with our customers? How will we measure our progress? How will we manage changes within our company after the relationship with our customers begins to deepen? Engaging the customer in a deeper relationship over time will require your company to change.
- *Technology.* This should be addressed only after the previous three steps are in place, to ensure that the appropriate technologies are selected. Technology identifies what applications are necessary to engage customers, meet the objectives, and support your online strategy.

The POST method is very important to understand because *there is no one right way to engage the groundswell.* This method helps guide the planning to begin engaging your customers in new ways. There are five main approaches to use when engaging your customers: listening, talking, energizing, supporting, and embracing. One of the five typical approaches to successfully engage the groundswell should be selected in order to provide focus. Over time, the additional methods can be added. The approaches are progressive, with those first in the list requiring less commitment. *Companies should start small, learning how to work with the groundswell to build success.* Success in that step can then be used to progress to the next step. As a company actively engages the groundswell, it will shape the direction of the company.

Listening

Listening helps clarify what the market is saying about your brand. Traditionally, companies conduct focused market research to understand customer perceptions of their brand. Traditional marketing is presented with the concept that a company owns its brands. According to groundswell theory, *it is actually the customers that own your brand.* Customers will speak vocally about your brand virtually anywhere online. The sheer volume of different mediums (blogs, online forums, Web pages, etc.) makes it difficult to obtain actionable information. There are two primary strategies for listening: private communities and brand monitoring.

Private communities are an active strategy for listening. These communities offer a two-way conversation between the company and the customer. While this is important, an even more powerful connection can be forged in these communities between your customers. These connections can provide insights to questions a company may never think to ask! Through listening on a private community, Memorial Sloan-Kettering Cancer Center learned that reputation was not the deciding factor for choosing a cancer center. A cancer diagnosis is frightening, and most people are not aware of how the treatment process begins, or where to go for treatment. The Center learned that the recommendation of the primary care doctor whom the patient trusts is more important than any national rankings. This helped them realize advertising their ranking is less important than making sure primary care doctors understand their services.

Brand monitoring is a passive strategy for listening that seeks primarily to hear what the groundswell is saying about your brand. Has someone started a fan group on Facebook? Are blogs speaking about products and services positively or negatively? Are videos posted about products on YouTube? Given the sheer volume of media content available on the Internet, brand monitoring may best be outsourced. Firms have been created to specialize in the aggregation of this information. They can provide aggregated data that are more actionable in order to minimize the time required for this activity.

Talking

Traditionally, talking with customers is fulfilled through advertising and public relations. Marketers create messages aimed at the mass market through television commercials and print ads. Public relations departments seek free publicity through news and magazine coverage. This publicity may be related to company sales, new product launches, or anything else that increases positive exposure of the company in the mass media. Traditional advertising and public relations typically focus on traditional sources. To engage the groundswell, the focus needs to move to online advertising. While there are several ways to do this, two potential approaches include utilizing social networking sites and creating blogs. Utilizing social networking sites requires joining sites like Facebook and MySpace. This allows a company to create content aimed at the specific audience that uses these sites. Depending upon the objectives previously determined using the POST method, for example, a page on Facebook could be used to allow customers to provide input on a particular product design. However, a clear strategy will need to be in place first due to the interactive content on these sites. Some questions to consider include: How will your fans connect with you? How will you respond to their postings? This approach works well when there is already strong brand loyalty for your product and your target audience utilizes these sites.

Creating blogs is another approach that can be used to reach your audience. Before launching a blog, carefully consider the process involved in creating and maintaining a blog, and ask a series of questions. Why will this blog be created? (Understanding the goals for the blog gives direction to shape the blog.) What will be accomplished by publishing on this blog? (There is a difference between blogging to announce new products for a company and blogging about a particular product or product line.) Who will write for the blog? (Finding an executive sponsor that is willing to commit the time to write for the blog and sponsor it are key components to this process.) Finally, how often will content be published, and how will the target audience know your blog exists? *None of the goals for blogging can be reached if your core audience does not even know you are there!*

Energizing

Energizing is used to start the word-of-mouth engine. Word of mouth succeeds because it is credible and self-spreading. The same characteristics that can work against a company when spreading negative publicity can be channeled to create a positive message when a customer has a good experience. Positive "spin" has been used in politics for many years. In the online space, creators are typically the group to focus on if energizing is used because they generate original content. There are three main considerations in energizing your customers. What is the Social Technographics profile of my customers (i.e., how do I engage them)? What is the problem my customers are trying to solve? Can I afford to stick around for the long haul? The final question is the most important. Once customers are engaged in a community, it is difficult to take that community away without generating negative backlash.

Supporting

Allowing the groundswell to support itself by enabling people to connect with each other is another key approach. Traditional customer support models are built to deal with issues after a product has been sold. If support systems are being utilized, it means there is an issue with the product. Proper levels of staffing to maintain support for products already sold can be very expensive. Creating the ability for customers to support each other can translate into cost savings for product support. Dell embarked on creating a community support forum to allow users to support each other. This allows customers to post questions, and other customers are able to answer questions. So why would anyone take the time to answer questions for a complete stranger? Dell learned that *customers who answer questions value the mental rewards they receive for helping people.* Some of these customers will spend many hours helping others without receiving any compensation from Dell. All parties benefit in this case: the customer with the question receives an answer, the customer assisting receives mental rewards, and Dell receives fewer support calls. This has translated to significant cost savings for Dell in the area of customer support. Systems that allow supporting each other should be designed with mental rewards in mind. This entices customers to participate in helping others.

Embracing

Embracing utilizes the groundswell to innovate with help from potential or existing customers. There are currently no unique technologies specifically used for embracing. This objective is the culmination of engaging the groundswell. The previous methods begin to shape a company, and embracing brings the customer more fully into the development life cycle. Customers want to be engaged and provide feedback. They will ask for products and services that a company may not even have designed yet. After a company is able to successfully engage the groundswell, they are more likely to continue to do it as part of their business. The evolutionary process for a company has now begun, and this becomes part of their identity over time.

THE GROUNDSWELL TRANSFORMS

The journey to engage the groundswell influences a company from the outside. While this is important, an internal groundswell can also be leveraged to change from the inside out. Just as listening and talking can be used with customers, they can also be used with employees. Best Buy, for example, successfully created an internal site called blueshirtnation.com to help engage employees. With over 1,200 stores, there are many employees in blue shirts at the stores. Employees have different levels of commitment to the company. This site was created to help these employees feel connected on a day-to-day basis and help each other solve problems. An associate at one store can post product questions or issues and get answers from an associate at another store. This saves the company time and money.

What is the future of the groundswell? How does a company prepare for the changes in the groundswell itself that will require them to respond? The best strategy for addressing these continuous changes is not found in technology. Remember, the groundswell is not about technology—it is about people and relationships. *Listening to your customers, developing relationships with them, and being collaborative will provide a solid long-term foundation as the groundswell continues to evolve.*

XIV

Management Fables and Lessons for Personal Success

Two major interrelated phenomena in business book publishing emerged in the past quarter century. The first was to use the format of a brief "managerial fable" (fabricated story line) to catch the reader's attention and as a format for presenting a few (usually four to eight) key lessons to readers in a simple, readable, straightforward form. The first book of significance to achieve substantial success with this format was *The One Minute Manager*, followed by dozens of similarly structured books. The second phenomenon involved the explosion in demand (and products provided) for managerial "guidance" books that offered suggestions for personal success. The model of this genre of book in the modern era is unquestionably *The Seven Habits of Highly Effective People*. This section of *The Manager's Bookshelf* brings you a sampling of both types of books.

Kenneth Blanchard and Spencer Johnson, in the enormously popular book *The One Minute Manager*, build their prescriptions for effective human resource management on two basic principles. First, they suggest that quality time with the subordinate is of utmost importance. Second, they suggest that employees are basically capable of self-management. These two principles provide the basis for their prescriptions on goal setting, praising, and reprimanding as the cornerstones of effective management. *The One Minute Manager* was identified as one of the "seven essential popular business books" by M. L. Jenson (*eBook Crossroads*, December 5, 2005).

Kenneth Blanchard was a professor of management at the University of Massachusetts, and remains active as a writer, management consultant, and cofounder of the Blanchard Companies. Blanchard has also published *The Power of Ethical Management, Gung Ho, The One-Minute Apology, Servant Leader, Whale Done, The Heart of a Leader, The Leadership Pill, The Secret*, and *Raving Fans*; his books have collectively sold over 17 million copies. Spencer Johnson, the holder of a medical doctorate, is interested in stress and has written the popular books *Who Moved My Cheese?* and *The Present*.

The second book summarized in this section of *The Manager's Bookshelf* has a simple and surprisingly nonbusiness-sounding title: *Fish!* Like several other books (e.g., *The One Minute Manager, Zapp!, Heroz*, and *Who Moved My Cheese?*), which have also sold in large numbers, *Fish!* is short (about 100 pages), easy and quick to read, engaging, and written in the form of a parable. The authors (Lundin, Paul, and

Christensen) provide a creative way to convey a central message—that work can (and should) be a joyful experience for all involved. Like any of the books summarized in this edition, we urge you to read the original source in its entirety and then reflect about what you have read. What are the roles of "fun" and "play" at work? Can such an environment be created? Is the conceptual foundation of the authors' message a solid one? Do negative implications as well as positive ones arise from creating a joyful experience at work?

Authors Lundin, Christensen, and Paul and Chart House Learning have also collaborated in the preparation of other products extending the Fish! philosophy and practice. Their follow-up books include *Fish! Tales, Fish! Sticks*, and *Fish! For Life*, and they also have a wide array of videos, calendars, training programs, apparel, and other related products available at their Web site, www.charthouse.com/home.asp. We think you will discover that despite the brevity, simplicity, and creative format of *Fish!*, useful ideas for action and debate can be found in this and almost any type of managerial literature. Like all ideas, of course, they need to be tested for their soundness, validity, and applicability.

Spencer Johnson (coauthor of *The One Minute Manager, The Present, "Yes" or "No": The Guide to Better Decisions, Peaks and Valleys,* and many others) has written *Who Moved My Cheese?*, which has sold over ten million copies. This book catapulted to the top of best-seller lists for *USA Today, Publisher's Weekly,* the *Wall Street Journal*, and *Business Week*, with some companies (e.g., Southwest Airlines and Mercedes-Benz) ordering thousands of copies to distribute to their employees. Written in the form of a fable about two mice and two small people living in a maze, Johnson suggests that change is rampant around us, and thus employees must anticipate, monitor, and adapt to change quickly in order to survive. Unfortunately, fear—and the tendency to cling to the familiar and comfortable past—prevents some people from letting go of old beliefs, attitudes, and paradigms.

Stephen R. Covey is a well-known speaker, author of several books, and chief executive officer (CEO) of the Franklin Covey Co. His first book, *The Seven Habits of Highly Effective People*, remains on best-seller lists and has sold over 20 million copies across the world. In it, he offers a series of prescriptions to guide managers as they chart their courses in turbulent times. Drawn from his extensive review of the "success literature," Covey urges people to develop a character ethic based on seven key habits: people being proactive, identifying their values, disciplining themselves to work on high-priority items, seeking win–win solutions, listening with empathy, synergizing with others, and engaging in extensive reading and studying for self-development.

Covey has also published *The Seven Habits of Highly Effective Families*, which adapts the basic effectiveness principles and applies them to families. *First Things First* urges people to manage their time and life well so as to achieve goals consistent with their values. His book *Principle-Centered Leadership* identifies seven human attributes—self-awareness, imagination, willpower, an abundance mentality, courage, creativity, and self-renewal—that, when combined with eight key behaviors (e.g., priority on service, radiating positive energy), help produce effective and principled leaders. His other books include *Living the Seven Habits, Reflections for Highly Effective People, Everyday Greatness, Predictable Results in Unpredictable Times*, and *Great Work, Great Career.* Covey's son and colleague, Stephen M. R. Covey, has followed in his father's footsteps by publishing *The Speed of Trust.*

The 8th Habit is another of Stephen R. Covey's major publication efforts. Driven by the dominance of the Knowledge Worker Age and the pervasiveness of employees who are unappreciated and undervalued, organizations require new leadership and a major change in thinking.

The 8th Habit urges managers everywhere to create workplaces where employees feel mentally engaged by establishing trust, searching for better alternatives, and developing a shared vision. This begins by leaders finding their own voice as a foundation for inspiring others.

Bob Pike, Robert Ford, and John Newstrom collaborated to produce a unique book, *The Fun Minute Manager.* They pick up on the theme that many organizations are actually toxic workplaces devoid of humor. Instead, they argue, managers should create a fun work environment that is characterized by humor, playful games, joyful celebrations, and recognition of achievements. Through an imaginative story line, they develop nine key insights about fun at work, and offer 10 useful guidelines for new fun minute managers.

Bob Pike, Chairman and CEO of the Bob Pike Group, is a member of the Speakers Hall of Fame. His creative presentations to annual conferences on participative approaches to training are legendary. Robert Ford holds a Ph.D. from Arizona State University and is currently a professor at the University of Central Florida. His best-known book is *Managing the Guest Experience in Hospitality.* Dr. John Newstrom taught at the University of Minnesota Duluth, and is a self-styled funologist. He is the coauthor of over 40 books, including *Games Trainers Play, Transfer of Training*, and *The Manager's Bookshelf.*

The One Minute Manager

Kenneth Blanchard and Spencer Johnson

Summary Prepared by Charles C. Manz

Charles C. Manz is Professor of Management at the University of Massachusetts at Amherst. He holds a doctorate in Organizational Behavior from Pennsylvania State University. His professional publications and presentations concern topics such as self-leadership, vicarious learning, self-managed work groups, leadership, power and control, and group processes. He is the author of the book The Art of Self-Leadership *and coauthor of* The Leadership Wisdom of Jesus.

The most distinguishing characteristic of *The One Minute Manager* by Kenneth Blanchard and Spencer Johnson is its major philosophical theme: Good management does not take a lot of time. This dominant theme seems to be based on two underlying premises: (1) *Quality* of time spent with subordinates (as with one's children) is more important than quantity; and (2) in the end, people (subordinates) should really be managing themselves.

The book is built around a story that provides an occasion for learning about effective management. The story centers on the quest of "a young man" to find an effective manager. In his search he finds all kinds of managers, but very few that he considers effective. According to the story, the young man finds primarily two kinds of managers. One type is a hard-nosed manager who is concerned with the bottom line (profit) and tends to be directive in style. With this type of manager, the young man believes, the organization tends to win at the expense of the subordinates. The other type of manager is one who is concerned more about the employees than about performance. This "nice" kind of manager seems to allow the employees to win at the expense of the organization. In contrast to these two types of managers, the book suggests, an effective manager (as seen through the eyes of the young man) is one who manages so that both the organization and the people involved benefit (win).

Kenneth Blanchard and Spencer Johnson. *The One Minute Manager.* La Jolla, CA: Blanchard-Johnson Publishers, 1981.

The dilemma that the young man faces is that the few managers who do seem to be effective will not share their secrets. That is only true until he meets the "One Minute Manager." It turns out that this almost legendary manager is not only willing to share the secrets of his effectiveness but is so available that he is able to meet almost any time the young man wants to meet, except at the time of his weekly two-hour meeting with his subordinates. After an initial meeting with the one-minute manager, the young man is sent off to talk to his subordinates to learn, directly from those affected, the secrets of one-minute management. Thus the story begins, and in the remaining pages, the wisdom, experience, and management strategies of the one-minute manager are revealed as the authors communicate, through him and his subordinates, their view on effective management practice.

In addition to general philosophical management advice (e.g., managers can reap good results from their subordinates without expending much time), the book suggests that effective management means that both the organization and its employees win, and that people will do better work when they feel good about themselves; it also offers some specific prescriptions. These prescriptions center around three primary management techniques that have been addressed in the management literature for years: goal setting, positive reinforcement in the form of praise, and verbal reprimand. The authors suggest that applications of each of the techniques can be accomplished in very little time, in fact in as little as one minute (hence the strategies are labeled "one-minute goals," "one-minute praisings," and "one-minute reprimands"). The suggestions made in the book for effective use of each of these strategies will be summarized in the following sections.

ONE-MINUTE GOALS

One-minute goals clarify responsibilities and the nature of performance standards. Without them, employees will not know what is expected of them, being left instead to grope in the dark for what they ought to be doing. A great deal of research and writing has been done on the importance of goals in reaching a level of performance (c.f., Locke, Shaw, Saari, and Latham, 1981). The advice offered in *The One Minute Manager* regarding effective use of performance goals is quite consistent with the findings of this previous work. Specifically, the authors point out through one of the one-minute manager's subordinates that effective use of one-minute goals includes the following:

- agreement between the manager and subordinate regarding what needs to be done;
- recording of each goal on a single page in no more than 250 words that can be read by almost anyone in less than a minute;
- communication of clear performance standards regarding what is expected of subordinates regarding each goal; and
- continuous review of each goal, current performance, and the difference between the two.

These components are presented with a heavy emphasis on having employees use them to manage themselves. This point is driven home as the employee who shares this part of one-minute management recalls how the one-minute manager taught him about one-minute goals. In the recounted story, the one-minute manager refuses to take credit for having solved a problem of the subordinate and is in fact irritated by the very idea of getting credit for it. He insists that the subordinate solved his own problem and orders him to go out and start solving his own future problems without taking up the one-minute manager's time.

ONE-MINUTE PRAISING

The next employee encountered by the young man shares with him the secrets of one-minute praising. Again, the ideas presented regarding this technique pretty well parallel research findings on the use of positive reinforcement (c.f., Luthans and Kreitner, 1986). One basic suggestion for this technique is that managers should spend their time trying to catch subordinates doing something *right* rather than doing something wrong. In order to facilitate this, the one-minute manager monitors new employees closely at first and has them keep detailed records of their progress (which he reviews). When the manager is able to discover something that the employee is doing right, the occasion is set for one-minute praising (positive reinforcement). The specific components suggested for applying this technique include the following:

- letting others know that you are going to let them know how they are doing;
- praising positive performance as soon as possible after it has occurred, letting employees know specifically what they did right and how good you feel about it;
- allowing the message that you really feel good about their performance to sink in for a moment, and encouraging them to do the same; and
- using a handshake or other form of touch when it is appropriate (more on this later).

Again, these steps are described with a significant self-management flavor. The employee points out that after working for a manager like this for a while you start catching yourself doing things right and using self-praise.

ONE-MINUTE REPRIMANDS

The final employee that the young man visits tells him about one-minute reprimands. This potentially more somber subject is presented in a quite positive tone. In fact, the employee begins by pointing out that she often praises herself and sometimes asks the one-minute manager for a praising when she has done something well. But she goes on to explain that when she has done something wrong, the one-minute manager is quick to respond, letting her know exactly what she has done wrong and how he feels about it. After the reprimand is over, he proceeds to tell her how competent he thinks she really is, essentially praising her as a *person* despite rejecting the undesired *behavior*. Specifically, the book points out that one-minute reprimands should include the following:

- let people know that you will, in a frank manner, communicate to them how they are doing;
- reprimand poor performance as soon as possible, telling people exactly what they did wrong and how you feel about it (followed by a pause allowing the message to sink in);
- reaffirm how valuable you feel the employees are, using touch if appropriate, while making it clear that it is their *performance* that is unacceptable in this situation; and
- make sure that when the reprimand episode is over it is over.

OTHER ISSUES AND RELATED MANAGEMENT TECHNIQUES

Good management does not take a lot of time; it just takes wise application of three proven management strategies—one-minute goals, one-minute praisings, and one-minute reprimands. Beyond this, the book deals with some other issues relevant to these strategies, such as "under what conditions is physical touch appropriate?" The authors suggest that the use of appropriate touch can be helpful when you know the person well and wish to help that person succeed. It should be done so that you are giving something to the person such as encouragement or support, not taking something away.

The authors also address the issue of manipulation, suggesting that employees should be informed about, and agree to, the manager's use of one-minute management. The key is to be honest and open in the use of this approach. They also deal briefly with several other issues. For example, Blanchard and Johnson suggest that it is important to move a subordinate gradually to perform a new desired behavior by reinforcing approximations to the behavior until it is finally successfully performed. The technical term for this is "shaping." A person's behavior is shaped by continuously praising improvements rather than waiting until a person completely performs correctly. If a manager waits until a new employee completely performs correctly, the employee may well give up long before successful performance is achieved because of the absence of reinforcement along the way.

The strategies can also be substituted for one another when appropriate. With new employees, for instance, dealing with low performance should focus on goal setting and then trying to catch them doing something right rather than using reprimand. Since a new employee's lack of experience likely produces an insufficient confidence level, this makes reprimand inappropriate, while goal setting and praise can be quite effective. The authors also suggest that if a manager is going to be tough on a person, the manager is better off being tough first and then being supportive, rather than the other way around.

Eventually, at the end of the story, the young man is hired by the one-minute manager and over time becomes a seasoned one-minute manager himself. As he looks back over his experiences, he recognizes numerous benefits of the one-minute management approach—more results in less time, time to think and plan, less stress and better health, similar benefits experienced by subordinates, and reduced absenteeism and turnover.

Conclusion

The bottom-line message is that effective management requires that you care sincerely about people but have definite expectations that are expressed openly about their behavior. Also, one thing that is even more valuable than learning to be a one-minute manager is having one for a boss, which in the end means you really work for yourself. And finally, these management techniques are not a competitive advantage to be hoarded but a gift to be shared with others. This is true because, in the end, the one who shares the gift will be at least as richly rewarded as the one who receives it.

Notes

Locke, E., K. Shaw, L. Saari, and G. Latham. "Goal Setting and Task Performance 1969–1980." *Psychological Bulletin,* 90 (1981), 125–152.

Luthans, F., and T. Davis. "Behavioral Self-management (BSM): The Missing Link in Managerial Effectiveness." *Organizational Dynamics,* 8 (1979), 42–60.

Luthans, F., and R. Kreitner. *Organizational Behavior Modification and Beyond.* Glenview, IL: Scott, Foresman and Co., 1986.

Manz, C. C. *The Art of Self-Leadership: Strategies for Personal Effectiveness in Your Life and Work.* Upper Saddle River, NJ: Prentice Hall, 1983.

Manz, C. C. "Self-Leadership: Toward an Expanded Theory of Self-influence Processes in Organizations." *Academy of Management Review,* 11 (1986), 585–600.

Manz, C. C., and H. P. Sims, Jr. "Self-Management as a Substitute for Leadership: A Social Learning Theory Perspective." *Academy of Management Review,* 5 (1980), 361–367.

Fish!

Stephen C. Lundin, Harry Paul, and John Christensen

Summary Prepared by John W. Newstrom

Mary Jane Ramirez is a manager who must create an effective team out of a set of employees who have historically been less than helpful to each other and generally unenthusiastic about teamwork. While taking a walk at lunchtime one day, she encounters a strange but compelling sight—the fishmongers of Seattle's Pike Street Fish Market. These employees have created a bustling, fun-filled, joyful work atmosphere both for themselves and for their customers. Through a series of conversations with Lonnie and some deep self-reflectiveness, she gradually uncovers some ideas that will guide her future behavior.

Using the fish market as a metaphor for other organizations, several key premises about employees are identified, and these lead logically to a short series of recommendations for personal effectiveness. The premises (underlying assumptions) include the following:

- Life is short, and our moments of life are precious. Therefore, it would be tragic for employees to just "pass through" on their way to retirement. Managers and employees both need to *make each moment count.*
- Most people prefer to work in a job environment that is *filled with fun.* When they find this fun or create it, they are much more likely to be energized and release their potential.
- People also like a work environment where they feel they can *make a difference* in the organization's outcomes. They need some capacity to assess their contribution toward those outcomes.
- Almost any job—no matter how simple or automated—has the potential to be performed with *energy and enthusiasm.*
- Employees may not always have the opportunity to choose whether to work or the work to be done itself. However, they will always have some degree of choice about the *way* in which they do their work. At the extreme, each employee can choose to be ordinary or world famous. One path is dull; the other exciting.

Stephen C. Lundin, Harry Paul, and John Christensen. *Fish!: A Remarkable Way to Boost Morale and Improve Results.* New York: Hyperion, 2000.

- Employees can legitimately act like a bunch of *adult kids* having a good time as long as they do so in a respectful manner (not offending coworkers or customers). When they do act as kids (along with choosing to love the work they do), they can find happiness, meaning, and fulfillment every day.

Based on these premises, four recommendations are offered to employees for their personal effectiveness:

1. Every morning, before you go to work, *choose your attitude* for the day (and make it a positive one).
2. Make an effort to introduce an element of **play** into your work environment; it will benefit you and all those around you.
3. Make a commitment to make someone else's day *special* for them. Do something that will create a memory, engage them in a meaningful interaction, or welcome them to your organization.
4. While you are at work, seek to be *present* with them. Focus your energy on them; listen attentively and caringly; pay attention to the needs of your customers and coworkers.

Following these simple prescriptions will make the work experience joyful for all involved, just as it has for the employees and customers of Seattle's Pike Street Fish Market.

3

Who Moved My Cheese?

Spencer Johnson, M.D.

Summary Prepared by Gary Stark

Gary Stark is a faculty member at Northern Michigan University. He earned his Ph.D. in Management from the University of Nebraska, and subsequently taught at the University of Minnesota Duluth and Washburn University. Gary's research interests include recruiting, work-life balance, and the study of how and why people seek feedback on their work performance. Prior to his academic life, Gary earned his B.S. and M.B.A. degrees at Kansas State University and worked in Chicago as a tax accountant.

A REUNION

Several former classmates met in Chicago one Sunday, the day after their class reunion. After discussing the difficulties they had been having with the many changes in their lives since high school, one of the classmates, Michael, volunteered a story that had helped him deal with the changes in his life. The name of the story was "Who Moved My Cheese?"

THE STORY

The story revolved around four characters who spent their lives in a maze. The maze was a giant labyrinth with many dead ends and wrong turns. But those who persisted in the maze were rewarded, for many rooms in the maze contained delicious **cheese**. Two of the characters in the maze were little people named Hem and Haw. Two were mice named Sniff and Scurry. The characters spent every day at Cheese Station C, a huge storehouse of cheese. However, the mice and the little people differed in their attitudes about Cheese Station C. These attitudes affected their behaviors. The mice, Sniff and Scurry, woke up early each day and raced to Cheese Station C. When they got there, they took off

Spencer Johnson, M.D. *Who Moved My Cheese?: An Amazing Way to Deal with Change in Your Work and in Your Life*. New York: Putman Books, 1998.

their running shoes, tied them together, and hung them around their necks so that they would be immediately available should they need to move on from Cheese Station C. And Sniff and Scurry did something else to make sure that they were ready to move on if the need arose. Every day upon arrival at Cheese Station C they carefully inspected the station and noted changes from the previous day.

Indeed, one day Sniff and Scurry arrived at Cheese Station C and found that the cheese was gone. Sniff and Scurry were not surprised because they had been inspecting the station every day and had noticed the cheese supply dwindling. In response to the cheeselessness, Sniff and Scurry simply did as their instincts told them. *The situation had changed so they changed with it.* Rather than analyze the situation, they put on their running shoes (taken from around their necks) and ran off through the maze in search of new cheese.

The little people, Hem and Haw, were different. Long ago, when they first found Cheese Station C, they had raced to get there every morning. But, as time went on, Hem and Haw got to the station a little later each day. They became very comfortable in Cheese Station C and, unlike Sniff and Scurry, never bothered to search for changes in the station. They assumed the cheese would always be there and even came to regard the cheese as their own. Unfortunately, unlike Sniff and Scurry, they did not notice that the cheese was disappearing.

When they arrived on the fateful day and discovered the cheese had run out in Cheese Station C, Hem and Haw reacted differently than Sniff and Scurry. Instead of immediately searching for new cheese, they complained that it wasn't fair. Finding cheese was a lot of work in their maze, and they did not want to let go of the life they had built around this cheese. They wanted to know who moved their cheese.

Hem and Haw returned the next day still hoping to find the cheese. They found none and repeated the behaviors of the day before. Eventually, Haw noticed that Sniff and Scurry were gone. Haw suggested to Hem that they do as Sniff and Scurry had and go out into the maze in search of new cheese. Hem rebuffed him.

A similar scenario played out day after day in Cheese Station C. Hem and Haw returned every day hoping to find the cheese they believed they were entitled to. They became frustrated and angry and began to blame each other for their predicament.

In the meantime, Sniff and Scurry had found new cheese. It had taken a lot of work, and they dealt with much uncertainty, but finally, in a totally unfamiliar part of the maze they found cheese in Cheese Station N.

Still, day after day, Hem and Haw returned to Cheese Station C in hopes of finding their cheese. And the same frustrations and claims of entitlement continued. Eventually, however, Haw's mindset began to change. He imagined Sniff and Scurry in pursuit of new cheese and imagined himself taking part in such an adventure. He imagined finding fresh new cheese. The more he thought about it the more determined he became to leave. Nevertheless, his friend Hem continued to insist that things would be fine in Cheese Station C. Hem figured that if they simply *worked harder* they would find their cheese in Cheese Station C. He feared he was too old to look for cheese and that he would look foolish doing so. Hem's concerns even made Haw doubt himself until finally one day Haw realized that he was doing the same things over and over again and wondering why things didn't improve. Although Haw did not like the idea of going into the maze and the possibility of getting lost, he laughed at how his fear was preventing him from doing those things. His realization inspired him to write a message to himself (and perhaps to Hem) on the wall in front of him. "What Would You Do If You Weren't Afraid?" (p. 48), it said. Answering his own question, Haw took a deep breath and headed into the unknown.

Unfortunately, a long interlude without food from Cheese Station C had left Haw somewhat weak. He struggled while searching for new cheese and decided that if he ever got another chance he would respond to a change in his environment sooner than he had to the situation in Cheese Station C.

Haw wandered for days and found very little new cheese. He found the maze confusing, as it had changed a great deal since the last time he had looked for cheese. Still, he had to admit that it wasn't as dreadful as he had feared. And whenever he got discouraged, he reminded himself that however painful the search for new cheese was, it was better than remaining cheeseless. The difference was that *he was now in control.* Haw even began to realize, in hindsight, that the cheese in Cheese Station C had not suddenly disappeared. If he had wanted to notice he would have seen the amount of cheese decreasing every day, and that what was left at the end was old and not as tasty. Haw realized that maybe Sniff and Scurry had known what they were doing. Haw stopped to rest and wrote another message on the wall. The message read: "Smell the Cheese Often So You Know When It Is Getting Old" (p. 52).

Haw was often scared in the maze for he did not know if he would survive. He wondered if Hem had moved on yet or was still frozen by his fears. However, Haw's confidence and enjoyment grew with every day as he realized that the times he had felt best in this journey was when he was moving. He inscribed this discovery on the wall of the maze: "When You Move Beyond Your Fear, You Feel Free" (p. 56).

Soon Haw began painting a picture in his mind of himself enjoying all his favorite cheeses. This image became so vivid that he gained a very strong sense that he would find new cheese. He stopped to write on the wall: "Imagining Myself Enjoying New Cheese Even Before I Find It, Leads Me to It" (p. 58). Outside a new station, Haw noticed small bits of cheese near the entrance. He tried some, found them delicious, and excitedly entered the station. But Haw's heart sank when he found that only a small amount of cheese remained in what was once a well-stocked station. He realized that if he had set about looking for new cheese sooner he might have found more cheese here. He wrote these thoughts on the wall: "The Quicker You Let Go of Old Cheese, the Sooner You Find New Cheese" (p. 60).

As Haw left this station, he made another important self-discovery. He realized what made him happy wasn't just having cheese. What made him happy was not being controlled by fear. He did not feel as weak and helpless as when he remained in Cheese Station C. Haw realized that moving beyond his fear was giving him strength and wrote that: "It Is Safer to Search in the Maze Than Remain in a Cheeseless Situation" (p. 62). Haw also realized that the fear he had allowed to build up in his mind was worse than the reality. He had been so afraid of the maze that he had dreaded looking for new cheese. Now he found himself excited about looking for more. Later in his journey he wrote: "Old Beliefs Do Not Lead You to New Cheese" (p. 64). Haw knew that his new beliefs had encouraged new behaviors.

Finally it happened. What Haw had started his journey looking for was now in front of his eyes. Cheese Station N was flush with some of the greatest cheeses Haw had ever seen. Sure enough, his mouse friends Sniff and Scurry were sitting in the cheese, their bellies stuffed. Haw quickly said hello and dug in.

Haw was a bit envious of his mouse friends. They had kept their lives simple. When the cheese moved, rather than overanalyze things, Sniff and Scurry moved with it. As Haw reflected on his journey, he learned from his mistakes. He realized that what he had written on the walls during his journey was true and was glad he had changed. Haw realized three important things: (1) the biggest thing blocking change is yourself; (2) things don't improve until you change yourself; and (3) there is always new cheese out there, whether you believe it or not. Indeed he realized running out of cheese in Cheese Station C had been a blessing in disguise. It had led him to better cheese and to discover important and positive things about himself.

Although Haw knew that he had learned a great deal, he also realized that it would be easy to fall into a comfort zone with the new store of cheese. So, every day he inspected the cheese in Cheese Station N to avoid the same surprise that had occurred in Cheese Station C. And, even though he had a great supply of cheese in Cheese Station N, every day he went out into the maze to make sure that he was always aware of his choices and that he did not have to remain in Cheese Station N. It was on one of these excursions that he heard the sound of someone moving toward him in the maze. He hoped and prayed that it was his friend Hem, and that Hem had finally learned to . . . "Move with the Cheese and Enjoy It!" (p. 76).

BACK AT THE REUNION

After the story, the former classmates recounted situations in which they had to face changes in their work and their personal lives and they discussed which maze character they had acted most like. Most resolved to act more like Haw when dealing with changes they would face in the future. All agreed the story was very useful and that they would use the wisdom contained within to guide them.

The Seven Habits of Highly Effective People

Stephen R. Covey

Summary Prepared by John W. Newstrom

There are two types of literature on how to succeed. The first type focuses on a *personality ethic*. It claims that you are what you appear to be; appearance is everything. It accents public image, social consciousness, and the ability to interact superficially with others. However, exclusive attention to these factors will eventually provide evidence of a lack of integrity, an absence of depth, a short-term personal success orientation, and basic deficiency in one's own humanness.

The second type of success literature revolves around a *character ethic*. It provides proven pathways to move from dependent relationships to independence, and ultimately to interdependent success with other people. It requires a willingness to subordinate one's short-term needs to more important long-term goals. It requires effort, perseverance, and patience with oneself. One's character is, after all, a composite of habits, which are unconscious patterns of actions.

Habits can be developed through rigorous practice until they become second nature. There are seven key habits that form the basis for character development and build a strong foundation for interpersonal success in life and at work:

1. *Be proactive.* Make things happen. Take the initiative and be responsible for your life. Work on areas where you can have an impact and pay less attention to areas outside your area of concern. When you do respond to others, do so on the basis of your principles.

2. *Begin with the end in mind.* Know where you're going; develop a personal mission statement; develop a sense of who you are and what you value. Maintain a long-term focus.

3. *Put first things first.* Distinguish between tasks that are urgent and not so urgent and between activities that are important and not so important; then

Stephen R. Covey. *The Seven Habits of Highly Effective People: Restoring the Character Ethic.* New York: Simon & Schuster, 1989.

organize and execute around those priorities. Avoid being in a reactive mode, and pursue opportunities instead. Ask yourself, "What one thing could I do (today) that would make a tremendous difference in my work or personal life?"

4. *Think "win–win."* Try to avoid competing, and search for ways to develop mutually beneficial relationships instead. Build an "emotional bank account" with others through frequent acts of courtesy, kindness, honesty, and commitment keeping. Develop the traits of integrity, maturity, and an abundance mentality (acting as if there is plenty of everything out there for everybody).

5. *Seek to understand, and then to be understood.* Practice empathetic communications, in which you recognize feelings and emotions in others. Listen carefully to people. Try giving them "psychological air."

6. *Synergize.* Value and exploit the mental, emotional, and psychological differences among people to produce results that demonstrate creative energy superior to what a single person could have accomplished alone.

7. *Sharpen the saw.* Do not allow yourself to get stale in any domain of your life, and don't waste time on activities that do not contribute to one of your goals and values. Seek ways to renew yourself periodically in all four elements of your nature—physical (via exercise, good nutrition, and stress control), mental (through reading, thought, and writing), social (through service to others), and spiritual (through study and meditation). In short, practice continuous learning and self-improvement, and your character will lead you to increased success.

The 8th Habit

Stephen R. Covey

Summary Prepared by David L. Beal

David L. Beal is a retired Operations Manager and Vice President of Manufacturing for Lake Superior Paper Industries and Consolidated Papers Inc. in Duluth, Minnesota. Under his leadership, the all-salaried workforce was organized into a totally self-reliant team system using the principles of sociotechnical design to create a high-performance system. Dave teaches in the Labovitz School of Business and Economics at the University of Minnesota Duluth, where his areas of interest include designing and leading self-directed team-based organizations, teamwork, and production and operations management. He received his B.S. in Chemical Engineering from the University of Maine in Orono, Maine, with a fifth year in Pulp and Paper Sciences.

INTRODUCTION

The challenges people face in their relationships, families, and professional lives and the complexities of powerful leadership in today's organizations have changed dramatically. Being effective as individuals and leaders in organizational environments is essential for success and goal achievement. While effectiveness drives success, *the higher calling for the future is to move beyond effectiveness to greatness.* Greatness means that we have mastered our human potential in every dimension of our life; the mind, body, heart, and spirit. Within each of us is an inner desire to live a life of greatness and to fulfill our purpose for existence and really make a difference. Greatness is fulfilling, allowing passionate execution and significant contribution for organizations to thrive, excel, and become leaders in today's global society.

The principles presented in *The Seven Habits of Highly Effective People* (see pp. 359–360) are enduring and timeless. These character principles affect who and what we are as individuals. The seven habits form the basis for character development and building a strong foundation for interpersonal success. These habits are

Stephen R. Covey. *The 8th Habit: From Effectiveness to Greatness.* New York: Free Press, 2004.

essential for individual effectiveness. *The 8th Habit* moves individuals from effectiveness to greatness by urging them to find their own voice and then subsequently inspiring others to find theirs as well. It moves people from independence to interdependence in a way that develops whole persons to excel in every aspect of their life. This passionate execution and fulfillment of life requires a whole new engrained behavior—the 8th habit.

Because most people feel unappreciated and undervalued at work, they soon become frustrated and victims of the organization and system they work and live in. With little or no sense of voice, they fail to develop their potential or unique contribution to the organization. Humanity's search for its "voice" is the answer to the soul's desire for greatness in life and the organization's need for achieving superior results. Human beings are not physical things that need to be motivated and controlled with an extrinsic approach. People make choices in life, and at work these choices determine how much of themselves they will give to the relationships that make them effective leaders. *Contemporary employees have an intrinsic ability, and hence they desire the freedom to reach full potential and to live in an environment that values and encourages developing all aspects of their life.* This can be accomplished by giving them the knowledge and ability to find their voice and the organizational system for their voice to flourish. This is why the 8th habit is essential for developing trusting relationships, achieving peace of mind, and excelling in all aspects of life.

Most of the inspiration and change in organizations that has sustained prosperity and achievement of overall objectives started with the exceptional leadership of one person, usually the CEO or president. These executives exercised their leadership in profound ways that sustained long-term growth and organizational success. They practiced the 8th habit and learned to identify and understand their voice so as to inspire others to find theirs.

FOUR PATHS TO GREATNESS

The 8th Habit assumes that everyone chooses one of two roads in life. One road is the familiar highway that most people take, while the other is the road to achieve real meaning in life and eventual greatness. How we eventually get there can be as different as black and white. Deep within each of us is an intrinsic desire to achieve greatness in chosen aspects of our life and, in so doing, make significant contributions to humankind. To make a significant difference and do what really matters in life, it is essential to

- Develop the whole person: Explore the mind, body, heart, and spirit.
- Discover your voice: Understand your inherent makeup; have the freedom and ability to choose your direction in life; and develop four capacities of intelligence directly related to the mind, body, heart, and spirit. *When we change our thinking, our life will change.*
- Express your voice: Live a life embodied in the human intelligences of vision, discipline, passion, and conscience and by integrating what you learned into your life.
- Inspire others to find their voice: Choose to expand your influence, increase your contribution, and exercise your leadership in a meaningful and profound way.

FOUR INTELLIGENCES

Corresponding to the four parts of our nature as human beings, the mind, body, heart, and spirit, are four intelligences that everyone possesses. These are the mental, physical, emotional, and spiritual intelligences. *Mental intelligence* enables us to comprehend, reason, solve problems, think, use languages for communication, and visualize the future. Everyone possesses *physical intelligence* that manages all of the complexities of the physical body system, much of it unconscious. *Emotional intelligence* involves knowing one's self in a way that develops compassion, empathy, the ability to translate and successfully communicate with others, and be aware of the impact and influence we have on others. *Spiritual intelligence* is the desire for meaning in life, the fulfillment of our purpose for existence, and the connection with something infinitely greater than ourselves. It is the highest of the four intelligences.

Developing the four intelligences and building capabilities requires knowledge and discipline. Mental intelligence requires disciplined study, learning through education, and having an acute awareness of one's self. Living a balanced life with regular exercise, good nutrition, proper rest, relaxation, and stress management improves physical intelligence. Developing good social and communication skills, self awareness, and a high level of intrinsic motivation develops healthy emotional intelligence. Finally, never compromising one's integrity by being true to the highest level of values and listening to the voice inside while developing meaning in life and practicing a life of service to others for the good of society develop spiritual intelligence.

Possessing a vision for life and seeing what is possible in people are the highest level of mental intelligence. Leading a disciplined life when vision joins with commitment develops physical intelligence. Igniting the fire within is passion, and with the desire and strength of conviction for life itself comes the development of emotional intelligence. Finally, listening to the voice inside and following our conscience are the greatest dimension of developing spiritual intelligence. These qualities represent the highest level of expressing our voice.

THE KEY ROLE OF TRUST

Trust is the most difficult value to attain in most organizations. Organizations today find that low trust exists almost everywhere and is chronic in nature. When vision and trust are neglected, the result will be a weak culture with no shared vision and value system. Under these conditions, any road will seem like the primrose path, but almost always to the detriment of achieving critical organizational goals. When there is no alignment built into the organizational design, systems, processes, or culture, the organization remains helpless in achieving goals and fulfilling its purpose. When there is no passion for the vision or the achievement of goals and work in the organization, there will be a profound disempowerment of the employees. It is for these reasons that the 8th habit is not just developing personal greatness, but just as importantly, it is the process of "Inspiring Others to Find Their Voice" through focus and execution. Focus involves the modeling and pathfinding roles, while execution involves the aligning and empowering roles.

Focus is practicing the modeling and pathfinding roles that inspire others to find their voice. When this happens and it becomes a means for achieving values, the high level of trust and vision that results will create a strong culture and successful organization. Developing the attitude, skill, and knowledge to inspire others to find their voice requires focus and modeling of the following principles:

1. "The Voice of Influence." Finding your own voice and passion to develop others is a first step. You cannot give to others what you fail to possess and put into practice yourself. By being able to expand your influence within your environments and choosing the attitude of initiative, others will be inspired to find their voice, and everyone will grow to achieve greatness. It's the fire within each one of us coming together to produce an inferno. Modeling is also the activity of a team, and as teamwork improves, organizational goals are achieved.

2. "The Voice of Trustworthiness." Trust comes from trustworthiness, the practice of trusting others first. Trusting relationships do not develop without a belief system that values the trust of others with open and truthful two-way communication. Knowing these principles and putting them into practice will open the path for influencing others and developing trusting relationships.
3. "The Voice and Speed of Trust." Developing strong relationships requires skills that build trust and helps to blend voices, which is literally creating a third alternative for solutions to differences and challenges with others. This rational process is usually a win–win for both parties by finding solutions that are better than either party's position taken alone.
4. "One Voice." The practice of one common voice being heard involves creating a single-minded vision with others about the priorities and values that will achieve critical outcomes.

Execution is the alignment of priorities and values while empowering others to find their voice and use it. The aligning and empowering roles are essential for others in the organization to develop the 8th habit. Execution of the aligning and empowering roles has two requirements:

1. "The Voice of Execution" requires the alignment of goals and systems for results. When the belief systems are untrustworthy, employees are not aligned with the organization's philosophy or values, and untrustworthy systems will dominate. Systems emerge out of necessity for the survival of employees when the behaviors in organizations are not aligned or supportive of the values the organization professes. Trustworthiness is paramount for alignment of values and operational goals within organizations, and when principle-centered alignment occurs, moral authority becomes institutionalized. This moral authority is the capacity to consistently serve the customer and be the supplier of choice with quality products and services, develop trusting relationships in all areas, and achieve organizational goals of efficiency, profitability, speed, and flexibility year after year.
2. "The Empowering Voice" is allowing your leadership abilities and passion for greatness to inspire others and then removing the obstacles that stand in the way for others to achieve their greatness. It's setting others free to grow, getting out of the way by empowering their abilities to achieve positive results no matter how small, and cheerleading their path to greatness.

Greatness Dimensions: Conclusions

The 8th habit is based on three dimensions of greatness: personal, leadership, and organizational. Personal greatness occurs when we put into practice the ability to choose our direction in life, understand and put into practice a principle-based existence, and fulfill the four human intelligences. When the voice within each of us is exercised in a profound and enduring way, others are inspired to find their voice and achieve leadership greatness. Organizational greatness occurs when a critical mass of employees within the organization puts into practice the principles and drivers of execution. There are four disciplines of execution. They are:

1. "Focus on the Wildly Important." The goals and objectives that have serious consequences if not met must be a supreme priority within the organization.
2. "Create a Compelling Scoreboard." The "Wildly Important" priorities promote accomplishment of critical organizational objectives if they are measurable. Without good measures of success, the goal or priority is never understood or achieved.

3. "Translate Lofty Goals into Specific Actions." Align the organization so that everyone on the team knows exactly what they're supposed to do. Teamwork is being creative, identifying better ways of doing things, and improving behaviors and translating goals into tasks that can be accomplished at all levels of the organization.

4. "Hold Each Other Accountable—All of the Time." Accountability ensures that critical organizational goals are accomplished.

When these four disciplines of execution are put into practice, they will enable an organization to achieve breakthrough performance.

6

The Fun Minute Manager

Bob Pike, Robert C. Ford, and John W. Newstrom

Summary Prepared by John W. Newstrom

John W. Newstrom *is the Chief Funologist for Funology, Inc., where his primary task is to help managers create and sustain a fun work environment for their employees. Additional information on fun at work can be found at http://www. thefunminutemanager.com/*

THE IMPORTANCE OF FUN AT WORK

A young manager, Bob Workman, is continually bombarded with problems at work that leave him and his colleagues emotionally drained at the end of each day. In sharp contrast, they find much enjoyment in activities that they engage in *away* from work (e.g., while participating in voluntary and nonprofit organizational settings, as well as truly recreational activities). Predictably, the manager embarks on a journey of discovery, in which he searches for an answer to his dilemma.

In his search for answers to his questions, Bob stumbles upon several key pieces of information. First, he discovers that most workers *want* a job that is fun (the strong interest is there). Second, he discovers a powerful fact—that "fun, play, and laughter" may actually exist at the pinnacle of the typical employee's need hierarchy as the *most sought-after environmental factor at work.* This provides a startling revelation for him: *It appears that a primary goal of any manager should be to provide opportunities for employees to have fun at work.*

After receiving an overview of the effects of fun at the physiological, psychological, and social levels, he resolves to help the people around him at work laugh more frequently. But how can he do this, he asks himself? This question challenges him to search for a set of tools by which he can create a fun work environment.

Bob Pike, Robert C. Ford, and John W. Newstrom. *The Fun Minute Manager: Create FUNomenal Results Now Through Using Fun at Work!* Minneapolis: CTT Press, 2009.

He explores what some other organizations have successfully done to implement fun at work and develops a set of initial conclusions. Fun workplaces are:

- easy to create,
- desired by most employees,
- easily identified by the presence of laughter, joy, happiness, surprise and spontaneity, and yet
- they can mean different things to different people. All of this makes intuitive sense to him as the reality about fun sinks in.

After reviewing the typical characteristics of many playful and recreational activities that bring out the joyful spirit within participants, Bob recognizes their applicability to the world of work. By studying the potential similarities between work settings and play, he discovered a set of criteria to apply in the creation of a fun work environment. For example, the fun activities should make people smile, be easy to prepare, be low-cost, involve a low risk of physical harm to people or resources, not be time consuming, be as inclusive as possible, combine both planned and spontaneous events, and be created and administered on a participative basis.

FUN FACTORS AND A DEFINITION

Now ready to jump in with both feet, he discovers a comprehensive research study that documents a surprisingly broad set of factors that contribute to having fun in any context (e.g., recognition of personal milestones, fun social events, public celebrations of achievements, stress release activities, friendly competitions, opportunities for community involvement, use of humor, opportunities for personal development, the use of games at work, and providing occasional entertainment at work). He experiments with several of these and concludes that they are

1. Generally easy to implement,
2. Inexpensive (often cost little or nothing), and
3. Are usually well received by his employees and colleagues.

As a consequence, he arrives at a working definition of a **fun work environment** as *one in which a variety of formal and informal activities regularly occur that are designed to uplift people's spirits, and positively and publicly remind people of their value to their managers, their organization, and to each other through the use of humor, playful games, joyful celebrations, opportunities for self development, or recognition of achievements and milestones.*

He invites his team members to create new job titles for themselves—ones that emphasize their evolving role as cocreators of fun work experiences. They enthusiastically participate (and have fun doing so). Their brainstormed list includes the titles of Corporate Cheerleader, Goddess (Empress) of Fun, Chief Energizing Officer, Funcilitator, Chief Funatic Manager, Fun 'R Us Team Leader, Joy Team Captain, Minister of Comedy, Glee Club Leader, Funologist, Funmaster (or Funmeister), Director of Fun, and Mutual Fun Manager. After a lot of laughs among the group, he chooses the title of *Fun Minute Manager* for himself, because he knows that many fun activities can be implemented in short periods of time—an important key to their success.

IMPORTANT OUTCOMES

When his proposal to formalize the fun process at work gets initially rebuffed by his boss, he carefully studies the possible impediments to a fun workplace. He discovers that a fun workplace *could* change the culture substantially, *may* lack the support of higher executives, *could* produce negative perceptions from outsiders, *may* raise some realistic fears among managers (e.g., lower productivity, dangerous behaviors, extra costs), and *might* cause managers to experience a certain degree of personal embarrassment. However, he concludes that these are not serious barriers that cannot be overcome.

Next, he searches the existing research literature on fun at work and identifies an array of work-related benefits that are reported to be likely products of a fun work environment. They include, in order of perceived importance:

Rank	Outcome
1	Greater employee enthusiasm
2	Higher ability to attract new employees
3	Increased employee satisfaction
4	Better communications among employees
5	Improved employee creativity
6	Richer employee friendships at work
7	Higher group cohesiveness
8	Increased levels of customer satisfaction
9	Elevated level of employee commitment to the organization
10	Stronger corporate culture (shared values and norms)

In addition, he is confident that fun at work will also reduce anxiety and stress and diminish the common complaints of boredom that he hears so often.

MAJOR FUN INSIGHTS

Finally, he prepares a set of key insights that he has gained from each step in his "journey into fun." These include the following:

INSIGHT #1: You can get a lot of people to do a lot of things if there is fun involved.

INSIGHT #2: Most people want to have fun while also doing meaningful and productive work.

INSIGHT #3: A wide range of activities exist that can provide fun at work.

INSIGHT #4: Fun at work is not traditionally viewed as an integral part of a manager's responsibilities, and consequently it will not be accepted easily by superiors without very convincing argument and solid evidence.

INSIGHT #5: Strong evidence is emerging that fun workplaces can and do produce a wide array of activities that lead to positive physiological and psychological outcomes for the individual and equally valuable benefits for work organizations.

INSIGHT #6: It is appropriate to outline—in advance—the criteria that a program for fun at work must meet, and then review them frequently.

INSIGHT #7: Using the principles of a high-involvement workplace, consultation with employees and solicitation of their ideas can provide a strong base of support and innumerable ideas for fun at work.

INSIGHT #8: The only way to conclusively determine (and demonstrate) the actual effects attributable to fun at work is to measure them on a pretest and posttest basis.

INSIGHT #9: Fun-at-work programs can be designed and implemented quickly, easily, and inexpensively by a truly committed "fun minute manager" and his/her team.

He then decides to conduct a systematic assessment of the readiness of his employees to engage in fun at work by surveying their self-reported receptivity. When the results are tabulated, they show that his employees have a strong desire to have fun and a clear sense that they aren't having much at the present time. Thus encouraged, he implements a high-involvement program that actively invites employees to design their own fun experiences. A year later, he follows up the original survey with another that assesses employee reactions to the fun workplace initiative. The results are powerfully supportive. The ultimate outcome is that Bob enjoys *his* work as a manager much more than previously, and he also achieves a high level of satisfaction from helping *others* to have fun at work, too.

IMPLEMENTATION PRINCIPLES

Then he concludes by carefully developing and defining a set of ten guiding principles that will help both him and other managers implement and sustain a fun work environment. The essential principles to be emphasized (and their implications) include the following:

1. *Address other employee needs first.* (Employees won't laugh at your humor if they are angry about environmental shortcomings or have jobs that are lacking in motivational content.)
2. *Make sure that "fun at work" will be a good fit with the organization's culture and with employee expectations.* (Ask yourself WHY you are trying to create a fun environment, who wants it, and whether it is needed.)
3. *Build a fun workplace on an underlying philosophical foundation, not just a set of mechanical practices.* (Make sure you aren't saying one thing [about having fun at work] and yet doing another [emphasizing work results exclusively].)
4. *Make a long-term commitment to fun as an ongoing process, not a short-term program.* (Don't be guilty of a splashy start and then a weak follow-through.)
5. *Become more playful yourself.* (Others won't follow you if you don't "walk the talk.")
6. *Involve others in creating fun experiences.* (Don't try to do it all yourself; invite others to participate.)
7. *Satisfy employee needs for recognition in new and unique ways.* (Remember that most people are hungry for appreciation and respect. Also, don't forget that "the sweetest sound in the world is the sound of our own name being called" when it is time for awards to be given out.)
8. *Use a wide variety of fun-related activities.* (Take advantage of the old adage to provide "different strokes for different folks." Keep the process new and fresh.)
9. *Capitalize on the surprise factor.* (Be unpredictable; try different things).
10. *Assess and monitor your success at creating a fun work culture.* (Remember that nothing speaks louder than data about the results of a fun work environment, coupled with supportive personal anecdotes and endorsements from employees about their experiences of fun at work.)

Concluding Thoughts

Several valuable appendices are included at the end of the book, including sample survey instruments, illustrations of fun-at-work activities, a listing of fun workplace organizations, fun and humor Web sites, and a bibliography of other resources on workplace fun.

XV

Contemporary Thinking About Management

In the evolution and growth of any field of science, there are usually thousands of relatively minor advances made across time, interspersed with occasional major developments (e.g., Albert Einstein's theory of relativity in physics, or Dr. Jonas Salk's development of the polio vaccine, or the creation of cloned sheep by biologists/geneticists). Sometimes, however, the greatest break-throughs emerge when an independent thinker or critic stands back and announces that "The emperor has no clothes!" (and thus allows others to "see" for the first time what should have been apparent to them all along).

In the field of management, there has been a paucity of major breakthroughs across the past century. It could be argued that the field has edged forward in a variety of narrower domains through the persistent efforts of many but that overall progress and "big picture" activity has been slow and fragmented. With rather rare exceptions (refer back to our references to books by Argyris, Kilmann, and Micklethwait/Wooldridge in Part I), few books have provided comprehensive and critical looks at the overall field of management. Therefore, we as editors felt the need to include summaries of two books to fill this void.

Jeffrey Pfeffer, in *What Were They Thinking?*, suggests that organizations—even when led by intelligent and dedicated executives—frequently make a variety of missteps and errors that would lead observers to wonder, "What is going on there? and Why in the world would they do that?" Pfeffer candidly points out that some business leaders fail to capitalize on simple yet powerful principles of org-anizational behavior, rely on naïve theories of human behavior, and neglect to consider the unintended by-products of their decisions and actions. Pfeffer propos-es that managers should think before they act, use common sense, draw upon the mass of available evidence on human behavior, and get beyond "conventional management wisdom."

Jeff Pfeffer holds a Ph.D. from Stanford University and has taught there in its School of Business for over 30 years. He is now the Thomas D. Dee II Professor of Organizational Behavior. His previous books include *The Human Equation, Managing with Power, Hidden Value*, and *The Knowing-Doing Gap*. Pfeffer is the recipient of the Academy of Management's Richard I. Irwin Award for scholarly contributions to management.

Pfeffer, along with Robert I. Sutton, wrote *Hard Facts, Dangerous Half-Truths, and Total Nonsense.* They suggest that managers often fall into the "doing-knowing" gap, wherein they take action without first learning enough about their underlying problems. They propose that executives at all levels embrace the practice of using *evidence-based management.* This perspective invites them to be cautious about "new" ideas, explore the pros and cons of new approaches, recognize the difference between anecdotal stories and research-based results, question their own assumptions, and look for data that might support the success or failure of intended actions. They conclude by offering a series of concrete suggestions for how managers might work toward evidence-based management.

Readers interested in a thorough explanation of both the principles of evidence-based management and the key factors that inhibit its use are encouraged to read Denise M. Rousseau and Sharon McCarthy's article, "Educating Managers From an Evidence-Based Perspective" (*Academy of Management Learning & Education*, 2007, Vol. 6, No. 1, pp. 84–101) as well as reviews of the Pfeffer–Sutton book on pp. 137–149 of the same issue and the authors' response to those reviews on pp. 153–155.

Pfeffer and Sutton—coauthors of *The Knowing-Doing Gap*—were both profiled earlier in *The Manager's Bookshelf.*

What Were They Thinking?

Jeffrey Pfeffer

Summary Prepared by Adam Surma

Adam Surma is in store management with Target Corporation. Adam has held several positions with Target, overseeing store operations in Minnesota and Iowa. Primary management responsibilities include team development, providing vision and accountability, and store process execution. Adam received a B.B.A. degree from the University of Minnesota Duluth, with a major in Organizational Management.

INTRODUCTION

Today's organizations face a myriad of challenges and pressures that allow the world outside to catch a glimpse of their operations and decisions as they confront and deal with these factors. Though most organizations in every sector of the economy are undoubtedly led by some of the best and brightest the labor pool has to offer, there are countless examples of actions undertaken by these organizations that leave an outsider to pose the question: "*what were they thinking?*" All too often it seems that organizations follow the dictates of the conventional wisdom of the day, only to discover that conventional wisdom is flat wrong. This error, along with underinformed leadership and poor judgment, often finds organizations making serious errors that can be categorized into three themes—disregarding feedback, using simplistic models, and overcomplicating simple issues.

COMMON THEMES

Though there are many reasons why organizations make poor decisions that seem obvious to a great many people, *three common threads seem to unify and categorize them well*:

Jeffrey Pfeffer. *What Were They Thinking? Unconventional Wisdom About Management.* Boston, MA: Harvard Business School Press, 2007.

1. Disregarding the feedback effects of decisions
2. Believing in and using overly simplistic models of people and organizational behavior
3. Overcomplicating reasonably straightforward issues

By making these three common errors, leaders doom the outcome and execution of their vision from the start; either through stifling their workforce's productivity, creativity, and morale, or through misdirecting scarce resources away from the most value-added option for the organization. These errors can be readily seen in the realms of people, process, leadership structure, the measuring of success, and public policy.

PEOPLE-CENTERED STRATEGIES

Much emphasis in recent years has been placed on self-led teams, the value of investing in your workforce, and removing bureaucratic barriers to promote creativity. Yet for all of the knowledge available on these subjects, many organizations still ignore the commonsense principles surrounding the motivation and retention of a great team. Businesses trying to cut costs or getting caught in the glamour of new technology invest more heavily in customer service software, computer hardware, and analysis than in the frontline workforce that sees their customers face to face everyday. Organizations feel, especially in the United States, that lower and lower labor costs and pushing more of the work to automated or off-site systems will create a competitive edge and ultimately higher profit margins. The gap, however, between Europe and the United States in productivity has been drastically reduced over the past 30 years with more and more of the highly skilled labor being outsourced to other nations where more resources are devoted to education and training. This "death spiral" of trying to cut costs and losing the talent and organizational knowledge of your employees poses a serious threat to the long-term competitive edge in the United States.

Another mistake that is commonly made is *the unforgiving nature that many organizations have adopted over time around making and admitting to mistakes.* Whether it is frontline workers admitting to production errors and thus increasing the chance of a major recall or senior executives "cooking the books" to cover up underperforming numbers from a misstep, the culture of many modern organizations does not leave much room for the inevitable mistake. This culture is counterintuitive to the very nature of what it takes to be competitive in today's world: innovation and the ability to try many new ideas to find the one that is ultimately a success.

Reluctance to admit mistakes also runs parallel to another error often found deeply seated in organizations that are not as successful as they could be, which is the fact that *people want to work and stay at organizations that treat them well.* Great pay and benefits alone will not achieve this, as much research has shown that pay is not the top motivator or reason why people join or leave an organization, but the sense of community one feels from their employer is a vital factor. Employees are asking themselves: Does the organization care about my family? Will they take care of me when I am sick? These are the questions that often are overlooked, as senior leaders discuss why they cannot create a culture that attracts and retains top talent.

CREATING EFFECTIVE WORKPLACES

Creating effective workplaces through the reduction of benefits and imposition of human resource controls is another area in which organizations can easily fall into one of the three common theme errors. Cutting benefits and pay when times get tough is a common approach seen in today's headlines. However, this can be a very detrimental and ultimately ineffective way to cut costs. It has been found that employees, when feeling slighted by their employer, will reduce their work output to create a natural balance (sense of equity) from their own perspective. This leads to lower productivity. Many organizations in countries that are thought to have high wages or "excessive labor costs" run surpluses and profits higher than U.S. companies that compete on the low-wage strategy. This is due to the fact that many leaders forget that labor costs equal wage rate combined with productivity, and what is important is what actually is completed for the hours worked. Similarly, the long hours and weekend work that plagues many organizational cultures in the United States are not a problem in many competing European companies. Research shows that a worker in the United States will work 40 percent more hours in their lifetime than someone from Germany, France, or Italy. However, many European countries' workforces rank higher in creativity indexes and are healthier in general according to the World Heath Organization. All these factors show that the old dogma of if you are not "burning the midnight oil" or you are undercontributing, then the organization will suffer is simply not true.

LEADERSHIP AND INFLUENCE

Another area in which executives often find themselves making poor choices is in the basic people skills of their leadership and the culture of their organization. This deficiency allows the lack of basic influencing traits and relationship-strengthening behaviors to be rewarded or cultivated. With so many demands on the time of the leaders in charge of organizations, it is easy to see how the basics of leadership taught in college classrooms can be thrown out during stressful times. An example of this is the need for appropriate framing and repetition of key messages and strategies of the company, and how many leaders never use this simple approach. Truly effective leaders know that the following four steps keep a large and complex organization going in the direction they want it to:

1. Define the criteria for success
2. Project clarity and confidence
3. Move fast to establish terms of discussion
4. Endlessly repeat the simple message

If more leaders took a step back in times of turmoil to keep these key points in mind, many of the decisions that find an outsider asking "what were they thinking?" could be avoided.

Clear communication and vision projection are not the only leadership behaviors that are prone to the three common errors of decision making. Problems can also occur when managers create a culture of not admitting mistakes (especially at the highest level), not accepting "it's impossible" as a valid answer to a challenge, and ensuring that leadership knows the foundations of an organization (what the business actually does on a day-by-day basis). These are all commonly seen behind the scenes of a major mistake as areas of deficit that ultimately contribute to failure. Even the use of basic psychology is often to blame in failures. The use of **psychological commitment** is a good example of this principle. This is the idea that people are interested and invested in other people's success when they have made a contribution to it and are familiar with and enjoy the company of an individual. This can be a powerful tool. More leaders need to use this to their advantage through the basics of turning on the charm, being polite, and focusing on people and family before business to ultimately gain more insight and commitment in their workforce.

MEASURES OF SUCCESS

Two serious issues that plague many organizations today as they try to measure their success are overrewarding forecasting and budgeting (vs. actual performance) and the overreliance on shareholder return as a valid measurement for success.

In the first, it is increasingly common for organizations to celebrate and benchmark their "successes" based on their own internal profit projections and budgets. Because many leaders at the top have incentive packages that are based on meeting and beating goals and expectations, it naturally becomes an exercise on how well leadership can sell the board of directors on goals that they are confident they can hit, thus insuring a positive outcome and continued goodwill of all involved. The real challenge that organizations need to address is the idea of using both internal and external benchmarks and creating systems that use competitors' success and potential market share along with basic yearly comparative sales projections versus meeting or beating what can be an arbitrary budget.

Second, studies have shown that stock price is neither reliable nor valid in terms of assessing the long-term success of a company or the quality of its management. Stock price cannot be used as a valid measure as you cannot measure a company with it time and time again and have a reliable predictor of future results. Evidence also points out that "earnings-oriented management" and the ability of a good investor relations department will have just as much sway as solid economic indicators like earnings and sales growth on the price of the stock. When organizations focus on stock price as a major objective, they are necessarily committing scarce resources to obtain a goal that is not the most value added for the total organization (which is not only the shareholders but also the employees, community, and customers that it serves).

ORGANIZATIONS AND PUBLIC POLICY

In relation to making large mistakes in the limelight of public opinion and in the midst of the hot issues of the day, there are three areas in which organizations often find themselves struggling to make effective decisions.

Labor unions are the first issue on which organizations can often make mistakes. Although there are many complex issues when dealing with union and business interaction, one issue that organizations often forget is that increased labor costs do not necessarily mean decreased profits in every industry. On the theory of "you get what you pay for," organizations must come to terms with the fact that productivity, training, and commitment are all factored in (along with the wage rate) to determine final outcomes. This may lead some industries and businesses to avoid unions when they may not actually be harmful to the bottom line in every situation.

The second issue is executive pay. With the average pay rate going up steadily in the past decade, and public outcry over such huge bonuses, organizations must take a hard look at their compensation approach if they are to avoid overpaying, and thus face negative media coverage and increased scrutiny, or underpaying, and miss out on top talent who would ultimately grow the business. The "**above-average effect**" suggests that everyone views themselves above average and demands at least the average executive pay. This along with the fact that many executives in large companies have literally become celebrities combines to make the choice of paying an organization's top people not really a decision at all when it comes to where on the sliding scale of pay they need to commit to if they are to keep top talent.

The last issue involves the many misdeeds that can be committed in organizations and how it deals with the aftermath of unethical business decisions. Our society has traditionally viewed white-collar crimes as significantly less serious than other forms of crime, and the stigmas associated with it are so reduced that even after committing serious misdeeds leaders can easily find a host of other organizations waiting to bring them aboard after being terminated or even sent to prison. Our culture has (unfortunately) made it clear—from business school to the boardroom—that the ends justify the means. Organizations must be aware of this and be extra vigilant if they are to avoid major blunders or to unconsciously reward unethical behavior.

Conclusion

Many of the mistakes and blunders that organizations make today could be avoided if they didn't overcomplicate simple business decisions, ignore the feedback effects of their decisions once implemented, or view their workforce as a complex and dynamic group of people. If these principles were acknowledged and used as guidelines more often by today's business leaders, many of the headaches and pains they now face would be eliminated and their organizations would be better positioned to be competitive and profitable—both domestically and abroad.

Hard Facts, Dangerous Half-Truths, and Total Nonsense

Jeffrey Pfeffer and Robert I. Sutton

Summary Prepared by Jannifer David

Jannifer David teaches Human Resource Management at the University of Minnesota Duluth. She received her Ph.D. in Labor and Industrial Relations from Michigan State University. Her research projects study the use of contingent workers and how they affect the work relationships of others within organizations. She is also interested in international human resource management practices. Her work has been published in Human Resource Planning, Journal of Leadership and Organizational Studies, and other human resources–related outlets.

CAUSES OF BAD DECISIONS

Evidence-based management—decisions based upon the best research, data, and experimentation available—should lead companies to make better decisions than if companies use the prevailing approach based upon incomplete and often non-factual hopes and fears. So why *don't* companies use evidence-based management? Three reasons stand out.

Business norms derived for decision making include many practices that hinder the use of solid evidence as the basis for decisions. First among these norms is the use of *casual benchmarking*, which happens when companies copy the visible practices of other successful companies but fail to adopt the underlying philosophy that drives these practices or fail to acknowledge that these successful companies may have different business strategies, competitive environments, and/or business models.

A second cause for not using evidence-based management is because *managers rely on (and repeat) past behaviors that seemed to be successful*, even if

Jeffrey Pfeffer and Robert I. Sutton. *Hard Facts, Dangerous Half-Truths, and Total Nonsense: Profiting from Evidence-Based Management.* Boston, MA: Harvard Business School Press, 2006.

these behaviors are not appropriate for the current situation. While learning from experience is important, it is equally important to recognize that the present is not always exactly like the past and what has worked before might not work now.

Finally, management may choose to implement a practice because *it conforms to their personal beliefs*. In these cases, it is often very difficult to convince managers that their beliefs are not supported by evidence and that these beliefs may be harmful to the organization.

Using evidence-based management requires managers to look at facts and experiment with different approaches to determine which of these approaches are the most successful rather than relying on conventional wisdom. Clearly there are many instances when data are not available to help make these decisions to. When reliable data are not available, it is important find new ways of collecting data to ensure that sound decisions can be made. At a minimum, managers should ask questions about the underlying assumptions related to a practice before implementing it.

Collecting data, doing research, and examining assumptions when making decisions are the basics of evidence-based management. They seem like common sense, but many managers do not act on these ideas. Managers are often overwhelmed by the amount of information around them. The plethora of business knowledge available may make it difficult for managers to sort through this information for reliable data. However, research has shown that where the data can be found, evidence-based management has positive results for companies.

HOW TO APPLY EVIDENCE-BASED MANAGEMENT

Practicing evidence-based management can lead to better outcomes for people and companies, but problems may arise. Consider the premise of evidence-based management—that good decisions are based on data. If decisions are made based upon solid evidence and information, then any employee may possibly hold information that will guide decisions. This will change the power dynamics of the organization so that managers in higher positions may not always be the best-informed people to guide decisions. Making decisions based upon the data rather than the intuition of leaders may be threatening to these leaders. Such leaders have to be willing to accept that others know things they do not know and then both gather and act on these data. As a corollary, these leaders must encourage employees to bring up problems and not just tell leaders that they are always right. Finally, managers must exert effort to wade through the plethora of business information available to them and decide which of this information is valuable.

How can managers overcome these barriers? Relying on sound logic and analysis is the best approach. Managers should sift through and study all of the information available to them. This means looking not only at practices of successful companies but also companies that fail. Managers should develop a habit of running small experiments within their companies to determine through data analysis which approaches are the most effective. Managers can change their thought processes about the information they use in the following ways:

- Be cautious of a "new" idea, because there are very few truly new ideas.
- Recognize that information rarely is generated by individuals and most likely comes from the efforts of a group of people.
- Acknowledge the positives *and* the negatives of any idea or approach.
- Use stories from other companies' successes and failures as interesting anecdotes, but not as research-based data.

- Before supporting or rejecting any ideology or theory, look for data that could indicate the success or failure of these ideas.
- Most importantly, evidence-based management suggests that managers should rely on gaining wisdom to make decisions. No approach to management will answer all of your questions definitively. Wise managers will recognize what they know, but also what they don't know. Find research and people to help you understand what you do not know.

EXAMPLES OF HALF-TRUTHS IN MANAGING PEOPLE AND ORGANIZATIONS

To illustrate the dangers of not using evidence-based management, here are some common business beliefs and a review of the data and research supporting and not supporting them.

Half-Truth #1: Separation of Work and Home Life Is Necessary

Employees' work lives are different from the rest of their lives. Employers often develop policies and practices to convey the idea that once employees are on the clock, none of their personal lives should ever enter into their thoughts or actions.

Companies require that employees dress in a particular manner to narrow, or eliminate (in the case of uniforms), the individuality expressed by employees. Employees are asked to follow directions without thinking about the consequences of these directions and without providing suggestions for improvements. Emotions displayed at work are sometimes expected to conform to the norms established for that company. These norms may frequently require employees to refrain from displaying their true emotions. Many companies have policies forbidding romantic relationships between coworkers and even attempting to limit friendships between employees. These policies about social interactions are reinforced by practices that encourage employees to compete against each other for promotions or other organizational benefits. Furthermore, behaviors such as bullying at work are seen as acceptable, although outside of work, such abusive behavior is clearly not socially acceptable. Lastly, while much of employees' personal lives are focused on finding personal fulfillment, work is seen as a job and nothing more.

What are the benefits of separating work life from other facets of life? By not allowing people to use work time to accomplish personal tasks, the amount of role conflict experienced by employees should diminish. Companies can focus on making objective decisions rather than decisions based on favoritism or nepotism. Defining clear boundaries between work and home life can help clarify consequences when people's home lives become impediments to their work lives.

But there may be benefits to *allowing* integration between work and home life. For example, building a strong culture of valuing employees and their personal lives can lead to lower turnover and greater employee efforts. Many companies encourage participation of family members either as a source of new employees or to help with personal responsibilities when employees are busy with company activities. Employees who hide their true emotions experience negative outcomes such as burnout and dissatisfaction. Allowing employees to express themselves (within reason, of course) can result in more creativity and better ideas being surfaced. Allowing employees to express themselves also extends to the leaders in the company. When leaders are viewed as honest and sincere, employees are more likely to believe in these leaders and be loyal to the company.

Half-Truth #2: Only Companies That Hire the Best People Will Be the Best Companies

Another common half-truth is that the best companies are that way because they hire only the best people. This argument is compelling because there is research showing that smart and skilled people perform at much higher levels than people of lesser ability. However, other assumptions about only hiring the best people make this half-truth dangerous. Many organizations claim they can spot top talent early in a person's career, but the research is inconclusive about which factors will best predict future performance. So companies engaging in this early identification are largely basing decisions on intuition. Does this early selection process create a Hawthorne effect leading to higher performance later? Another assumption is that great employees will hire other great employees and that mediocre or poor employees will hire other mediocre or poor employees. Successful organizations then need to find a few great people and let them hire others like them. A similar-to-me effect may play a role here as research shows that conscientious people tend to hire other conscientious people, but research does not speak to whether or not poor performers will hire other poor performers.

This obsession on hiring great talent is somewhat misleading since organizations cannot easily identify talent. Also people's performance will vary naturally over time due to external constraints on their ability to focus and their levels of experience. Research shows that talent is not necessarily a given, but rather talent can be developed overtime through motivation and effort and effective training. Finally, some evidence supports the conclusion that truly great people will be squashed by a truly terribly system. If an organization institutes a bureaucratic system that fails to enhance or capitalize on peoples' abilities, then no amount of talent will shine through.

So what approach to talent should organizations embrace to be successful? First, acknowledge that talent can be learned and demonstrated by anyone, not just the few people who walk in the door with it. Next, focus on developing good systems in which people can demonstrate their abilities. Encourage employees to ask questions and talk about what is going on at work. If employees are unable or afraid to discuss problems, nothing will ever get better.

Half-Truth #3: Financial Incentives Are a Must for Executives

Offering financial incentives to employees is so popular in the United States that the practice and the rationale behind it frequently go unquestioned. Organizations offer financial incentives as a means to make employees think like owners. Incentives are thought to motivate performance, but this assumption presumes that performance is under the control of the employees. On the positive side, incentives provide employees with useful information about what is valued by the organization and therefore where to focus their efforts. Incentives may create a self-selection effect where employees who will have higher performance are attracted to companies with incentives, and employees who will have lower performance seek out companies that have pay structures based on seniority, but this assumption presumes that money is the primary motivator of an employee in choosing a particular place of employment. Through financial incentives, social messages will be sent about the employees who are more important to the organization than others. This message may impact negatively the performance of employees who believe their efforts are just important, but find themselves not valued by the company.

Research shows that most people are not motivated by money when choosing a career, but rather they choose careers based upon which jobs will make them feel fulfilled. Extrinsic rewards like financial incentives rank significantly lower in importance to people than enjoying their work. Further, financial incentives may not motivate the desired results or behaviors because they are blunt instruments. There are often unintended consequences of these incentive programs that will reflect negatively on the organization.

This is not to say that incentives should never be used, but they should be used judiciously. Relying heavily on financial incentives will limit the efforts of employees to those related to achieving the financial objectives. Using fewer financial incentives will allow employees to broaden their focus on a wider array of opportunities in the organization.

Half-Truth #4: Strategy is Destiny

The prevailing belief in the business world is that doing the right thing, even if it is not done well, is better than doing the wrong thing well. This idea suggests that companies must have an overall plan to reach their objectives. It is based on the assumptions that each company is equipped to do some things better than other companies and that focusing on these things will result in better outcomes because of the limited time and resources available to the organization.

Again, however, the research is not always supportive of this strategic view of the world. Empirical studies show inconsistent support for the idea that strategic planning improved organizational performance. There are some external constraints on companies, such as industry structure, that will powerfully affect overall performance beyond company strategy.

Additionally, there are reasons not to engage in significant strategic planning. The time and money spent annually on strategic planning can be extraordinary. This time spent on planning and budgeting can divert peoples' attentions away from solving fundamental problems within the organization. In addition, focusing all of peoples' energies on a specific strategic plan may limit the ideas that surface within a company, thereby limiting the discovery of profitable opportunities.

Nevertheless, some planning is probably better than none. A balance between focusing so much time and money on strategic planning and ignoring the planning process altogether should be achieved. First, instead of top executives developing these plans, perhaps a simpler approach like using customer feedback would work just as well. Second, once a good strategy has been developed, be careful not to abandon it because the implementation went wrong. Fix the implementation. Third, be certain that employees understand the strategy. If a strategy is too complex, employees will not comprehend it or buy into it, thus making it virtually impossible for them to act upon it. Finally, be flexible enough to change the strategy in light of changes in the industry. Learning as you go and adapting to current conditions may be more important than blind commitment to a long-term strategic plan.

Half-Truth #5: Change Is Inevitable

Experts will tell you that if your company doesn't change it will die. But is all change good? Some change is surely valuable to organizations, but many changes are not for the best. The trick to good management is determining (ahead of time) which changes will help the company and which ones won't. Which changes are worth doing? There are a series of questions that you could ask yourself as you decide if a particular change is right for your company:

- Will this change improve what you are already doing? And is anyone in your company already doing it?
- Are the benefits of this change really worth the costs?
- Do you need to make a real change, or would it be better to make a symbolic change?

- Is the change good for the company or just good for you?
- If you want to champion a change, do you have enough power in the organization to make it happen?
- How many changes have been implemented recently?
- Can the planned change be altered during the adoption process as people learn?
- Can this change be abandoned without significant costs or loss of face?

A review of many research studies and cases suggests that organizations can adapt quickly and easily to new realities. There are a few elements that need to be present to make the change successful. First, people must be dissatisfied with how things are currently happening. Second, they need clear direction on where the change is headed. Third, leadership must consistently convey high levels of confidence that this change will fix the problems the organization faces. Finally, the message conveyed and enacted should be that the change will be messy and that anxiety is a normal part of change. When organizations embrace these elements, a worthwhile change can be achieved quickly and successfully.

Half-Truth #6: Leaders are Everything

We are obsessed with leaders. We reward leaders handsomely, reflecting the organization's belief that they are in complete control of a company's fate. There is much research that leadership can affect the performance of a company and/or work group. Leaders, however, do not control everything about company outcomes. In fact, some research suggests that industry and company effects are much more influential than leaders when measuring company outcomes.

So why do we believe leaders are so important? When an organization does very well or poorly, we attribute these good or bad outcomes to the leader of the organization, because it is he or she who is the most obvious symbol of the company and we cannot see all of the individual efforts that went into making these outcomes possible. Since the complexities that make up the operations of a large company are impossible for most of us to understand completely, our attribution of the company's performance to an individual leader simplifies and clarifies our thinking.

Despite our belief that leaders are in control, we worry that they should not be in control. Complete control can lead to complete corruption. Also, by giving complete control to one person in an organization, it lessens the ability of other employees to have control over their work lives and lowers their commitment to work. This lower commitment speaks to the truth that most leaders have far less power than would be suspected by others—and most leaders admit to this fact.

Good leaders recognize the substantial limits on their abilities to direct the efforts of others. These leaders should project confidence in the direction of the organization, but simultaneously understand the limits of their abilities. By staying unimpressed by their own authority, leaders should be able to see more clearly when to step aside and let others make decisions for the direction of the company.

Leadership cannot be learned from a book or a class. Good leaders learn their craft by experience. This is why many companies rely on internal promotions for leaders. Outside succession of leadership can complicate the job of new leaders because they do not always understand the company very well. Continually learning and practicing at being a better leader will lead to higher performance of the leader and ultimately of the organization.

HOW TO IMPLEMENT EVIDENCE-BASED MANAGEMENT

The half-truths outlined here not only highlight the potential problems of following the crowd but also illustrate the potential value of evidence-based management. Managers committed to evidence-based management can help their organizations to be more successful. A commitment to evidence-based management is not a one-time fix, but rather a permanent change in how people think and engage information. Here are some guidelines for working toward this method:

- Keep an attitude that things can always be improved and that continual learning about what you know and don't know will lead to improvements.
- Stick to facts and not what people want to believe.
- Learn your facts from many sources.
- See both the positives and the negatives of your organization and the practices you wish to implement.
- Check your ego at the door.
- Make evidence-based management a company-wide objective.
- Recognize that switching an organization's philosophy of management to an evidence-based approach will take some selling—and some time.
- Use evidence-based management to slow the spread of bad practices.
- Learn from failures, not only your own organization's but also those of other companies.

Conclusion

We have learned that managers are not magicians. Managers recognize the imperfections of their worlds and learn over time how to deal with these problems. An attitude of wisdom bent toward continual learning is crucial to evidence-based management. Being open to creating, collecting, and analyzing data about organizational issues can lead managers to make better decisions for their companies.

XVI

Retrospective Views on the Best Sellers

It should be apparent from your reading of the best-seller summaries in this book that there are currently several types of author "voices" that provide messages relevant to management education. One is the *organizational scholar* (e.g., Edward E. Lawler III, or Wayne Cascio), who by training and a lifetime of careful work has a strong foundation of rich theories of management and organization and rigorous empirical observations of organizations in action to draw upon. Another source includes *management consultants and management practitioners* (e.g., Bill George, Jim Collins, or Stephen Covey), who offer us perspectives from their lives on or near the "organizational firing line." A third source of ideas lies in the *professional writers* (e.g., Malcolm Gladwell, Tom Friedman), who identify an interesting idea, trend, or concept and proceed to develop and expand it into a book appropriate for a managerial audience.

Traditional academics—students of tight theory and rigorous empirical study of organizational behavior—often find a large disparity among these three perspectives on management and organization. Confronted with the increasing popularity of the "best-sellers," the editors of *The Manager's Bookshelf* have raised a number of questions about this nontraditional management literature. For example:

- Is this material "intellectual pornography," as some have claimed?
- Should college and university students read this material?
- Should managers of today's organizations be encouraged to take this material seriously?
- What contributions to management education and development come from this array of management books?
- What are the major deficiencies or limitations of these books?

For answers to these questions—and to provide some closure on *The Manager's Bookshelf*—we turned to three colleagues (Professors Larry L. Cummings, Brad Jackson, and Anne Cummings). We asked each of them to reflect upon the current and continued popularity of this "best-seller" literature. The questions we asked them (and their responses) are intended to help you frame, reflect back upon, and critically and cautiously consume this literature. Their reflections on the role of the popular books in management education are included in Reading 1 in this part.

Reflections on the Best Sellers

Jon L. Pierce and John W. Newstrom,

with Larry L. Cummings, Brad Jackson, and Anne Cummings

Dr. Larry L. Cummings *was the Carlson Professor of Management in the Carlson School of Management at the University of Minnesota. He previously taught at Columbia University, Indiana University, the University of British Columbia, the University of Wisconsin in Madison, and Northwestern University. Dr. Cummings published more than 80 journal articles and 16 books. He served as the editor of the* Academy of Management Journal, *as a member of the Academy's Board of Governors, and President of the same association. Dr. Cummings was a consultant for many corporations, including Dow Chemical, Cummins Engine, Eli Lilly, Prudential, Samsonite, Touche-Ross, and Moore Business Forms.*

Dr. Brad Jackson *is Head of School at the Victoria Management School at Victoria University of Wellington in New Zealand. Dr. Jackson taught previously at Denmark's Copenhagen Business School in Denmark and at the University of Calgary in Canada. Jackson's research interests include the changing role of the CEO, the global management fashion industry, and organizational political processes associated with managing change. He has taught courses in Organizational Behavior, Change Management, Intercultural Management, Organizational Communication, and Management Learning. Jackson has pub-lished three books—*Management Gurus and Management Fashions, The Hero Manager, *and* Organisational Behaviour in New Zealand.

Dr. Anne Cummings *taught General Management, Organizational Behavior, Teams, Negotiations, and Leadership for undergraduate, M.B.A., Ph.D., and Executive Education audiences at the University of Pennsylvania's Wharton School, and is now on the Management Studies faculty at the University of Minnesota Duluth. Dr. Cummings won the David W. Hauck teaching award at Wharton in recognition of her outstanding ability to lead, stimulate, and challenge students. She holds a Ph.D. in Organizational Behavior from the University of Illinois at Urbana-Champaign, and her research has appeared in the* Academy of Management Journal, Journal of Applied Psychology, California Management Review, *and* Leadership Quarterly.

This closing section provides our reflections upon management (both the body of knowledge and its practice), as well as upon the wave of management books that has almost become an institutionalized part of the popular press. We hope it will provide some helpful perspectives and point you in some new directions.

One of the world's premier management gurus, the late Peter F. Drucker, suggested that managing is a "liberal art." It is "liberal" because it deals with not only fundamental knowledge but also self-knowledge, wisdom, and leadership; it is an "art" because it is also concerned with practice and application. According to Drucker, "managers draw on all the knowledge and insights of the humanities and the social sciences—on psychology and philosophy, on economics and history, on ethics—as well as on the physical sciences."* Building on this, we note that management can be defined as the skillful application of a body of knowledge to a particular organizational situation. This definition suggests that management is an art form as well as a science. That is, there is a body of knowledge that has to be applied with the fine touch and instinctive sense of the master artist. Peter Drucker reminds us that the fundamental task of management is to "make people capable of joint performance through common goals, common values, the right structure, and the training and development they need to perform and to respond to change" (p. 4). Consequently, execution of the management role and performance of the managerial functions are more complex than the simple application of a few management concepts. The development of effective management, therefore, requires the development of an in-depth understanding of organizational and management concepts, careful sensitivity to individuals and groups, and the capacity to grasp when and how to apply this knowledge.

The organizational arena presents today's manager with a number of challenges. The past few decades have been marked by a rapid growth of knowledge about organizations and management systems. As a consequence of this growth in management information, we strongly believe that it is important for today's manager to engage in lifelong learning by continually remaining a student of management. It is also clear to us that our understanding of organizations and management systems is still in the early stages of development. That is, there remain many unanswered questions that pertain to the effective management of organizations.

Many observers of the perils facing today's organizations have charged that the crises facing American organizations today are largely a function of "bad management"—the failure, in large part, to recognize that management is about human beings. It is the ability, according to Drucker, "to make people capable of joint performance, (and) to make their strengths effective and their weaknesses irrelevant. This is what organization is all about, and it is the reason that management is the critical, determining force" (p. 10). Similarly, Tom Peters and Bob Waterman have observed that the growth of our society during the twentieth century was so rapid that almost any management approach appeared to work and work well. The real test of effective management systems did not appear until recent decades, when competitive, economic, political, and social pressures created a form of environmental turbulence that pushed existing managerial tactics beyond their limits. Not only are students of management challenged to learn about effective management principles, but are also confronted with the need to develop the skills and intuitive sense to apply that management knowledge.

Fortunately, there are many organizations in our society from which they can learn, and there is a wealth of knowledge that has been created that focuses on effective organizational

---

* Page references are to Peter F. Drucker, "Management as a social function and liberal art," *The Essential Drucker: The Best of Sixty Years of Peter Drucker's Essential Writings on Management.* Harper Business, 2003.

management. There are at least two literatures that provide rich opportunities for regular reading. First, there is the traditional management literature found in management and organization text-books and academic journals (e.g., *Academy of Management Journal, Administrative Science Quarterly, Harvard Business Review, Managerial Psychology, Research in Organizational Behavior,* and *California Management Review*). Second, the past few decades have seen the emergence of a nontraditional management literature written by management gurus, manage-ment practitioners, and management consultants who describe their organizational experiences and provide a number of other management themes. Knowledge about effective and ineffective management systems can be gleaned by listening to the management scholar, philosopher, and practitioner.

Since not all that is published in the academic journals or in the popular press meets com-bined tests of scientific rigor and practicality, it is important that motivated readers immerse themselves in both of these literatures. Yet, neither source should be approached and subse-quently consumed without engaging in critical thinking.

CRITICAL THINKING AND CAUTIOUS CONSUMPTION

We believe that the ideas promoted in these best sellers should not be integrated blindly into any organization. Each should be subjected to careful scrutiny in order to identify its inherent strengths and weaknesses; each should be examined within the context of the unique organiza-tional setting in which it may be implemented; and modifications and fine-tuning of the tech-nique may be required in order to tailor it to a specific organizational setting and management philosophy. In addition, we strongly encourage juxtaposing the concepts, ideas, and management practices presented in these books with the scientific management literature. To what extent have these "popular press" ideas been subjected to investigation following the canons of the scientific method? Have they been supported? Are they endorsed by other respected management philoso-phers and practitioners? If these ideas or similar ones have not been rigorously examined scien-tifically, it would be prudent to ask the important question "Why not?" If these ideas have not been endorsed by others, we should once again raise the question "Why not?" before blindly entering them into our storehouse of knowledge and "bag of management practices." Finally, the process that is used to implement the management technique may be as important to its success as the technique itself, as good ideas (techniques, programs) may still fail if the processes employed to implement them are seriously flawed.

This is an era of an information–knowledge explosion. We would like to remind consumers of information of the relevance of the saying *caveat emptor* (let the buyer beware) from the product domain, because there are both good and questionable informational prod-ucts on the best-seller market. Fortunately, advisory services like Consumer Reports exist to advise us on the consumption of consumer goods. There is, however, no similar guide for our consumption of information in the popular management press. Just because a book has been published or even become a best seller does not mean that the information contained therein is worthy of direct consumption. It may be a best seller because it presents an optimistic message, it is enjoyable reading, it contains simple solutions that appeal to those searching for easy answers, the author is a recognized figure, or it has been successfully marketed to the public.

The information in all management literature should be approached with caution; it should be examined and questioned. We suggest that a more appropriate guide for readers might be *caveat lec-tor, sapeat lector* (which loosely translates to "Let the reader beware, but first let the reader be informed"). The pop-management literature should not be substituted for more scientific-based knowledge about effective management. In addition, this knowledge should be compared and contrasted with what we know about organizations and management systems from other sources—the opinions of other experts, the academic management literature, and our own prior organizational experiences.

We invite you to question this best-seller literature. In the process, there are many questions that should be asked. For example: What are the author's credentials, and are they relevant to the book? Has the author remained an objective observer of the reported events? Why did the author write this book? What kind of information is being presented (e.g., opinion, values, facts)? Does this information make sense when it is placed into previously developed theories? Could I take this information and apply it to another situation at a different point in time and in a different place, or was it unique to the author's experience? These and similar questions should be part of the information screening process.

INTERVIEWS WITH THREE ORGANIZATIONAL SCHOLARS

As we became increasingly familiar with the best sellers through our roles as editors, we began asking a number of questions about this type of literature. We then sought and talked with three distinguished management scholars—Professors L. L. Cummings, Brad Jackson, and Anne Cummings. Following are excerpts from those interviews.

Exploring the Contributions of Best Sellers

We have witnessed an explosion in the number and type of books that have been written on management and organizations for the trade market. Many of these books have found themselves on various "best-seller" lists. What, in your opinion, has been the impact of these publications? What is the nature of their contribution?

LARRY CUMMINGS'S PERSPECTIVE Quite frankly, I think these books have made a number of subtle contributions, most of which have not been labeled or identified by either the business press or the academic press. In addition, many of their contributions have been inappropriately or inaccurately labeled.

Permit me to elaborate. I think it is generally true that a number of these very popular "best-seller list" books, as you put it, have been thought to be reasonably accurate translations or interpretations of successful organizational practice. Although this is not the way that these books have been reviewed in the academic press, my interactions with managers, business practitioners, and MBA students reveal that many of these books are viewed as describing organizational structure, practices, and cultures that are thought to contribute to excellence.

On the other hand, when I evaluate the books myself and when I pay careful attention to the reviews by respected, well-trained, balanced academicians, it is my opinion that these books offer very little, if anything, in the way of generalizable knowledge about successful organizational practice. As organizational case studies, they are the most dangerous of the lot, in that the data (information) presented has not been systematically, carefully, and cautiously collected and interpreted. Of course, that criticism is common for case studies. Cases were never meant to be contributions to scientific knowledge. Even the best ones are primarily pedagogical aids, or the basis for subsequent theory construction.

The reason I describe the cases presented in books like *In Search of Excellence* as frequently among the most dangerous is because they are so well done (i.e., in a marketing and journalistic sense), and therefore, they are easily read and so believable. They are likely to influence the naive, those who consume them without critically evaluating their content. They epitomize the glamour and the action orientation, and even the machoism of American management practice; that is, they represent the epitome of competition, control, and order as dominant interpersonal and organizational values.

Rather, I think the contributions of these books, in general, have been to provide an apology, a rationale, or a positioning, if you like, of American management as something that is not just on the defensive with regard to other world competitors. Instead, they have highlighted American management as having many good things to offer: a sense of spirit, a sense of identification, and a sense of clear caricature. This has served to fill a very important need. In American management thought there has emerged a lack of self-confidence and a lack of belief that what we are doing is proactive, effective, and correct. From this perspective, these books have served a useful role in trying to present an upbeat, optimistic characterization.

BRAD JACKSON'S PERSPECTIVE   It is very difficult to assess the true nature of the impact that the best sellers have on management practice. We might infer from the huge number of books that are sold each year that their impact might be quite substantial. Corporations and consulting firms purchase many business best sellers on a bulk basis. It is difficult to ascertain how many of these are actually distributed and received. The next question to consider, of course, is the extent to which these books are actually read. Anecdotal evidence (as well as personal experience!) suggests that, even with the best intentions, most readers manage to peruse the book jacket, the testimonials, the preface, and, at best, the introductory chapter. Few find the time to read the book's entire contents.

Most crucially, however, we should try to understand the nature of the impact that the reading of a best seller, even if it is very partial, has on how the individual manager perceives the world and how he or she acts on that world as a result of being exposed to the ideas expressed in this genre of books. This is a task that is fraught with difficulty, as managers are exposed to so many different influences and are shaped and constrained by a wide range of organizational environments. In my book, *Management Gurus and Management Fashions* (Jackson, 2001), I suggest that business best sellers not only make an intellectual contribution, but also provide quite important psychological and emotional support to managers. It is no accident that we can observe the swelling of the personal growth section of the business book section during times of widespread turbulence.

During the 1990s, organizations across all sectors embraced new management ideas (management fashions) that were promoted by management gurus in business best sellers. Organizational improvement programs such as Total Quality Management, Business Process Reengineering, the Balanced Scorecard, and Knowledge Management were seized upon as the panacea for organizations desperate to retain their competitive edge or merely survive. Vestiges of these and older programs can still be traced in the language, systems, and structures of these organizations, but their influence and attention are well past their peak. We have very little to go on in terms of understanding how these management fashions are adapted and institutionalized, but a few studies have shown that these ideas tend to be only selectively adopted or they are reworked or even actively resisted by managers and employees. The bottom line is that it is very difficult to accurately trace the impact of best sellers. However, we should be prepared to accept that the final impact is likely to be quite different than what the best-selling author originally intended!

ANNE CUMMINGS'S PERSPECTIVE   These best-selling business books have offered my teaching a variety of important contributions:

- They offer powerful corporate examples that I use for illustrating conceptual points in class. I often find the examples of what didn't work (and the ensuing discussion about why) as useful (if not more useful!) than the examples of what did work.
- They update me on the newest terminology and techniques that managers are reading about, which helps me to communicate efficiently and effectively with them, using their vocabulary.
- They stimulate interesting conversations with Executive Education participants, who often question the value of the latest fads and want to explore how these new ideas compare to their managerial experience and to the conceptual foundations about management that they learned a decade earlier.
- Some of the books offer basic frameworks for viewing problems and issues, and this encourages students to begin thinking conceptually. I can then nudge students toward thinking further about cause–effect relationships, contingencies, and the utility of academic research.
- Some of the books offer important insights into environmental trends, shifting managerial pressures, and even new ways of thinking about things—sometimes long before academics explore these areas.

Possible Concerns about Best Sellers

In addition to a large volume of sales, surveys reveal that many of these books have been purchased and presumably read by those who are managing today's organizations. Does this trouble you? More specifically, are there any concerns that you have, given the extreme popularity of these types of books?

LARRY CUMMINGS'S PERSPECTIVE   I am of two minds with regard to this question. First, I think that the sales of these books are not an accurate reflection of the degree, the extent, or the carefulness with which they have been read. Nor do I believe that the sales volumes tell us anything about the pervasiveness of their impact. Like many popular items (fads), many of these books have been purchased for desktop dressing. In many cases, the preface, the introduction, and the conclusion (maybe the summary on the dust jacket) have been read such that the essence of the book is picked up, and it can become a part of managerial and social conversation.

Obviously, this characterization does not accurately describe everyone in significant positions of management who has purchased these books. There are many managers who make sincere attempts to follow the management literature thoroughly and to evaluate it critically. I think that most of the people with whom I come in contact in management circles, both in training for management and in actual management positions, who have carefully read the books are not deceived by them. They are able to put them in the perspective of representations or characterizations of a fairly dramatic sort. As a consequence, I am not too concerned about the books being overly persuasive in some dangerous, Machiavellian, or subterranean sense.

On the other hand, I do have a concern of a different nature regarding these books. That concern focuses upon the possibility that the experiences they describe will be taken as legitimate bases or legitimate directions for the study of management processes. These books represent discourse by the method of emphasizing the extremes, in particular the extremes of success. I think a much more fruitful approach to studying and developing prescriptions for management thought and management action is to use the method of differences rather than the method of extremes.

The method of differences would require us to study the conditions that gave rise to success at Chrysler, or McDonald's, or which currently gives rise to success at Merck or any of the other best-managed companies. However, through this method we would also contrast these companies with firms in the same industries that are not as successful. The method of contrast (differences) is likely to lead to empirical results that are much less dramatic, much less exciting, much less subject to journalistic account (i.e., they're likely to be more boring to read), but it is much more likely to lead to observations that are more generalizable across managerial situations, as well as being generative in terms of ideas for further management research.

Thus, the issue is based on the fundamental method that underlies these characterizations. My concern is not only from a methodological perspective. It also centers on our ethical and professional obligations to make sure that the knowledge we transmit does not lead people to overgeneralize. Rather, it should provide them with information that is diagnostic rather than purely prescriptive.

The method of extremes does not lead to a diagnostic frame of mind. It does not lead to a frame of mind that questions why something happened, under what conditions it happened, or under what conditions it would not happen. The method of differences is much more likely to lead to the discovery of the conditional nature of knowledge and the conditional nature of prescriptions.

BRAD JACKSON'S PERSPECTIVE   I tend to be less concerned about the large volume of business best sellers than a lot of my academic colleagues. While I wish that there were bigger public appetites for more academically oriented management books, I am generally encouraged by the widespread interest in business and management. It's important for managers to take an interest in what is going on beyond their immediate work environment and to ask questions about why things are being done in a certain way and what could be done differently. Best sellers typically challenge the status quo in provocative and dramatic ways that readily engage managers' attentions. Subsequently, many managers wish to learn more and sign up for some form of formal management education. It is in this forum that they can become exposed to alternative and more rigorously researched accounts of management theory and practice that challenge some of the assumptions made in the best sellers. I have found that encouraging managers to take a more critical reading of the business best sellers can be highly instructive for both them and me, especially when they are presented alongside academically oriented texts, which they find to be slightly less accessible, but ultimately more rewarding.

ANNE CUMMINGS'S PERSPECTIVE   My greatest concern with these books is that many readers do not have the time, motivation, or managerial experience to appropriately apply the contents. Unfortunately, a few students seem to be mostly interested in "speaking the language" with bravado just to demonstrate how up-to-date they are. Others seem to want to simply imitate the successful examples that they have read about, as though these reports of alleged best practices represent a "cookbook" approach that can be easily applied elsewhere. Most managers consider their time an extremely valuable resource and consider this reading a "luxury"; they tell me they therefore approach these readings looking for "take-aways" from each one—short lists of guiding principles, practical procedures they can implement immediately, or a simple diagram or model to organize a project or change they are leading. All students of management can benefit from remembering that the process of building solid theories and best practices from isolated case examples (i.e., inductive learning) is a complex one; some discipline and patience are required to avoid premature generalizing before valid evidence is available and well understood. The challenge is for readers to expend some real effort and apply critical thinking to these products—to analyze when and why the practices might be successful. Demanding conversations with colleagues, mentors, and competitors; comparing apparent discrepancies; and asking tough "why" and "how" questions are all useful techniques to achieve this discipline.

Recent Changes in Best Sellers

The modern era of business best-seller popularity now spans roughly a quarter century. Have you witnessed any changes or evolution in the nature of these best-seller books over the past decade or so?

BRAD JACKSON'S PERSPECTIVE   Looking back, I characterize the 1990s as the "guru decade." This was the era in which a few highly influential management gurus such as Michael Hammer, Tom Peters, Michael Porter, Peter Senge, and Stephen Covey reigned supreme among the best sellers. Their larger-than-life presences helped to spawn a few very powerful management ideas that drove a lot of conventional management thinking in North America and beyond. I do not see the same concentration of interest in either management gurus or management fashions in the current business book market. Instead I see a lot of niche-based ideas that are being promoted by specific consulting firms. None of these seem to have had the same pervasive influence that the gurus previously held. On the other hand, I see a lot of interest in biographical accounts of what I call "hero managers" such as Jack Welch, Richard Branson, and Lou Gerstner. Most of these are inspirational self-celebratory accounts, but, of course, there has also been a lot more interest in exposing some of the darker sides of corporate life in the wake of the Enron and other corporate scandals.

Words of Advice

Do you have any insights or reflections or words of advice to offer readers of business best sellers?

BRAD JACKSON'S PERSPECTIVE   I like to share the advice that Micklethwait and Wooldridge (*The Witch Doctors*, 1996) give at the end of their excellent exposé on the management theory industry. They argue that because management theory is comparatively immature and underdeveloped, it is vital that managers become selective and critical consumers of the products and services offered by the management theory industry. In particular, they suggest that managers should bear in mind the following advice when making book purchase decisions:

1. Anything that you suspect is bunk almost certainly is.
2. Beware of authors who aggrandize themselves more than their work.
3. Beware of authors who argue almost exclusively by analogy.

4. Be selective. No one management theory will cure all ills.

5. Bear in mind that the cure can sometimes be worse than the disease.

6. Supplement these books with reactions from academic reviewers to get an informed and critical perspective on the value of new management theories and their proponents.

All I would add to this succinct list is to encourage managers to read more widely and to look to other disciplines such as philosophy, history, psychology, and art for supplemental insights into management practice and organizational life. I'm always surprised by how much I learn when I browse through books in the other sections of the library or bookstore.

Conclusion

We hope that you have enjoyed reading the views of these management scholars (Professors Larry Cummings, Brad Jackson, and Anne Cummings) on the role of popular management books. In addition, we hope that the readings contained in the ninth edition of *The Manager's Bookshelf* will stimulate your thinking about effective and ineffective practices of management. We reiterate that there is no single universally applicable practice of management, for management is the skillful application of a body of knowledge to a particular situation. We invite you to continue expanding your understanding of new and developing management concepts. In a friendly sort of way, we challenge you to develop the skills to know when and how to apply this knowledge in the practice of management.

GLOSSARY OF TERMS

Above-average effect The perception by many employees that they are better than most others and hence deserve additional compensation. (Pfeffer)

Abstract attitude The capacity to reflect explicitly on the ways in which one does, or does not, fulfill a certain role. (Gardner)

Achievement To take pride in one's accomplishments by doing things that matter and doing them well; to receive recognition for one's accomplishments; to take pride in the organization's accomplishments. (Sirota, Mischkind, and Meltzer)

Activists Highly engaged followers who have strong feelings (pro or con) about their leaders and are heavily invested in their group. They possess the energy and ability to enlist the help of other followers. (Kellerman)

Adaptive unconscious The part of one's brain that makes perceptions, impressions, motivations, and decisions very quickly. (Gladwell)

Affirmation bias The belief that the focus is (and should be) on the positive assets and strengths of people. (Cameron)

Amygdala The part of the brain that triggers emotional reactions before the thinking brain has a chance to pick up the signal. (Frost)

Authentic leadership Actions by people of high integrity who are committed to building enduring organizations by relying on morality and character. (George)

Authority Person who is an expert in a field (a niche player). (Reardon)

Bad bosses Managers who abuse their power, lose their temper, micromanage, and exhibit insecurity and incompetence. (Van Fleet and Van Fleet)

Bad followers Persons who knowingly and deliberately commit themselves to "bad leaders" and who generally mirror bad leaders for a variety of complex reasons. (Kellerman)

Bad leadership Actions—ineffective or unethical—that are a result of leaders behaving poorly because of who they are, and because of what they want, and acting in ways that do harm (either intentional or as a result of carelessness or neglect). (Kellerman)

Balanced life Leading a life that recognizes the importance of work, family, friends, faith, and community

service, with none of them excluding any of the others. (George)

Balanced path The approach that harmonizes worker fulfillment with enterprise performance. (Katzenbach)

Battered bystanders Innocent coworkers and family who also (perhaps indirectly) suffer the effects of ugly work incidents. (Sutton)

Behaving with urgency Demonstrating (and expecting) efficiency, openness, and passion for accomplishments. (Kotter)

Big losers Companies that have demonstrated a persistent lack of competitive advantage through stock market performance significantly poorer than their respective industry average over the period 1992–2002. (Marcus)

Big winners Companies that have demonstrated sustainable competitive advantage through stock market performance that significantly exceeds their respective industry average over the period 1992–2002. (Marcus)

Bringing the outside in Obtaining valuable information from customers, suppliers, and the business community, and building strong relationships with those groups. (Kotter)

Burnout The effects of a mismatch between the needs of an employee and the demands of a job, which can be manifested by an erosion of emotions, frustration, and health symptoms. (Cascio)

Bystanders Followers who are aware of their leaders and the dynamics of their group, but make a conscious choice to disengage. (Kellerman)

Camaraderie The feeling of having warm, interesting, and cooperative relations with others in the workplace. (Sirota, Mischkind, and Meltzer)

Capabilities The clearly identifiable and measurable value-adding activities that describe what the organization can do. (Lawler and Worley)

Capitalize Using an asset, skill, or resource in the most effective and efficient way. (Buckingham)

Capitulation To end all resistance; to give up; to go along with or comply; to end all resistance because of loss of hope. (Collins)

Cheese A metaphor for anything that employees are seeking (as rewards for their efforts) or elements of their environment with which they are familiar (that cause confusion if changed). (Johnson)

Choice points   Natural places during a conversation where the course of action can be altered. (Reardon)

Choice-structuring process   A process whose goal is to produce sound strategic choices that lead to successful action. (Argyris)

Circumstance-based categorization   Segmentation of products and services. (Christensen Raynor and Anthony)

Climbers   Companies that lagged their peers in the first period, but achieved performance better than their peers in the second. (Joyce, Nohria, and Roberson)

Collaborative work system   A form of organization that practices a disciplined system of collaboration and a set of 10 principles to achieve superior results so as to be successful in a rapidly changing environment. (Beyerlein, Freedman, McGee, and Moran)

Commoditization   The process that transforms profitable, differentiated, proprietary products into undifferentiable commodities. (Christensen Raynor and Anthony)

Compassion   Empathy and caring in action, which enables managers to understand people's wants and needs and feel motivated to act on their feelings. Compassion is the third of three keys for renewal. (Boyatzis and McKee)

Compassionate organization   Organizations that promote a culture of and a set of practices and respectful policies that produce generative responses from their people and link the emotional health of the organization with the bottom line. (Frost)

Competitive advantage   Structure, human resources, processes, knowledge, culture, and other aspects of the organization that provide a sustainable edge in the marketplace. (Lawler); the edge a firm can gain over its competitors by providing equivalent benefits at a lower price or greater benefits that compensate for a higher price than competitors charge. (Porter)

Complacency   A feeling of contentment or self-satisfaction, especially when coupled with unawareness of organizational danger, threat, or trouble. (Kotter)

Conscious decision making   Processing information on a conscious level to reach a decision. This process is intentional, typically slow, and entails gathering information, employing logic, and coming up with a definitive answer to a problem, before the action can follow the decision. (Gladwell)

Constructive confrontation   Rather than attacking people, deciding when and how to fight by using evidence and logic to deal with problems. (Sutton)

Conversational coherence   Knowing when an issue is relevant to an ongoing discussion. (Reardon)

Core competencies   Technical areas of organizational expertise that can support the pursuit of strategic objectives and provide the basis for sustained competitive advantage. (Lawler); A combination of technology and production skills that underlie the product lines and services of an organization. (Lawler and Worley)

Countercyclical   Moving in the opposite direction (Kidder)

Creative mind   A mind that goes beyond existing knowledge and synthesis to pose new questions and offer new solutions to the same problem. (Gardner)

Critical configuration   The effect produced when an organization's strategic intent describes a path that is proximate to both its environment and its identity. (Lawler and Worley)

Culture   Pattern of commonly held values and beliefs within a group or organization. (Kidder)

Customer-focused quality   A quality measurement that focuses externally on customers and uses customer feedback as the ultimate measurement of quality. (George)

Death spiral   The opposite of a virtuous spiral, this deteriorating condition flourishes in organizations that mishandle their human capital, in turn causing both individual and organizational performance decline. (Lawler)

Deliberate strategy   Improved understanding of what works and what doesn't based on deliberate, conscious, and analytical decision making. (Christensen)

Diehards   Deeply engaged followers who are devoted to their leaders (or to removing them) and to their group. They are willing to die for their cause. (Kellerman)

Differentiation   Providing something unique that is valuable to buyers and for which they are willing to pay a price premium. (Porter); Realizing that we are all unique individuals, responsible for our own survival and well-being, while enjoying the expression of our being in action. (Csikszentmihalyi)

Disciplined mind   The ability to master in depth at least one way of thinking about the world such that the individual is capable of applying oneself diligently, improving steadily, and continuing beyond formal education. (Gardner)

Disruption   An act of delaying or interrupting the continuity; in the management context, disruption creates an opportunity to examine and evaluate the status quo and improve upon it. (Buckingham)

Disruptive innovations A strategy that targets new, less-demanding customers with products and services that, although not as good as the currently available products, appeal due to simplicity, cost, or convenience. (Christensen Raynor and Anthony)

Dissonance Loss of resonance; out of tune, out of sync; lacking clarity and awareness. (Boyatzis and McKee)

Dissonant leaders Persons who are emotionally volatile and reactive; they are known to drive people too hard for the wrong reasons and in wrong directions, leaving a trail of frustration, fear, and antagonism because they often lack awareness of their emotions and impact on others. (Boyatzis and McKee)

Downsizing An intentional, proactive management strategy, which can include reductions in the firm's financial, physical, and human assets. (Cascio)

Dynamic alignment The result created when the strategic intent drives the nature and quality of an organization's competencies, capabilities, and design. (Lawler and Worley)

Effective managers Managers who manage themselves and others so that both employees and the organization benefit. (Blanchard and Johnson)

EGO Acronym for a person's heart's motivation to either Edge God Out or Exalt God Only. (Blanchard)

8th habit The passionate execution and fulfillment of life that moves people from effectiveness to greatness through finding their voice and helping others to do the same. (Covey)

Empathy The ability to sense what people are feeling through receiving and interpreting verbal and nonverbal messages. (Goleman); Entering the private perceptual world of another person; being sensitive moment to moment to the changing feelings that flow from the other person. (Reardon); The ability to identify with others and, to a certain extent, feel what they feel. (Forni); The process of considering another's needs, feelings, and emotions by aligning one's own feelings with that of the other person. (Dean)

Employee enthusiasm A state of high employee morale that derives from satisfying the three key needs of workers, which results in significant competitive advantages for companies with the strength of leadership and commitment to manage for true long-term results. (Sirota, Mischkind, and Meltzer)

Energy-climate era A period during which energy and climate change are the predominant social, political, biological, and economic issues. (Friedman)

Energy Internet An electricity grid that includes centralized and distributed electrical production, abundant battery storage, and computer-controlled vehicles, buildings, appliances, and so on that all communicate with one another to efficiently produce and consume electricity. (Friedman)

Energy poverty Living without regular access to an electricity grid, usually caused by misgovernance and nonfunctioning utilities. (Friedman)

Enriched jobs Jobs that create three psychological conditions: experience of meaningfulness, experience of responsibility, and feedback or knowledge of results. (Lawler)

Espoused theories The beliefs and values people hold about how to manage their lives. (Argyris)

Ethical dilemmas Complex situation involving equally undesirable alternatives. (Kidder)

Ethical mind A mind that can and will respond sympathetically and constructively to differences among individuals and among groups, seek to understand and work with those who are different, and extend beyond mere tolerance and political correctness. (Gardner)

Evidence-based management The use of research, data, and experimentation to determine if a particular company practice will be helpful to the organization. (Pfeffer and Sutton)

Evolutionary Gradual process of change (Kidder)

Evolved capacities Features of the brain that are a function of both genes and the learning environment, with examples including language, recognition memory, emotions, and imitation. (Gigerenzer)

Execution The disciplined and systematic process of exposing reality (key information) through robust dialogue and acting on it with intensity and rigor. (Bossidy); The alignment of priorities and values while empowering others to find their voice and use it. (Covey)

External commitment Commitment that is triggered by management policies and practices that enable employees to accomplish their tasks. (Argyris)

Facilitating the best of the human condition The belief that people are intrinsically good. (Cameron)

False sense of urgency A sense of urgency that is filled with energy and activities that come from anxiety and anger and create behaviors that do not address the real threats or problems. (Kotter)

False spiral A spiral that occurs when an organization or individual believes it has started a virtuous spiral, when in fact it is simply an illusion. (Lawler)

Feedback   Information regarding results of one's efforts (how well one is performing). (Blanchard and Johnson)

Finding opportunities in crises   Using potentially damaging situations to generate creative solutions. (Kotter)

Flow   Full involvement with life. (Csikszentmihalyi)

Focal asset   The main product or organizational capability that creates an advantage over the competition, which makes an organization unique and different from competitors. (Buckingham)

Followers   Subordinates who have less power, authority, and influence than do their superiors and who therefore usually, but not invariably, fall into line. (Kellerman)

Followership   An implied relationship (rank) between subordinates and superiors and a response (behavior) of the former to the latter. (Kellerman)

Fraudulent spiral   A spiral that can be easily mistaken for a virtuous one, but is caused by deceitful activities. (Lawler)

Fundamental state of leadership   The condition in which leaders transform themselves from their normal state to become results centered, internally directed, other focused, and externally open. (Quinn)

Fun minute manager   Person who knows that many fun activities can be implemented in short periods of time and produce multiple payoffs. (Pike, Ford, and Newstrom)

Fun work environment   One in which a variety of formal and informal activities regularly occur that are designed to uplift people's spirits and positively and publicly remind people of their value to their managers, their organization, and to each other through the use of humor, playful games, joyful celebrations, opportunities for self-development, or recognition of achievements and milestones. (Pike, Ford, and Newstrom)

Global ethics recession   The apparent reduction in (business) ethical behavior across the world. (Kidder)

Good followers   Subordinates who are strong, independent partners with leaders; they think for themselves, self-direct their work, and hold up their end of the bargain. (Kellerman)

Groundswell   The major trends in online technologies and shifting consumer behavior that are forcing companies to reexamine their traditional marketing and customer interaction models. (Li and Bernoff)

Gut feelings   Also known as hunches or intuition, these are judgments that appear quickly in consciousness, whose underlying reasons are not in awareness, and are strong enough to act upon. (Gigerenzer)

Habits   Actions taken to renew one's commitment to God. (Blanchard)

Hands   A leader's actions and behaviors. (Blanchard)

Head   A person's belief system and point of view on leadership. (Blanchard)

Heart   A person's leadership motivations and intentions (Blanchard)

Hope   Optimistic belief that challenging goals can be successfully achieved, and if one way of getting there doesn't work, another one will be successfully applied. (Luthans)

Hubris   Excessive pride, pretentiousness, self-importance, ambition, or arrogance. (Collins)

Inner jerk   The capacity of anyone to turn into a jerk in certain situations and become caustic and cruel. Anger, fear, and contempt are highly contagious when exhibited by others. (Sutton)

Innovation   The process of transforming discoveries into products, goods, and services. (Drucker)

Inside-out management   Commitment derived from energies internal to human beings that are activated because getting a job done is intrinsically rewarding. (Argyris)

Institutional-building pride   Intrinsic pride that is based on emotional commitment that tends to further collective rather than strictly individual sets of interest. (Katzenbach)

Integration   Creating conditions at work such that individuals can best achieve their own goals by directing their efforts toward the success of the enterprise. (McGregor); Realizing that however unique and independent people are, they are also completely enmeshed in networks of relationships with other human beings. (Csikszentmihalyi)

Intentional change   Deliberate, focused identification of one's personal vision and current reality, and conscious creation of and engaging in a learning agenda. (Boyatzis and McKee)

Interdependence   Mutual dependence that creates a reciprocal relationship between independent entities. (Buckingham)

Intermediary   In the management context, managers act as intermediaries, taking the employee's talents and distributing them to the organization in pursuit of organizational goals. The manager must understand the talents of the employee and the needs of the organization to create a good match. (Buckingham)

Isolates   Detached and alienated followers who do not know or care about their leaders, and don't respond to them in any way. (Kellerman)

Knowledge workers   Employees with high levels of education, skills, and competencies. (Drucker)

Lateral thinking   Coined by Edward de Bono, this is the capacity to shift frameworks, wear different hats, and/or come up with a plethora of ingenious solutions to a nagging dilemma. (Gardner)

Leader attribution error   Leaders (and others) tend to believe that leaders have more power to achieve results than they actually do. (Kellerman)

L.E.A.D.E.R.S. Method   A model of leadership that focuses on seven critical leadership skills, including Listen to learn, Empathize with emotions, Attend to aspirations, Diagnose and detail, Engage for good ends, Respond with respectfulness, and Speak with specificity. (Dean)

Leadership characteristics   A desired combination of heart, purpose, values, relationships, and self-discipline. (George)

Logotherapy   A method (developed by Viktor Frankl) by which the therapist helps the client become fully aware of his or her freedom of choice. (Pattakos)

Losers   Companies that lagged peers in both periods. (Joyce, Nohria, and Roberson)

Low-end disruptions   The process of attacking the least profitable and most overserved customers at the low end of the original value network. (Christensen)

Management by objectives (MBO)   A process where employees set goals, justify them, determine resources needed to accomplish them, establish timetables for their completion, and perform accordingly. These goals reflect the overall objectives of the organization. (Drucker)

Management structure   The way managers divide, share, coordinate, and evaluate the work they do in planning and organizing the firm's overall operations. (Drucker)

Mindfulness   The capacity to be fully aware of all that one experiences inside the self—body, mind, heart, spirit—and to pay full attention to what is happening around us—the people, the natural world, our surroundings, and events. (Boyatzis and McKee)

Mind-mapping   A technique for expanding thought and encouraging insight by identifying a number of potential options and omitting ones that seem too risky. (Reardon)

Mission-driven organization   An organization that utilizes its mission statement as an integral part of managing the organization, not merely a plaque that hangs on the CEO's wall. (George)

Model I   The management theory that individuals use to protect themselves, while unilaterally treating others in the same (undifferentiated) way. (Argyris)

Model II   The management theory that relies upon valid information, free and informed choice, and internal commitment. (Argyris)

Moral competence   The skill of doing the right and moral thing (i.e., the action itself). (Lennick and Kiel)

Moral courage   Mindset of adhering to one's values. (Kidder)

Moral intelligence   The mental capacity to determine how universal human principles should be applied to our values, goals, and actions. (Lennick and Kiel)

New-market disruptions   The process of creating new value networks and products that are more affordable to own. (Christensen)

NONOS   People who resist any form of change and undermine the efforts of others who attempt it. (Kotter)

Optimism   Belief that positive events will happen in the future and the reasons for those positive events are attributed to oneself, are permanent, and are likely to happen now and in the future. (Luthans)

Organizational restructuring   Planned changes in a firm's organizational structure that affect its use of people, including the possibility of workforce reductions. (Cascio)

Participants   Engaged followers who have clear feelings (pro or con) about their leaders and their group, and they are willing and able to become involved. (Kellerman)

Partnership relationship   A highly effective method of creating and maintaining high levels of long-term organization performance in which a bond develops among adults working collaboratively toward common, long-term goals and having a genuine concern for each other's interests and needs. (Sirota, Mischkind, and Meltzer)

Peak performers   Any group of employees whose emotional commitment enables them to deliver products or services that constitute a sustainable competitive advantage for their employers. (Katzenbach)

Persuasion   The ability to position ideas in an appealing manner so others will accept them. (Reardon)

Petrodictatorships   Authoritarian states that are highly dependent on oil production for the bulk of their exports and government income. (Friedman)

Play   The introduction of joy, fun, and enthusiasm into a work environment. (Lundin, Paul, and Christensen)

Political insight   The use of empathy and creativity to understand and respond to the way things work in organizations. (Reardon)

Ponzi scheme   A type of illegal pyramid scheme, often involving soliciting new money from investors to pay off earlier investors until the situation collapses (Kidder)

Positive organizational behavior (POB)   A movement in positive psychology which focuses on the micro individual level and deals with positive attributes that are open to development and relate to an individual's work performance. (Luthans)

Positive organizational scholarship   Research that studies macro organizational issues and personal attributes. (Luthans)

Positively deviant performance   Situation where the results exceed expectations and go above and beyond. (Cameron)

Power stress   A unique brand of leadership stress that stems from choices that are unclear, the incredible complexity of communication and decision making, the need to lead with ambiguous authority, and loneliness at the top. As a result of power stress, leaders may become dispirited, forget their own deeply held values, act out in unhealthy ways, or burn out completely. (Boyatzis and McKee)

Problem   The difference between what is actually happening and what you want to happen. (Blanchard and Johnson)

Processes   The patterns of interaction, coordination, communication, and decision making through which inputs are transformed into outputs. (Christensen)

Productivity   Employee output in terms of the quantity and quality of work completed. (Blanchard and Johnson)

Professional intimacy   Working in a way that honors the integrity of the position, the person, and the organization at a level of connection deeper than normal. (Frost)

Psychological capital (PsyCap)   A person's positive psychological state that is characterized by the person displaying self-efficacy, optimism, hope, and resiliency. (Luthans)

Psychological commitment   Interest and investment in other people's success when they have made a contribution to it and are familiar with and enjoy the company of the other person. (Pfeffer)

Rapid cognition   The act of unconscious decision making, in which situational decision-making clues are gathered quickly by the adaptive unconscious and a decision is made based on limited information. This process is not intentional. (Gladwell)

Really simple syndication (RSS) Feeds   A technological process that allows readers to subscribe to areas of content interest, and automatically receive updates in a standardized form from a site when new content is published. (Li and Bernoff)

Recall memory   The capacity to retrieve episodes, facts, or reasons from memory, based on cues or signals that help people make decisions. (Gigerenzer)

Reciprocity   Doing a favor for another to induce an obligation for repayment at a future time. (Reardon)

Recognition memory   The ability to tell the novel from the previously experienced or to decipher the old from the new. Gigerenzer)

Reframing   Changing your mindset about something stressful to help you cope with the bad situation and limit the damage to yourself. (Sutton)

Requisite organization   An organizational structure that explicitly recognizes the time horizon each hierarchical level deals with as its organizing principle. (Raynor)

Requisite uncertainty   An organizational structure that explicitly recognizes the strategic uncertainties each hierarchical level deals with as its organizing principle. (Raynor)

Renewal   A conscious holistic process (involving body, mind, heart, and spirit) that helps people step out of destructive patterns to renew themselves physically, mentally and emotionally. (Boyatzis and McKee)

Reprimand   Negative verbal feedback provided when undesirable employee behavior and performance occur. (Blanchard and Johnson)

Resiliency   Ability to bounce back and encourage/inspire others to bounce back in the face of extreme adversity or to bounce back from even positive occurrences. (Luthans)

Resonant leaders   Individuals who are awake, aware, and attuned to themselves, to others, and to their world; they chart the path, inspire people, create hope in the face of fear and despair, and move people powerfully, passionately, and purposefully while giving of and caring for themselves so they can sustain resonance over time. (Boyatzis and McKee)

Resonant leadership   The ability to move others in a positive direction by being responsive to their feelings. (Goleman, Boyatzis, and McKee)

Respectful mind   A mind that seeks to note and welcome differences between human individuals and groups while also trying to effectively work with them. (Gardner)

Responsible restructuring   An alternative to "slash and burn" workforce reductions, wherein employees' ideas and efforts form the basis of sustained competitive advantage by addressing underlying competitive problems. (Cascio)

Revolutionary   Quick, radical process of change. (Kidder)

Sacrifice syndrome   A trap that leaders may fall into when they sacrifice too much for too long and reap too little, resulting in exhaustion, burning out, or burning up. (Boyatzis and McKee)

Safe zones   Created spaces where toxin handlers are moved out of the stressful situations within the organization for a period of time in order to let them reenergize and rest. (Frost)

Scarcity   The ability to create a high demand by controlling and providing resources that are perceived to be rare. (Reardon)

Scenarios   Possible future situations that an organization could encounter, and likely responses to them. (Raynor)

Selective adaptation   Choice of a method or action that accommodates identified conditions rather than ignoring or going against those facts. (McGregor)

Self-efficacy   Confidence that one will be successful even given difficult circumstances. (Luthans)

Self-managed teams (SMTs)   Teams of workers who, with their supervisors, are delegated various managerial functions to perform and the authority and resources needed to carry them out. (Sirota, Mischkind, and Meltzer)

Self-serving pride   Individualistic pride that comes from drives for power, ego, and materialism. (Katzenbach)

Sense of urgency   Strong organizational motivation to succeed by capturing the hearts and minds of a critical mass of employees. (Kotter)

Shared vision   The capacity to create and hold a shared picture of the future across a set of individuals. (Senge)

Slush fund   A special financial account used for illegal activities. (Kidder)

Social instinct   The result of special gut feelings versus complex calculation. The two basic social instincts are family instinct and community instinct. (Gigerenzer)

Social responsibility   The contribution a firm makes to its society. To some, this means making a profit, while others expect the firm to do more than this by ameliorating social problems. (Drucker)

Social technographics profile   The product of categorizing online participants into groups based on how they participate in online technologies. This is used along with age and gender to refine classifications of customers. (Li and Bernoff)

Soul   The energy a person or organization devotes to purposes beyond itself. (Csikszentmihalyi)

Sour spot   A highly contested market position affording incumbents little opportunity to control the five classic industry forces. (Marcus)

Strategic intent   The overall guide that an organization uses to decide how it will create value and design itself. (Lawler and Worley)

Strategic flexibility   The ability of an organization to effect change in its strategy. (Raynor)

Strategic options   The opportunities to pursue alternative technologies or business models that will redirect the organization's strategy without an attendant obligation to do so. (Raynor)

Strategy paradox   The observation that the trait that distinguishes successful companies—commitment to an extreme strategy—is also the trait that distinguishes those that fail. (Raynor)

Summum bonum (chief good)   The belief that whereas people desire other goods (such as money or power) because they believe those things will make them happy, they really want happiness for its own sake. (Csikszentmihalyi)

Sustained individual success   Using the talents in work that a person finds rewarding and fulfilling over a long period of time. (Buckingham)

Sustaining innovations   A strategy that offers demanding high-end customers better performance than that which was previously available. (Christensen)

Sweet spot   An attractive market position characterized by a lack of direct competition, and presenting incumbents with the opportunity to control the five classic industry forces. (Marcus)

Synthesizing mind   A mind that is able to select crucial information from the vast amounts available and arrange the information in a way that is understandable by the masses. (Gardner)

Team of rivals   Work group that is constructed by assembling previously competitive individuals and drawing upon their expertise. (Goodwin)

Theories in use   The actual rules or master programs that individuals use to achieve control. (Argyris)

Theory X   A set of assumptions that explains some human behavior and has influenced conventional principles of management. It assumes that workers want to avoid work and must be controlled and coerced to accept responsibility and exert effort toward organizational objectives. (McGregor)

Theory Y   A set of assumptions offered as an alternative to Theory X. Theory Y assumes that work is a natural activity, and given the right conditions, people will seek responsibility and apply their capacities to organizational objectives without coercion. (McGregor)

The rule   (Also known as the *no-asshole rule*) A combination of formal policies, rules, behavioral norms, and culture, which together communicate expectations for civil human interactions and provide the tools necessary for enforcement. (Sutton)

Thin slicing   The ability of the unconscious mind to find patterns in situations and behavior based on very narrow slices of experience. (Gladwell)

Three factor theory of human motivation   A model that asserts that there are three primary sets of goals of people at work—equity, achievement, and camaraderie. (Sirota, Mischkind, and Meltzer)

Topicality shift   Knowing how and when to introduce a new concept into a conversation. (Reardon)

Tough love   The leadership practice of living in the balance of being both simultaneously compassionate/concerned and assertive/bold. (Quinn)

Toxin handlers   Those leaders, managers, and staff that tend to the emotional pain of the people in the organization and work to bring harmony and balance and remove stress and tension. (Frost)

True urgency   Legitimate urgency that focuses on critical issues and problems in the organization, particularly from the external environment. (Kotter)

Tumblers   Companies who exhibited better-than-peer performance in the first period, followed by underperformance in the second. (Joyce, Nohria, and Roberson)

Unconscious intelligence   The use of prior knowledge about a person, situation, or concept, combined with hidden rules of thumb that drive intuition and gut feelings. (Gigerenzer)

Uniqueness   The skills, abilities, personality traits, attitudes, and aptitudes that are present in different amounts and combinations in each person. (Buckingham)

Urgency   The experience of pressing importance in addressing the real threats and problems an organization faces. (Kotter)

Value chain   The discrete value-producing activities within a firm that are potential sources of competitive advantage. (Porter)

Values   The standards by which employees make prioritized decisions. (Christensen)

Victims   Persons who work for abusive bosses and subsequently suffer psychologically, physiologically, and in their careers. (Sutton)

Virtual organizations   Companies that have groups of individuals working on shared tasks while distributed across space, time, and/or organizational boundaries. (Beyerlein, Freedman, McGee, and Moran)

Virtuous spiral   The ultimate competitive advantage, it is a win–win relationship that is a source of positive momentum that creates higher and higher levels of individual and organizational performance. (Lawler); A potentially powerful competitive advantage produced when both critical configuration and dynamic alignment exist for long periods of time. (Lawler and Worley)

Vision   A vivid mental image of a potential future for an organization, which can include possible goals, products, customers, and so on. (Buckingham)

Will to meaning   The authentic commitment to meaningful values and goals (a basic human drive) that only individuals can actualize. (Pattakos)

Winners   Companies outperforming their peers in both periods of examination. (Joyce, Nohria, and Roberson)

Workforce   All of the employees across the baseline of the organization who either make the products, design the services, or deliver the value to the customer. (Katzenbach)

BIBLIOGRAPHY OF INCLUSIONS

Argyris, Chris (2000). *Flawed Advice and the Management Trap.* New York: Oxford University Press, Inc.

Beyerlein, Michael M., Freedman, Sue, McGee, Craig, and Moran, Linda (2003). *Beyond Teams: Building the Collaborative Organization.* San Francisco, CA: Jossey-Bass/Pfeiffer.

Blanchard, Kenneth, and Hodges, Phil (2005). *Lead Like Jesus: Lessons from the Greatest Leadership Role Model of All Times.* Nashville, TN: Thomas Nelson.

Blanchard, Kenneth, and Johnson, Spencer (1981). *The One Minute Manager.* LaJolla, CA: Blanchard-Johnson.

Boyatzis, Richard, and McKee, Annie (2005). *Resonant Leadership: Renewing Yourself and Connecting with Others Through Mindfulness, Hope, and Compassion.* Boston, MA: Harvard Business School Press.

Buckingham, Marcus (2005). *The One Thing You Need to Know . . . About Great Managing, Great Leading, and Sustained Individual Success.* New York: Free Press.

Cameron, Kim (2008). *Positive Leadership: Strategies for Extraordinary Performance.* San Francisco, CA: Berrett-Koehler Publishers, Inc.

Cascio, Wayne F. (2003). *Responsible Restructuring: Creative and Profitable Alternatives to Layoffs.* San Francisco, CA: Berrett-Koehler.

Christensen, Clayton M., and Raynor, Michael E., and Anthony, Scott D. (2003). *The Innovator's Solution: Creating and Sustaining Successful Growth.* Boston, MA: Harvard Business School Press.

Collins, James C. (2009). *How the Mighty Fall—And Why Some Companies Never Give In.* New York: Harper Collins.

Covey, Stephen R. (1989). *The Seven Habits of Highly Effective People: Restoring the Character Ethic.* New York: Simon and Schuster.

Covey, Stephen R. (2004). *The 8th Habit: From Effectiveness to Greatness.* New York: Free Press.

Csikszentmihalyi, Mihaly (2003). *Good Business: Leadership, Flow, and the Making of Meaning.* New York: Penguin Putnam.

Dean, Peter J. (2006). *Leadership for Everyone: How to Apply the Seven Essential Skills to Become a Great Motivator, Influencer, and Leader.* New York: McGraw-Hill.

Deming, W. Edwards (1986). *Out of the Crisis.* Cambridge, MA: MIT Press.

Drucker, Peter F. (1954). *The Practice of Management.* New York: Harper and Row.

Friedman, Thomas (2008). *Hot, Flat, and Crowded: Why We Need a Green Revolution—And How It Can Renew America.* New York: Farrar, Straus and Giroux.

Frost, Peter J. (2003). *Toxic Emotions at Work: How Compassionate Managers Handle Pain and Conflict.* Boston, MA: Harvard Business School Press.

Gardner, Howard (2008). *Five Minds for the Future.* Boston, MA: Harvard Business Press.

George, Bill (2003). *Authentic Leadership: Rediscovering the Secrets to Creating Lasting Value.* San Francisco, CA: Jossey-Bass.

Gigerenzer, Gerd (2007). *Gut Feelings: The Intelligence of the Unconscious.* New York: Viking Press (Penguin).

Gladwell, Malcolm (2005). *Blink: The Power of Thinking Without Thinking.* New York: Little, Brown.

Goodwin, Doris Kearns (2005). *Team of Rivals: The Political Genius of Abraham Lincoln.* New York: Simon and Schuster.

Johnson, Spencer, M.D. (1998). *Who Moved My Cheese? An Amazing Way to Deal with Change in Your Work and Your Life.* New York: Putnam Books.

Joyce, William, Nohria, Nitin, and Roberson, Bruce (2003). *What (Really) Works: The 4 + 2 Formula for Sustained Business Success.* New York: Harper Collins.

Katzenbach, Jon R. (2003). *Why Pride Matters More than Money: The Power of the World's Greatest Motivational Force.* New York: Crown Business.

Kellerman, Barbara (2004). *Bad Leadership: What It Is, How It Happens, Why It Matters.* Boston, MA: Harvard Business Press.

Kellerman, Barbara (2008). *Followership: How Followers Are Creating Change and Changing Leaders.* Boston, MA: Harvard Business Press.

Kidder, Rushford M. (2009). *The Ethics Recession: Reflections on the Moral Underpinnings of the Current Economic Crisis.* Rockland, ME: Institute for Global Ethics.

Kotter, John (2008). *A Sense of Urgency.* Boston, MA: Harvard Business Press.

Lawler III, Edward E. (2003). *Treat People Right! How Organizations and Individuals Can Propel Each Other Into a Virtuous Spiral of Success.* San Francisco, CA: Jossey-Bass.

Lawler III, Edward E., and Worley, Christopher G. (2003). *Built to Change: How to Achieve Sustained Organizational Effectiveness.* San Francisco, CA: Jossey-Bass.

Lennick, Doug, and Kiel, Fred (2005). *Moral Intelligence: Enhancing Business Performance and Leadership Success.* Pennsylvania, PA: Wharton School Publishing.

Li, Charlene, and Bernoff, Josh (2008). *Groundswell: Winning in a World Transformed by Social Technologies.* Boston, MA: Harvard Business Press.

Lundin, Stephen C., Paul, Harry, and Christensen, John (2000). *Fish! A Remarkable Way to Boost Morale and Improve Results.* New York: Hyperion.

Luthans, Fred, Youssef, Carolyn M., and Avolio, Bruce J. (2007). *Psychological Capital: Developing the Human Competitive Edge.* New York: Oxford University Press.

Marcus, Alfred (2005). *Big Winners and Big Losers: The 4 Secrets of Long-Term Business Success and Failure.* Pennsylvania, PA: Wharton School Publishing.

Maslow, Abraham H. (1998). *Maslow on Management.* New York: John Wiley & Sons.

McGregor, Douglas (1960). *The Human Side of Enterprise.* New York: McGraw-Hill.

Pattakos, Alex (2004). *Prisoners of Our Thoughts: Viktor Frankl's Principles at Work.* San Francisco, CA: Berrett-Koehler.

Pfeffer, Jeff (2007). *What Were They Thinking? Unconventional Wisdom About Management.* Boston, MA: Harvard Business School Press.

Pfeffer, Jeffrey, and Sutton, Robert I. (2006). *Hard Facts, Dangerous Half-Truths, and Total Nonsense: Profiting from Evidence-Based Management.* Boston, MA: Harvard Business School Press.

Pike, Bob, Ford, Robert C., and Newstrom, John W. (2009). *The Fun Minute Manager: Create FUNomenal Results Now Using Fun at Work!* Minneapolis, MN: CTT Press.

Porter, Michael E. (1985). *Competitive Advantage: Creating and Sustaining Superior Performance.* New York: Free Press.

Quinn, Robert E. (2004). *Building the Bridge As You Walk On It: A Guide for Leading Change.* San Francisco, CA: Jossey-Bass.

Raynor, Michael E. (2007). *The Strategy Paradox: Why Committing to Success Leads to Failure (And What to Do About It).* New York: Currency Books.

Reardon, Kathleen Kelley (2005). *It's All Politics: Winning in a World Where Hard Work and Talent Aren't Enough.* Currency Books.

Senge, Peter M. (1990). *The Fifth Discipline: The Art and Science of the Learning Organization.* New York: Doubleday.

Sirota, David, Mischkind, Louis A., and Meltzer, Michael Irwin (2005). *The Enthusiastic Employee: How Companies Profit by Giving Employees What They Want.* Pennsylvania, PA: Wharton School Publishing.

Sutton, Robert I. (2007). *The No Asshole Rule: Building a Civilized Workplace and Surviving One That Isn't.* New York: Business Plus.

Van Fleet, Ella W., and Van Fleet, David D. (2007). *Workplace Survival: Dealing with Bad Bosses, Bad Workers, and Bad Jobs.* Baltimore, MA: PublishAmerica.

INDEX